CONSUMER NEUROSCIENCE

CONSUMER NEUROSCIENCE

EDITED BY MORAN CERF AND

MANUEL GARCIA-GARCIA

THE MIT PRESS

CAMBRIDGE, MASSACHUSETTS • LONDON, ENGLAND

This book was set in Melior and MetaPlus by Toppan Best-set Premedia Limited. Printed and bound in the United States of America.

Library of Congress Cataloging-in-Publication Data

Names: Cerf, Moran, editor. | Garcia-Garcia, Manuel, editor.
Title: Consumer neuroscience / Moran Cerf and Manuel Garcia-Garcia.
Description: Cambridge, MA : MIT Press, [2017] | Includes bibliographical references and index.
Identifiers: LCCN 2016059705 | ISBN 9780262036597 (hardcover : alk. paper)
Subjects: LCSH: Consumers--Psychology. | Consumer behavior. | Brand choice--Psychological aspects. | Neurons--Physiology. | Neural transmission.
Classification: LCC HF5415.32 .C658673 2017 | DDC 658.8/342--dc23 LC record available at https://lccn.loc.gov/2016059705

10 9 8 7 6 5 4 3 2 1

Contents

FOREWORD   VII
PHILIP KOTLER

PREFACE   IX
MORAN CERF AND MANUEL GARCIA-GARCIA

1   **INTRODUCTION TO CONSUMER NEUROSCIENCE**   1
MANUEL GARCIA-GARCIA, MORAN CERF, AND ANA IORGA

2   **BRAIN PHYSIOLOGY AND ANATOMY**   21
YUPING CHEN, MING HSU, AND MORAN CERF

3   **SENSATION AND PERCEPTION**   35
IRIT SHAPIRA-LICHTER AND MORAN CERF

4   **METHODS**   63
MORAN CERF

5   **ATTENTION**   103
MANUEL GARCIA-GARCIA
APPENDIX: USE OF NEUROIMAGING IN THE EVALUATION OF TELEVISION COMMERCIALS   122
GIOVANNI VECCHIATO, PATRIZIA CHERUBINO, ARIANNA TRETTEL, AND FABIO BABILONI

6   **MEMORY**   133
INGRID L. C. NIEUWENHUIS

7   **EMOTIONS**   151
CARL MARCI AND BRENDAN MURRAY

8   **DECISION MAKING**   177
MORAN CERF

9   **REWARD SYSTEM**   207
NEAL J. ROESE, HANS MELO, THALIA VRANTSIDIS, AND WILLIAM A. CUNNINGHAM
**APPENDIX: NEURO-AESTHETICS: THE ROLE OF DOPAMINERGIC REWARD IN PROCESSING
AESTHETICALLY APPEALING PACKAGE DESIGN**   219
MARTIN REIMANN

10   **BRAND EQUITY**   223
MING HSU

11   **PRICING**   241
HIRAK PARIKH, DAVIDE BALDO, AND KAI-MARKUS MÜLLER

12   **SOCIAL MARKETING**   255
DANTE M. PIROUZ

13 **USING KNOWLEDGE FROM NEUROSCIENCE TO MAKE BUSINESS PREDICTIONS** 267
MORAN CERF

14 **APPLICATIONS IN MARKET RESEARCH** 281
DAVID BRANDT

15 **ETHICS IN CONSUMER NEUROSCIENCE** 303
JULIA F. TRABULSI, MARIA CORDERO-MERECUANA, DANIELA SOMARRIBA,
AND MANUEL GARCIA-GARCIA

16 **FUTURE OF CONSUMER NEUROSCIENCE** 321
KIMBERLY ROSE CLARK

CONTRIBUTORS 343
INDEX 345

FOREWORD

I am glad to welcome this comprehensive book on the new field of consumer neuroscience. I want to compliment Professor Moran Cerf for assembling this superb collection of experts on the many aspects of consumer neuroscience.

This book comes after a long history of marketing studies of how consumers make their judgments and their decisions. Marketing scholars were among the first to depart from accepting the economists' assumption that consumers always make rational decisions. The idea was that consumers would choose rationally what would serve their best interests. But if this was the case, why would consumers smoke? Why would consumers fail to save enough money for retirement? Why would low-income consumers buy an expensive car when a cheaper car would save them money and get them everywhere they want to go?

We would postulate that many consumers make multiple irrational decisions, by which we mean: decisions that are not objectively in their best interest. The new field of behavioral economics is built on the notion of nonrational decision making and the effort to reason out the sources of such behavior. With the amalgamation of psychology and behavioral economics and the increase in the number of scientists involved in studying the underlying mechanisms of the psychology of behavioral economics, neuroscience has largely contributed recently to our understanding of human psychology in the context of both behavior and decision making (specifically in the applications of those to the business world at large) and marketing.

As one of the leaders in the field, Professor Cerf has shown how neuroscience and its breakthrough understandings of our psychology can contribute to the study of irrational behavior and to improvement in our ability to predict behavior and choice, as well as ways to help us improve them.

An increasing number of consumer companies have adopted these tools to better understand how their customers are reacting to their products, brands, and communications.

This book on consumer neuroscience is the best starting point for marketers, managers, and lay readers to develop a better understanding of how the human mind actually works in transacting with the world of products and services.

Philip Kotler
S. C. Johnson & Son Distinguished Professor of International Marketing

> Neuroscience and its breakthrough understandings of our psychology can contribute to the study of irrational behavior and to improvement in our ability to predict behavior and choice, as well as ways to help us improve them.

Preface

Welcome to the first edition of the textbook *Consumer Neuroscience*.

The field of consumer neuroscience has grown immensely in recent years, with more businesses electing to entirely replace traditional marketing methods or to enhance the use of neural methods.

Along with these changes, which inevitably bring new skills to the world of marketing, we see an increased movement to more quantitative and data-based marketing at the expense of qualitative methods. Big data, analytics, and statistical inferences are becoming part of everyday marketing solutions, and the requirements for a modern marketing manager exceed those of yesterday.

We expect that being able to use implicit measures of preferences and values will become an ever-growing trend among marketing managers and accordingly offer this book as a first step toward that world.

While the field of consumer neuroscience has grown vastly, the number of textbooks and references in the field falls short. Various popular books offer an overview of the potential and the importance of the field, but none addresses the practical set of information a marketing manager actually needs to know in order to become a significant player in the field.

As such, the majority of solutions are offered by companies, typically mostly made of neuroscientists, who offer a black-box solution. The jargon barriers and the inevitable lack of understanding among the neuroscience community and the marketing community at times generates a gap in the ability to translate the myriad of offerings the field carries into a tangible set of opportunities.

This book, first and foremost, aims to address this problem.

The book is written as a textbook to accompany a class or an educational program that takes a person with no knowledge in neuroscience and carries him or her to an understanding of the tools, techniques, options, and opportunities in this new field. Chapters include discussion questions, case studies, and a variety of examples and summary points that will help an incoming marketing manager to identify a path to understanding the field at his or her level of interest. From a deep mathematical background on the various methods to a broader coverage of the possibilities, we hope that this book will be specific for someone who wants to learn the details of the solutions or all-encompassing if the reader is interested in simply knowing superficially what the field is offering. We hope that readers from many levels will find the book helpful and relevant.

The book is structured in a format that was tried and tested in a number of classes on consumer neuroscience at New York University's Stern School of Business, Northwestern University's Kellogg School of Management, the Burke Institute, through Coursera, and elsewhere. We hope that the combined years of experience of the authors and collaborators will amount to a useful academic experience for readers.

We begin in chapter 1 with an overview of the field, its place among existing disciplines, and the possibilities and potential for neuroscience to shape consumer insights in the years to come. This chapter, written by Manuel Garcia-Garcia (SVP, Research and Innovation at the Advertising Research Foundation, a nonprofit organization that focuses on assessing the opportunities and possibilities in new technologies to lead the advertising industry to the cutting edge), Moran Cerf (a professor studying consumer neuroscience and business and a consultant to a variety of institutions on the use of implicit measures to gather consumer insights), and Ana Iorga (founder of Buyer Brain, a company specializing in the field of consumer neuroscience), will provide an incoming marketing manager with an understanding of the history and background of the field and highlight the journey we are embarking on together.

In chapter 2, Professors Yuping Chen (National Taiwan University), Ming Hsu (University of California, Berkeley), and Moran Cerf (Kellogg School of Management and the MIT Media Lab) will overview the necessary physiologic systems and terms one needs to know in order to pursue a journey in the field. Without going too broadly into neurophysiology, the authors offer a bridge between the jargon neuroscientists often use in their work and the terminology marketing managers should be aware of to better understand later chapters and interact with the tools available.

In chapter 3, Professors Irit Shapira-Lichter (Rabin Medical Center) and Moran Cerf will dive into the systems that govern our senses, the systems used to evaluate and experience the world around us, and the mechanisms that share our perception.

Equipped with the right jargon to understand how the brain is studied, and armed with the knowledge of the ways by which our brain perceives the world and creates our experience of it, we will investigate in chapter 4 the tools offered to marketing managers to study the brain. Tools such as functional magnetic resonance imaging (fMRI), electroencephalography (EEG), eye tracking, biometrics, facial coding systems, and many more will be discussed, giving the reader a deep and profound grasp of the multiple options and assessments. The pros and cons of each tool, the capabilities and challenges of each, and the multitude of possibilities a marketing manager should be aware of will be discussed by Moran Cerf. The reader is welcome to read through all of the options or instead find the tools that may be more relevant to his or her need and focus on those. The chapter is written such that it allows for a deep understanding—at the level required by a practitioner who aims to actually use the tools in her work or that is useful for a manager who is interested in being able to assess the possibilities.

In chapter 5, Manuel Garcia-Garcia introduces us to one of the systems that marketing managers focus on in trying to study the effect of content and experiences on the brain, one that is key to any future evaluation of content—whether we actually attended to it. The mechanisms that navigate and manipulate our attention will be described, along with the ways in which neuroscience can determine the amount of attention we allocate to a resource and the use of attention in understanding the consumer.

Chapter 6 will continue this journey when Ingrid Nieuwenhuis from Nielsen Consumer Neuroscience explores another important mechanism that marketing managers are interested in: memory. How do we make a message memorable and make sure that it is consolidated and used in the long term? These questions will be addressed by the discussions of how memory works and how neuroscientists know what affects it.

In chapter 7, Carl Marci (chief science officer at Nielsen Consumer Neuroscience and assistant professor at Harvard Medical School) together with Brendan Murray (director of neuroscience and client service at Nielsen Consumer Neuroscience) describe the neurologic processes that underlie emotion and how they relate to advertising and consumer behavior. They will also explore the methods used in the industry to measure different aspects of emotion, such as valence and arousal.

Chapter 8 will take us on the journey of decision making, where Moran Cerf explores theories of decision making and the cognitive factors that play a role in the decision-making process. He will also discuss free will and a number of studies that will help the reader understand the way consumers make purchase decisions.

Continuing the path toward an understanding of the functions that we employ in exercising choice in a marketing environment, we will explore the ways by which our brain codes a selection as positive. In chapter 9, Neal Roese (professor of consumer behavior at Kellogg School of Management, Northwestern University) and William Cunningham (Rotman School of Management, University of Toronto) describe the neurologic attributes of the reward system in our brain. The system that is activated as we expect an appetitive experience is key to understanding how events are coded as positive and end up being sought after. The reward system is the main target of promotion and is crucial to understanding why content may impact consumer behavior.

After this, we will dive into the use of all those systems to actually generate a value for a brand. In chapter 10, Ming Hsu (professor at the Haas School of Business, University of California, Berkeley) describes how consumers build implicit associations around a brand and the insights from neuroscience that help us understand the effect of brand equity on the consumer's behavior.

Having covered the functions and the ways in which people code the brand associations in their head, we will proceed to look at the marketing mix and marketing strategies through the lens of neuroscience. In chapter 11, Hirak Parikh, Davide Baldo, and Kai-Markus Müller of The Neuromarketing Labs will take us through different cognitive processes that explain the way in which consumers perceive and respond to pricing. In chapter 12, Dante Pirouz (professor of consumer neuroscience at the Ivey Business School, University of Western Ontario) describes the issue of social marketing and how consumer neuroscience can provide a force for good to help promote healthy behaviors.

All those methods, techniques, functions, and tools ultimately should be used for one purpose—making better predictions about future behavior. This is how marketing managers can assess the value of these, and this is what neuroscience is effectively bringing to the table. In chapter 13, Moran Cerf describes how prior knowledge combined with "big data" analytics and machine learning can and should be used to ultimately make *predictions* about the future. In chapter 14, David Brandt (executive vice president for ad effectiveness strategy at Nielsen Consumer Neuroscience) describes the consumer research industry and how neuroscience changes it. David will address topics such as ad testing, brand equity, package testing, and more in the context of neuroscience and the impact and value added by nonconscious measurement in each one of these applications.

In chapter 15, Julia Trabulsi (global engineer manager at Nielsen Consumer Neuroscience), together with Maria Cordero-Merecuana (Emory University School of Medicine), Daniela Somarriba (Nielsen Consumer Neuroscience), and Manuel Garcia-Garcia, will take us through a number of ethical issues raised in society by the application of neuroscience knowledge and techniques and the response and actions taken by the consumer neuroscience industry.

Finally, in chapter 16, Kimberly Rose Clark (professor of Consumer Neuroscience at Tuck School of Business, Dartmouth College, and chief research officer at Merchant Mechanics) will describe some burning issues and potential platforms that might represent the future of this field.

Following this outline that has been used in numerous consumer neuroscience courses worldwide, we aim at providing a very actionable overview of the value of neuroscience in consumer research that the student can easily apply in his or her professional development. This textbook combines the point of view of academics and of practitioners in order to reach a balance between scientific rigor and applicability for future and current leaders in the consumer research industry.

We truly hope you will find this textbook helpful and relevant to your work and a good introduction to the growing field.

Moran Cerf and Manuel Garcia-Garcia

CHAPTER 1

INTRODUCTION TO CONSUMER NEUROSCIENCE

MANUEL GARCIA-GARCIA,
MORAN CERF, AND ANA IORGA

1.1 INTRODUCTION

> Consumers don't think how they feel. They don't say what they think and they don't
> do what they say.
> —David Ogilvy

Consumers do not think how they feel. They do not say what they think and they
do not do what they say. This is the main value proposition of consumer neuroscience and the reason why understanding the way our brain responds to marketing
stimulation is a very powerful tool for understanding and trying to affect the
behavior of the consumer.

In the world of market research, there are multiple examples in which traditional testing could not have predicted the incredible success of some advertising
campaigns that even challenged common sense. Professor Robert Heath likes to
mention the curious case of O2 in the United Kingdom (Heath 2012). It was 2001
when the small network operator Cellnet was spun off and relaunched under the
name O2 at an event held in front of a gigantic Vodafone, which was then becoming the world's largest operator of its kind. O2 spent a lot of money in an advertising
campaign that mostly featured blue water with bubbles and some lilting music in
the background. Rather inexplicably, in 4 years O2 achieved market leadership.
One could now argue that the water and the bubbles created an equity of freedom
around the new brand that made it unique in a world of locked up contracts with
cell phone service providers. The truth is that we do not really know what made
that campaign so successful.

As said, understanding the consumer is not an easy task, but marketers and advertisers are seeing a great opportunity to shed some light into the *black box* by looking at the consumer at the most fundamental level: the human brain.

We will look at the variety of questions that can be answered through consumer neuroscience research and the types of questions that cannot be answered. It is easy to imagine how exaggeration of the effectiveness of these research tools could create a false expectation that consumer neuroscience will solve all your problems. We will then discuss the advantages and limitations of this type of research and will provide a guideline to choosing the most appropriate methodology on the basis of the question that needs to be answered and criteria such as sample size, duration, and optimal cost. You will learn how to evaluate a consumer neuroscience vendor and what to ask for when you want to commission a new project.

As we will discuss further, consumer neuroscience has its limitations, and you need to take them into account when assessing the results that you get from a study. Bear in mind that consumer neuroscience is just a tool (although a powerful one) that provides deep insights but does not replace your critical thinking, and it is not a single-source panacea.

The one big source of misunderstanding was that often, clients thought about consumer neuroscience as a tool to implant thoughts into the minds of consumers.

The one big source of misunderstanding was that often, clients thought about consumer neuroscience as a tool to implant thoughts into the minds of consumers. It is a great responsibility to diligently explain as researchers and to clearly understand as clients that the purpose of these tools is to better assess the presence and valence of the reaction of consumers to our stimuli in order to create and shape for them better products and services and not to manipulate their brains.

1.2 The Brain as the Seat of Behavior

Multiple studies have proved the capacity of brain activity to predict human behavior at very different levels, from anticipating memory retrieval or clinical symptoms in epilepsy to product purchase and use of services. This case below illustrates the drastic impact of brain malfunction on behavior.

August 1, 1966, seemed like a typical day in Austin, Texas. The news reported calm and sunny weather, and the headline in the morning focused on the local U.S. Senate race debate. However, the events of that day will forever be remembered among the people of Austin as one of the most horrific days the city has experienced.

On that morning, Charles Whitman, an American engineering student who was in his mid-twenties, drove to the University of Texas at Austin where he was a student. He was not known to be particularly violent or outspoken. Whitman arrived at the university wearing coveralls over his white shirt and blue jeans and pretended to be a research assistant delivering equipment. No one suspected that he had rifles, pistols, and ammunition in the box on his hand truck. Once Whitman reached the observation deck of the main building ("the tower") on campus, he killed three people inside the tower and then began to take aim at the people within range on the grounds of the campus below: he proceeded to kill 11 and wound 33 individuals. He had also killed his wife and mother in the early-morning hours of August 1 before arriving at the campus.

The police arrived after the rampage began and surrounded the tower, but Whitman would not stop shooting. Finally, an officer ended Whitman's rampage by shooting and killing him.

A week prior, Whitman sat at his desk, writing in his journal. He wrote that he was feeling rather strange and that he was scared that he would "snap" at some point. A few months earlier, Whitman had gone to see the staff psychiatrist at the university health center for an examination. The psychiatrist, Dr. Heatly, noted Whitman's feelings of hostility and sent him home with simply a suggestion for a follow-up visit. Whitman did not return.

In a suicide note written before the rampage, Whitman had requested that an autopsy be performed on his body when he died. An autopsy was performed after his death, and a large tumor was found near the part of the brain that controls violent urges, anxiety, and anger, called the amygdala, but no cause-and-effect relationship between the tumor and Whitman's behavior could be established.

Now, if readers feel that the example is in any way far removed from the norm and not relevant to us—think again. We can in fact all imagine situations where a little molecule of ethanol in a certain concentration makes us all behave differently and not be ourselves. Ethanol is the molecule commonly referred to as alcohol. And a little sip of alcohol in the right concentration can in fact make many of us less inhibited, our jokes become funnier, and generally we find ourselves a bit different. Our brain is controlling our personality and our choices, and we suddenly are not the same. Could neuroscientists use this understanding of our brain to better predict who we are and what we will be like in certain situations?

To understand how this applies to marketing, it is necessary to historically review the way in which the world has understood decision making and market research and find the point where they converged and started influencing each other.

1.3   THE NEUROSCIENCE OF DECISION MAKING THROUGHOUT HISTORY

Contemporary marketing has advanced in use of technology, but many of the guiding principles and the driving forces and motivations of marketers remain similar: understanding and predicting human behavior. One of the monumental changes that the world has arrived at in the past decades is the ability to look at the brain for answers.

Beginning in the early eleventh century, Avicenna (Ibn Sina; 980–1037), originally from Bukhara, could be considered an early visionary of consumer neuroscience, as he developed a system that relates biomarkers to inner emotional states. These biomarkers, such as pulse rate, skin conductance (sweat), pupil dilation, and so forth, are currently used in the consumer neuroscience industry as a way to infer emotional states elicited by advertising through very flexible and nonintrusive systems that can provide high face validity. In one of Avicenna's autobiographical books, *The Road to Isfahan*, he reports how he came across a man who was suffering from melancholia (depression); Avicenna recited aloud the names of provinces, districts, towns, streets, and people while performing a digital (i.e., manual) examination of the patient's pulse rate. Through changes in the patient's pulse rate, Avicenna was able to find out the name and residence of the woman that the patient was in love with. Similar to some modern industry players, he was able to infer an individual's inner emotional state elicited by the illustration of some places that are associated with the source of the change in the emotional state—the woman he loved (Mohamed 2008). Unfortunately, at those times Avicenna had no way to register information directly from the brain, so he could only infer the state of the *soul* from peripheral biomarkers.

During the sixteenth century and the scientific revolution, Europe recovered many of Galen's theses as well as the influence of the scientific advances that had occurred in the Arab world while Christian Europe was immersed in religious dogmatism. Dissections of the human body became a common practice, leading to the birth of neuroanatomy. Having the ability to see what the brain looks like, scientists would start to take positions in an emergent debate: Are mental functions and abilities located in specific brain regions or are they scattered across that organ? Scientists would soon begin to locate mental functions in specific areas of the brain.

Some impressive advancements occurred in neuroscience: an illustrated and detailed description of brain anatomy was published by Thomas Willis (1621–1675), and reflexes and involuntary movements were described; more important, the relevance of those reflexes. While reflexes were first thought to be independent of the brain, Robert Whytt (1714–1766) demonstrated that the pupillary reflex was linked to midbrain activity, and he stressed the protective function of these reflexes as survival mechanisms that evolved so our bodies can make quick decisions. Marshall Hall (1790–1857) established the idea of these reflexes being unconscious and involuntary (and modifiable by drugs). But many questions still remain: How are reflexes really different from most decisions we make? Do we rule our daily lives on the basis of reflexes? Are they mindless? Are they brainless?

Around the second half of the eighteenth century, after Benjamin Franklin had performed extensive research on electricity, it was the time for Galvani and many others to discover the capacity of animals to generate electricity and even to observe muscle contraction and movements induced by external electrical impulses. The concept of electrophysiology had been invented, and it set the stage for future techniques that would register electrical activity directly from the brain, or even on the human head.

One of the most influential and disputed thinkers in the field was the New Yorker William James (1842–1910). His theses about consciousness, emotion, and habits are still very relevant in fields with interest in decision making, such as consumer neuroscience. His viewpoints in many aspects are very interesting to the field nowadays. Let us have a quick look at some of them so you can extract your own conclusions:

1. "The habits to which we have an innate tendency are called instincts"; other than those innate instincts or reflexes, he claims that habits are formed on the basis of the plasticity of the organism; that is, *our nervous system grown to the modes in which it has been exercised.* These habits would simplify the movements required to achieve a given result, make them more accurate. and diminish fatigue. Notably, *habit diminishes the conscious attention with which our acts are performed.* He described that *the simultaneous combination of movements is thus in the first instance conditioned by the facility with which in us, alongside of intellectual processes, processes of inattentive feeling may still go on.* Now, think how many of your decisions are made on the basis of habits and how many of them are rationalized. Think of every step on your way to work, whether riding the subway or driving down the highway, and all the decisions you are forced to make within one minute, some of them of vital importance, such as stepping on the brake pedal of your car or turning the wheel. This view on decision making that challenges the traditional view of consciousness and willingness would be fought during the most part of the twentieth century and would later be recovered. It now plays a big role in the fields of decision making, neuroeconomics, and definitely in consumer neuroscience.

2. Together with Carl Lange, James developed a theory (figure 1.1) whose basic premise is that *physiologic arousal instigates the experience of a specific emotion.* They proposed that instead of feeling an emotion and then experiencing a body response, the body change occurs first, and the emotion is then experienced when the brain reacts or interprets the body information. In other words, they postulated that instead of *think* and then *feel*, we *feel* and then *think.* More specifically, this theory states that a stimulus (like a car suddenly merging into your lane or a car approaching at a very high speed while you cross the street) evokes a physiologic response (rise in heart rate, respiration, to prepare your body for a fast reaction); this physiologic change will be perceived by the cerebral cortex, which will send this information to the muscles in order to respond to the stimulus (run to the other side of the street or step on your car's brake pedal). Finally, impulses from the muscles are sent back to the cerebral cortex, so the individual feels the emotion

James-Lange Theory

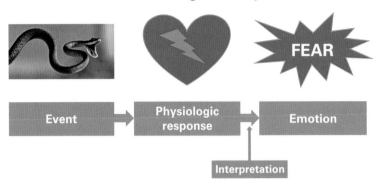

Figure 1.1
The James-Lange model.

(fear). James explains that while common sense would dictate that a person sees a bear, becomes afraid, and runs away, he thought that first the person has a physiologic response to the bear (trembling), and then runs and becomes afraid. This theory has critical implications in consumer neuroscience: by measuring the brain activity that leads to the body change or the body change itself, we would be collecting much more information than the individual himself would ever be able to report.

3. James described the existence of different mechanisms of decision making, one being led by rational arguments and one that is the consequence of our voluntary choice; most of our decision making, as described by James, will not derive from our own will, but as a response to external stimuli, *as a response prompted by a submission to our own selves*, such as a habit, or as a result of a sudden change of mood. This demeaning of the personal will or capacity to rationally make our own decisions would become very controversial for the decades to come and a very exciting matter of research when tools were available to explore our brains in search of answers.

4. James's theses on attention have been repeatedly quoted and discussed in the literature: "Everyone knows what attention is. It is taking possession by the mind, in clear and vivid form, of one out of what seem several simultaneous possible objects and train of thoughts. … It implies withdrawal from some things in order to deal effectively with others, and is a condition which has a real opposite in the confused, dazed, scatter-brain state which in French is called distraction and Zehrstreuheit in German." All his postulates about attentional processing, and the impossibility of dealing effectively with simultaneous objects, including those external stimuli that cause (what we now in English call) distraction, served as inspiration for many researchers to find out how attention processes work. Furthermore, the notion of being unable to effectively deal with a train of thoughts and with distracting objects is controversial in terms of personal will and crucial in understanding how advertising works.

The first half of the twentieth century witnessed the emergence of *behaviorism*, which interestingly was only concerned with observable behavior. Proponents maintained that behavior could be described without looking into internal events or thoughts. Some names that resonate with the times of behaviorism are Watson, Skinner, or even Pavlov, although the latter was not a fan of this school of thought. I am sure most people are familiar with Pavlov's experiments in behavioral mechanisms performed on dogs. In simple terms, the dog was presented with a stimulus, such as a light or a sound, and then was given food. After a few repetitions, the dog would associate that stimulus with the food; therefore the dog would salivate after the presence of the stimulus, also if there was no food involved (Buchman and O'Connell, 2006). While this stimulus-response experiment is not concerned with any non-observable event, the association between the stimulus and the food was being built in the brain. Now think of the association of Coca-Cola and Santa Claus and how it has been built.

Similarly, Skinner's behavioral experiments were just concerned with observable events and were tuned more finely to these behaviorist insights. According to Skinner's conditioning, behavior operates in the environment and is modified by its consequences. Therefore, a behavior followed by a reinforcement or a reward would be maintained, while a behavior followed by punishment would be withdrawn. Besides the obvious repercussion of these postulates for education, now think for a moment about the relevance of these theses in advertising. The general goal of advertising is to perpetrate a purchase behavior though the reinforcement of that behavior with the positive outcome of enjoying a product. The advertiser might first need to create some associations between your product and some positive outcome, which makes the consumer "salivate" in the presence of your product, brand, or label and feel the desire to purchase it in the first place. And as you might be thinking, we wished things were this simple.

During the second half of the twentieth century, a new school emerged as a response to behaviorism's neglect of cognition. While behaviorists identified thinking as behavior, cognitivists argued that the way people think does impact their behavior. Although it emerged as a response to behaviorism, cognitive psychology represented rather an expansion of the previous school that also accepted mental states, and they both combined well in the development of the psychological practice through the cognitive-behavioral therapies.

We have to go back some years to describe an event that will entail a revolution in the way of thinking about personality and decision making in relation to the brain. This case would be studied for many decades to come, all the way through to our times. Phineas P. Gage (1823–1860) was an American railroad construction foreman who suffered a rock-blasting accident in which a large iron rod was driven completely through his head. Surprisingly, he did survive, although the iron rod destroyed a large part of his left frontal lobe. The interesting fact about this case is that this injury caused significant changes in his personality and behavior that would remain for the 12 years he lived after this accident. His doctor reported that before the accident, Gage was hardworking, responsible, and considered to be the most efficient and capable foreman by his employers. These same employers thought the change in his mind to be so significant that they would not let him continue as foreman after the accident. Gage's physician, Dr. Harlow, wrote:

> The equilibrium or balance, so to speak, between his intellectual faculties and animal propensities, seems to have been destroyed. He is fitful, irreverent, indulging at times in the grossest profanity (which was not previously his custom), manifesting but little deference for his fellows, impatient of restraint or advice when it conflicts with his desires, at times pertinaciously obstinate, yet capricious and vacillating, devising many plans of future operations, which are no sooner arranged than they are abandoned in turn for others appearing more feasible. A child in his intellectual capacity and manifestations, he has the animal passions of a strong man. Previous to his injury, although untrained in the schools, he possessed a well-balanced mind, and was looked upon by those who knew him as a shrewd, smart businessman, very energetic and persistent in executing all his plans of operation. In this regard his mind was radically changed, so decidedly that his friends and acquaintances said he was no longer Gage.

Gage was not capable of adapting his behavior to the social situation. Now we know that social inhibition is located in the orbitofrontal cortex, and we observe similar behavior in patients with a lesion in this brain region. This case is so important that it has generated publications even during the twenty-first century and has motivated much research work in clinical populations and in healthy subjects. After the development of neuroimaging techniques, this new knowledge would be tested in order to understand the role of frontal brain regions in decision making, personality, and social behavior.

After Hans Berger registered human brain electrical activity from the surface of the head in 1928—inventing *electroencephalography*—the second half of the twentieth century witnessed the emergence of a number of human neuroscience techniques that allowed us to look inside the brain for answers about its shape and function (figure 1.2). In 1970, computerized axial tomography (CAT) scanning gave us a tool to obtain detailed anatomic images of the brain for diagnostic and research purposes. During the early 1980s, better images of the brain could be obtained with single-photon emission computed tomography (SPECT) and positron emission tomography (PET). During that time, magnetic resonance imaging (MRI) was developed and was quickly introduced in clinical practice for refined diagnostic applications. Soon after, scientists learned that the blood flow changes measured by PET

Techniques in the 20th Century

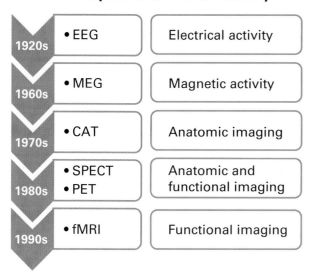

1920s	• EEG	Electrical activity
1960s	• MEG	Magnetic activity
1970s	• CAT	Anatomic imaging
1980s	• SPECT • PET	Anatomic and functional imaging
1990s	• fMRI	Functional imaging

FIGURE 1.2
A timeline of techniques.

could also be imaged by functional magnetic resonance imaging (fMRI) with a much lower level of invasiveness and lack of radiation exposure.

The development of these technologies that allow us to look into the brain, together with the great advancement in computing capacity, has given researchers tools to answer many questions that remained historically unanswered about human behavior and decision making.

Moreover, it gave us the opportunity to take this knowledge into practice and develop algorithms and devices that facilitate the interaction between our brain and a machine through brain-computer interface (BCI). The early twenty-first century has been marked by the application of these techniques to different areas, such as consumer research or health self-monitoring, and that has led to great developments in the portability of these methodologies to bring them out of the lab and provide higher face validity.

A contemporary neuroscientist who studied Gage's case and answered some of the remaining historical questions about human decision making is the Portuguese-American Antonio Damasio. Through his work on Gage's case and with other patients who had lesions in brain frontal regions, Damasio recovered some of William James's perspective on *feelings* as a readout of the body and the concept about emotion leading decision making and social cognition. Damasio's *somatic marker hypothesis* explains how emotions and their biological underpinnings are involved in decision making, quite often nonconsciously. Through extensive work

The development of these technologies that allow us to look into the brain, together with the great advancement in computing capacity, has given researchers the tools to answer many questions that remained historically unanswered about human behavior and decision making.

that will be reviewed in later chapters, he uncovered cortical and subcortical brain sites for emotion that are crucial for decision making, such as the amygdala and the ventromedial prefrontal cortex (Kandel, Schwartz, and Jessell 2000).

The great influence of Damasio's theses on neuroeconomics and in consumer neuroscience is indisputable. Other authors, such as Daniel Kahneman, also wrote about different systems for making decisions, one of them being nonconscious, quick, and driven by emotions. Robert Heath took this school of thought one step further into our field and applied this implicit decision-making process guided by emotions to the world of advertising and the success of advertising campaigns in driving purchase decisions.

With all this knowledge on the table and among the numerous applications that neuroscience has found in the past decade, consumer neuroscience has already been helping advertisers, manufacturers, brands, and so forth, understand their consumers and optimize their marketing communications and advertising campaigns, driving success among very well-known companies.

1.4   Consumer and Advertising Research throughout History: Decision Making

The history of advertising can also be traced back to papyrus used by ancient Egyptians to make sales messages and wall posters. Rock and wall painting is an ancient advertising form that can be found in Indian rock art painting around 6,000 years ago and also in some parts of the world today.

In Europe during the Middle Ages, where the general population was unable to read, traders would use images associated with their products, and sometimes street callers on the main plazas, to advertise their wares for the convenience of the consumer.

During the eighteenth century, print advertising started to appear in weekly newspapers in England. It was in the nineteenth century when Thomas J. Barratt from London, known as the father of modern advertising, created an effective campaign with slogans and images and led Pears' soap to be the first legally registered brand. He worked on the equity of Pears' to create an association of the brand with high culture and quality. He emphasized the relevance of an exclusive brand image and of highlighting the product's availability through saturation campaigns.

The twentieth century started with some influence of the most accepted psychological school of the times on advertising. While some of its postulates were not accurate, psychoanalysis had an enriching influence in popular culture, clinical psychology, and also in advertising. In fact, a nephew of Sigmund Freud, Edward Bernays, would adopt the doctrine that human instincts can be targeted and directed toward the desire to purchase a product. This is an interesting early adoption of the enormous relevance of emotion in consumer behavior.

During the 1920s, psychologist Walter D. Scott developed that same idea further: "Man has been called the reasoning animal but he could with greater truthfulness be called the creature of suggestion. He is reasonable, but he is to a greater extent suggestible." He implemented the concepts of behaviorism described above into advertising, focusing on appealing to *love, hate,* and *fear.*

In the 1960s, advertising witnessed media diversification from print and radio to television. Similar to what is happening in the early twenty-first century, campaigns diversified featuring heavy spending in different media. The same campaigns would be displayed across the three different touchpoints: magazine, radio, and television.

The most prominent theory of advertising dates back to 1899 when E. St. Elmo Lewis described the AIDA model as follows: "The mission of an advertisement is to attract a reader, so that he will look at the advertisement and start to read it; then to interest him, so that he will continue to read it; then to convince him, so that when he has read it he will believe it. If an advertisement contains these three qualities of success, it is a successful advertisement." AIDA is an acronym that describes the four steps that an ad has to elicit, each one being a necessary condition for the next step to happen: attention, interest, desire, and action (figure 1.3).

AIDA MODEL

"The mission of an advertisement is to attract...so that he will look at the advertisement and start to read it; then to interest him, so that he will continue to read it; then to convince him, so that when he has read it he will believe it."

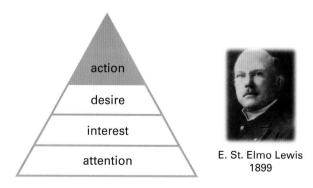

action

desire

interest

attention

E. St. Elmo Lewis
1899

FIGURE 1.3
The AIDA model.

In the past decades, as stated above, advances in neuroscience have made it feasible to prove the postulates indicating the relevance of emotion in decision making. The theses of Kahneman and the studies of Damasio among others have established solid theories on decision making that are obtaining further development through rigorous scientific research. The work of Heath and many other academics led the way to integrate these scientific findings into consumer research and advertising, and the recent emergence of consumer neuroscience is allowing advertisers to better understand their consumers' behavior by looking at them at their most fundamental level: the brain.

1.5 Consumer Neuroscience

Consumer neuroscience emerged as the natural result of the development of human neuroscience techniques and the added value that those deeper insights could provide to consumer research. But moreover, the mindset of how people make decisions started rooting into the philosophy of marketers. The relatively recent confirmation of some of James's postulates on decision making through neuroscience methods made necessary complementary consumer research with some insights coming directly from the brain.

Consumer research relies on a cognitive-behavioral model, such as the stimulus-organism-response model, in which the "black box" is the organism representing the underlying brain processes. Consumer research has existed for some time already, characterizing individual consumers as socio-demographic and personality variables, in order to understand and predict their behavior.

Traditionally, consumer researchers have intended to infer motivational, perceptual, and higher cognitive processes at different stages of the consumer experience, through observation of behavior and articulated survey research. While great insights were obtained using more traditional techniques, the availability of neuroscience methods permitted researchers to go directly to the "black box" to look for insights about consumers' motivational and cognitive processes and ultimately to predict their behavior.

The development of more insightful theories about decision making led to the emergence of a new field called neuroeconomics. This new field uses neuroscientific insights to understand economic decisions and guide models of economics.

However, there is much more to consumer neuroscience than understanding and predicting consumers' decisions. On the basis of these premises, consumer neuroscience can help advertisers optimize their marketing communication at very different stages of the process, the flow of their television commercials, their online user interfaces, the design of their packages, and so forth. As a combination

> The development of more insightful theories about decision making led to the emergence of a new field called neuroeconomics. This new field uses neuroscientific insights to understand economic decisions and guide models of economics.

of consumer research and neuroscience, the goal of consumer neuroscience is to use insights and methods from neuroscience to improve the understanding of consumer behavior at many different levels. There are many current applications of consumer neuroscience in consumer research extending from advertising, concepts, and package research to branding and other forms of marketing communication.

One of the most interesting areas of consumer neuroscience is advertising. After decades of advertising research, it is still hard to explain how advertising works, how to create effective advertising, and to predict the in-market outcome of an advertising campaign. Until the recent breakthrough of neuroscience in the field of market research, the dominant theory, the AIDA model described earlier, identified a successful campaign as one that first is able to capture a consumer's attention, then generate some interest, and after that induce some desire that ultimately leads to action. It is interesting to note how this prevailing assumption of a linear rationale, when translated into daily decision making, involves the belief that we are provided with unlimited cognitive resources, as well as unlimited time.

In the advertising world, there are numerous cases of unpredicted successful campaigns that are yet hard to explain. Having a window into the black box brings us a step closer to predicting in-market success. However, the multiple variables playing a role in in-market performance make it very hard to predict the success of a campaign only from its advertising effectiveness, no matter how far we get in understanding consumers' reaction to it. In any case, these insights play a big role, and it is certain that every advertiser would like to enhance understanding of their campaign's effectiveness in the consumers' brains.

Understanding branding has been a great opportunity for consumer neuroscience to shine both in the lab and in the market research industry. Focusing on the reward system, which activates in anticipation of a reward, researchers have been able to show how different brands could work as social reinforcers and activate the reward system. Moreover, neuroscience is helping us to understand how the *brand-building* process works. Frequent questions are: How long does it take for a brand to build its equity? What does it take to build those associations with a brand in consumers' minds?

1.6 WHY CONSUMER NEUROSCIENCE?

Why do we need another market research technique? Aren't there enough tools on the market already? We gather too much data that we do not actually know how to take advantage of, so why should we bother?

Practitioners from the research field can attest, as Ogilvy once said, that "Consumers don't think how they feel. They don't say what they think and they don't do what they say." That might be because we, as human beings, are striving

Focusing on the reward system, which activates in anticipation of a reward, researchers have been able to show how different brands could work as social reinforcers and activate the reward system.

to please and be accepted by our peer group (Lieberman 2013), so most people would rather conform than be different. This explains why socially desirable answers could become such an issue in market research. In general terms, this is being traditionally accepted as a systemic error and even called "consumer over-claim." Complex post hoc validations have been used to calibrate and attempt to factor out these biases. That's at least one place where consumer neuroscience comes into play and proves its value. As it goes beyond consumers' declarative states, it sheds some light into the real motivators behind people's actions and attitudes.

Furthermore, another reason for which consumer neuroscience is worth its price comes from Zaltman's observation that as much as 95% of our purchasing decision-making process takes place at the nonconscious level (Zaltman 2003). Consumer neuroscience thus becomes extremely useful, as it collects both conscious and nonconscious reactions. This is crucial given that "We are really far less rational than standard economic theory assumes," as Ariely notes in his book (Ariely 2008).

Consumer neuroscience reduces companies' risks associated with product development and marketing and communication campaigns by identifying emotional and nonconscious triggers that drive brand preference and purchasing behavior.

1.6.1 ADVANTAGES OF CONSUMER NEUROSCIENCE

Here we list some of the main advantages of consumer neuroscience:

- Consumer neuroscience goes beyond the declarative state of customers.

- By recording and analyzing customers' brain activity when exposed to different stimuli, we get a glimpse of what's going on in their brains in those moments. This in turn can help us by giving a higher granularity to the assessment data.

- It can capture transient processes (e.g., emotions) that people might not be aware of or may omit to mention because the processes are very short or weak (Lee, Broderick, and Chamberlain 2007). These processes leave a physiologic trace that is picked up by the recording device and can further be analyzed.

- In cases in which the issue or material that is tested is socially sensitive, thus creating an extra incentive to deceive or give a socially desirable answer, consumer neuroscience is especially useful as it records brain activity, which people cannot control. Thus, it is able to rule out biases such as strategic behavior and social desirability that oftentimes alter traditional research methods (Camerer, Loewenstein, and Prelec 2005).

- By studying brain activity, researchers can assess the price point at which the gain (the expected pleasure derived from consuming the product) exceeds the pain of paying (Knutson et al. 2007). In 2013, Kai-Mueller, of The Neuromarketing Labs in Germany, performed the *Starbucks Study*, one of the most mediatized studies on pricing. He recorded and analyzed consumers' brain reactions to the price of a "Tall" Starbucks coffee and arrived at the conclusion that people would be willing to pay around 33% more on their indulgence. This comes as counterintuitive because Starbucks is already perceived as being at the upper end of the coffee business.

- Importantly, consumer neuroscience allows companies to increase their return on investment (ROI) on media and advertising spending. By fine-tuning their messages and selecting the elements that have the highest impact on consumers, companies will make a better use of their advertising money.

> Consumer neuroscience allows companies to increase their return on investment (ROI) on media and advertising spending.

1.6.2 LIMITATIONS OF CONSUMER NEUROSCIENCE

Although a powerful instrument, consumer neuroscience presents some limitations that spring from the tools that are used and the methodologies developed by different areas of research.

One of the main limitations that consumer neuroscience faces comes from the fact that it does not tell us *why* people develop the reactions we observe. We see that customers love our new ad, and we can also detect which elements of the ad are the ones people love the most (and which ones they hate), but we do not know why people like (or hate) them. We can only assume certain causalities on the basis of previous results and historic behavior, and we can compute some correlations, but we do not know for sure why people reacted the way they did (Perrachione and Perrachione 2008). One could argue that this is not even important because, as long as we know what are the elements that have the highest impact or the products that people love the most, we can still build an efficient communication campaign and have a successful launch.

Another drawback is represented by the artificial lab setting where most of the studies are performed, which might distort people's reactions compared to those in real-life situations. Further limitations derive from issues related to the tools' temporal (fMRI, PET) and spatial (EEG, SST) resolution limitations, ethical issues (TMS, fMRI, MEG), and cost barriers (fMRI, TMS, MEG).

However, some of these techniques have little to no application to consumer research, and the constant technological developments are bringing many of these tools outside the lab, enabling collection of nonconscious reactions with nonintrusive devices at a much lower price, providing great face validity. Some vendors are still far from adopting these new developments, but such a cutting-edge field will not stay outdated.

One of the difficulties neuroscience encounters is reverse inference, which represents the assumption that a specific mental process took place on the basis of

> One of the difficulties neuroscience encounters is reverse inference, which represents the assumption that a specific mental process took place on the basis of the occurrence of a brain pattern.

the occurrence of a brain pattern (Poldrack 2011). Like any applied science, consumer neuroscience relies on reverse inference, which is not flawed per se. It would be perfectly legitimate if we had a perfect understanding of the relationship between the brain and the mind, argues Thomas Ramsøy in his latest book on neuromarketing (Ramsøy 2014). As we are not there yet, researchers agree that reverse inference should be used cautiously and that they should not rely solely on this practice to draw the main conclusions of their papers.

By shedding some light on how the brain works and by introducing a science-based approach to marketing, consumer neuroscience creates a framework that allows researchers to validate, reassess, or improve conventional marketing theories (Fugate 2007). It also brings a deeper understanding of the mental processes that underlie consumer behavior, thus allowing companies to create better communication strategies (Hubert and Kenning 2008).

Box 1.1
How to Evaluate a Consumer Neuroscience Vendor

You are considering doing a consumer neuroscience research study in your organization, but you are not sure where to start from. There are several steps that you can take in order to ensure that your future project will be a success.

First, you must assess whether it is the timing is right for such a study in your organization—are the key people willing to embrace change and committed to implement the results?

Second, it is important to clearly define what your objectives for the study are and what are the questions that you want to answer. Then, you need to decide on the material that you want to test—you might want to find out whether your company's positioning is right in the minds of your customers, or maybe you want to test your newest television commercial before spending a huge budget on media, or you are involved in product development and you want to make sure that the new and improved version of your product is everything people are waiting for.

After deciding on these aspects, you need to discuss with the consumer neuroscience vendor the most suitable tool to be used in order to get the answers that you are looking for. Very likely, there is a mix of several techniques that can be used to address your subject as they each provide slightly different insights and have specific shortcomings, but taken together they produce a balanced result. For example, you can test a television commercial by using EEG with eye tracking, galvanic skin response (GSR), facial coding, and other biometric tools. Or you can use fMRI. All these techniques come at different price points, and, unless you have an unlimited budget, you need to reach a compromise between the insights that you get and the money you can afford to spend.

Furthermore, the process of data collection is of equal importance, and special care should be taken to avoid potential situations that might contaminate the data. For example, for an IAT (implicit-association test) study performed online, where people respond from their homes, one potential issue is related to the speed and the

Box 1.1
(continued)

signal of the Internet connection: if the speed varies and the connection gets lost during the test, then the data collected should be discarded. You might want to ask the consumer neuroscience vendor about the specific safeguards they have put in place to prevent those situations.

When searching for a consumer neuroscience vendor, you should evaluate the method's validity (the tools should be properly designed in order to measure what they claim they measure) and reliability (getting the same results in the same conditions). You can also ask for case studies of past projects where you can assess that the above metrics are met.

One particular aspect that needs special attention is related to overclaiming. As in any new field, where practices are not yet standardized, there might be companies that claim more than they can deliver. Such cases may occur when there are issues related to the validity or reliability of the methodologies or when the studies are poorly designed. The overclaiming game has been fueled by media outlets that are hungry for sensationalist news and would pick up any claims, regardless of whether they are backed up by solid science or not, in order to increase their audience.

According to Carla Nagel,[1] the head of the Neuromarketing Science and Business Association (NMSBA), the organization is taking the first steps in reducing the incidence of overclaiming by introducing the Corporate Accreditation Process that acts as a quality mark for companies in providing neuromarketing research. The quality mark ensures that a company offers valid and scientifically based neuromarketing services.

Here, we provide a checklist that can be used when selecting a consumer neuroscience partner for your projects.

VENDOR CHECKLIST

- Company profile: experience in market research and in using specific neuroscience techniques.
- Technique portfolio: what kind of techniques does the company employ (traditional vs. neuroscience or both).
- Specific tools and metrics: what metrics does the company measure (emotions, memory, attention, etc.).
- Portability: what is the setting required to run a study (lab only, in-store, or online).
- Sample size and composition: what is the minimum sample size (and has it been validated); what are the cooperation and dropout rates of participants; are there specific restrictions regarding the people that can take part in a study.
- Statistics analysis and database comparisons: significance testing, database norms, other modeling analytics.
- Data quality and validity: data quality-control processes for data recording and analysis.
- Policies and compliance: protection and privacy policies for respondents.

1. Personal e-mail correspondence with one of the authors (A.I.).

Key Takeaways

In the past decade, there has been a growing understanding among marketing managers that knowledge from neuroscience can play an essential part in helping shape the marketing message and the ability to improve our understanding of the customer. As marketing has been changing in the past decade to introduce digital marketing into the mainstream, so will consumer neuroscience shape our understanding of the marketing landscape. In this chapter, we learned about the history of decision-making studies and neuroscience, about why understanding the brain is crucial to understanding behavior, and how marketing managers have been using neuroscience to better understand the consumer.

Here are a few questions to think about after your reading:

1. Can you think of ways in which neuroscience can inform your understanding of a company that you are familiar with?

2. How many of your decisions are governed by rational thinking versus emotional or irrational decision-making processes?

3. If you could make a choice now between two products (say, two types of toothpastes), do you know how to decide solely on the basis of the dimensions you believe to be useful for you?

These questions and more will be discussed further in the coming chapters about rational and irrational decision-making processes.

Discussion Questions

1. What are the hurdles that neuromarketing still needs to overcome?

2. What is neuromarketing's main selling proposition? Why is that important to customers?

3. Do you believe that overclaiming poses a real threat to neuromarketing? Why?

4. Why is reverse inference a problem in neuromarketing?

5. What are the most important insights that you get from a neuromarketing study?

6. You are the head of research of a large retailer. Your CEO is pushing you to provide more insight, and you are pondering whether to give neuromarketing a try. What should you look for, and what methodologies should you use?

How do you choose the right partner for the study? Split into small groups and discuss.

7. You are in charge of business development within a medium-sized research agency and are continually assessing new methodologies that would allow your company to grow. You just came back from an industry event where people were hyped about neuromarketing, and you want to share that with your colleagues. Split into small groups and discuss the advantages and limitations of neuromarketing.

8. You are the vice president of marketing of a large sweets manufacturer, and you want to run an fMRI study to test some flavors for a new product line that you are going to launch. Unfortunately, your CEO is not so keen about this project because he fears a consumer backlash driven by the perception of manipulating and reading the minds of consumers. Pair with another colleague and discuss the benefits and risks that a neuromarketing study would bring to your company. How can you mitigate the risks that your CEO fears?

REFERENCES

Ariely, D. 2008. *Predictably irrational: The hidden forces that shape our decisions*. New York: HarperCollins.

Camerer, C., G. Loewenstein, and D. Prelec. 2005. Neuroeconomics: How neuroscience can inform economics. *Journal of Economic Literature* 43:9–64.

Fugate, D. L. 2007. Neuromarketing: A layman's look at neuroscience and its potential application to marketing practice. *Journal of Consumer Marketing* 24 (7): 385–394.

Heath, R. 2012. *Seducing the subconscious: The psychology of emotional influence in advertising*. Hoboken, NJ: Wiley-Blackwell.

Hubert, M., and P. Kenning. 2008. A current overview of consumer neuroscience. *Journal of Consumer Behaviour* 7 (4–5): 272–292.

Kandel, E. R., J. H. Schwartz, and T. M. Jessell. 2000. *Principles of neural science* (4th ed.). New York: McGraw-Hill.

Knutson, B., S. Rick, G. E. Wimmer, D. Prelec, and G. Loewenstein. 2007. Neural predictors of purchases. *Neuron* 53 (1): 147–156.

Lee, N., A. J. Broderick, and L. Chamberlain. 2007. What is "neuromarketing"? A discussion and agenda for future research. *International Journal of Psychophysiology* 63:199–204.

Lieberman, M. D. 2013. *Social: Why our brains are wired to connect*. Oxford, England: Oxford University Press.

Mohamed, W. M. Y. 2008. History of neuroscience: Arab and Muslim contributions to modern neuroscience. *IBRO History of Neuroscience*.

Perrachione, T. K., and J. R. Perrachione. 2008. Brains and brands: Developing mutually informative research in neuroscience and marketing. *Journal of Consumer Behaviour* 7 (4–5): 303–318.

Poldrack, R. A. 2011. Inferring mental states from neuroimaging data: From reverse inference to large-scale decoding. *Neuron* 72 (5): 692–697.

Ramsøy, T. Z. 2014. *Introduction to neuromarketing & consumer neuroscience*. Rørvig, Denmark: Neurons, Inc.

Zaltman, G. 2003. *How customers think: Essential insights into the mind of the market*. Cambridge, MA: Harvard Business Press.

CHAPTER 2

BRAIN PHYSIOLOGY AND ANATOMY

YUPING CHEN, MING HSU,
AND MORAN CERF

2.1 INTRODUCTION

Because all thoughts and behavior ultimately comes from the brain (Gazzaniga 2004), it is unlikely that managers and firms can truly understand their customers without understanding what goes on inside the brain. This chapter will provide some basic knowledge of the brain regions and circuits that will be discussed in the rest of the book.

The human brain is a unique structure that boasts a complex three-dimensional architecture. An adult human brain weighs ~3 lb (1,500 g) and is about the size of a cantaloupe (Carpenter and Sutin 1983). The brain looks a little like a large pinkish-gray walnut and is composed of neurons that generate our thoughts, feelings, and choices. The human brain is made up of approximately 100 billion neurons of different kinds, with about 100 trillion connections between them, making each 1 mm of brain cell have more connections than there are stars in the Milky Way Galaxy. Each individual cell includes all our genetic makeup. The neurons connect through long, spidery arms and communicate with each other through electrochemical signals (figure 2.1). Among this web of cells there are our neurons, which are the building blocks of our thoughts, emotions, memories, and identities (known as the gray matter in our brain), and the glue that sets the scaffolding for this network, which is made of myelin (and known as the white matter). The gray matter is where the core processing happens. As you will see in later chapters (i.e., chapter 4), in many of our analyses of brain data we start by filtering out the white matter, which is not involved in the actual thinking, to make sure

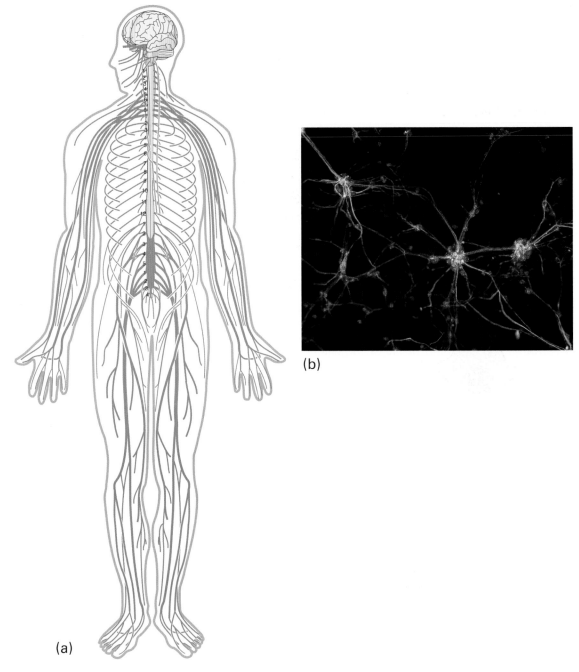

(a)

(b)

Figure 2.1
(a) The nervous system and (b) neurons in the brain. Credit: William Crochot

we only learn about the processes that lead to our behavior and not the mechanisms that oversee the mechanics of brain function.

Neurons—our brains cells—are typically described as a combination of three components (figure 2.2): the input areas known as the *dendrites* (Greek for "tree" because of their resemblance to branches) feed into the center of the neuron, known as the cell body (soma), where information from multiple other neurons feeding into the dendrites is aggregated. Based on the timing of the input from other cells and the strength of the input, the cell combines all the inputs it received in the cell at a certain moment and calculates the total. If the total passes a threshold of inputs needed to generate a response from that cell, the cell body triggers a response output through its single output branch—the axon. Each neuron therefore processes the activity of multiple neurons feeding into it and ends up generating a single output at a time. This input is effectively an electrochemical signal propagated from the axon into the dendrite of a different neuron. This set of activities is what leads to our thoughts. The actual signal that cells send is made of changes in

The human brain is made up of approximately 100 billion neurons of different kinds, with about 100 trillion connections between them, making each 1 mm of brain cell have more connections than there are stars in the Milky Way Galaxy.

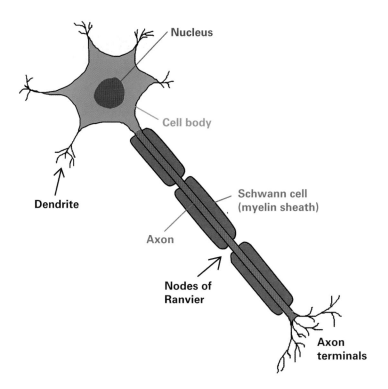

FIGURE 2.2
Structure of a neuron. Credit: Nick Gorton

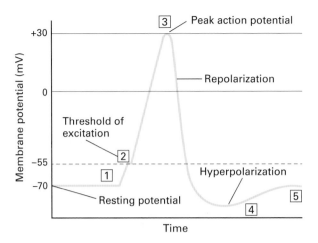

FIGURE 2.3
Schematic of an action potential (spike).

chemicals that are registered as changes in voltage. Each cell is made of a combination of sodium, potassium, calcium, and chloride, and the changes in concentrations of these inside and outside of the cells are what generates the burst of activity. Neuroscientists call this burst a *spike* (see figure 2.3 for an image of a spike). Neurons can spike fast (of the order dozens or even hundreds of spikes per second) or spike only once or twice a year. The spiking activity is typically associated with indication of the cell's main activity. That is, neurons fire a burst of spikes when an occurrence in the world that they are responsible for is happening (i.e., when you think of a certain word or feel a certain emotion). Accordingly, knowing when neurons spike, and how much they spiked, is a way for us to understand what the brain is processing at a given moment.

Knowing when neurons spike, and how much they spiked, is a way for us to understand what the brain is processing at a given moment.

Importantly, the spiking activity of neurons is usually measured by a change from their typical number of spikes per second. A typical neuron is never silent. It fires at times irrespective of its preferred stimulus being there. As such, neuroscientists often measure first the baseline activity of a neuron and compare that to the activity when a relevant occurrence happens. Neurons can increase their firing when something happens (an event known as excitation) or can decrease their activity below the baseline (known as inhibition). One cell firing a lot at one time can signal to another cell to fire below its baseline at the same time. Thus, the complex way a brain codes a signal is a matter of many dimensions. Neuroscientists spend much of their time and resources on learning how the brain codes functions and experiences. Once these coding mechanisms are discovered, we, as marketing managers, can use them as ways to assess the specific processing that a person is going through. For example, once neuroscientists have understood the mechanisms that lead to a movement of the hand—starting with a burst of activity in neurons in a part of the brain known as the motor cortex—we as users of this information can now simply use imaging methods to eavesdrop on the activity of motor cortex cells and know that once we see a burst of firing in those neurons, we can expect a movement of the arm within fractions of a second. The same pertains to our ability to then decode a specific emotion in an individual without asking him or her about it, or even a specific memory being elicited in the brain of a subject—before the subject is even aware of the thought emerging in his or her head.

The brain can be divided into cortical and subcortical regions, with the cortical region consisting of the cerebral cortex and the subcortical regions consisting of the thalamus, hypothalamus, cerebellum, and brain stem. The cerebral cortex directs the brain's higher cognitive and emotional functions. The word *cortex* comes from the Latin word for "bark" (of a tree). This is because the cortex is a sheet of tissue that makes up the outer layer of the brain. The cerebral cortex is divided into two hemispheres connected by the corpus callosum, a bridge of wide, flat neural fibers that act as communication relays between the two sides (Carpenter and Sutin 1983). While several popular books suggest this lateralization is important to function (i.e., the right hemisphere of the brain is the creative side while the left hemisphere dabbles more in analytical processing), most cognitive processes are represented by activation on both hemispheres (Gazzaniga 2004).

The two hemispheres are nearly symmetrical, and each one is further subdivided into four major lobes: the occipital, the temporal, the parietal, and the frontal (figure 2.4). Areas within these lobes oversee all forms of conscious experience, including perception, emotion, thought, and planning, as well as many unconscious cognitive and emotional processes. Below the cerebral cortex is a variety of other structures, called subcortical (literally "below the cortex") structures (see appendix).

2.2 UNDERSTANDING CONSUMER BEHAVIOR USING NEUROSCIENCE

Understanding how the brain makes decisions requires understanding not just activity in a single brain region but also how networks of them work together and their functions (Gazzaniga 2004). Whether one is trying to understand customers, employees, competitors, or the CEO, it is important to realize that our brains share important features at a fundamental level. In the following, we discuss four neural circuits and how they contribute to our understanding of consumers (see table 2.1 for mapping of the connection between those circuits and key marketing attributes).

The brain can be divided into cortical and subcortical regions, with the cortical region consisting of the cerebral cortex and the subcortical regions consisting of the thalamus, hypothalamus, cerebellum, and brain stem.

The two hemispheres are nearly symmetrical, and each one is further subdivided into four major lobes: the occipital, the temporal, the parietal, and the frontal.

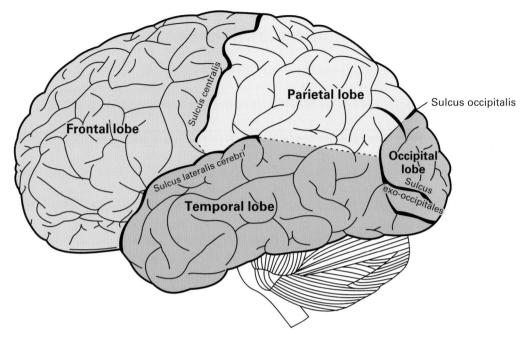

FIGURE 2.4
Cortical regions of the brain.

TABLE 2.1
Effect of marketing mix on neural circuits

Marketing actions	Primary effects on neural circuits
Product	Decision making, emotion
Price	Decision making
Promotion	Emotion, memory, attention
Place	Attention

When you first experience pleasure, your brain releases a neurotransmitter called dopamine. The dopamine is primarily produced in the ventral tegmental area (VTA).

2.2.1 REWARD AND DECISION MAKING: UNDERSTANDING HOW YOUR CUSTOMERS MAKE PURCHASE DECISIONS

Think about a time when you felt happy; these times are particularly rewarded. Perhaps somebody gave you a hug, you received some verbal praise, or you ate an excellent piece of cake. Although the reasons differ, a similar set of neural circuits is being engaged in these cases (Wise 2004; Haber and Knutson 2010). This is the reward pathway or circuit.

When you first experience pleasure, your brain releases a neurotransmitter called dopamine. The dopamine is primarily produced in the ventral tegmental area (VTA), which is located in the midbrain (Schultz, Dayan, and Montague 1997; Schultz 2002). When the VTA releases dopamine, it is transmitted to the broader reward circuit including amygdala, striatum, and parts of the prefrontal cortex (Missale et al. 1998; Spanagel and Weiss 1999). When you experience a stimulus and the dopamine in the VTA is released and travels along these pathways, it basically tells your body that this was good, let's do it again. This is your natural response to some pleasurable stimuli such as food, sex, social integrations, and certain drugs (Pierce and Kumaresan 2006). When the VTA releases dopamine to all these different parts of the brain with dopamine receptors, these brain regions take up dopamine.

Reward is an objective way to describe the positive value that an individual ascribes to an object, behavioral act, or an internal physical state; for example, food, sexual contact, and money. A reward is an appetitive stimulus given to a human to alter his or her behavior. In neuroscience, the reward system is a collection of brain structures that attempts to regulate and control behavior by inducing pleasurable effects. It is a brain circuit that, when activated, reinforces behaviors. The circuit includes the dopamine-containing neurons of the ventral tegmental area, the nucleus accumbens, and part of the prefrontal cortex.

2.2.2 EMOTION: UNDERSTANDING WHAT DRIVES YOUR CONSUMERS

Underneath our desire for tangible rewards such as money, food, or housing, our behavior is driven by a host of feelings and emotions, some of which are only partially accessible to our conscious awareness (Chartrand 2005; Dijksterhuis et al. 2005). For example, the fact that we desire money is partly due to its instrumental value, namely the things that money can buy for us, but also due to the more intangible ways in which money makes us feel. For example, it alleviates fears in that money brings us feelings of security or promotes positive feelings by signaling social status to others.

For marketers, understanding the emotional drives behind purchase decisions is important because they can provide actionable insights for managers (Westbrook and Oliver 1991; Bagozzi, Gopinath, and Nyer 1999). Most managers intuitively understand that customers can value the same good for very different reasons. For example, one customer can buy a new Apple Watch for its functionality, whereas for a different customer the watch is a status symbol. However, because the reasons are not directly observable to managers, and sometimes to the consumers themselves, neuroscience provides a way to uncover these feelings.

One of the key brain regions involved in detecting emotions, in particular fear, is the amygdala (LeDoux 1998). The amygdala is an almond-shaped structure in the brain. Each amygdala is located close to the hippocampus, in the frontal portion of the temporal lobe. Your amygdalae are essential to your ability to feel certain emotions, especially fear, and to perceive emotions in other people. In fact, the amygdala seems to modulate all of our reactions to events that are very

For marketers, understanding the emotional drives behind purchase decisions is important because they can provide actionable insights for managers.

Your amygdalae are essential to your ability to feel certain emotions, especially fear, and to perceive emotions in other people.

important for our survival. Events that warn us of imminent danger are therefore very important stimuli for the amygdala, but so are events that signal the presence of food, sexual partners, rivals, children in distress, and so on.

2.2.3 ATTENTION: STANDING OUT FROM YOUR COMPETITION

More than ever, consumers are being bombarded by an immense array of goods and services that were unimaginable just a decade ago, let alone a generation ago (Lynch and Srull 1982; Teixeira 2014). In these cases, the competition is not only out for a share of the wallets of consumers, but also for their attention. This is particularly true for many industries, ranging from ice cream to high-tech electronics, where new products and services are the primary ways for companies to attract consumers (Teixeira 2014).

Neuroscientists distinguish between two types of attention: bottom-up and top-down attention.

Neuroscientists distinguish between two types of attention: bottom-up and top-down attention (Sarter, Givens, and Bruno 2001; Buschman and Miller 2007). For marketers, by far the most important is bottom-up attention, which is a reflexive, automatic response for example when a sudden movement in the corner of our eye catches our attention (Sarter, Givens, and Bruno 2001). The seat of bottom-up attention includes the insula and frontoparietal circuits. This type of attention is particularly important for advertising and other promotional activities. Most marketers have an intuitive sense of the features that will capture bottom-up attention; for example, Tiffany's famous shade of blue. In recent years, neuroscientists have begun to "reverse-engineer" salience detection by directly tapping into the brain to understand which features are salient to the brain (Cerf et al. 2008; Zhao and Koch 2011). This potentially provides a data-driven and scientifically principled method to construct and predict what will be salient to consumers.

2.2.4 MEMORY: LEAVING LASTING IMPRESSIONS ON YOUR CUSTOMERS

It is a popular sentiment that modern consumers are driven by their immediate desires. Although it may well be true that consumers are more "impulsive" than they were in the past (and there is no compelling data to even suggest that), it remains true that consumers remain loyal in their purchasing and consumption decisions and habits (Bettman 1979). Data from consumer research on shopping behavior reveals that about 45% of people's purchases and consumption is repeated almost daily and usually in the same context (Wood and Neal 2009). For example, consumers tend to buy the same brands of products (Seetharaman 2004), purchase the same amounts (Vogel, Evanschitzky, and Ramaseshan 2008), and eat similar types of foods (Khare and Inman 2006).

All this is to simply say that consumer memories and habits play an important role in shaping consumer purchase decisions, especially when viewed over time (Alba, Hutchinson, and Lynch Jr. 1991; Hutchinson, Raman, and Mantrala 1994). Memory researchers distinguish between two types of memory, short-term and long-term (Milner, Squire, and Kandel 1998). Short-term memory involves holding on to a piece of information temporarily in order to complete a task. Engagement of short-term memory relies on brain regions including the prefrontal lobe (Baddeley 1966).

Perhaps more important from a managerial perspective is long-term memory, which consists of our entire autobiographical history as well as our knowledge of the world (Milner, Squire, and Kandel 1998; Schacter and Slotnick 2004). Long-term memory is formed when information is transferred from short-term memory through engagement of the hippocampus. The hippocampus is a very old part of the cortex evolutionarily, and it is located in the inner fold of the temporal lobe (Moscovitch et al. 2006; Squire and Wixted 2011). When we remember new facts by repeating them or by employing various mnemonic devices, we are actually passing them through the hippocampus several times. The hippocampus keeps strengthening the associations among these new elements until, after a while, it no longer needs to do so. The cortex will have learned to associate these various properties itself to reconstruct what we call a memory.

> **Perhaps more important from a managerial perspective is long-term memory, which consists of our entire autobiographical history as well as our knowledge of the world.**

2.3   APPENDIX: DESCRIPTION OF BRAIN REGIONS

Site	Description
Cortical regions	
Occipital lobe	The occipital lobe, located at the back of the brain, is the seat of the primary visual cortex, the brain region responsible for processing and interpreting visual information and for recognition of written text (not the content—merely its existence and allocation of resources to interpret it). The occipital lobe processes visual information and passes its conclusions to the parietal and temporal lobes.
Temporal lobe	Reaching from the temple back toward the occipital lobe, the temporal lobe is a major processing center for language and memory. For example, the temporal lobe assists in auditory perception, language comprehension, and visual recognition. Namely, it is the seat of memory acquisition and the final spot for much of visual perceptions where a set of inputs is aggregated to a single concept. As such, it is also highly involved in categorization of objects. Also in the temporal lobe are key sites of emotion processing. Essentially, the temporal lobe is where information that was processed before by auditory/visual/tactile/olfactory senses gets aggregated into a meaningful concept that we can name as a word or classify as an item in a category. Accordingly, the temporal lobe is also the seat of Wernicke's area and Broca's area, which guide receptive and expressive language processing.

Site	Description
Parietal lobe	Above the temporal lobe and adjacent to the occipital lobe, the parietal lobe houses the somatosensory cortex and plays an important role in touch and spatial navigation. The parietal lobe assists in sensory processes, spatial interpretation, attention, language comprehension, and in the allocation of visual attention. Additionally, it is involved in tactile perception in the form of touch perception, temperature perception, and goal-oriented voluntary movements. It is also involved in the manipulation of objects (i.e., the actual holding of a product in your hands) and the integration of different senses that allows understanding of a single concept. Simply put, this is the core site where our personality (emotions, memories, and percepts) sits.
Frontal lobe	The frontal lobe, extending from behind the forehead back to the parietal lobe, is the brain region that separates humans from our primate cousins. This large brain lobe is the seat of the so-called executive function, with a hand in reasoning, decision making, integration of sensory information, and the planning and execution of movement. Simply put, this is the site where our identity and high-level processing get established. Our consciousness, our ability to set goals and plan the future, and our ability to inhibit thoughts or allocate attention to resources are also here. Additionally, the frontal lobe is implicated in our time perception, the control of emotional responses (feeding back to the temporal lobe), and even the internalization of language (feeding back to the language areas). Complex processing such as volition, or the initiation of responses to changes in the environment, as well as judgment and imagination are all centered in our novel frontal lobe.
Subcortical regions	
Cerebellum	The cerebellum is located behind the brain stem. The word cerebellum is derived from the Latin word for "little brain." It plays an important role in motor control. The cerebellum does not initiate movement, but it contributes to coordination, precision, balance, equilibrium, and accurate timing. Additionally, it is the seat of memory for reflex motor acts, which is involved in muscle memory.
Brain stem	The brain stem refers to the area of the brain between the thalamus and spinal cord. Structures of the brain stem include the pons, medulla oblongata, tectum, reticular formation, and tegmentum. The brain stem is important for maintaining basic life functions such as breathing, heart rate and blood pressure, swallowing, response to startling stimulus, control of level of alertness, the sense of balance, as well as the connection to the autonomic nervous system and the ability to sleep.

Site	Description
Hypothalamus	The hypothalamus is composed of several different areas and is located at the base of the brain. One function of the hypothalamus is the control of body temperature, and it also controls the pituitary.
Thalamus	The thalamus receives sensory information from other areas of the nervous system and sends this information to the cerebral cortex. The thalamus is also important for processing information related to movement.
Limbic system	The limbic system (or the limbic areas) is a group of structures that includes the amygdala, the hippocampus, mammillary bodies, and cingulate gyrus. These areas are important for controlling the emotional response to a given situation. The hippocampus is also important for memory.
Basal ganglia	The basal ganglia is a group of structures, including the globus pallidus, caudate nucleus, subthalamic nucleus, putamen, and substantia nigra, that are important in coordinating movement.
Midbrain	The midbrain includes structures such as the superior and inferior colliculi and the red nucleus. The midbrain plays an important role in vision, audition, eye movement, and body movement.
Hippocampus	A major component of the consolidation of information from short-term memory to long-term memory. It is also involved in spatial navigation and is essential to high-level processing.
Amygdala	Primarily involved in the formation and storage of emotional events. Implicated in the alertness to fearful stimulus and essentially involved in much of emotion processing.
Insula	Highly involved in emotion processing, social emotions, introspections, and primarily painful experience markers. For example, it is shown that the pinch of a needle in your arm makes the insula activated—signaling pain. Notably, social pain like jealousy or the "pain of paying" have also been shown to activate insular cortices. Generally, saliency of content, heightened emotions, and social processing all show activation in the insula.
Nucleus accumbens	The nucleus accumbens (NAc) is implicated in much of reward processing and reinforcement learning processing.
Anterior cingulate	The anterior cingulate (AC) is known to be involved with "error detection." Simply put, if you're making a mistake or identifying an anomaly, the AC is firing to alert you of its existence so you can make a correction. In the context of marketing, we can use this activity to identify a written report that is incongruent with the experience of the subject; possibly, the neuroscience response is more predictive of the behavior than the written response.

Site	Description
Orbitofrontal cortex	A frontal lobe subsite that is essential for decision making, assessment of options, and integration of multiple sets of information to arrive at a choice that is then acted upon by motor areas. The orbitofrontal cortex (OFC) also acts as a control hub for many prior sites, sending inputs back and feeding back to emotions and memories to change them prior to a future choice.

KEY TAKEAWAYS

This chapter provided a brief overview of brain regions, their locations, and their approximate functions. For marketers, this chapter emphasized the functions of four important neural circuits that are of particular importance for understanding consumer behavior. First, a decision-making circuit, centered on the striatum, cingulate, and medial prefrontal cortex, is responsible for consumers' ability to weigh costs and benefits and to choose actions that maximize consumer preference. Second, an emotion circuit, which includes a number of evolutionarily ancient nuclei such as the amygdala, is critical for understanding the deep-seated desires and fears of consumers, some of which are only partially accessible to conscious awareness. Third, an attention circuit, centered on the insula, lateral prefrontal cortex, and lateral parietal cortex, is responsible for detecting and responding to salient stimuli and events, such as a particularly eye-catching ad. Finally, a set of memory systems, which includes the hippocampus and much of the neocortex, provides the basis for a consumer's memory, including all of one's autobiographical details as well as one's knowledge of the world. Although there are many important neural circuits that are not described here, for example those dealing with language, these four circuits provide a useful starting point to understand consumer behavior, and in particular how marketing actions might affect these circuits.

DISCUSSION QUESTIONS

1.   What is the weight of the brain?

2.   How many neurons does the brain contain approximately?

3.   What is a neuron?

4. What is a spike?

5. Which are the major lobes in the human cortex?

6. Describe the main structures involved in the reward system and their connections.

7. Name the main structures involved in emotion.

8. Which brain regions regulate bottom-up attention?

9. What is the hippocampus?

REFERENCES

Alba, Joseph W. J., Wesley Hutchinson, and John G. Lynch Jr. 1991. Memory and decision making. In *Handbook of Consumer Behavior*, 1–49. Englewood Cliffs, NJ: Prentice-Hall.

Baddeley, Alan D. 1966. Short-term memory for word sequences as a function of acoustic, semantic and formal similarity. *Quarterly Journal of Experimental Psychology* 18 (4): 362–365.

Bagozzi, Richard P., Mahesh Gopinath, and Prashanth U. Nyer. 1999. The role of emotions in marketing. *Journal of the Academy of Marketing Science* 27 (2): 184–206.

Bettman, James R. 1979. Memory factors in consumer choice: A review. *Journal of Marketing* 43 (2): 37–53.

Buschman, Timothy J., and K. Earl Miller. 2007. Top-down versus bottom-up control of attention in the prefrontal and posterior parietal cortices. *Science* 315 (5820): 1860–1862. doi:10.1126/science.1138071.

Carpenter, Malcolm B., and Jerome Sutin. 1983. *Human neuroanatomy*. Baltimore, MD: Williams & Wilkins.

Cerf, Moran, Jonathan Harel, Wolfgang Einhäuser, and Christof Koch. 2008. Predicting human gaze using low-level saliency combined with face detection. *Advances in Neural Information Processing Systems* 20:1–7.

Chartrand, Tanya L. 2005. The role of conscious awareness in consumer behavior. *Journal of Consumer Psychology* 15 (3): 203–210.

Dijksterhuis, Ap, Pamela K. Smith, Rick B. Van Baaren, and Daniël H. J. Wigboldus. 2005. The unconscious consumer: Effects of environment on consumer behavior. *Journal of Consumer Psychology* 15 (3): 193–202.

Gazzaniga, Michael S. 2004. *The cognitive neurosciences*. Cambridge, MA: MIT Press.

Haber, Suzanne N., and Brian Knutson. 2010. The reward circuit: Linking primate anatomy and human imaging. *Neuropsychopharmacology* 35 (1): 4–26.

Hutchinson, J. Wesley, Kalyan Raman, and Murali K. Mantrala. 1994. Finding choice alternatives in memory: Probability models of brand name recall. *JMR, Journal of Marketing Research* 31 (4): 441–461. doi:10.2307/3151875.

Khare, Adwait, and J. Jeffrey Inman. 2006. Habitual behavior in American eating patterns: The role of meal occasions. *Journal of Consumer Research* 32 (4): 567–575.

LeDoux, Joseph. 1998. *The emotional brain: The mysterious underpinnings of emotional life*. New York: Simon and Schuster.

Lynch, John G., and Thomas K. Srull. 1982. Memory and attentional factors in consumer choice: Concepts and research methods. *Journal of Consumer Research* 9 (1): 18–37. doi:10.2307/2488934?ref=no-x-rou te:39b8faf9e1d98d774368ba275342a391.

Milner, B., L. R. Squire, and E. R. Kandel. 1998. Cognitive neuroscience and the study of memory. *Neuron* 20 (3): 445–468.

Missale, C., S. R. Nash, S. W. Robinson, M. Jaber, and M. G. Caron. 1998. Dopamine receptors: From structure to function. *Physiological Reviews* 78 (1): 189–225.

Moscovitch, Morris, Lynn Nadel, Gordon Winocur, Asaf Gilboa, and R. Shayna Rosenbaum. 2006. The cognitive neuroscience of remote episodic, semantic and spatial memory. *Current Opinion in Neurobiology* 16 (2): 179–190. doi:10.1016/j.conb.2006.03.013.

Pierce, R. Christopher, and Vidhya Kumaresan. 2006. The mesolimbic dopamine system: The final common pathway for the reinforcing effect of drugs of abuse? *Neuroscience and Biobehavioral Reviews* 30 (2): 215–238. doi:10.1016/j.neubiorev.2005.04.016.

Sarter, Martin, Ben Givens, and John P. Bruno. 2001. The cognitive neuroscience of sustained attention: Where top-down meets bottom-up. *Brain Research Reviews* 35 (2): 146–160. doi:10.1016/S0165-0173(01) 00044-3.

Schacter, Daniel L., and Scott D. Slotnick. 2004. The cognitive neuroscience of memory distortion. *Neuron* 44 (1): 149–160. doi:10.1016/j.neuron.2004.08.017.

Schultz, Wolfram. 2002. Getting formal with dopamine and reward. *Neuron* 36 (2): 241–263.

Schultz, W., P. Dayan, and P. R. Montague. 1997. A neural substrate of prediction and reward. *Science* 275 (5306): 1593–1599.

Seetharaman, P. B. 2004. Modeling multiple sources of state dependence in random utility models: A distributed lag approach. *Marketing Science* 23 (2): 263–271.

Spanagel, Rainer, and Friedbert Weiss. 1999. The dopamine hypothesis of reward: Past and current status. *Trends in Neurosciences* 22(11):521–527. doi:10.1016/S0166-2236(99)01447-2.

Squire, Larry R., and John T. Wixted. 2011. The cognitive neuroscience of human memory since H.M. *Annual Review of Neuroscience* 34:259–288. doi:10.1146/annurev-neuro-061010-113720.

Teixeira, Thales S. 2014. *The rising cost of consumer attention: Why you should care, and what you can do about it.* Harvard Business School Working Paper, No. 14-055.

Vogel, Verena, Heiner Evanschitzky, and Balasubramani Ramaseshan. 2008. Customer equity drivers and future sales. *Journal of Marketing* 72 (6): 98–108.

Westbrook, Robert A., and Richard L. Oliver. 1991. The dimensionality of consumption emotion patterns and consumer satisfaction. *Journal of Consumer Research* 18 (1): 84–91.

Wise, Roy A. 2004. Dopamine, learning and motivation. *Nature Reviews. Neuroscience* 5 (6): 483–494. doi:10.1038/nrn1406.

Wood, Wendy, and David T. Neal. 2009. The habitual consumer. *Journal of Consumer Psychology* 19:579–592. doi:10.1016/j.jcps.2009.08.003.

Zhao, Qi, and Christof Koch. 2011. Learning a saliency map using fixated locations in natural scenes. *Journal of Vision (Charlottesville, Va.)* 11 (3): 9.

SENSATION AND PERCEPTION

IRIT SHAPIRA-LICHTER AND MORAN CERF

Our senses are the gateways to our environment. Sensation is carried out by dedicated sense organs equipped with unique neurons—called *receptors*—that absorb physical energy from the environment and convert it to electrical pulse, a process termed *transduction*. The electrical signal is then transmitted to the brain, where it is processed and interpreted, creating a perception. Each sense organ detects a particular kind and range of energy and is insensitive to other types and ranges of energy (table 3.1). Traditionally, five sensory modalities were identified in humans: vision (seeing), audition (hearing), olfaction (smelling), gustatory (tasting), and somatosensory (touching). Over the years, a more delicate parcellation distinguished the detection of pressure, vibration, temperature changes, and tissue damage (perceived as pain) as different types of body senses. Also, the vestibular system and kinesthesis were recognized as additional senses that provided information regarding position and movements of the head and body, respectively. Notably, other species that may lack some of the human senses can sense other types of energy that humans cannot detect and have different ranges of sensitivity. In this chapter, we will describe some of the key properties of the most studied human senses: vision, audition, taste, and smell. Readers should keep in mind that current understanding of almost all aspects of human sensation and perception is limited. Contemporary influential theories regarding the principles of coding and organization will be described; however, there is yet much to be discovered.

Each sensory system is composed of a designated sense organ and primary, secondary, and associative areas in the cortex. The sensory information is processed mostly in a hierarchical manner. Initial processing is carried out by the peripheral sense organs, and processing continues sequentially by subcortical

Each sensory system is composed of a designated sense organ and primary, secondary, and associative areas in the cortex.

Table 3.1
The traditional division of the human senses and the type of energy related to each sense

Sense	Sense organ	Type of energy
Vision	Eyes	Light energy
Audition	Ears	Mechanical energy
Smell	Nose	Chemical energy
Taste	Mouth	Chemical energy
Touch	Skin	Mechanical/thermal energy

structures and then by primary, secondary, and association cortices. Each region receives information from the region beneath it in the hierarchy, processes it, and sends it to the region above it in the hierarchy. Usually, neurons lower in the hierarchy of the sensory system collect and process information from smaller parts of the environment—manifested as smaller spatial receptive fields. The primary sensory cortices are the earliest and simplest sensory area in the cortex. They receive sensory input from the receptors with only a few synapses interposed and are highly specialized for detecting simple sensory qualities such as simple contours or color in vision or pitch in audition. Primary cortices are surrounded by secondary sensory cortices, which integrate information coming from the primary sensory areas but still process relatively basic dimensions of sensory stimuli. Higher up in the hierarchy are the sensory association cortices, which combine and process information coming from earlier cortices and other sources to represent complex stimuli. The highest association cortices integrate multimodal information to serve high-order mental processes not dependent on specific sensory information, such as language, planning, and decision making.

Notably, additional to the sequential, feed-forward transmission mode described above, also termed *bottom-up processing*, many sensory areas are also directly connected with subcortical or cortical areas through connections that bypass the hierarchical order. These connections transmit sensory information via different routes, bypassing the hierarchy and allowing feedback. Additional interconnections exist between sensory cortices and different parts of the cerebral cortex outside the sensory system, setting the stage for modulation of perception by high-level processes, termed *top-down processing*. Evidence shows that all levels of sensory processing in the cortex are subjected to top-down modulation. For example, some neurons in the primary auditory cortex of cats exhibited stronger response to a particular sound frequency when it appeared as part of a specific sequence (McKenna, Weinberger, and Diamond 1989). This result tells us that high-order properties such as context influence the ways in which low-order neurons operate. Thus, perception is not deterministically determined by the incoming sensory input: it is rather affected, at early and later phases of processing, by factors such as context, expectations, emotions, and attention (Moran and Desimone 1985).

Perception is not deterministically determined by the incoming sensory input: it is rather affected, at early and later phases of processing, by factors such as context, expectations, emotions, and attention.

3.1 MEASURING STIMULI DETECTION

Our sensory system is very sensitive, indicated by the very low intensities needed in order to reliably detect a stimulus, a measure that is termed *absolute threshold*. Humans are also able to differentiate between very similar stimuli—a measure termed *difference threshold*. The difference threshold varies as a function of stimuli intensity: the more intense the stimuli are, the larger the difference threshold becomes ("Weber low"). Both the absolute threshold and the difference threshold are empirically quantified in psychophysical experiments. A typical experiment consists of multiple trials: in each the stimulus is either present or absent, and the participant indicates whether he or she detected a stimulus. Such experiments are the basis of the current knowledge regarding the relative sensitivity of various species, senses, and sensory qualities. For example, humans are more sensitive to light intensity than to sound intensity and are more sensitive to the frequency of sounds than to their intensity. This kind of information is used in subliminal advertising (box 3.1). One has to keep in mind that on top of the differences between different species, there are also interindividual differences in thresholds within each species.

A hidden assumption in an experiment like the one described above is that a "yes" response equals the detection of a stimulus. However, thresholds are not fixed, and they are not affected solely by a sensory barrier. Rather, judgments regarding near-threshold stimuli are difficult perceptual decisions, conducted in conditions of uncertainty. Thus, a decision is affected by two factors: the participant's sensitivity to the stimulus and the subject's criteria. The criteria reflect

> Humans are more sensitive to light intensity than to sound intensity and are more sensitive to the frequency of sounds than to their intensity.

Box 3.1
Subliminal Advertising

> Subliminal advertising is the use of subliminal stimuli with commercial content embedded into other content in order to promote a message and alter the behavior of participants. Frequently, the stimuli are briefly presented for a period that is too short to create a conscious perception yet is prolonged enough to allow detection by the sense organ.
>
> The idea of subliminal advertising aroused much hype since it was first introduced in the middle of the previous century, yet its effectiveness is still extremely controversial. The effect of subliminal advertising seems to be rather limited in scope and duration; for instance, to occasions when the subliminal message is relevant to the participant's goals. For example, subliminal exposure to a brand label increased the intention to drink the prime brand, but only in thirsty participants (Karremans, Stroebe, and Claus 2006).
>
> Use of subliminal advertising frequently gives rise to public criticism and antagonism, and it is illegal in some countries.

Table 3.2
Possible outcomes in a signal detection theory experiment

		Response	
		Respond "present"	Respond "absent"
Signal	Present	Hit	Miss
	Absent	False alarm	Correct rejection

response biases that may arise from the psychological and/or physiologic states of the participant (e.g., fatigue, strategy, expectations). For example, an engineer that is not sure whether he saw a flash signifying the presence of a car crossing the railroad track would adopt a lower criteria and stop the train, preferring a false alarm (table 3.2) over the potential accident caused by a miss. The same ambiguous flash signal may be dismissed (i.e., regarded as an absence) by a statistician who counts the number of vehicles passing a certain road at a certain time window, applying a higher criteria. In signal detection theory, each decision is categorized into one of four cells according to participants' judgment and the real conditions (table 3.2). The proportions of trials in these categories is used to infer both the sensitivity and the criteria (Swets, Tanner, and Birdsall 1961).

3.2 Adaptation

Across the day we do not feel our clothes because our somatosensory receptors adapt to constant mechanical pressure.

Organisms are constantly flooded by huge amounts of multimodal sensory information. One key property that helps the system to efficiently deal with this abundance is its predisposition to reduce responses to unchanging incoming information. This leaves more available resources to process new incoming information, which may require a behavioral change or response. Adaptation occurs unconsciously and uncontrollably in all senses (perhaps less so in pain). For example, across the day we do not feel our clothes because our somatosensory receptors adapt to constant mechanical pressure. Likewise, we gradually lose awareness to the noise created by the car's engine, and after a while in a restaurant, the smells of the kitchen that hit one upon arrival seemingly disappear. Physiologically, sensory adaptation due to exposure to a constant stimulus occurs at multiple levels, from the diminished response of receptors, through alteration in the response of single cortical neurons, to changes in the distributed mental representations of stimuli across multiple brain regions (Solomon and Kohn 2014). Adaptation can be rather selective, for example, to movement in a certain direction and to a certain speed.

3.3   THE VISUAL SYSTEM

Light: Electromagnetic radiation in the human visible range.

Photoreceptors: The receptors of the visual system, which traduce light energy into electrical signal.

3.3.1   THE STIMULUS

Human vision arises from exposure to electromagnetic radiation at wavelengths between approximately 400 and 700 nm, termed *light*. The physical properties of the wave, namely, wavelength, intensity, and purity, are perceived as hue, brightness, and saturation, respectively (figure 3.1).

Human vision arises from exposure to electromagnetic radiation at wavelengths between approximately 400 and 700 nm, termed light.

3.3.2   ANATOMY OF THE VISUAL SYSTEM

Rays of light reflect from all objects in the environment and propagate in all directions. Rays of light that enter our visual sense organ—the eye—produce a small inverted image of the visual environment in it. Some key components that underlie this process are demonstrated in figure 3.2. These include: the cornea, which refracts light, bending the rays into a point of sharp focus on the retina; the lens, which alters its shape to focus on various distances and also inverts the image (up-down and left-right); the pupil, a small opening in the iris whose size regulates the amount of light that enters the eye; the retina, a thin layer at the inner surface of the eyeball where visual receptors, termed *photoreceptors* (table 3.3), are located

FIGURE 3.1
Demonstration of color-related properties. Credit: SharkD.

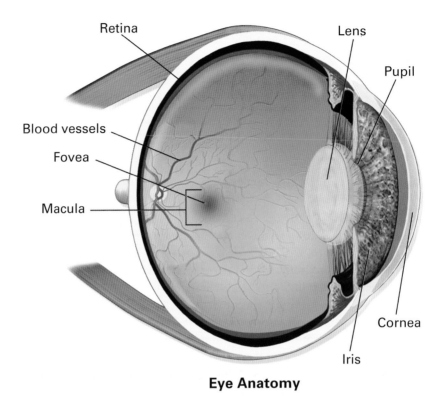

Eye Anatomy

Figure 3.2
Schematic view of a human eye. Credit: BruceBlaus.

Table 3.3
Key properties of the various types of photoreceptors in the human retina

Name	Number	Density in retina	Sensitivity to low intensity	Wavelength*	Perception	Use
Cone (three subtypes)	6 million to 7 million	High in the fovea, low in the periphery	Low	~419 nm ("blue") ~531 nm ("green") ~558 nm ("red")	Sharp vision of details, color vision	Day vision
Rod	~120 million	Only in the periphery	High	~496 nm	Poor acuity, color blind	Dim light, night vision

* Wavelength of maximal response/absorbance (Dartnall, Bowmaker, and Mollon 1983).

Box 3.2
Tracking Eye Movements to Infer Where Attention Is Deployed

The limited processing capacity does not allow an organism to consciously attend all sensory inputs, necessitating selection. Directing foveal vision to specific locations in the visual environment is a key mechanism for visual selection. Gaze direction is determined by multiple factors related to both the viewer (e.g., goals and expectations; Einhäuser, Rutishauser, and Koch 2008) and the stimuli (e.g., salience, object recognition; Schütz, Braun, and Gegenfurtner 2011). As the direction of gaze is closely related to the locus of attention, tracking of eye movements has the potential to provide a relatively direct measure of where attention is deployed (Duc, Bays, and Husain 2008).

Remarkably, as eye tracking does not require active cooperation of the viewer, this technique can be used with children and infants. For example, it has been shown that similar to adults, healthy infants from Western cultures typically direct their gaze to the eyes of others (Jones and Klin 2013).

Eye tracking is widely used to assess the effectiveness of various commercial media (Duchowski 2002), investigating the processing of information related to packages, brands, ads, websites, shelf displays, and so forth. Multiple measures are employed, including scan paths that depict the sequence of eye movements, fixation length, the number of fixations, time to first fixation, and more.

and the locus in which the inverted image of the visual environment emerges; and the fovea, a small region in the center of the retina that subserves accurate color vision. Unproportionally large portions of the optical nerve and the visual cortex are devoted to carry and process the information detected by the fovea (Daniel and Whitteridge 1961). During both reflexive and intentional exploration of the visual environment, our eyes constantly move in fast, jerky movements called *saccades*. Saccades are interleaved with periods of a few hundreds of milliseconds during which the eyes remain relatively still, termed *fixations* (Rayner 1998). Consequently, in each moment a slightly different portion of the environment falls onto the fovea and is sensed with highest resolution. The fact that foveal vision is essential for perceiving complex visual stimuli makes the use of eye tracking to infer where attention is deployed so effective (box 3.2).

3.4 CODING AND ANALYZING VISUAL INFORMATION

Object constancy: The phenomenon where an object's properties remain constant in consciousness despite considerable changes in its retinal image.

Monocular depth cues: Depth cues that rely on the information obtained in each eye.

Binocular depth cues: Depth cues that rely on small differences between the retinal images of the two eyes.

The detection of light commences when light strikes a molecule of photopigment in a photoreceptor. This initiates a cascade of events that eventually changes the firing rate of a ganglion cell. The identity of the firing ganglion signifies the location of light on the retina and accordingly in the real world. Most ganglion cells have a circular spatial receptive field, with opposite response of the inner and outer aspects of the field. For some cells, light that falls in the inner circle causes excitation, while light that falls in the outer circle causes inhibition (figure 3.3). Other ganglion cells have the opposite circular receptive field. Some ganglion cells encode brightness, while others are color sensitive, responding to yellow/blue or red/green in opposite ways in the inner and outer circle. Coding via opponent color-pairs explains the human inability to perceive something as reddish-greenish or bluish-yellowish; the former mixture is typically experienced as yellow, and the latter as white. The psychological effects of color and their application in neuro-marketing are described in box 3.3. The axons of the ganglion cells project from the eye to the brain, forming the optic nerve, which primarily relays to the dorsal lateral geniculate nucleus of the thalamus. From there, information is transmitted to the visual cortices.

The primary visual cortex (called *striate cortex*) is located on the posterior pole of the occipital lobes. It preserves the retina's spatial organization, with adjacent neurons responding to adjacent locations on the retina (and in the real world).

(a)   (b)

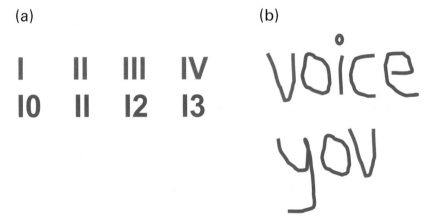

FIGURE 3.3
Top-down contributions to visual perception. (a) The sign II is perceived as the number 2 in the upper row and as the number 11 in the bottom row. (b) The letter in orange color appears as V in the upper row and as U in the bottom row.

Box 3.3
Color

PART 1: PSYCHOLOGICAL EFFECTS OF COLOR

Different colors convey symbolic meanings and cultural connotations, but each individual also has subjective preferences. The meaning, preference, and impact of colors vary between countries, cultures, genders, ethnic groups, ages, and personality characteristics (Whitfield and Wiltshire 1990; Aslam 2005; Bakker et al. 2015). Color experience is the joint product of three key physical dimensions described at the beginning of this section; namely, hue, brightness, and saturation. These dimensions, along with other visual parameters (e.g., the type and amount of light, distance from the object [Elliot 2015], as well as the physical and psychological contexts [Elliot and Maier 2014]) profoundly affect the perceived color. Color combinations are qualitatively different from the sum of their ingredients. Here we will focus on the most studied aspect of color perception—the effects of specific hues (wavelengths).

An early influential assumption was that colors influence arousal, ascribing cool and calming effects to short-wavelength colors (blue, violet, green) and warm, anxious, and arousing effects to long-wavelength colors (yellow, red) (Goldstein 1942; Jacobs and Suess 1975). Though there is little scientific support to the arousal notion (Elliot and Maier 2014), scientific investigation confirms that colors can influence initial processing of visual stimuli (Castelhano and Henderson 2008), behavior (Frank and Gilovich 1988), cognition (Elliot et al. 2007), motivation (Mehta and Zhu 2009), and emotional state (Hamid and Newport 1989). For example, under specific circumstances, red hampers performance (Elliot et al. 2007; Elliot and Maier 2014), blue enhances creativity (Mehta and Zhu 2009), and black enhances aggressive behavior (Frank and Gilovich 1988). Color can affect individuals without necessitating conscious elaboration of the conveyed message (Friedman and Forster 2010). Current theories suggest that changes in motivation (Mehta and Zhu 2009) and/or scope of attention (Friedman and Forster 2010) modulate the effects of colors. For example, a red color that signifies danger narrows an individual's scope of attention in the context of achievement challenges, resulting in poorer performance (Elliot and Maier 2014).

PART 2: COLOR AS A PERSUASIVE FORCE AT THE SERVICE OF MARKETING

Colors play a pivotal role in marketing strategies. Their effect is multilevel, starting from the colors of the product and its packaging, through the colorfulness of the displays in shops, malls, and websites, up to the level of the color schema of the brand's logo and the colors associated with the product's advertising. Colors are used to create the desirable mood or impression, convey messages, and create expectations. They can affect the shopping experience, purchase intentions, and product or company appraisal. Like other background attributes, colors have larger effects in low-involvement purchases (Grossman and Wisenblit 1999). The intricate nature of

Box 3.3
(continued)

color perception described in the first part of this box prevents formulation of firm, all-embracing rules regarding the effect of specific colors. Yet several rules of thumb hold for certain circumstances and populations. For example, stores with a blue exterior are often perceived as less crowded compared to stores with an orange exterior (Yüksel 2009), blue websites can be perceived as more trustworthy (Lee and Rao 2010; Alberts and van der Geest 2011), and judgment of flavor identity is commonly affected by its coloring (Spence et al. 2010). Notably, color preferences are product-specific (Grossman and Wisenblit 1999) and are commonly related to a product's functionality (Bottomley and Doyle 2006). For example, luxurious and status-related merchandise, such as sports cars, are often colored red. Likewise, expensive, elegant products often have cold, dark-color packaging, whereas products designated for price-sensitive consumers usually have light-color packaging (Ampuero and Vila 2006).

Colors can also be used to differentiate a product or brand (Grossman and Wisenblit 1999). This approach was employed by Pepsico, the maker of Pepsi, who used the red-white-blue color scheme to distinguish the product from the red color used by its primary competitor, Coca-Cola.

As stated above, the retina embodies an inverted image of the visual field, such that the right aspect of the visual field falls on the left side of each retina, and the upper part of the visual field falls on the lower part of each retina. In the brain, each side of the environment is represented in the opposite hemisphere. Neurons in the primary visual cortex respond to elementary features such as colors, sine wave gratings, lines at specific orientation, and retinal disparity or movement and are excellent in edge detection. Some neurons in the primary visual cortex of macaque monkeys changed their preferable orientation (i.e., the orientation to which a neuron responds most vividly) over time (Ringach, Hawken, and Shapley 1997). More complex visual features are represented in higher visual areas, many of which maintain the retinotopic arrangement. In the extrastriate cortex, some subregions, such as areas v4 and v5, are specialized in processing a specific visual feature, such as color and motion, respectively (Livingstone and Hubel 1988). Processing visual information is conducted in two parallel streams (Ungerleider and Mishkin 1982). The ventral stream, which ends in the inferior temporal cortex, is mainly dedicated to perception of form and object recognition. Subregions in it specialize in processing specific types of stimuli such as faces, landscapes, written words, and body parts (Kanwisher 2010). Moreover, some neurons within the ventral stream selectively respond to different instances of certain individuals, landmarks, or objects, indicating invariant and sparse representation of specific exemplars (Quiroga et al. 2005). The dorsal stream, which ends in the posterior parietal cortex, is mainly dedicated to perception of location and movement.

3.4.1 OBJECT RECOGNITION

Bottom-up visual object recognition starts with detection of simple lines and angles, integrating them into more complex forms, and matching the generated form to stored representations of objects. Object recognition is based first and foremost on shape. Secondary contributors are the object's size, color, texture, and visual context. Top-down processing aids object recognition using prior knowledge and expectations (see figure 3.3), particularly when the visual information is vague. Object recognition requires both segregation of objects from one another and grouping of related elements into a whole. Gestalt psychologists described several principles that guide grouping of elements, including proximity in space (grouping close elements; figure 3.4a), closure (ignoring gaps and filling them up to complete contour lines; figure 3.4b), good continuation (grouping elements that create a continuance contour), and similarity in shape or movement (grouping similar elements or elements that are moving together) or distance (grouping elements that are perceived in similar distances from the viewer). A fundamental property of object recognition is our ability to recognize an object across visual conditions that produce different retinal images. For example, one can recognize a mug despite the fact that its retinal size changes significantly as a function of its distance, its retinal shape continually changes from cylinder to circle as a function of viewing

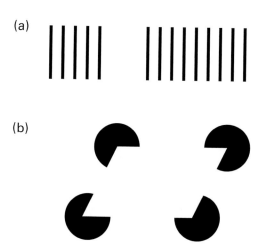

FIGURE 3.4
Illustration of some Gestalt grouping principles. (a) Grouping based on proximity in space: the lines are perceived as two separate groups. (b) Grouping based on closure: a rhombus partially hiding four circles is perceived.

angle and tilt, and its retinal color dramatically changes as a function of illumination. This phenomenon is termed object constancy.

3.4.2 OBJECT LOCALIZATION

Localization of an object requires information about its location and movement. An object's spatial location in a three-dimensional world should be inferred from the two-dimensional image created on the retina. This is achieved by monocular and binocular depth cues that rely on the retinal image, on comparisons of images obtained by the two eyes or in successive time points, and on the muscular adjustments of the eyes. In order to figure out if an object is moving, changes in the location of the object on the retina should be integrated with information regarding the head and/or eye movements of the observer. When an object is moving, it conceals different sections of the background, resulting in changes on the retina that provide additional cues for movement.

3.4.3 THE BINDING PROBLEM

The visual features that are processed separately in distributed brain regions must be bound together in order to generate a unified, integrated perceptual experience (Damasio 1989). How and where in the brain this is done is still an enigma. At the cellular level, temporal synchronization in oscillating neural assemblies has been suggested as a possible mechanism for binding (Singer and Gray 1995). At a higher processing level, the feature integration theory suggests that a spatial attention mechanism binds visual features (Treisman and Gelade 1980), while others claim that it binds features across different sensory modalities.

Human audition results from exposure to sound waves at frequencies of approximately 20–20,000 Hz.

3.5 AUDITORY SYSTEM

3.5.1 THE STIMULUS

Sounds are produced by vibrations that move air molecules, producing an oscillating wave of pressure changes that propagate through media such as the air. Sounds can be described as sine waves. One measure to quantify a sine wave is the number of cycles (i.e., from one wave crest to the following one) that occur in 1 second. The measure is termed *frequency*, and it is represented in units of hertz (1 Hz equals 1 cycle per second). Human audition results from exposure to sound waves at frequencies of approximately 20–20,000 Hz. Notably, as you will read below, some acoustic features are processed and coded differently for high and low frequencies. Simple sounds (termed *pure tones*) consist of a single sine wave. Sine waves can be further characterized in terms of amplitude, duration, and phase (figure 3.5a–e). Complex sounds are the sum of multiple sine waves, which can differ in frequency, intensity, and phase (figure 3.5f). Wave amplitude, also termed *intensity*, is closely related to the perceived dimension of loudness (high intensity

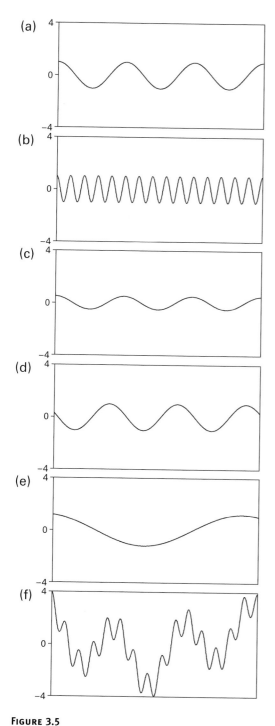

FIGURE 3.5

Simple (a–e) and complex (f) sounds. (a) A sinusoidal wave. (b) Same intensity and phase as (a), but higher frequency. (c) Same frequency and phase as (a), but lower amplitude. (d) Same frequency and amplitude as (a), but different phase; that is, different parts of the oscillating sine wave occur at a given time point compared to the sine wave in (a). (e) Different intensity, phase, and frequency. (f) A complex wave consisting of the sum of waves (a) to (e).

= loudness), while frequency is closely related to the perceived dimension of pitch (high frequency = high pitch tone). Complexity underlies the perceived dimension of timbre. That is, each combination triggers a particular pattern of neural activity, which is identified as a particular sound (e.g., the difference between musical instruments).

3.5.2 Anatomy of the Auditory System

The hearing organs are the ears. Their anatomy and particularly the mechanical composition of the membranes and small bones in the outer and middle parts of the ear are designed for sound transmission and amplification (figure 3.6). Specifically, wave sounds vibrate the eardrum membrane, an effect that initiates a movement in a set of small bones, which in turn vibrate another membrane called the *oval window*. These vibrations lead to pressure changes and vibrations in a part of the inner ear called the *cochlea*. This is a coiled tube of bone filled with fluid and contains the basilar membrane on which the receptors of the auditory system are located. These receptors, which are called *hair cells*, owing to their shape, bend in response to the vibrations of the basilar membrane, producing an electrical impulse,

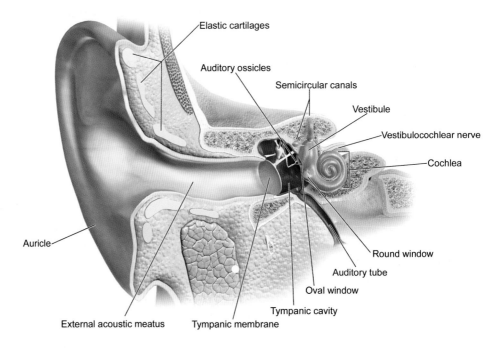

Figure 3.6

Schematic view of a human ear. Source: Blausen.com staff. Blausen gallery 2014. *Wikiversity Journal of Medicine*. doi:10.15347/wjm/2014.010. ISSN 20018762.

Sound wave
↓
The eardrum vibrates
↓
The first, second, and third bones move one after the other
↓
The oval window vibrates
↓
Parts of the basilar membrane vibrate,
in accordance with the frequency of the sound
↓
Pressure changes in the cochlear fluid
↓
Hair cells bend, an electrical impulse is created

FIGURE 3.7
The transmission, amplification, and transduction of sound in the human ear.

thereby transducing mechanical energy into an electrical signal. Figure 3.7 summarizes the steps that precede auditory signal transduction.

3.5.3   CODING AND ANALYSIS OF AUDITORY INFORMATION

Hair cells: The receptors of the auditory system. They traduce mechanical energy into an electrical signal.

Tonotopic map: Topographical organization of the representation of the frequency of sounds, such that adjacent locations respond to successive frequencies.

3.5.3.1   CODING FREQUENCY
Sound frequency is coded differently for high and low frequencies. Moderate to high frequencies are coded by the location of the hair cells (also termed *place coding*). The thickness and elasticity of the basilar membrane change along its length. This feature creates a unique coupling between sound frequency and response in a specific location of the membrane. That is, because of the anatomic property of the basilar membrane, each frequency initiates a vibration in a specific part of the membrane (von Bekesy 1949; see figure 3.8). Accordingly, the location of the hair cells that were bent represents the sound's frequency. The topological arrangement of frequency coding sets the stage for place coding of frequency via tonotopic maps. Low frequencies are coded by other means; namely, the vibration

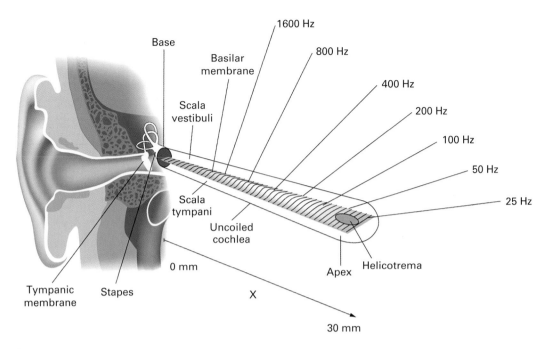

Figure 3.8
Frequency tuning along the basilar membrane. Credit: A. Kern, C. Heid, W-H. Steeb, N. Stoop, and R. Stoop.

rate of a specific portion of the basilar membrane dedicated to representation of lower frequencies. Studies have shown that stimulating this particular area using an electrical signal with low frequency rates creates an experience of hearing in deaf people (Pijl and Schwarz 1995).

3.5.3.2 Coding Intensity

In high frequencies, firing rate codes the intensity of the sounds. The intensity of a low-frequency sound wave is coded by the number of neurons that are firing. The coding of frequency and intensity in high and low frequencies is summarized in table 3.4.

Multiple types of neurons have been identified in auditory systems. Some neurons respond to simple features, such as frequency or intensity, or to modulation in these feature. Some neurons increase firing rate in response to a specific band of frequencies and decrease firing rate in response to adjacent frequencies. Yet other neurons respond to certain binaural structures, or respond in a time-dependent manner, or to conjunctions of features (deCharms, Blake, and Merzenich 1998). Multiple neural response patterns related to stimulus duration have been identified. One example is exclusive response at the stimulus onset or at its offset, while another example is different response patterns at stimuli onset, offset, and in between. Some neurons in auditory associative cortices respond only to particular combinations of frequencies that create specific complex sounds. For example, in the auditory cortex of squirrel monkeys, neurons that are sensitive to vocalizations of their own species were identified (Wollberg and Newman 1972).

After processing in several subcortical relay stations, auditory information reaches the primary auditory cortex located in the upper bank of the lateral fissure. This area preserves the tonotopic map arrangement of the basilar membrane, with the medial-lateral axes corresponding to the lower and upper aspects of the basilar membrane, respectively (Romani, Williamson, and Kaufman 1982). Auditory information is transmitted from primary to secondary and associative auditory cortices, where sounds are imbued with meaning. In humans, adjacent to the primary auditory cortex some specialized regions preferentially respond to speech sounds, probably owing to their unique acoustic features (Binder et al. 2000). Interestingly, some areas are specialized in both language and music perception, suggesting common mechanisms. Box 3.4 describes the psychological effects of music. A region known as Wernicke's area, located posterior to the primary auditory cortex in the dominant hemisphere for language (usually the left hemisphere), plays a pivotal role in auditory word recognition and understanding of language (Petersen et al. 1988). Contemporary models acknowledge the key contribution of anterior parts of the superior temporal gyrus to word recognition (DeWitt and Rauschecker 2012).

TABLE 3.4
Coding of frequency, intensity, and location in the auditory system

| Sound wave | The coded property | | Location of source |
	Frequency	Intensity	
High frequency	Location	Firing rate	Intensity
Low frequency	Firing rate	Number of neurons firing	Phase difference

Box 3.4
Psychological Effects of Music

Music can elicit emotions (Krumhansl 1997), and this property was identified as the primary drive for listening to music (Juslin and Laukka 2004). Accordingly, music can modulate the activity of brain structures that are generally implicated in emotion processing, such as the limbic system (Frühholz, Trost, and Grandjean 2014). Emotion can be elicited from fast and coarse low-level processing as well as from more complex aspects of the musical piece. The amygdala has been implicated in the former, while the hippocampus has been implicated in the latter, possibly because it provides memory-based and contextual associations (Frühholz, Trost, and Grandjean 2014).

Table 3.5
Similarities and differences between visual and auditory systems

	Visual system	Auditory system
A. The stimuli		
Type of physical stimulus	Electromagnetic radiation	Oscillating mechanical wave of pressure changes
Only a limited subrange of the energy is detectable	~400–700 nm	~20–20,000 Hz
The effect of mixture	Synthetic—a mixture of wavelengths is merged into a single color	Analytical—a mixture of tones preserves the two original tones
B. The sense organs		
Organ	Eyes	Ears
Spatial coverage	Highest resolution for a small part of the visual field (foveal sight), gradually reduced resolution as moving away from it; the nearby surroundings that do not fall onto the retina are not seen	Sounds erupting from the entire surroundings are detectable
The use of discrepancies between the sense organs	Binocular differences aid depth perception	Binaural differences aid source localization
C. Neural organization		
Receptive fields	Spatial receptive field (e.g., ganglion cells that increase firing rate for stimuli appearing in their center and decrease firing rate for stimuli appearing in the periphery)	Frequency receptive field (e.g., neurons that increase firing rate for particular frequencies and decrease firing rate for adjacent frequencies)
Hierarchical processing	From simple edges to complex objects and scenes	From pure tones and simple sound features to complex sounds
Topological correspondence between periphery and primary sensory cortex	Retinotopic organization of the periphery and the primary visual cortex	Tonotopic organization of the periphery and the primary auditory cortex
Examples of specialized regions in the human brain	Fusiform face area that specializes in face perception	Wernicke's area that specializes in language perception

TABLE 3.5
(continued)

	Visual system	Auditory system
D. Signal interpretation		
Localization	Localization is inferred from retinotopic maps and depth cues	Localization is inferred from phase and intensity differences
The segregation challenge	Distinguishing figure (i.e., the object) from ground (i.e., the background)	Distinguishing different sound's sources
Examples of principles for grouping similar elements (low-level principle of segregation, perceived fast and automatically)	Proximal elements, elements that move in the same direction and speed (Gestalt roles)	Sounds with similar patterns over time
Examples of learned schemas (high-level features, analyzed slowly, learned)	Accumulating knowledge regarding regular visual patterns (e.g., a treetop usually appears above the trunk)	Accumulating knowledge regarding regular auditory patterns (e.g., a mixture of certain frequencies jointly create a sound of a clarinet)

Upon completing the fundamental task of sound detection, the auditory system encounters the challenges of sound recognition and localization.

3.5.3.3 SOUND RECOGNITION

People are able to identify and distinguish a continually changing mixture of complex sounds simultaneously erupting from various sources. For example, reading this textbook in the library, you possibly hear the voice of several students chatting, a book that someone mistakenly dropped, a ringtone of a cell phone, and typing on laptops. Auditory pattern recognition requires grouping of the various frequencies that compose a distinctive sound, as well as segregating them from other frequencies belonging to different sounds. These processes rely on multiple cues, including the unique spectrum, location, onset, duration, and loudness of each source. Sounds that have similar patterns over time or similar frequency spectra are grouped together (Bregman 1990).

A region known as Wernicke's area, located posterior to the primary auditory cortex in the dominant hemisphere for language (usually the left hemisphere), plays a pivotal role in auditory word recognition and understanding of language.

3.5.3.4 SOUND LOCALIZATION

For low frequencies (below 3,000 Hz), location is mainly determined by interaural differences in arrival time or phase. That is, if the source of the sound is located to the right or left of the head, in each given moment, different portions of the oscillating sine waves arrive at each ear, a situation that is termed *out of phase*. Only if the source is located exactly in front or behind the head, the same portion of the sound wave reaches both ears at the same time. Some auditory neurons receive information from both ears and detect arrival time or phase differences. For distinct sounds, such as a click, differences in arrival time at each ear indicate the location of the source. Whereas for continuous sounds, such as a long tone, phase differences between the ears indicate location. In high frequencies, differences in phase are too short to be detected, thus location is inferred by another means. The auditory system takes advantage of the absorption of high frequencies by the head. This physical property produces differences in intensity of the arriving signal such that the ear that is closer to the source of the sound receives the signal with greater intensity. The mechanisms for coding the location of sound are summarized in table 3.4.

Table 3.5 summarizes the similarities and differences between visual and auditory systems.

3.6   Olfactory System

3.6.1   The Stimulus

Our most primitive sense is smell. The brain interprets an airborne chemical called *deodorant*: the chemical composition of deodorants slows the brain's processing of information about an object without having direct contact. The human sense of smell can detect a trillion different types of odors. However, our sense of smell cannot compare to that of other animals, such as the dog, who have 125–300 scent glands (dependent on breed).

3.6.2   Anatomy of the Olfactory System

The nose is the primary organ of smell. Inside the nose is the olfactory system that passes the deodorant to the brain to be identified. On both sides of the nose deep within the nasal cavity, neurons that detect deodorants reside. These neurons are located in the olfactory epithelium at the top of the nasal cavity. They are also connected to the cells of the olfactory bulb. The olfactory bulb is a small section of the brain at the base and below the frontal bulbs. The olfactory bulb transfers information from the olfactory tract to the olfactory bulb. Cilia (hair-like strands) and mucus coat the epithelium.

3.6.3   Coding and Analysis of Olfactory Information

When molecules of odor are breathed in through the nose, they dissolve the mucus in the nasal passage. The odors are then recognized by the odorant receptors of the olfactory sensory neurons. The odor stimulus is then sent to the brain when the odor molecules react with the receptor on the cilia. The neurons that send signals are randomly distributed in the epithelium regions called *expression zones*. The signals are sent from the olfactory cells to the olfactory bulb. The axons then make sure to express the same receptor on the same area of the olfactory bulb. These bands of axons are called the *olfactory tract*. The olfactory tract projects to the olfactory cortex. The olfactory bulb receives information back from the amygdala, neocortex, hippocampus, locus caeruleus, and substantia nigra.

3.6.4   USE OF SMELLS IN MARKETING

Smell is considered one of the senses that are most closely linked to emotional memory rather than factual memory (Halloway 1999). Smell has also been known to trigger memories of all different types of emotion (Aggleton and Waskett 1999). Retailers can potentially use smell to evoke memories of positive emotions, such as the smell of freshly baked bread (Davies, Kooijman, and Ward 2012). These triggers are produced by outside experiences that are not directly linked back to the retail environment. Another potential use of smell is the recall of a smell that is specific to a certain retail environment. This can evoke a memory of a pleasant experience or a memory that the consumer had at that retail environment. This trigger is produced by the retailer. It is hard to quantify results from using smell as a form of retail marketing. Consumers are sometimes unsure if they are actually processing the stimuli of the different smells. However, smell is one of the most powerful senses to create a "bond" between the retailer and the consumer. Because smell has been shown to trigger past memories, this would be a powerful tool in developing retail loyalty.

> Smell is considered one of the senses that are most closely linked to emotional memory.

3.7   TASTE SYSTEM

3.7.1   THE STIMULUS

Taste is closely related to the more primitive side of the behavioral function of the human nervous system. Taste is produced from the chemicals in foods. These chemicals are broken down in the mouth with saliva. The chemicals reach the taste cells by going through the taste pores. A chemical then reacts with the taste receptor protein or the ion-channel proteins. This will cause electrical changes in the taste cells that will send chemical messages to the brain. Through neurotransmitters, the chemical message is sent to the brain. The stimuli that are sent to the brain can be interpreted as five different basic flavors: sweet, sour, salty, bitter, and umami. The ion channels are responsible for channeling the chemicals that produce the five different flavors. The chemicals that produce the salty and sour flavors go directly through the ion channels. However, the chemicals that produce the sweet and bitter flavors bind to surface receptors to send signals to close and open the ion channels. The sweet tastes are produced by organic chemicals. These chemicals are typically composed of carbons. The sour tastes are produced by hydrogen ions.

> The stimuli that are sent to the brain can be interpreted as five different basic flavors: sweet, sour, salty, bitter, and umami.

This is why acids tend to taste more sour than bases. Ionic salts produce a salty taste that activates multiple types of taste receptors. Like sweet tastes, bitter tastes are also typically produced by organic chemicals. This means that small modifications to the molecular structure could change a bitter taste to sweet or vice versa. Alkaloids or bases often tend to be bitter. Umami is the newest type of taste and is the Japanese word for "savory." This flavor is produced by the amino acid glutamate. Glutamate is known to be a flavor enhancer and is considered the second most pleasant taste after sweet.

3.7.2 Anatomy of the Taste System

We taste with the muscular organ called the *tongue*. The taste is identified by the taste buds of the tongue. Taste cells make up these taste buds, allowing them to perceive taste. The taste buds on the tongue can be found in papillae, the small bumps that give the tongue its rough texture. The papillae look like scattered pink bumps on the tongue. In the posterior of the tongue there are several circumvallate papillae. The actual taste buds are small spheres. The taste buds consist of three different groups of cells: supporting cells, taste cells, and the basal cells. Basal cells perform as stem cells. The basal cells split into the supporting cells and then differentiate to the final maturely grown taste cell. The taste bud is mostly composed of supporting cells. The supporting cells insulate taste cells from each other and from the tongue epithelium. The supporting and taste cells have long microvilli (gustatory hairs) that project through a taste pore to the tongue epithelium. The pores are a gateway for molecules and ions to reach the receptor cells.

3.7.3 Coding and Analysis of Taste Information

Receptor cells actually interpret the different chemical substances as taste. All receptor cells are attached to a sensory neuron that links back to the brain. The nerve fibers help communicate the taste sense from the tongue to the brain. The nerve fibers first signal the gustatory nuclei of the medulla, then the ventral posterior nucleus, and then the primary and secondary gustatory cortex. The nerve fiber discharge frequency increases until it reaches its peak of a fraction of a second. The taste nerves then connect the brain stem, then the thalamus, and finally the insula and frontal operculum core. The brain will then recognize the signals and determine the taste. It is known that eating favorite foods can cause endorphins to be released in the brain. These endorphins can promote relaxation and decrease pain.

Key Takeaways

Sensory information is processed mostly in a hierarchical manner, termed *bottom-up processing*, with neurons gradually representing larger parts of the environment and more complex dimensions. Additional routes bypass the hierarchical order, allowing feedback and modulation of perception by high-level processes, termed *top-down processing*.

The response to unchanging incoming information is typically reduced, leaving more available resources to process new incoming information.

Visual features are processed separately in distributed brain regions and are bound together to generate a unified perceptual experience. The ventral stream is mainly dedicated to the perception of form and object recognition, with some regions specialized to specific types of stimuli. The dorsal stream is mainly dedicated to perception of location and movement.

Visual object recognition requires segregation of objects from one another, grouping of related elements into a whole, and object constancy despite different retinal images in terms of shape, size, color, texture, and visual context.

Auditory pattern recognition requires grouping and segregation of frequencies, processes that rely on the unique spectrum, location, onset, duration, and loudness of each source.

Smell is the most primitive human sense and is closely linked to emotional memory.

The human brain translates the information in the world into brain signals using machinery to take the signal in its raw form (photons, sound waves, etc.) and convert it into an electrochemical signal. On the basis of the site in the brain where the signal gets processed, we name the experience hearing, seeing, smelling, and so on.

Our machinery for sensing the world is limited, and we are only able to see, hear, smell, or sense a portion of the world around us.

Vision makes for the largest brain real-estate in humans. Nearly a fifth of the brain is allocated to seeing. Information from the eyes travels to the back of the brain where it is processed by the visual system and then propagates forward until it reaches our perception.

Similarly, our auditory system translates wave interference in the air into a movement of the eardrum that is interpreted as sound.

Taste and smell use air molecules that bind with our nose or tongue and activate the processes that make for the experience of smelling.

Pain is regarded as a sense as well, albeit different than the other five senses. It does not work in the same way in multiple aspects. However, it is often connected strongly to the sense of touch, which is also unique. Touch is made from temperature and pressure sensors located all over our skin that transmit the tactile feelings into our brains. Our body is mapped to brain sites, and the feeling of the world on our body is therefore allocated to a specific location. Our tactile abilities are very sensitive. The movement of a piece of hair on the back of our hand will be felt easily.

DISCUSSION QUESTIONS

1. Some people say that the senses of smell and taste are actually a manifestation of the same sense. Explain why this idea could be entertained and what is and is not true about it.

2. People that are born blind have no signal activating their visual cortex. Accordingly, other senses often "take over," and they might develop acute hearing or sense of smell. This gives rise to a theoretical idea where our brain can in fact reallocate its abilities if we train it to "learn" new senses. This field, termed *sensory addition*, suggests that we can have a better sense of smell, hearing, or taste. In fact, oftentimes sommeliers or chefs describe developing such better senses through experience. Discuss the idea of what it would mean to enhance sensations in humans and what it would mean to have improved sight or hearing in our world. (How would the world change if we were able to see the rays of a mobile phone or have a sense of smell as acute as that of a dog?)

3. Describe the difference between absolute and difference thresholds in stimuli detection.

4. When we put on a new perfume or cologne, most often after a few minutes of wearing the odor we will not smell it again. This is known as habituation. However, senses such as pain do not go result in the same experience. Why do you think the sense of pain is not prone to such habituation?

5. Pick one of the two senses, vision or audition, and explain the process by which a signal is transmitted from the moment a photon hits the retina or a wave of sound interferes with the eardrum until the brain codes the experience as seeing or hearing. At the brain level—once the process of parsing the signal is over—is there a difference between hearing and seeing in the pathways they converge in and bind?

6. While light is faster than sound, our neural processing of sight is actually slower than that of sound given the architecture of the brain. Accordingly, we often process sound faster than sight. Explain why this is in line with the fact that the "go" sign for the start of a 100-m foot race is the sound of a gun rather than a green light like the ones used in car racing.

7. Explain how the following phenomenon can affect consumer behavior, and describe creative applications of these principles in neuromarketing.

   • Sensory adaptation

   • Top-down modulation of perception by prior knowledge and expectation

8. Identify campaigns that successfully use color or music to induce emotional states. Describe how the learned principles were applied in these campaigns.

9. Identify a campaign that could better use color and music to induce emotional states, and apply the learned principles to portray a better creative solution.

10. Demonstrate the utilization of Gestalt roles for grouping of elements in neuromarketing.

REFERENCES

Aggleton, J. P., & Waskett, L. (1999). The ability of odours to serve as state-dependent cues for real-world memories; Can Viking smells aid the recall to Viking experiences? *British Journal of Psychology*, 90(1), 1–7.

Alberts, W. A., & van der Geest, T. M. (2011). Color matters: Color as trustworthiness cue in web sites. *Technical Communication (Washington)*, 58(2), 149–160.

Ampuero, O., & Vila, N. (2006). Consumer perceptions of product packaging. *Journal of Consumer Marketing*, 23(2), 102–114.

Aslam, M. M. 2005. Are you selling the right colour? A cross-cultural review of colour as a marketing cue. In *Developments and trends in corporate and marketing communications: Plotting the mindscape of the 21st century: Proceedings of the 10th International Conference on Corporate and Marketing Communications*, edited by I. Papasolomou, 1–14. Cyprus: InterCollege, Marketing Department, School of Business Administration.

Bakker, I., van der Voordt, T., Vink, P., de Boon, J., & Bazley, C. (2015). Color preferences for different topics in connection to personal characteristics. *Color Research and Application*, 40, 62–71.

Bregman, A. S. (1990). *Auditory scene analysis: The perceptual organization of sound*. Cambridge, MA: Bradford Books, MIT Press.

Binder, J. R., Frost, J. A., Hammeke, T. A., Bellgowan, P. S., Springer, J. A., Kaufman, J. N., et al. (2000). Human temporal lobe activation by speech and nonspeech sounds. *Cerebral Cortex*, 10(5), 512–528.

Castelhano, M. S., & Henderson, J. M. (2008). The influence of color on the perception of scene gist. *Journal of Experimental Psychology: Human Perception and Performance*, 34(3), 660–675.

Damasio, A. R. (1989). The brain binds entities and events by multiregional activation from convergence zones. *Neural Computation*, 1, 123–132.

Daniel, P. M., & Whitteridge, D. (1961). The representation of the visual field on the cerebral cortex in monkeys. *Journal of Physiology*, 159, 203–221.

Dartnall, H. J., Bowmaker, J. K., & Mollon, J. D. (1983). Human visual pigments: Microspectrophotometric results from the eyes of seven persons. *Proceedings of the Royal Society of London. Series B, Biological Sciences*, 220(1218), 115–130.

Davies, B., Kooijman, D., & Ward, P. (2012). The sweet smell of success: Olfaction in retailing. *Journal of Marketing Management*, 19(5), 611–627.

deCharms, R. C., Blake, D. T., & Merzenich, M. M. (1998). Optimizing sound features for cortical neurons. *Science*, 280(5368), 1439–1443.

DeWitt, I., & Rauschecker, J. P. (2012). Phoneme and word recognition in the auditory ventral stream. *Proceedings of the National Academy of Sciences of the United States of America*, 109(8), E505–E514.

Duc, A. H., Bays, P., & Husain, M. (2008). Eye movements as a probe of attention. *Progress in Brain Research*, 171, 403–411.

Duchowski, A. T. (2002). A breadth-first survey of eye tracking applications. *Behavior Research Methods, Instruments, & Computers*, 34(4), 455–470.

Einhäuser, W., U. Rutishauser, and C. Koch. 2008. Task-demands can immediately reverse the effects of sensory-driven saliency in complex visual stimuli. *Journal of Vision* 8 (2): 2, 1–19.

Elliot, A. J. (2015). Color and psychological functioning: A review of theoretical and empirical work. *Frontiers in Psychology*, 6, 368.

Elliot, A. J., & Maier, M. A. (2014). Color psychology: Effects of perceiving color on psychological functioning in humans. *Annual Review of Psychology*, 65, 95–120.

Elliot, A. J., Maier, M. A., Moller, A. C., Friedman, R., & Meinhardt, J. (2007). Color and psychological functioning: The effect of red on performance in achievement contexts. *Journal of Experimental Psychology. General*, 136, 154–168.

Frank, M. G., & Gilovich, T. (1988). The dark side of self and social perception: Black uniforms and aggression in professional sports. *Journal of Personality and Social Psychology*, 54(1), 74–85.

Friedman, R. S., & Forster, J. (2010). Implicit affective cues and attentional tuning: An integrative review. *Psychological Bulletin*, 136(5), 875–893.

Frühholz, S., Trost, W., & Grandjean, D. (2014). The role of the medial temporal limbic system in processing emotions in voice and music. *Progress in Neurobiology*, 123, 1–17.

Goldstein, K. (1942). Some experimental observations concerning the influence of colors on the function of the organism. *Occupational Therapy and Rehabilitation*, 21, 147–151.

Grossman, R. P., & Wisenblit, J. Z. (1999). What we know about consumers' color choices. *Journal of Marketing Practice*, 5(3), 78.

Halloway, M. (1999). The ascent of scent. *Scientific American*, 99(281), 42.

Hamid, P. N., & Newport, A. G. (1989). Effects of colour on physical strength and mood in children. *Perceptual and Motor Skills*, 69, 179–185.

Hanss, D., Böhm, G., & Pfister, H. R. (2012). Active red sports car and relaxed purple-blue van: Affective qualities predict color appropriateness for car types. *Journal of Consumer Behaviour*, 11, 368–380.

Jacobs, K. W., & Suess, J. (1975). Effects of four psychological primary colors on anxiety state. *Perceptual and Motor Skills*, 41, 207–210.

Jones, W., & Klin, A. (2013). Attention to eyes is present but in decline in 2–6 month-olds later diagnosed with autism. *Nature*, 504(7480), 427–431.

Juslin, P. N., & Laukka, P. (2004). Expression, perception, and induction of musical emotions: A review and a questionnaire study of everyday listening. *Journal of New Music Research*, 33, 217–238.

Kanwisher, N. (2010). Functional specificity in the human brain: A window into the functional architecture of the mind. *Proceedings of the National Academy of Sciences of the United States of America*, 107, 11163–11170.

Karremans, J., Stroebe, W., & Claus, J. (2006). Beyond Vicary's fantasies: The impact of subliminal priming and brand choice. *Journal of Experimental Social Psychology*, 42(6), 792–798.

Krumhansl, C. L. (1997). An exploratory study of musical emotions and psychophysiology. *Canadian Journal of Experimental Psychology*, 51(4), 336–353.

Lee, S., & Rao, V. S. (2010). Color and store choice in electronic commerce: The explanatory role of trust. *Journal of Electronic Commerce Research*, 11(2), 110–126.

Livingstone, M., & Hubel, D. (1988). Segregation of form, color, movement & depth: Anatomy, physiology and perception. *Science*, 240, 740–749.

McKenna, T. M., Weinberger, N. M., & Diamond, D. M. (1989). Responses of single auditory cortical neurons to tone sequences. *Brain Research*, 481(1), 142–153.

Mehta, R., & Zhu, R. J. (2009). Blue or red? Exploring the effect of color on cognitive task performances. *Science*, 323, 1226–1229.

Moran, J., & Desimone, R. (1985). Selective attention gates visual processing in the extrastriate cortex. *Science*, 229, 782–784.

Petersen, S. E., Fox, P. T., Posner, M. I., Mintun, M., & Raichle, M. E. (1988). Positron emission tomographic studies of the cortical anatomy of single-word processing. *Nature*, 331(6157), 585–589.

Pijl, S., & Schwarz, D. W. (1995). Melody recognition and musical interval perception by deaf subjects stimulated with electrical pulse trains through single cochlear implant electrodes. *Journal of the Acoustical Society of America*, 98(2 Pt 1), 886–895.

Quiroga, R. Q., Reddy, L., Kreiman, G., Koch, C., & Fried, I. (2005). Invariant visual representation by single neurons in the human brain. *Nature*, 435(7045), 1102–1107.

Rayner, K. (1998). Eye movements in reading and information processing: 20 years of research. *Psychological Bulletin*, 124(3), 372–422.

Ringach, D. L., Hawken, M. J., & Shapley, R. (1997). Dynamics of orientation tuning in macaque primary visual cortex. *Nature*, 387(6630), 281–284.

Romani, G. L., Williamson, S. J., & Kaufman, L. (1982). Tonotopic organization of the human auditory cortex. *Science*, 216(4552), 1339–1340.

Schütz, A. C., Braun, D. I., & Gegenfurtner, K. R. (2011). Eye movements and perception: A selective review. *Journal of Vision (Charlottesville, Va.)*, 11(5), 1–30.

Singer, W., & Gray, C. M. (1995). Visual feature integration and the temporal correlation hypothesis. *Annual Review of Neuroscience*, 18, 555–586.

Solomon, S. G., & Kohn, A. (2014). Moving sensory adaptation beyond suppressive effects in single neurons. *Current Biology*, 24(20), R1012–R1022.

Spence, C., Levitan, C. A., Shankar, M. U., & Zampini, M. (2010). Does food color influence taste and flavor perception in humans? *Chemosensory Perception*, 3, 68–84.

Swets, J., Tanner, W. P., & Birdsall, T. G. (1961). Decision processes in perception. *Psychological Review*, 68, 301–340.

Treisman, A., & Gelade, G. (1980). A feature-integration theory of attention. *Cognitive Psychology*, 12, 97–136.

Ungerleider, L. G., & Mishkin, M. (1982). Two cortical visual systems. In D. J. Ingle, M. A. Goodale, & R. J. W. Mansfield (Eds.), *Analysis of visual behavior* (pp. 549–586). Cambridge, MA: MIT Press.

von Bekesy, G. (1949). The vibration of the cochlear partition in anatomical preparation and in models of the inner ear. *Journal of the Acoustical Society of America*, 21, 233–245.

Whitfield, T. W., & Wiltshire, T. J. (1990). Color psychology: A critical review. *Genetic, Social, and General Psychology Monographs*, 116(4), 385–411.

Wollberg, Z., & Newman, J. D. (1972). Auditory cortex of squirrel monkey: Response patterns of single cells to species-specific vocalizations. *Science*, 175(4018), 212–214.

Yüksel, A. (2009). Exterior color and perceived retail crowding: Effects on tourists' shopping quality inferences and approach behaviors. *Journal of Quality Assurance in Hospitality & Tourism*, 10(4), 233–254.

CHAPTER 4

METHODS

MORAN CERF

A variety of techniques can be used to understand the brain. These range from imaging methods to study the inside of the brain; direct measurement methods—invasive in nature—that eavesdrop on the activity of individual neurons directly by listening to, manipulating, activating, or damaging a set of neurons; and various derivative measures that infer brain activity from the residual changes in bodily performance (movement of the eyes, changes in skin conductance, facial muscle movements, and so forth).

This chapter discusses the variety of tools, their advantages and disadvantages, price, complexity, ease of accessibility, typical and common-use cases, and problems to note and address as one begins using neuroscience in marketing research.

4.1 WHAT METHODOLOGY SHOULD I CHOOSE?

Before diving into the merits of each tool, one might ask what research methodology is best-suited for a particular research question, and, accordingly, which tool is most effective in answering relevant questions efficiently. The tools used in consumer neuroscience research can be roughly divided into two main categories: those that record brain activity (either directly or indirectly, metabolic or electrical activity) and those that pick up other recordings (like biometric responses, facial and eye movements, and the speed of reaction) and infer from it the workings on the brain. Following is an overview of the most important tools currently used in this field (figure 4.1).

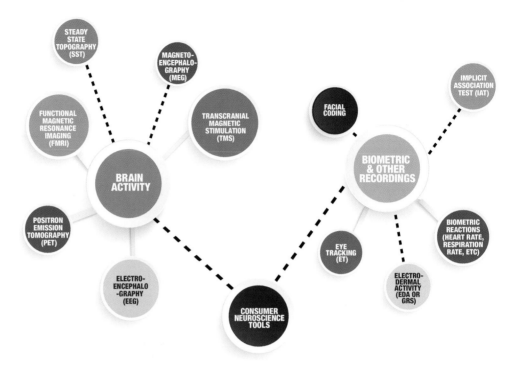

FIGURE 4.1
Consumer neuroscience tools.

Each tool has its own strengths and limitations, and these should be taken into account when devising the study. Based on the objectives of the research, there are tools that do the job better than others in answering strategic and everyday marketing management questions (table 4.1). Furthermore, each tool and its usage can play different roles based on the stage of the marketing mix one is engaged with.

Most of the consumer neuroscience studies aim to answer the last question in table 4.1 (*What to do?*) and to assess the impact of creative concepts and communication materials on consumers. The creative process behind a new campaign is one of the most sensitive areas of research. Often times, the creative people in agencies are very skeptical of any research method that could be used in assessing their work. The abusive use of qualitative methods in some instances does justify their resistance. We showcase a simplified structure of how consumer neuroscience could be used in such cases, covering all four stages, from testing the concept, to the creative (or product prototype), to the final product, and the overall impact of the communication (figure 4.2).

TABLE 4.1
Mapping the neuromarketing tools against typical business questions

Strategic marketing questions	Marketing management tools	Consumer neuroscience tools

Where to play?	*Market segment*
	  • Who are the customers?
	  • How do they cluster?
	  • What are the market offerings?
		• IAT

How to win?	*Brand positioning*
	  • What matters in the category (category drivers)?
	  • Which brand owns/is associated with what attribute?
		• fMRI
		• IAT

What to do?	*Product lineup*
	  • Variants assortment (flavors, colors, etc.)
	  • Size assortment
	  • Packaging
		• fMRI
		• IAT
		• EEG
		• EDA (GSR)
		• ET

	Pricing • How much are the customers willing to pay?	• fMRI • IAT • EEG • EDA (GSR)

	Communication
	  • How to communicate best (content, execution, sequencing, channels)?
	  • Is this best or competitive enough?
		• fMRI
		• IAT
		• EEG
		• Facial coding
		• ET
		• EDA (GSR)
		• Biometric recordings

	Distribution
	  • Presence
	  • Shelving (placement)
	  • Merchandising (communication tools)
		• fMRI
		• IAT
		• EEG
		• Facial coding
		• ET
		• EDA (GSR)
		• Biometric recordings

Abbreviations: EEG, electroencephalography or electroencephalograph; ET, eye tracking; fMRI, functional magnetic resonance imaging; GSR, galvanic skin response; IAT, implicit association test; EDA, electrodermal activity.

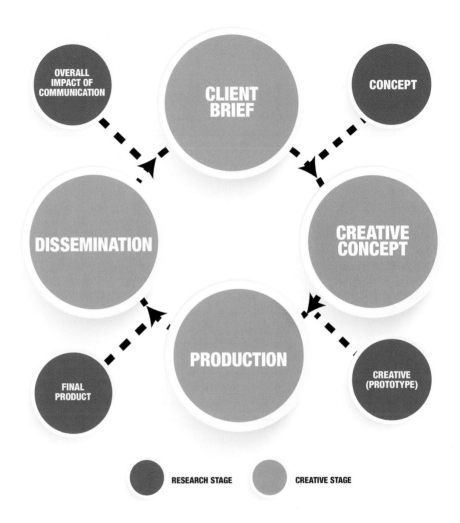

FIGURE 4.2
Research stages in the creative workflow process.

In the first stage, we can test the attributes and claims that are going to be used in building the concept of the campaign. For example, we can find out what are the most important attributes in the category, which brand owns those attributes, and which ones are free consistent with our strategy.

Once the creative concept is approved, we can test storyboards or animations of different executions and see which ones have the best impact on the company's users and non-users. We can also evaluate which elements enhance or decrease the impact of the message on both users and non-users.

Although ideal, it is not always possible to test perceptions from the beginning of the creative process, so if you already produced your television commercial or website, you can evaluate its impact using the same approach as described above: test different elements of the layout, and assess whether your tagline works or the claims are credible.

If your campaign is already on-air or if you have been communicating on the same positioning for a while, you can test your communication performance after a period of time and evaluate the overall impact and how the perception changed over time. This will allow you to react swiftly to subtle changes in perception and brand image, before those changes become overt and influence the behavior of customers.

The insights and added value brought by neuromarketing in each stage of the creative process are summarized in table 4.2.

A similar approach can be used to test each stage of the product development process, starting with testing the benefits and positioning of the new product, to evaluating the prototype and final product, and, after the product is launched, assessing the perceptions of customers.

4.2 TOOLS

There are numerous ways to classify the tools used frequently by neuroscientists to test marketing messages. Those can be evaluated by price, ease of use, speed, etc.. One common way of classifying methods often used by neuroscientists involves ranking the tools on the dimensions of temporal resolution and spatial resolutions of the acquisition data. Given the brain's rapid activity (of the order milliseconds), a higher temporal resolution yields a more accurate readout of the brain signal but would generate a tremendous amount of big data that makes for more difficult analysis. Contrary, tools with very low temporal resolution—of the order seconds—like fMRI or positron emission tomography (PET) can easily miss a number of rapid events. However, they can capture the action of a brain structure involved in a specific function or a residue thereof if it involves multiple mechanisms that altogether amount to a longer set of activities.

In the same vein, higher spatial resolution of recording can yield an understanding of connections and interaction across brain structures. A resolution of recording at the level of an individual neuron can hint to changes at that level, including an understanding of the inputs/outputs to a single cell and the changes within a cell that drive learning and adaptation. Here, too, the higher resolution involves a large data set and also requires a large set of recording devices, presumably implanted deep inside a brain. Therefore, a lower-spatial-resolution device, such as EEG, allows for a broader view of the activity of millions of neurons altogether. This means that one cannot tell, for example, whether a person thinks of

Given the brain's rapid activity (of the order milliseconds), a higher temporal resolution yields a more accurate readout of the brain signal but would generate a tremendous amount of big data that makes for more difficult analysis.

Table 4.2
Insights and added value from using consumer neuroscience to test different stages of the creative process

Stage	Concept	Creative	Final product	Overall impact
Neuromarketing insights	• What are the attributes that customers appreciate most (or least) in the category (at the nonconscious level)? • Who owns certain attributes? • Am I credible if I use this particular attribute? • What about my competition—what are their most powerful attributes? • Do customers believe my brand promises or positioning?	• Which creative does the best job in conveying the message? • Which execution has the best impact on actual customers? What about potential customers—are they impressed to the same extent? • Are there elements in the execution of the message that enhance/decrease the overall message?	• Are there elements in the execution of the message that enhance/decrease the overall message? • What is the impact of the message on customers? • For communication messages (or products) that have been used for a while: Does my tagline work? Do customers believe my claims? Are they willing to purchase?	• How does the true perception of your brand change in time? • What about the perceived image of your competitors?
Added value brought by neuromarketing	• Maximize the impact of future campaigns by focusing on the right concept (and message). • Minimize the risks by choosing a message that really works. • Increase ROI. • For new products: find the best positioning or message to build upon.	• Maximize the impact of future campaigns by choosing the most efficient creative execution to convey the message. • Minimize the risks related to producing and disseminating a message that might not work.	• Increase return on investment (ROI) by focusing on the products (or messages) that have the highest impact. • Minimize the risk of spending money on the wrong messages.	• React swiftly to subtle (nonconscious) changes in perception and brand image, before those changes become powerful enough to change customers' behavior.

his or her "mom" or "dad" (knowledge encoded at the level of individual neurons) but can tell that a subject is thinking of a "person" rather than an "object" or a "place." Even higher spatial resolutions amount to knowledge that a person is "awake" or "asleep" or is engaged in "mathematical processing" versus "emotional processing," but not the extent of the content that drives those.

Combinations of both high spatial resolution and high temporal resolution arrive using invasive tools such as single-neuron recording (see section 4.3.3)—a method in which scientists implant electrodes in the brains of animals or humans undergoing surgery for clinical purposes. This method is very telling, but not likely to be readily available to marketing managers. However, the insights gained from this method should be highly regarded by marketing managers as they shed light on some of the key processes that underlie thinking. For example, using this method one can learn how many repetitions of a stimulus are needed in order to generate an association within the brain of an individual, how pairing between two different contents might happen in the brain, or how some memories or feelings get registered in the brain. This firsthand look at the brain is key to this understanding, and accordingly should not be ignored by marketing leaders, albeit they are not likely to be its immediate users.

4.2.1 fMRI

There are many different methods that scientists use to trace patterns in the brain and body. One of the most accurate of these methods is functional magnetic resonance imaging (also referred to as fMRI). An fMRI scanner calculates and measures the variances in blood oxygenation and blood flow that take place throughout the brain as a result of neural activity. When a specific portion of the brain is more active, it requires a larger amount of oxygen flow to power it. To provide this increased amount of oxygen, the blood flow will increase to the active region of the brain. Consequently, fMRI scanners can produce diagrams that show which parts of the brain are in use at a given time because they can trace where the highest densities of blood flow are. Another reason why the fMRI scanners can trace activity in the brain is because oxygen-rich blood and oxygen-poor blood have a noticeably different magnetic resonance. The regions with more blood flow have oxygen-rich blood. The measurement of blood flow, blood volume, and oxygen use is called the blood oxygen level–dependent (BOLD) signal.

Scientists choose to use fMRI scanners (figure 4.3) for a variety of reasons. One of the biggest reasons is that an fMRI scanner is noninvasive and does not involve a significant amount of radiation. This makes it safer for users because they are not at risk for damaging effects of radiation, and it is easy to use. Another benefit of fMRI is that it can go further in detail to assess what a person is feeling. This is because it can accurately show which parts of the brain are active at a given time, allowing doctors to determine what emotions or changes are occurring. fMRI is also especially useful for measuring three-dimensional brain activity compared with the EEG's more two-dimensional structure.

However, there are some disadvantages. An fMRI scanner is extremely expensive to make and to purchase (often reaching up to $2 million), and it can only sum up the action of the brain within the past few seconds. Functional MRI tests also require a specialized person to conduct the test and also require a lab or clinic location. It cannot state exactly when a certain emotion was evoked, only that it occurred. These are some huge drawbacks when trying to investigate research for neuromarketing. However, there are other less costly methods, including the EEG scanner.

Combinations of both high spatial resolution and high temporal resolution arrive using invasive tools such as single-neuron recording— a method in which scientists implant electrodes in the brains of animals or humans undergoing surgery for clinical purposes.

fMRI scanners can produce diagrams that show which parts of the brain are in use at a given time because they can trace where the highest densities of blood flow are.

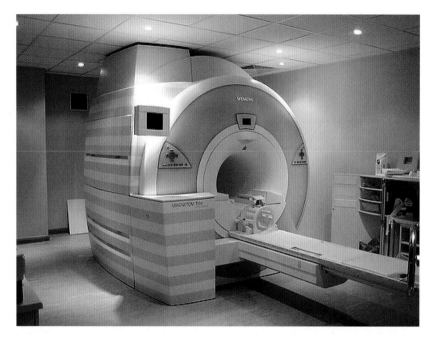

FIGURE 4.3
fMRI machine image. The magnetic coils are embedded in the large cylinder, where the head is mounted and scanned.

While fMRI data is typically hard to collect for marketing managers because of the logistical hurdles involved in the need for a big expensive machine and some knowledge of its operation, there are some companies that offer marketing solutions using fMRI. Studies of pricing mostly have benefited recently from these works. A work by academics has also shown how pricing of products gets registered in the reward systems in the brain—these systems are nearly inaccessible to methods other than fMRI because of the depth of the location of the nucleus accumbens (see chapter 2) in the brain (far from the cortex and therefore not reachable using EEG).

Ultimately, the key challenges in using fMRI arise from the expenses attached to it and the fact that it cannot be used with many subjects because of the limitations imposed by the high magnetic field. (For example, some tattoo ink might trigger a metallic heating, and therefore people with tattoos cannot be subjects. The same goes for people with metal in their bodies—typically following injury where some prosthetic rods were installed during surgery. Even some types of clothing that have metal in them are a potential problem.) Additionally, many subjects are simply unwilling to participate in fMRI studies because of the claustrophobic nature of the machine, which requires caging the head of the subject in a way that makes it nearly impossible to move, and then inserting the subject into a massive, loud machine.

The key challenges in using fMRI arise from the expenses attached to it.

Once the study has been run, independent of the type of analysis that one is interested in conducting, an initial limitation arises merely from the difficulty of pre-processing the data. Scientists analyzing fMRI data need to first register the head size to a standard size (given that every subject has a different head shape, a standard normalized head is often used). Once this registration has been done, one needs to clear all the artifacts that emerged due to inevitable head movement in the machine. Following this noise cleaning, one has to filter out any additional ghost images in the magnet that come from white matter that is not to be analyzed because it carries no functional relevance to cognitive tasks. Finally, because every brain's oxygenation levels might differ, there is a need to normalize the data for every subject. All of these preprocesses happen before a single analysis is done. Existing tools can aid scientists in the process but are quite expensive and are not made for popular use and often deemed difficult to use and unfriendly.

The high price per subject (hundreds to thousands of dollars) for magnet time, along with a typical need for roughly ~15–20 subjects for each comparison cell, makes the experiments quite pricey—of the order tens of thousands of dollars.

All of these make fMRI a less popular tool among marketing managers. That said, its ability to access deep areas in the brain is second to none. And if the particular research question requires understanding of reward, cognitive decision-making processes, valuation, or complex sets of memory activations, fMRI is still a necessity.

Once the data are preprocessed and translated to an accessible format, scientists essentially end up with a set of roughly one hundred thousand time-series. Each series corresponds to the activity over time of one brain volume pixel (voxel). That is the blood oxygenation activity within every ~1.5 seconds in one location in the brain. These can be seen as a typical cube of about $50 \times 50 \times 50$ such time-series, corresponding to a three-dimensional image of the brain as a cube and time. So for a recording of, say, 30 minutes (30 minutes = 30×60 seconds = $30 \times [40$ samples per 1.5 seconds]), we get about $50 \times 50 \times 50 \times 30 \times 40 \times 1.5$ = a quarter-million samples.

Given that most studies record data for 1 hour (as fMRI pay slots usually go by hours) and a typical study involves about 20 subjects, we easily obtain multiple gigabytes of raw data. This in itself poses some logistical problems with respect to analysis tools, the memory of the analyzing system, the need for lengthy computer time for processing, and storage needs for backups.

Ultimately, the processing itself is quite easy after all the complex preprocessing. Scientists typically identify the x, y, z coordinates of a brain area that they care about (e.g., the amygdala), and either using a preliminary task that would activate the amygdala above and beyond other areas (known as a localization task) or simply using estimated coordinates of its location, they now identify the voxels that are important and monitor the activity of those voxels during the task—when a given stimulus was shown or removed. That is, was there an increase/decrease

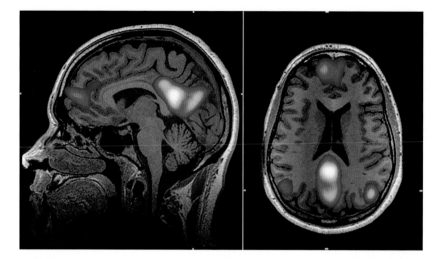

FIGURE 4.4
fMRI scan image. Slices of the brain from various angles are used to highlight locations that are active during the scan. The colored (yellow/red) highlight in the image reflects areas of significantly higher activity during the scan.

above/below a baseline established before the stimulus onset once it appeared or disappeared?

To get robust data, stimuli need to appear multiple times—to ensure that whichever analysis was used does not simply capture a noisy environment.

The analysis itself is done with either commercial tools or standard analysis tools such as MATLAB, Python, R, or other known analysis software.

Because of the many steps involved in the analysis and the fact that there are multiple places in which a mistake could lead to a fluke in the responses, there has been a lot of scrutiny of fMRI studies. Many works have recently been refuted by respectable scientists who found flaws in the statistics, the registration, the normalization, or the data-analysis methods.

With the technique becoming mainstream, there are now more and more existing standards and tools that make the process easier, but it is still regarded as more advanced than other tools.

Typically, fMRI data are depicted by highlighting (as a heat map overlaid on an MRI image of a brain) the brain areas that were active during the task (figure 4.4).

4.2.2 EEG

An electroencephalograph (EEG) is another tool that can be used to measure activity in the brain. The EEG has been a universal neuroscience tool for decades. It records the immediate electrical activity from neuron firing. The typical EEG has anywhere from 32 to 64 brain sensors. EEGs are also noninvasive: they work by placing a given number of electrodes on the human scalp by use of a head cap (figure 4.5). These electrodes can then trace the electrical signals that are made by the brain, typically searching for increased activity in a certain region, similar to the fMRI scanners. These signals are transmitted to a galvanometer, which is an instrument that measures all of the small electrical currents.

EEGs allow scientists to track these currents occurring all around in the brain and then observe changes within fractions of a second after they occurred. However, a drawback of EEGs is that they cannot depict the different structures of the brain,

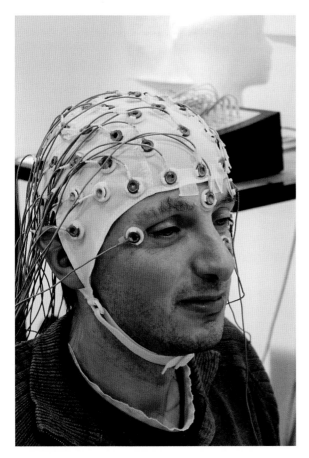

FIGURE 4.5
EEG cap mounted on a subject's head. The electrodes are placed on various locations across the head using a specific organizations ("montage") and connect to an acquisition system in the back that reads the voltage activity on the surface of the head emitted by the brain.

which means they cannot show which specific regions of the brain are responsible for what. The EEGs are very powerful and can detect activity at every moment: this makes it easier to identify triggers in the brain. The EEG is able to measure emotional engagement, attention levels, and certain memory indicators. The EEG is also very portable and can be used in various environments. The entire cost of an EEG system can be from $30,000 to $40,000 for one with high signal-to-noise ratio and large number of electrodes. The EEG also requires specialists in data collection as well as interpretation. The effort and time it takes to set up an EEG head cap on a subject can also be taxing. Regardless, there is a wide range of uses for the EEG, and it has proved valuable to neuromarketing research.

A rule of thumb is that higher resolution of electrodes and higher coverage is typically better for any study.

Unlike fMRI, an EEG is much easier to use and administer and is regarded as a cheaper tool despite its above-mentioned price. Good EEG systems range in pricing (table 4.3) of the order tens of thousands of dollars, and once acquired they are easy to operate. The market now offers a variety of even-cheaper EEG tools with limited numbers of electrodes. While those become more and more popular, they are still regarded as less reliable. A rule of thumb is that higher resolution of electrodes and higher coverage is typically better for any study. Some trivial studies that focus on whether the subject is asleep or awake, dozing off or paying attention, or feeling something or not feeling something might benefit from even a smaller number of electrodes, but for the most part, a set of 32 electrodes is still today's de facto standard. Similarly, 20–25 subjects are a typical number for a 1-cell study (i.e., a study comparing subjects in one condition).

The analysis is quite similar to fMRI once preprocessing is done. Because of the ease of use, there is typically less preprocessing altogether, and most EEG machines output the raw data in a format that can be read by standard tools.

The data are in a format similar to the fMRI data. A series of 32 (electrodes) × 30 (minutes) × 60 (seconds) × 500 (typical sampling rate of 500 samples per second) for a 30-minute study yields data of the order hundreds of megabytes.

Once the data are in a time-series format, it is typically plotted (figure 4.6), and high-resolution moments where a particular event has happened are extracted. Scientists then compare the average activity of many trials where the same event occurred to times with no event and identify average minute increase/decrease in the signal. In a single trial, it is almost impossible to identify any difference because of the noisiness of the data (the signal goes up and down all the time as the brain activity moves in "phases" or "waves"). However, averaging (typically hundreds) of trials smooths the noise and extracts the actual changes due to the stimulus. This process is known as event-related potential (ERP) and is the key way in which EEG is analyzed. For each brain area under a certain electrode, there would be different timing for the activity evoked by the stimulus—based on the order in which it was processed. For example, when a subject sees a face, we expect the part of the occipital lobe that processes faces to become active before

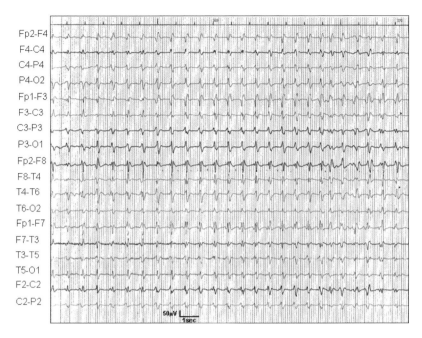

FIGURE 4.6
Illustration of the EEG signal. Each row reflects the voltage activity of a single electrode in the subject's brain, coming from various locations across the scalp.

the part in the temporal lobe that recognizes the identity of the person. Therefore we expect, say, an increase in activity of occipital lobe cells around 100 milliseconds after stimulus onset and potentially an increase in activity of temporal lobe cells after, say, 50 milliseconds more (150 milliseconds after stimulus onset). Accordingly, averaging the activity of the occipital electrodes in all the trials when a picture of the participant's favorite female model appeared in an ad would result in an increased activity 100 milliseconds after onset. This heightened activity is typically named by neuroscientists as P100 (corresponding to a "positive" peak at 100 milliseconds; a negative—inhibitory—response would be accordingly named N100). A following average temporal activity might result in N150, for example.

Neuroscientists by now have mapped multiple such positive/negative peaks implicated in specific functions, and those can be used by marketing managers to identify specific functions (i.e., to know if memory is being active when a person sees a specific content—one might want to repeat the content and check for N180 in the electrode above a temporal area). Marketing managers to-date are not involved in the identification of such activities, but rather refer to "dictionaries" of known

Table 4.3
Metrics to help assess method

Method	Number of subjects for valid typical study	Ease of use (1–5)*	Price	Timing for study/ analysis	Resolution (spatial/ temporal)	What can be studied	Mobility (for marketing studies)
EEG with many electrodes (>32)	25	4	Equipment, $80,000 Study, $25,000	Hours to days	Low/high	Emotion, memory, attention, engagement	Not optimal, but possible
EEG with few electrodes	30	3	Equipment to run in-house, $500 Study, $20,000	Hours to days	Low/high	Emotion, engagement	Possible
fMRI	15	5	Days to weeks	Days to weeks	High/low	Emotion, memory, attention, engagement, pricing, reward, pain	Impossible
TMS	20	4	Machine, $2,000 Study, $2,000	Days to weeks	Low/high	Accessibility to functions such as emotion, cognition, and executive functions	Not used previously; possible but is not necessary
Surveys	80	1	Place/personnel, ~$10,000 Study, $15,000	Hours to days	No neural data	Subjective/ perceived emotion, memory, subject/ perceived engagement, estimated willingness to pay and answer to any possible question involving self-perception, response time	Possible
IAT	80	2	$200 (typically done online, and the costs are for the web, content or statistical analysis sassistance)	Minutes to hours	No neural data	Associations, response time	Impossible

TABLE 4.3
continued

Method	Number of subjects for valid typical study	Ease of use (1–5)*	Price	Timing for study/ analysis	Resolution (spatial/ temporal)	What can be studied	Mobility (for marketing studies)
Eye tracking	20	4	Equipment, $20,000 Study, $4,000	Hours to days	Low/high	Arousal, engagement, response time, attention, low-level features, recognition, content-salient features	Possible
Facial coding	80	3	~500 minutes of analysis, $1,000	Minutes to hours	Low/low	Emotion	Possible
Skin conductance	80	3	Equipment, $2,000 Study, ~3,000	Hours to days	Low/low	Arousal	Possible
Wearable devices	100	3	App development using very inexpensive tools, ~$1,000 Study, ~$2,000	Minutes to days (based on number of samples and devices used together)	Low/low	Location, movement, as proxies for some emotion; ultimately, non-neural	Possible
Electrophysiology	10	5	Equipment, ~$300,000 (not offered for commercial use thus far)	Days to Months	High/high	Emotion, attention, memory, engagement, pain, reward, willingness to pay, associations, decision-making processes, unconscious processes	Impossible

Abbreviations: EEG, electroencephalography or electroencephalograph; fMRI, functional magnetic resonance imaging; IAT, implicit association test; TMS, transcranial magnetic stimulation.
*1, no knowledge in programming and easy to set up and to process the data; 5, requires extensive knowledge in neuroscience and programming skills or tools.

phenomena that they can use for their analysis. A qualified neuroscientist would typically recognize many of the known sets of expected responses and could help a team of marketing managers generate a study that would measure the specific response that they care about. See table 4.4 for some of the key expected functions that EEG can inquire about currently. These sets of functions grow daily with more neuroscience research identifying more and more areas and activities.

In addition to the change in average amplitude over many trials, neuroscientists have also discovered that the frequency of the EEG waves typically changes in specific areas with change in stimulus. That is, from typically 3 waves per second (regardless of their amplitude) in the occipital lobe observed by virtually every human when the eyes are open, once the eyes close we see a jump to a much higher number of waves per second (about 8) that decrease immediately as the eyes open again. Such changes in the frequency in various areas can also be identified and categorized to signal changes in function. Again, neuroscientists characterized many of those changes and named the frequencies in ways that allow for easy notations of the change (the change highlighted above to 8 waves per second in eyes closed, for example, might be named "alpha band" activity). A simple mathematical function known as the Fourier transform allows us to quickly isolate those changes and highlight areas in the brain that code a specific function change with them. This is known as spectral analysis and is a method neuroscientists also use to identify functional differences that are associated with behavior.

Importantly, once those tools of analysis—spectral analysis and time-series/event-related analysis—are mastered, they are essentially the same tools used to analyze *most* of the following techniques. Similar to fMRI/EEG being essentially the same after preprocessing, only that the dimensionality is different (fMRI = many voxels but little time yielding $50 \times 50 \times 50 \times 30 \times [40 \times 1.5]$ time-series; EEG = ~32 times-series but many time points: $32 \times 30 \times [60 \times 500]$), all tools in the end give us a similar analysis metric: a time-series with either many time points or many space points.

Facial coding, for example, will give us ~128 face muscles × a sample every ~0.5 second, but the analysis would otherwise be the same.

4.2.3 Facial Action Coding System

The facial action coding system (FACS) is used to assess different types of human facial movements on the basis of the appearance of the face. FACS was originally created by a Swedish scientist by the name of Carl-Herman Hjortsjö on the basis of studies conducted by an evolutionary biologist and psychologist who identified that facial expressions tend to be similar across cultures in reflecting the emotional state. A key work by Paul Ekman mapped the muscles involved in generating each facial expression that is tied with an emotion in such a way that it is effectively decodeable. FACS uses facial recognition software that is built into the system.

A key work by Paul Ekman mapped the muscles involved in generating each facial expression that is tied with an emotion in such a way that it is effectively decodeable.

This software identifies the muscular patterns of the facial reactions. This process occurs while the subjects are videotaped, and the software translates the movement of the facial action to expressive emotions. The advantage of facial coding is that it provides real-time emotional reaction. Facial coding is also relatively affordable as it mainly requires the system, webcam, and television to display the advertisement. Although the facial coding system is proven to work, there is still room for improvement in accuracy. The current system can interpret the overall intensity of the six basic Ekman emotions: sadness, anger, surprise, fear, disgust, and contempt. An improvement in the system can expand to different emotions such as boredom, confusion, alertness, and attraction. Facial coding also is limiting in capturing the full response of the subjects. They can only measure the facial response from the subject. There is also a debate whether this method is applicable to different cultures as there are different types of facial response depending on different responses.

Facial coding analysis is typically done using off-the-shelf open-source tools that were made to categorize a set of images of a face to an emotion two times per second. These yield graphs of "how much smile is in the face every half-a-second," "how much sadness is in the face," "how much anger," and so on. Most of those classifications are based on studies of faces of many people that were preclassified. Now the computer simply asks: "How similar is this face to that of a stereotypical smile, frown, and so forth."

Alternatively, some marketing managers choose to train themselves as facial coding system administrators and acquire the ability to code facial expressions from movie clips manually. A method that has become more popular recently involves crowdsourcing of individual images by asking people online to classify the image to a certain emotion. Enough subjects agreeing on the specific emotion for a frame of a movie × many such frames yields the facial coding.

See figure 4.7 for an example of a set of facial expressions that make the input for a facial coding software. The still images depict emotions like (top left to right): happiness, sadness, doubt, surprise, fear, disgust and anger.

4.2.4 EYE TRACKING

Eye tracking is a method of tracing and recording the motion of a person's eye in relation to the head and body. Scientists can collect eye-tracking data by using an eye-tracker that can be mounted to either the subject's head or to a computer. Prior to new technology, scientists used a video camera to track eye movement and collected data manually. In each of these methods, the goal is to assess and record the location of the pupil of the eye in fragments of time. For example, if the subject is looking at an image for 10 seconds, scientists search for the location of the eye on the image each second. Eye tracking is a useful tool for neuromarketing and other neuroscience fields because it can be used to analyze human tendencies or

TABLE 4.4
Summary of methods and features

Technology	Metric/measure	Units of measurement	Technological specifications	Targeted mental processes	Potential marketing uses
Electroenceph-alography (EEG)	Voltage fluctuations of thousands of neurons per millisecond at a spatial resolution of up to a single centimeter.	The hertz (frequency) and micro-voltage (amplitude) together define characteristic wave forms. These include alpha, beta, delta, gamma, theta, and mu waves.	Thousands of surface electrodes arranged in headgear (cap, helmet, etc.). The noninvasive electrodes are painless and relatively comfortable. The cost associated with EEG can range from $500 (single scan) to upwards of $10,000 for the set up of an entire EEG hardware and software set.	Ideal for targeting and exploring cognitive mechanisms that occur rapidly. Well suited to explore general cognitive decision making, initial responses, problem solving, etc., due to the high temporal resolution of the data sets acquired.	*Branding*: Identifies brain-wave patterns that emerge when presented words or images that are strongly associated in memory. *Advertising*: Measure of attention, changes in certain brain-wave patterns over regions of the brain.
Functional magnetic resonance imaging (fMRI)	Blood oxygen level–dependent (BOLD) brain tracking that resolves activity to the micrometer scale per second.	Voxel (3D-pixel and volume) intensity is color coded to indicate relative brain activity, with red normally depicting high brain activity and blue representing lower brain activity.	Two magnetic fields are used to stabilize and excite brain nuclei and measure the resulting changes in energy via magnetic coils. fMRI scans are noninvasive and safe with the only major proven health risk being claustrophobia. Recent research into the carcinogenic effects of fMRI are debated. fMRI ranges from $500 to $800 for a single scan and entire setups cost from $1 million to $3 million, with more recent advanced (7 tesla) fMRI scanners yet to hit the commercial market and expected to be upwards of $5 million.	Designed to resolve brain processes at fine spatial resolution to pinpoint brain regions responsible for corresponding behavior. Best for studies attempting to localize brain regions responsible for sustained behaviors such as food or drink seeking, judgment, etc.	*Branding*: Identify brain regions that attract greater blood flow when strong associations are triggered.

TABLE 4.4
(continued)

Technology	Metric/measure	Units of measurement	Technological specifications	Targeted mental processes	Potential marketing uses
Magnetoencepha-lography (MEG)	Magnetic fields that arise from the electrical signals in the brain. Magnetic measurement allows resolution of these fields to within a millisecond.	The tesla (1 weber/m^2), a unit of magnetic flux density. Typical recordings fluctuate between 1 and 3 teslas.	Large nonmobile setup used to detect magnetic fields via magnetometers such as superconducting quantum interference devices (SQUIDs). MEG is both noninvasive and medically approved for people of all ages. MEG costs ~$5,000 for a single scan and $2 million to $4 million for an entire machine and analysis setup.	Best suited for temporal processes that require higher spatial resolution than EEG. Useful for detecting brain changes within the fusiform face area as well as specific regions within sensory lobes.	Used in academic studies but has not caught on as a practical method for commercial neuromarketing. Limited availability of equipment in the world.
Transcranial magnetic stimulation (TMS)	Magnetic fields are used to activate or inhibit regions of the brain by interfering with its normal electrical activity.	The tesla (1 weber/m^2). See above for description.	Magnetic coils output electrical pulses via electromagnetic induction, which, depending on high or low frequency, can stimulate or inhibit the brain. TMS has been FDA approved for clinical use, however it has been associated with slight side effects such as headaches, unawareness, occasional fainting, and in rare cases even seizures. TMS scans can range from $300 to $500, and hardware setup and training costs are ~$100,000.	Excitation or inhibition of brain regions can help to discover the role of various neuronal areas in behavior.	*Advertising*: Product and package design. Analyzes the subject in front of a marketing stimuli while certain brain areas are disabled, stimulated, or normal.

TABLE 4.4
(continued)

Technology	Metric/measure	Units of measurement	Technological specifications	Targeted mental processes	Potential marketing uses
Facial action coding system (FACS)	User-coded criteria classifies various facial movements and features into different action units (AUs). Combinations of these AUs and their relative intensities can be used to indirectly assess a person's mood or behavior.	No SI unit of measurement. The system employs more than 50 facial action unit characterizations along with another 50 related to general head and specific subfacial movements.	Users are trained to accurately identify the various (50+) AUs through a paid course (~$300–$400) after which most associated costs are primarily labor. Recent work has focused on automating AU classification via facial recognition software.	Well suited to identify a person's underlying mood or intended behaviors that may otherwise not be explicitly expressed by analyzing subtle facial movements that correlate to particular mindsets or attitudes.	*Product testing*: Analyze customer reactions to proposed product features. *Advertising testing*: Choose between ad versions. Determine why ad campaigns fail. *Brand emotions*: Measures emotional responses to brands.
Eye tracking	Video recordings track the pupil via infrared or near-infrared light used to generate corneal reflections on the subject's eyes. Additional hardware can be employed to further track a subject's gaze when moving.	Fixations per second, saccade linear mapping, blinks per second, voxels (for attentiveness heat maps).	Small, high-resolution video cameras are placed near the eyes without obstructing the subject's view; a small noninvasive light is used to guide the camera in tracking the view in parallel with other cameras that capture the scene. Eye-tracking hardware and software packages vary greatly depending on specifications and data sets generated and can cost anywhere from hundreds to tens of thousands of dollars.	Useful for investigating the visual system, particularly the length and order in which a subject views various aspects of a scene.	*Product and package design*: Tests visual attention and emotional arousal while viewing an object. *Advertising*: It can measure the number of fixations per second (fps) when a person is viewing an ad. *Shopper marketing*: Measures where consumers are looking in the aisle, at the shelf, and when examining individual products.

FIGURE 4.7
Illustration of the muscle involved in a facial coding of a specific emotion.

behavior. Scientists can use eye tracking to determine what will catch the attention of people first, because the human brain will automatically focus the eyes to whatever it is analyzing. Therefore, scientists can simply look for what the subject focuses on initially. An example of this is when a person focuses on a red apple in an otherwise black-and-white photo first, then scientists can determine that the apple caught the viewer's attention first. By figuring out what a person is focusing their attention on at given times, scientists can better understand how the human takes in visual stimuli and how this information is processed. Importantly, most eye-tracking devices to-date measure, in addition to the location of the eyes, also the pupil size—which is a proxy to arousal or level of lighting in the room—and often the head's distance and alignment from a screen. Eye-tracking devices can be stationary or mobile, where a mobile set could be used in field studies to measure purchase choice (e.g., in a supermarket).

While seemingly complex in its nature, the reality of eye-tracking data is that it is very similar to EEG or fMRI data in its making. A typical eye-tracking machine yields a seven-column CSV file of data, typically at high sampling rate (about 500–1,000 samples per second). The data are often in the format:

Time stamp, xL, yL, pL, xR, yR, pR

where time stamp corresponds to the frame time (i.e., first frame in the first second, giving about 1,000 numbers for every second in a 1,000-Hz eye-tracking device. Such that the 1,000th row corresponds to 1 second of eye-tracking data. Then, xL, yL correspond to the location of the left eye (*x*, *y*) coordinates on the screen and xR, yR to the right eye. pL and pR are a measure of the size of the pupil at a given moment.

If the light in the room (and the brightness of the screen!) are kept constant in the time of the experiment, the pupil size change typically corresponds to a change in arousal, which is indicative of interest and emotion in the course of the viewing of content (i.e., a commercial).

Analysis of the data typically tries to discover where the eyes were at a given critical moment in the viewing; say, when a person was navigating a website, how fast did his eyes go to the ad on the left? How much time did he spend on said ad? Was his pupil growing (indicative of arousal) when he viewed the product in the ad? When the eyes moved from the beautiful model in the ad, did they move to the product she was holding in her hand? Did the subject look at the phone number in the commercial? And so forth.

Eye-tracking data is easy to analyze and accordingly is more and more useful among marketing managers for studies involving product design, attention, shelf organization, print and commercial ads, and more.

See figure 4.8 for an example of the saccades (numbered) of an individual subject viewing a website. A typical first saccade to the face is prominent but the immediate departure from the screen before a return to the yellow highlighted text could indicate that the site organization is not ideal for maintaining attention.

4.2.5 POSITRON EMISSION TOMOGRAPHY

Positron emission tomography (PET) is a tool that provides both two- and three-dimensional images of brain activity. It does so by measuring the radioactive signals that are transmitted into the bloodstream. Many doctors use PET scans of the brain because they can be used to detect and locate tumors or otherwise diseased or impaired tissue. Tissue can be damaged as a result of a change in blood flow, illness, age, and injury. Scientists have used PET scans to diagnose patients with

---

Analysis of the data typically tries to discover where the eyes were at a given critical moment in the viewing; say, when a person was navigating a website, how fast did his eyes go to the ad on the left?

FIGURE 4.8
Illustration of eyes scanpath when viewing an image on a website. The numbers indicate the order of the fixations as the subject was first exposed to the site.

seizure disorders that do not respond to medical therapy, patients with certain memory disorders, and patients with a history of alcohol or drug abuse. They can locate the damaged regions in the brain and use this knowledge for a more accurate treatment. Scans are used at hospitals or other types of medical centers on outpatients, similar to use of an fMRI scanner. Although fMRI scans are also used to locate alterations in the brain, PET scans are more accurate and show more information than other types of scanners. A low-level radioactive isotope, which binds to chemicals that flow to the brain, is injected into the bloodstream and can be traced as the brain performs different functions.

4.2.6 OTHER BIOMETRIC TECHNIQUES

There are also other methods to measure consumer response using biometrics such as blood pressure, heartbeat, respiration, and skin perspiration. Fluctuations in these biometrics can indicate simulation or relaxation level. Biometrics tends to have less specific data than neurometrics on the trigger of the stimulation. However, the data collected from biometrics are important because they provide nonarticulated responses. Galvanic skin response (GSR) is used with EEG and eye tracking. GSR works with a sensor attached to a finger to record the change in perspiration level of the skin. A belt can also be easily attached to a consumer to measure changes in that person's heart rate. These methods make great supplements to other forms of collecting reaction data.

In addition to the above-mentioned devices, improvement in wearable devices gave rise recently to an abundance of inexpensive and easily accessible tools for additional measures of states. These include accelerometers (measuring position in space and movement pace), gyroscopes, magnetometers, pressure sensors, temperature sensors, and high-resolution spatial positioning using GPS that can work not just outdoors using satellite geolocation but indoors as well.

These tools are not only cheap and easily accessible but are also robust in that they can generate big data that can later be compared and generalized across a wide population. Recent works, for example, use merely biometric data to identify depression (notable difference in the amount of movement or departure from home, for example) or other psychiatric conditions or social states. Machine-learning decoding techniques that enable comparison of behavior in distinct states show potential in the ability to use those seemingly simple tools to derive very complex understanding of a user's personality traits.

Given that phones and handheld devices are used by nearly 5 billion people (nearly twice the amount of computers used in the world) and are connected to the Internet even in rural areas, and given that they are often used by individuals nearly at all times the phones and devices are turned on, many companies focus their efforts on using these tools for behavior prediction. Marketing managers are no different here in their desire to access the information. Not surprisingly, the value of the information here is high, and therefore numerous companies vie for the control of and access to the personal information of individuals derived from those phones and devices. Marketing analytics companies and marketing researchers are employing sophisticated techniques here to maximize the ability to parse the information and use it for an improved understanding of the customer.

4.3   PSYCHOMETRIC METHODS

Another form of testing responses using software is called psychometric or implicit testing. These tests capture instinctive responses. A common test used is the implicit association test (IAT). Psychometric methods can be used in various types of studies and also produce real-time results. Psychometric methods are also relatively inexpensive. However, the results from these tests are less direct than those from neurometrics. Psychometrics also requires expertise to analyze the data.

Machine-learning decoding techniques that enable comparison of behavior in distinct states show potential in the ability to use those seemingly simple tools to derive very complex understanding of a user's personality traits.

Marketing analytics companies and marketing researchers are employing sophisticated techniques here to maximize the ability to parse the information and use it for an improved understanding of the customer.

4.3.1 TRANSCRANIAL MAGNETIC STIMULATION

Transcranial magnetic stimulation (TMS) is another method scientists use to observe and treat the brain. It is a noninvasive system that can stimulate small regions within the brain. It has a magnetic field generator that looks like a coil that is able to produce small electrical currents. This coil is also connected to a pulse stimulator, which sends the electrical currents into the coil. The focus of the coil is to send these currents into a specific region of the brain. Available stimulators can generate as much as 2.5 teslas in the magnetic field and frequencies as high as 30 Hz. Typically, doctors use TMS to test the connection between a specific muscle and the brain. For example, they often use it in multiple sclerosis, stroke, and other types of movement disorders. They also often use it to treat other ailments, such as chronic migraines, by targeting the regions of the brain causing the pain.

While TMS is surprisingly easy to acquire and use and is available without any regulation in the United States, it is a powerful way to induce a momentary "lesion" in the participant and learn what functions get lost in the process—to infer crucial steps for processing (i.e., we momentarily stop occipital areas from functioning and observe if the individual sees a stimulus presented in this key moment or can report it subconsciously despite not "seeing" it with the visual areas).

See figure 4.9 for an image of the butterfly-like coil above a subject's head as she is participating in a TMS study.

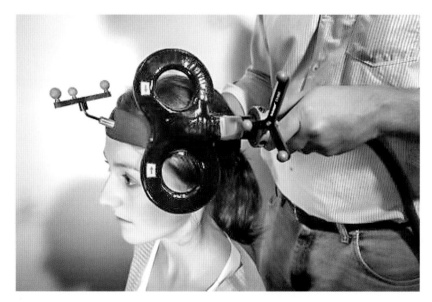

FIGURE 4.9
Stimulation using TMS. The butterfly-looking coil is placed close to the scalp and a magnetic stimulation is induced to generate an activation that leads to a momentary behavioral change.

4.3.2 IMPLICIT ASSOCIATION TEST

The implicit association test (IAT) assumes that people can make quick connections to concepts that are familiar to them. This test is a neuro-based method to test unconscious association such as bias. The subjects may be unaware of these biases. The test has many practical uses in both psychology and marketing. Marketers might be interested in the unconscious attention of a certain brand. The IAT is a low-cost test that has great flexibility in the type of things that may be tested. However, the results of these tests are up for interpretation and are inferences rather than hard scientific data.

4.3.3 ELECTROPHYSIOLOGY

The basic building blocks of the brain are neurons. Neurons in the same part of the brain and even adjacent to each other can have very different functions and respond to different stimuli (Cerf and MacKay 2011). Thus, much can be learned, in terms of how the human brain functions, by studying the activity of individual neurons. Yet even a single voxel in an fMRI study typically contains several thousand neurons (Grill-Spector and Malach 2001), and the differences in brain activation observable using fMRI or EEG are due to the collective activity of many thousands or even millions of neurons.

While considerable research has examined the activity of individual neurons, most of this work has studied non-human animals, such as rats or monkeys (Shadlen and Kiani 2013), though this research has provided many insights applicable to human behavior and economic decision making (Levy and Glimcher 2012; Glimcher and Fehr 2014). More recently, researchers have begun studying the activities of single neurons in humans. Certain surgical treatments for patients with epilepsy require placing electrodes, either as probes fairly deep in the brain or as a grid on the surface of the cortex (Fried et al. 2014). Thin microwires, placed in the hollow center of these probes, often contact neurons and give reliable readings of individual neurons for a relatively extended period. Though understandably absent in marketing literature, single-neuron research in humans has provided insights of interest to marketers and consumer researchers.

Initially, single-neuron work was done exclusively with non-human animals. However, advances in surgical treatments for epilepsy patients whose seizures could not be managed by pharmacological means created an opportunity to observe single-neuron activity in humans. Epileptic seizures, which are massive and uncontrollable firings of neurons, usually originate in a particular region of the brain for a given patient. Physicians found that surgically removing the area of origin could stop many patients' seizures, permanently curing them of epilepsy.

To identify the exact neural region where seizures originate, neurosurgeons implant thin, hollow electrodes or probes (typically 1 to 12), about a millimeter in diameter and up to several inches long, into several areas surrounding the suspected site of seizure origin. The implant sites are determined only by clinical criteria. Probes are often implanted in the medial-temporal lobe, frontal areas, or motor cortices and less often (or not at all) implanted in other areas. In general, the implant sites are associated with neural functions such as memory consolidation or retrieval (hippocampus, entorhinal cortex), fear and social behavior encoding (amygdala), high-level perception (all), navigation (parahippocampal cortex), analysis and perception of specific concepts (right amygdala and parahippocampal cortex), high-level cognitive control and regulation (orbitofrontal cortex), motor planning (supplementary motor area), and general planning and volition as well as error correction (anterior cingulate, orbitofrontal cortex, and other frontal sites).

Note that though we focus on the method involving microwires, alternative methods, such as electrocorticography and intracranial EEG, use electrodes placed on the surface of an exposed brain to record activity from the cortex alone. The recorded activity is typically field voltage rather than the activity of individual neurons, but it still benefits from direct access to the brain of a human subject.

Much of the single-neuron research in humans has focused on basic neural processes of interest to the greater neuroscience community, such as memory, perception, navigation, or neural coding. Understandably, this research has not focused on the usefulness of these findings to applied fields such as marketing. However, some of the findings do have relevance for marketing and consumer behavior.

Of interest to marketing managers, 4.5 provides a list of measures along with explanations and available tools. Figure 4.10 presents a schematic rendering of the spatial and temporal resolutions of different techniques to study the brain.

APPENDIX: SPECIFIC QUANTITATIVE ANALYTICS FOR NEURAL STUDIES PROCESSING (ADAPTED FROM BARNETT AND CERF 2017)

Oftentimes, scientists venturing into the field of consumer neuroscience are interested in the specifics of the tools. "How do I actually set up the machines?" "How do I actually analyze the data?" And so forth. This appendix details a specific example of the analytics used by commercial groups to analyze neural activity. The activity in the specific example (which reflects a standard setup used in many labs) was recorded by means of a portable EEG system (BEmicro and Galileo software, EBneuro, Italy). Informed consent was obtained from each subject after explanation of the study, which was approved by the local institutional ethics committee. All subjects were comfortably seated on a reclining chair in an electrically shielded,

TABLE 4.5
List of functions that can be measured using neural tools

Measure	Explanation	Accuracy	Method	Complexity
Engagement	Measure of engagement in the content experienced (visual, auditory, etc.).	80%	EEG	Medium
Engagement	Higher-resolution measure of engagement in the content experienced (visual, auditory, etc.).	90%	fMRI	High
Emotion	Was the content emotional? (yes/no)	80%	EEG	Medium
Emotion	Was the emotion positive/negative?	80%	fMRI	High
Emotion	Specifically, what emotion was the subject experiencing (happiness, sadness, disgust, anger, fear, surprise, neutral) or were there high-level emotions (awe, jealousy, embarrassment, etc.)?	60%	FACS Biometrics	Low
Memory I	Recognition = "I know I have seen it before."	80%	EEG	Low
Memory II	Recall = remembered when asked to recall freely things seen before.	80%	EEG	Medium
Memory III	Visual = subject can recall fine details like the handedness of the character in the movie or the number of sunflowers in the van Gogh painting (really seeing it in the mind's eye).	70%	EEG	Medium
Attention	Measuring the profile of attention in content. Gives a moment-to-moment assessment.	80%	EEG	Medium
Taste	Whether the subject will like it or—in comparing it to other items—which will taste better? This one can also be broken down to dynamic tastes (i.e., will taste great for desert but not in the morning, or the first two bites will be tasty but not any bite after, etc.).	70%	fMRI	High
Reward	Assessment of the activity of the reward system when experiencing the product (useful for estimating how addictive content is).	60%	fMRI	High
Price	Effect of manipulating the price. For example, seeing if two prices are perceived as "same" or "different" (4.99 versus 5.00) or measuring the effect of price changes on perception of the content ("will increasing the price from 4.65 to 4.66 be perceived as changing the value?").	90%	fMRI	High
Impulse	Level of impulse in purchase, and level of likelihood to resist temptation to buy in a certain situation where self-control is relevant.	40%	EEG	Medium

TABLE 4.5
(continued)

Measure	Explanation	Accuracy	Method	Complexity
Personal biases	Study of an individual to identify specific parameters to their choice (relevant for subjects who want to learn about their own biases to improve choice or estimate decision parameters).	70%	Combined	High
Speed of effects	Measuring speeds of choice or speed of effects of content on the brain. Relevant for measures where rapid choice leads to different outcomes than slow choice (i.e., making investment decisions in high frequency).	40%	EEG	Medium
Low-income preferences	Measures of decision making of individuals in situations of resource scarcity. As scarcity leads to high "cognitive load," this allows for assessing the choice in high pressure (typically relevant for estimation of choice under time pressure, under high load of options, or in low-income populations where a choice is made with limited information).	40%	fMRI	High
Intertemporal choice	Assessment of individuals' ability to perform temporal discounting in choice.	20%	Combined	Medium
Internal competition and deliberation	Measuring and accessing the internal deliberation process and the competitive mechanisms in an individual's brain that guide his or her decision-making processes.	90%	Combined	High
Decision making under uncertainty	Assessing the metrics involved in an individual's decision metric with low information.	60%	Combined	High
Risk assessment	An assessment of the unconscious perceived risk, as well as the personal guidelines to assessing risk within an individual, and their tolerance for risky choices (especially relevant in financial choices).	90%	GSR	Low
Effect of emotion on choice	Prediction of the involvement of nonconscious aspects in seemingly conscious decision-making.	40%	Combined	Medium
Saliency	Measure of conspicuity of visual content (how likely is it to be watched?, how early?, etc.).	90%	Combined	Medium

Measure	Explanation	Accuracy	Method	Complexity
Associations	Using single-neuron recordings (SNR) to identify the number of repetitions required to establish an association (associations between brand and endorser or between brand and category, etc.). This can be used to measure both the strength of association as well as the establishment of an association.	60%	SNR	High
Casting	Using engagement metrics to help in casting decisions for specific visual content.	80%	EEG	Medium
Compression	Using engagement metrics to identify moments that can be removed from a clip while maintaining the same level of engagement (useful for shortening television ads to lower expenses).	80%	EEG	Medium
Intent to buy	Conscious intent to purchase as perceived by the subject (with ~40% predictive power to actual purchase intent).	80%	EEG	Medium

Shaded measures: measures that are relevant to the individual making the decisions, rather than the content observed/experienced.

Methods:

• **EEG**: an acquisition of brain activity using external readout of voltage from the scalp.

• **fMRI**: imaging method that uses magnetic resonance to read the energy consumption of a volume of brain cells. Reads activity from the entire brain, including deep structures.

• **FACS**: reads the involuntary muscular changes in the facial expression, which indicate subtle emotional changes that are governed by neural activity that cannot be overtly controlled by a subject.

• **Biometrics**: a combination of skin conductance, heart rate, respiration, oxygen level, muscular movement, acceleration, pressure, and body movement metrics. Indicates arousal, fear, emotional responses, and engagement.

• **DNA measures**: assays of subjects pre/post measures, which indicate hormonal changes that are driven by performance (adrenaline, oxytocin, etc.).

• **SNR** (single-neuron recording): direct readouts of neural activity using electrodes implanted in the brains of patients undergoing neurosurgery. The ultimate and most precise measure, but rare in applications outside of cognitive neuroscience research.

Accuracy: level of accuracy in predicting behavior from the data.

Complexity: an estimated combination of the time, the price, and the length of the study. Medium = approximately 20 subjects needed, 24-hour turnaround to produce the results, and $2,000 for a study. High = 20 subjects needed, 1-week turnaround to produce the results, and an estimated $20,000 for a test. Low = less than 20 subjects, only minutes or hours of analysis, cheap and easy-to-learn analysis and overall popular and accordingly highly accessible with less experience needed.

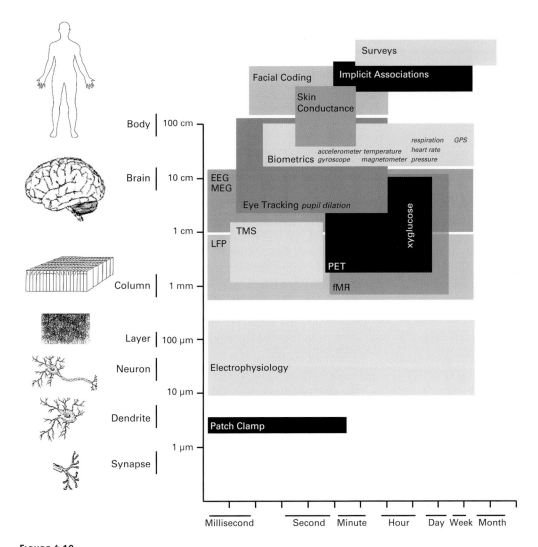

FIGURE 4.10
A schematic rendering of the spatial and temporal resolutions of different techniques to study the brain. The *x* axis describes temporal resolutions from milliseconds to months, and the *y* axis describes spatial resolutions from micrometers to centimeters. EEG, electroencephalography; fMRI, functional magnetic resonance imaging; LFP, local field potential; MEG, magnetoencephalography; PET, positron emission tomography; TMS, transcranial magnetic stimulation. Credit: Moran Cerf.

dimly lit room. As this study focused on EEG recordings, electrodes were arranged according to an extension of the 10–10 international system, which is a standard organization of the electrodes on the surface of the brain. Electrodes are named in this "montage" (this is the term used by neuroscientists to reflect the organization and the names/locations of the electrodes) by their location above the head (Fp for frontal pole, T for temporal, O for occipital, and so on), based on the lobe above which the electrode is placed. The numbers reflect the specific location of each electrode about the lobe, with even/odd numbers indicating left/right hemisphere, and the letter *z* reflecting an imaginary line across the center of the brain—known as the "midline." In addition to EEG data, galvanic skin resonance was measured, as well as heart rate. Because a clear role of the frontal areas has been depicted for the investigated phenomena (Erk et al. 2002; Braeutigam 2005; Knutson et al. 2007; Vecchiato et al. 2011), we used the following channels: AF7, Fp2, Fpz, Fp1, AF6, F5, AF3, AFz, AF4, and F6. Recordings were initially extracerebrally referred and then converted to an average reference off-line. We collected the EEG activity at a sampling rate of 256 Hz while the impedances were kept below 5 kΩ. Each EEG trace was then converted into the Brain Vision format (BrainAmp, Brainproducts GmbH, Germany) in order to perform signal preprocessing such as artifact detection, filtering, and segmentation. The EEG signals have been band pass–filtered at 1–45 Hz and depurated of ocular artifacts by employing independent component analysis (ICA). The EEG data have been re-referenced by computing the common average reference (CAR). Individual alpha frequency (IAF) has been calculated for each subject in order to define the bands of interest as theta. A number of metrics were distilled from the recorded data, which reflect the measures of emotionality of an individual, as well as measures of attention and memory activation. Those standard readings are not easy to isolate from the activity. Therefore, we will show below the data analysis used in order to extract the measures.

AUTONOMIC RECORDINGS AND SIGNAL PROCESSING

The galvanic skin response (GSR) and the heart rate (HR) have been recorded by means of the PSYCHOLAB VD13S system (SATEM, Italy) with a sampling rate of 10 Hz. Skin conductance was recorded by the constant voltage method (0.5 V). Ag-AgCl electrodes (8-mm diameter of the active area) were attached to the palmar side of the middle phalanges of the second and third fingers of the subject's non-dominant hand by means of a Velcro fastener. SATEM also provided disposable Ag-AgCl electrodes to acquire the HR signal. Before applying the sensors, a subject's skin was cleaned by following the procedures and suggestions published in the literature (Boucsein 2012). GSR and HR signals were continually acquired for the entire duration of the video and then filtered and segmented with in-house MATLAB software. As to the GSR signal processing, we used a band pass filter with a low cutoff frequency of 0.2 Hz in order to split the phasic component of the electrodermal activity from the tonic one, and a high cutoff frequency of 1 Hz to filter out noise and suppress artifacts caused by Ebbecke waves (Boucsein 2012).

MEMORIZATION INDEX

The EEG signal is filtered in the theta band and, for the subsequent computation, only the left frontal channels have been selected. From the neuroscientific point of view, there is evidence that trace for successful encoding of novel information can be detected by measuring an increase of EEG theta power from the left frontal cerebral regions (Summerfield and Mangels 2005; Werkle-Bergner et al. 2006). Of these channels, we compute the spatial average through the following formulation defining the memorization index (MI):

$$MI = \frac{1}{N_Q} \sum_{i \in Q} x_{\theta_i}^2(t) = \text{Average power}_{\theta_{\text{left,frontal}}}$$

where x_{θ_i} represents the ith EEG channel in the theta band that has been recorded from the left frontal lobe. In addition, Q is the set of left channels, and N_Q represents its cardinality. In such a way, an increase of MI is related to an increase of memorization. In the following, we will refer to the memorization index as memorization.

ATTENTION INDEX

The frontal EEG signals are filtered in the alpha band for defining the following index. There is evidence that cerebral activity related to attention can be detected at frontal sites by measuring the variation of the alpha rhythm (Klimesch 1999; Petersen and Posner 2012). Of these channels, we compute the spatial average through the following formulation defining the attention index (AI):

$$AI = -\frac{1}{N_Q} \sum_{i \in Q} x_{\alpha_i}^2(t) = \text{Average power}_{\alpha_{\text{frontal}}}$$

where x_{α_i} represents the ith EEG channel in the alpha band that has been recorded from the left frontal lobe. In addition, Q is the set of frontal channels, and N_Q represents its cardinality. In such a way, an increase of AI is related to an increase of memorization. In the following, we will refer to the attention index as attention.

APPROACH/WITHDRAWAL INDEX

To define an approach/withdrawal index (AW) according to the theory related to the EEG frontal asymmetry theory (Coan and Allen 2003; Davidson 2004), we computed such imbalance as the difference between the average EEG power of the right and left channels. The formula we used is the following:

$$AW = \frac{1}{N_P} \sum_{i \in P} x_{\alpha_i}^2(t) - \frac{1}{N_Q} \sum_{i \in Q} y_{\alpha_i}^2(t)$$

$$= \text{Average power}_{\alpha_{\text{right,frontal}}} - \text{Average power}_{\alpha_{\text{left,frontal}}}$$

where x_{α_i} and y_{α_i} represent the ith EEG channel in the alpha band that has been recorded from the right and left frontal lobes, respectively. In addition, $P = \{\text{Fp2, AF6, AF4, F4}\}$ and $Q = \{\text{Fp1, AF7, AF3, F5}\}$, N_P and N_Q represent the cardinality of the two sets of channels. In such a way, an increase of AW will be related to an increase of interest and vice versa. The AW signal of each subject is z-score transformed and then averaged across subjects. In the following, such index is used as a measure of interest.

EMOTIONAL INDEX

The emotional index is defined by taking into account the GSR and HR signals. With respect to the construction of such a variable, we refer to the affect circumplex (Russell and Barrett 1999), where the coordinates of a point in this space are defined by the HR (horizontal axis) and the GSR (vertical axis). Several studies have highlighted that these two autonomic parameters correlate with valence and arousal, respectively (Critchley 2002; see Mauss and Robinson [2009] for a review).

To have a mono-dimensional variable, we describe the emotional state of a subject by defining the following emotional index (EI):

$$EI = 1 - \frac{\beta}{\pi}$$

where

$$\beta = \begin{cases} \dfrac{3}{2}\pi + \pi - \vartheta & \text{if } \text{GSR}_Z \geq 0, \text{HR}_Z \leq 0 \\[2mm] \dfrac{\pi}{2} - \vartheta & \text{otherwise} \end{cases}$$

GSR_Z and HR_Z represent the z-score variables of GSR and HR, respectively; ϑ, in radians, is measured as $\arctan(\text{HR}_Z, \text{GSR}_Z)$. Therefore, the angle β is defined in order to transform the domain of ϑ from $[-\pi, \pi]$ to $[0, 2\pi]$ and obtain the EI varying between $[-1, 1]$. This is why we have two ways to calculate β. According to the equations for EI and β and the affect circumplex (Russell and Barrett 1999), negative ($\text{HR}_Z < 0$) and positive ($\text{HR}_Z > 0$) values of the EI are related to negative and positive emotions, respectively, spanning the whole affect circumplex.

THE SETUP ITSELF

Finally, because this chapter offers a tool for incoming scientists to venture into the field of consumer neuroscience, the author felt it was important to also add a very specific guideline and toolkit for the setup of an EEG system. Granted, the tools used by marketing researchers in neuroscience vary, and EEG is by no means the only tool; however, given its growing popular use, we focus on it as an example.

1. Before subjects are seated, EEG caps needed to be prepared for the study. A typical experimenter would have access to multiple cap sizes for different head diameters (e.g., 54 cm and 58 cm), and the appropriate cap should be selected for each subject. The electrodes are then snapped into the correct holders according to a specific scalp location (e.g., the 10–10 montage that was mentioned earlier). It is helpful to label each electrode with a number and label the corresponding number to the appropriate plastic holder on the EEG cap. Also, it is easier to attach the electrodes to the plastic holders if the cap is placed on a foam model head (see figure 4A.1, left panel).

2. An EEG cap (which resembles a cloth swim cap with round, plastic holders for EEG electrodes) is placed on each subject's head with the subject's assistance. The experimenter ensures that the cap fits the subject closely and is worn symmetrically so that the location of a particular electrode on one subject corresponds to the same anatomic location on other subjects (for future group-level analyses). A fabric

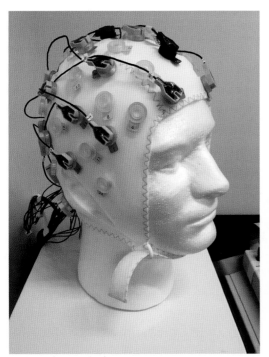 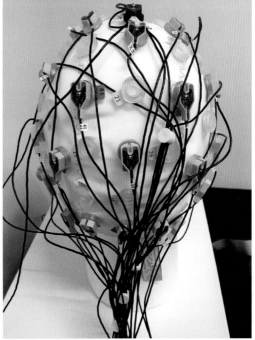

FIGURE 4A.1
Preparing an EEG cap. Photo credit: Moran Cerf.

fastener below the subject's chin is tightened so that the cap does not move, but it should not be uncomfortably tight. Additionally, to maximize each subject's comfort, the thin cables extending from each electrode are angled away from the subject's face by rotating the electrodes in place in their holders (i.e., forming a "ponytail" of cables behind the head; see figure 4A.1, right panel).

3. The EEG electrode cables converge to a ribbon, which connects to a control box (see figure 4A.2, left side of image). The impedance button, denoted Z, is pressed to activate an LED in each electrode. If there is high impedance, the electrode will

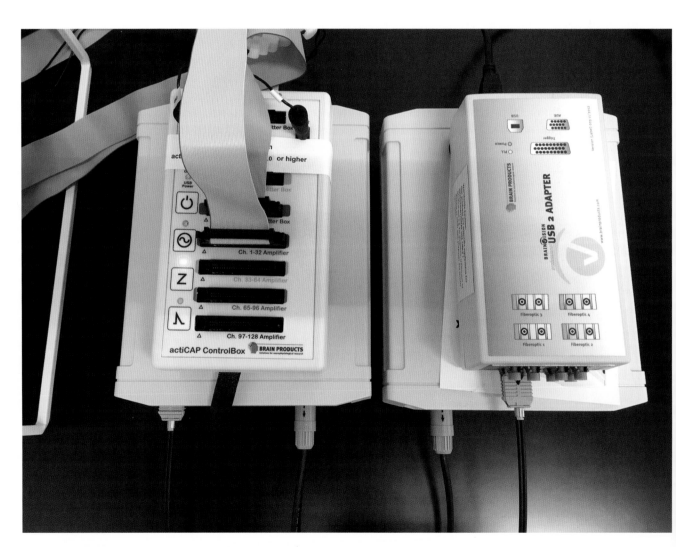

FIGURE 4A.2
EEG system components. Photo credit: Moran Cerf.

be lit red (see figure 4A.1), indicating that conductive gel needs to be applied at that site. Gel was applied via a syringe and a blunt needle, which was shown to subjects to alleviate any potential concerns. Additionally, we preferred to call the needle a "tube" to avoid raising any alarm. A pea-sized amount of gel usually sufficed to establish electrical conduction at a given site, but the process required practice and patience. The first two sites to apply gel need to be the ground ("GND," black) and reference ("REF," blue) electrodes; after gel is sufficiently applied to both of those sites, their LEDs will turn green. Then, gel is applied to the 32 data-collecting electrodes; each site's LED will turn green when it has enough gel to conduct the signal (i.e., sufficiently low impedance). Once all LEDs are green, which takes approximately 15 minutes per subject, the signal button (denoted with a circled "~") is pressed. EEG recording is then initiated from the system's software suite on a laptop connected to the equipment.

4. If the study involves other readings, like galvanic skin responses, heart rate, respiration, and so forth, the other physiologic recording equipment is connected to each subject. For the cardiac data collection, the subject is instructed to place three electrode leads under clothing on either side of the chest and on the left lower abdomen, forming a triangle around the heart. For the respiratory data collection, the subject is asked to place an expandable band around the torso just below the chest. For the electrodermal activity recording, electrodes were taped to the index and middle fingers of the subject's nonwriting hand. These electrodes are connected to a relay device that is worn like a watch around the wrist. Lastly, a video camera was placed near the movie screen angled and zoomed to view the subjects. All of these devices are recording before the onset of the experiment.

5. At the initiation of the experiment, preselected audiovisual stimuli are presented.

6. After the study is completed, all recording equipment is shut down and disconnected from the subjects.

7. The gel washes out easily with water, so subjects were offered wet towels to clean their scalp at the conclusion of the viewing session.

KEY TAKEAWAYS

- There are many tools available nowadays to marketing managers to study the brain without asking the customers for their opinions.

- Tools vary in the ways they measure neural response. Some look directly at the neurons in the brain, some look at the residue of large-population neural activity, some look at the amount of oxygen needed to work the neural circuits, and some even look at the residual activity of the nervous system by testing the facial muscles or the eyes as a proxy.

- Each tool has advantages and disadvantages. Some are more accurate temporally, some spatially. Some are cheaper, some are faster. In choosing our method, we need to think about the specific question we want answered, the function we will be testing, and the price, speed, and other factors that help determine the choice of method.

DISCUSSION QUESTIONS

1. Name the key differences between fMRI and EEG and the advantages/disadvantages of using either one in a consumer neuroscience study.

2. Lisa wants to have a group of 30 subjects watch a commercial and learn about their emotional experience while watching it. Give Lisa three different tools and ways by which she can get some understanding of the affect and valence of the commercial without asking her directly.

3. Pick any two methods for studying subject preferences, and name three advantages and three disadvantages to conducting a study using this method compared to simply asking the participant about his or her preferences using a survey.

4. A perfectly square product appears exactly at the center of a 1280×960 pixels, 15-inch monitor while a person is viewing a commercial. The product's image is 100 pixels wide. A subject's eye coordinates are at:

   a. $x = 591$; $y = 434$

   b. $x = 589$; $y = 434$

   c. $x = 600$; $y = 600$

   d. $x = 640$; $y = 540$

   For each location, say where the subject is gazing at the product.

5. A client is interested in learning which ad to launch at the coming Super Bowl. They are at the stage where they have a product (an anti-dandruff shampoo) but do not yet have a complete idea for the Super Bowl ad. Nor do they have the talent they want to use for the ad (they are considering George Clooney alongside a cute puppy). Normally, they would develop a few ads (typically, three) and run them by a focus group both during the development phase and when the product is finalized to know what time in the game they

should place the ad, how long it should be, whether the puppy and actor are right for the roles, and so forth. This time, the innovative company decided to come to you instead and have you do the customer insights for them. Instead of a focus group, they want to use a consumer neuroscience approach for the work. Using your knowledge of available tools and techniques, advise them which method to use and what experiments they could run to choose the best ad, the right talent, the right length, and ways to measure attitudes.

REFERENCES

Barnett, S. B., and M. Cerf. 2017. A ticket for your thoughts: Method for predicting content recall and sales using neural similarity of moviegoers. *Journal of Consumer Research* 44 (1): 160–181.

Boucsein, W. 2012. *Electrodermal Activity*. Medford, MA: Springer Science & Business Media.

Braeutigam, S. 2005. Neuroeconomics—From neural systems to economic behaviour. *Brain Research Bulletin* 67:355–360.

Bruce, A. S., J. M. Bruce, W. R. Black, R. J. Lepping, J. M. Henry, J. B. C. Cherry, et al. 2014. Branding and a child's brain: An fMRI study of neural responses to logos. *Social Cognitive and Affective Neuroscience* 9 (1): 118–122.

Cerf, M., and M. Mackay. 2011. Studying consciousness using direct recording from single neurons in the human brain. In *Characterizing Consciousness: From Cognition to the Clinic? Research and Perspectives in Neuroscience*, ed. S. Dehaene and Y. Christen, 133–146. Berlin: Springer.

Coan, J. A., and J. J. Allen. 2003. Frontal EEG asymmetry and the behavioral activation and inhibition systems. *Psychophysiology* 40 (1): 106–114.

Critchley, H. D., C. J. Mathias, and R. J. Dolan. 2002. Fear conditioning in humans: The influence of awareness and autonomic arousal on functional neuroanatomy. *Neuron* 33 (4): 653–663.

Davidson, R. J. 2004. What does the prefrontal cortex "do" in affect: Perspecitives on frontal EEG asymmetry research. *Biological Psychology* 67:219–233.

Erk, S., M. Spitzer, A. P. Wunderlich, L. Galley, and H. Walter. 2002. Cultural objects modulate reward circuitry. *Neuroreport* 23:2433–2438.

Fried, I., U. Rutishauser, M. Cerf, and G. Kreiman. 2014. *Single Neuron Studies of the Human Brain: Probing Cognition*. Cambridge, MA: MIT Press.

Glimcher, P. W., and E. Fehr, eds. 2013. *Neuroeconomics: Decision Making and the Brain*. 2nd ed. New York: Academic Press.

Grill Spector, K., and R. Malach. 2001. fMR-adaptation: A tool for studying the functional properties of human cortical neurons. *Acta Psychologica* 107 (1): 293–321.

Klimesch, W. 1999. EEG alpha and theta oscillations reflect cognitive and memory performance: A review and analysis. *Brain Research. Brain Research Reviews* 29:169–195.

Knutson, B., S. Rick, G. E. Wimmer, D. Prelec, and G. Loewenstein. 2007. Neural predictors of purchases. *Neuron* 53 (1): 147–156.

Levy, D. J., and P. W. Glimcher. 2012. The root of all value: A neural common currency for choice. *Current Opinion in Neurobiology* 22 (6): 1027–1038.

Mauss, I. B., and M. D. Robinson. 2009. Measures of emotion: A review. *Cognition and Emotion* 23 (2): 209–237.

Petersen, S. E., and M. I. Posner. 2012. The attention system of the human brain: 20 years after. *Annual Review of Neuroscience* 35:73–89.

Russell, J. A., & L. F. Barrett. 1999. Core affect, prototypical emotional episodes, and other things called emotion: dissecting the elephant. *Journal of Personality and Social Psychology* 7 6(5): 805.

Shadlen, M. N., and R. Kiani. 2013. Decision making as a window on cognition. *Neuron* 80 (3): 791–806.

Summerfield, C., and J. A. Mangels. 2005. Coherent theta-band EEG activity predictsitem-context binding during encoding. *NeuroImage* 24 (3): 692–703.

Vecchiato, G., L. Astolfi, F. De Vico Fallani, J. Toppi, F. Aloise, F. Bez, et al. 2011. On the use of EEG or MEG brain imaging tools in neuromarketing research. *Computational Intelligence and Neuroscience* 2011:643489.

Venables, P. H. 1991. Autonomic activity. *Annals of the New York Academy of Sciences* 620:191–207.

Werkle-Bergner, M., V. Müller, S.-C. Li, and U. Lindenberger. 2006. Cortical EEG correlates of successful memory encoding: Implications for lifespan comparisons. *Neuroscience and Biobehavioral Reviews* 30:839–854.

ATTENTION

MANUEL GARCIA-GARCIA

5.1   INTRODUCTION

Consumers are constantly being fed information from advertising, but they can only process so much as cognitive resources are limited. While individuals can be exposed to up to 11 million bits of information through sensory receptors, we are only capable of processing about 50 bits of the information, which is only a fraction of what is being sent (Wilson 2002). Attention is the cognitive process that decides what is being processed. Let's remember William James's quote in 1890 about how attention is defined (figure 5.1):

Everyone knows what attention is. It is taking possession by the mind, in clear and vivid form, of one out of what seem several simultaneous possible objects and train of thoughts. ... It implies withdrawal from some things in order to deal effectively with others, and is a condition which has a real opposite in the confused, dazed, scatter-brain state which in French is called distraction and Zehrstreutheit in German.

Attention is a very relevant factor in information processing as it decides what has priority to enter our brain systems. James's postulates about attentional processing assumes that we need to withdraw from some things in order to deal effectively with others. The impossibility of dealing effectively with simultaneous objects served as an inspiration for many researchers to find out how attention processes work. The most interesting angle is to understand what happens when our attention shifts, out of our control, toward external elements.

Attention is often broken down to two types: bottom-up and top-down. Top-down attention is the type we normally think of when we use the term—the things

Attention is a very relevant factor in information processing as it decides what has priority to enter our brain systems.

Top-down attention is the type we normally think of when we use the term.

FIGURE 5.1
William James.

we choose to focus on and shift our attention to. This could be looking at an object, moving our head in the direction of a statue in a museum that we want to observe more thoroughly, or focusing on a specific piece of detail in a big picture. Bottom-up attention is the one that intrigued neuroscientists for a while. This is the spotlight that lives inside our head and is highlighting the world without our conscious determination. When you look at a picture of a group of 4-year-olds in their preschool picture, you cannot avoid seeing your daughter first. Your eyes somehow are drawn to her face, even though she might be standing in the third row, next to two taller kids whose faces are not half-hiding behind. When you walk in the forest and suddenly hear a sound coming from the bush, your brain immediately has drawn your attention to the looming danger that may rise from there. These types of changes in attention are involuntary, unconscious, and they happen at a rapid speed that is far faster than our ability to process information. They are governed by parts of our brain that are made to alert us and keep us focused on cues that are essential to our survival. Their rapidness and dominance is important not only to understand our biology, but also to capitalize on it and create a world in which the important things get seen first.

Distraction is in fact a form of what we call *bottom-up* attention. There is a reason why bottom-up attention occurs. The human brain is wired to ensure survival of oneself and of the species. In order to do so, it has to ensure individuals will approach appetitive stimuli that promote survival and reproduction and avoid potential threats. Our brain needs to monitor the surroundings in search of emotionally salient stimuli that might appear as a threat (or appetitive objects). This is why our brain is constantly finding a balance between focusing and allocating all attention resources to the main event of interest, but also allowing some attention resources to monitor the surroundings in the event that something relevant or emotionally salient appears. Imagine yourself focusing on an interesting read and voluntarily deciding to allocate most attention resources on that text. In the event that a glass breaks, a fire alarm sounds, or someone walks in, your brain needs to allow some resources to evaluate those events. Those events will elicit distraction, during which you will process those events and assess whether they are relevant enough to keep your attention, and if they are not, your focus will just go back to the exciting read you were immersed in. This all can happen in as short as half a second.

The notion of being unable to effectively deal with a train of thought as well as with distracting objects is crucial in understanding how advertising works, especially in the days of multiscreen phenomena. It is known that viewers often switch their attention across different devices while the television is running in the background. Picture yourself sitting on your couch in the evening effectively focusing your attention on your IM chat with a friend or relative on WhatsApp. Our brain is constantly monitoring the environment in search of potential threats or salient events. Although the television is on and you are ignoring all television ads and focusing on texting, if you hear something that is relevant to you, your attention focus might quickly switch toward the advertisement. Given that some resources need to be allowed to monitor the surroundings, advertisers will try to bring your attention back to the television, capitalizing on those available cognitive resources; however, this is not an easy task.

In this chapter, we will explore some concepts that are fundamental to understand how to attract the consumer's attention, such as saliency filters, top-down control, competitive visual selection, and working memory (Knudsen 2007). We will start by describing the two main types of attention and their relevance for consumer research: *bottom-up* and *top-down* attention.

Distraction is in fact a form of what we call *bottom-up* attention.

Being unable to effectively deal with a train of thought as well as with distracting objects is crucial in understanding how advertising works, especially in the days of multiscreen phenomena.

5.2   Top-Down Attention: Consciously Driven Goal-Oriented Attention

Top-down attention is the intentional allocation of attention resources to a predetermined object or space. It is driven by the individual and her or his interest. The top-down attention is based off both the consumer as well as the product. It also refers to the processes of attention as a result of prior experiences, knowledge, and the goals of the person. Prior experiences with a product or a specific aspect of an image will draw in attention before foreign information. This can be affected by both negative and positive experiences. For example, when looking for a car, the consumer's attention can be drawn toward "flashy" or expensive looking cars or cars they have researched previously.

The specific goals and passions of the person can also affect top-down attention. Research has shown that our attention to one detail may be enhanced based off consumers' needs. For example, when looking for a Coke can, the consumer's attention toward red areas is enhanced (Theeuwes 2010).

5.3   Saliency Models of Attention: *Bottom-Up Attention*

When we process new stimuli, we do not have enough resources to process all the information at once.

When we process new stimuli, we do not have enough resources to process all the information at once. Our brain already consumes about 20% of our energy and needs to function in an economic way. This is why some elements in the environment need to be prioritized over others, and knowing which ones will be prioritized presents a huge advantage for advertisers. Our brain uses a systematic method to determine the objects of interest, or "salient objects" (Riche et al. 2012). According to saliency-based models of interest, our cognitive systems will determine what elements are the most relevant to process according to the amount of information that it might contain. This is why salient stimuli show an advantage to attract our attention, even though the individual did not intend to attend to these stimuli (Schreij, Owens, and Theeuwes 2008).

For instance, if an individual is engaged in a conversation, but a loud bang occurs, this bang may attract attention. Something that happens unexpectedly will attract our attention because it contains new information that might be relevant. Imagine a red package among a number of blue packages on a shelf. A mismatching element contains novel information by definition because it is the only other set of information in a given set, so it is more likely to be processed.

Bottom-up attention can be considered the first step of the attention process because it relies on pre-attention mechanisms. A large body of literature has reported the impact of an unexpected event in very early stages of stimulus processing leading to a stronger evaluation of such stimulus. A brain electrical indicator has been described in pre-attention stages for unexpected or *mismatching* stimuli (named *mismatch negativity*; Escera and Corral 2007). Processing unexpected stimuli is so relevant in human evolution that this brain pattern has even been found in babies and patients in a coma (Fischer, Morlet, and Giard 2000).

There are certain factors that facilitate bottom-up attention:

1. *Emotionally relevant.* Primary emotional stimuli are those that represent a basic or primary need to promote survival, such as food, sex, or threats we need to avoid. There is a clear preference to this kind of stimuli because in case they present a threat, we need to prioritize their processing in order to react to them and protect ourselves. If you are walking down the street and witness a potential threat (such as a car driving your way, or an armed person, etc.), your brain will take you out of your deep thoughts so you can evaluate the situation and react accordingly with no delay. Similarly, food and water, as well as sex-related events, will be preferred by your brain as they serve our primal needs, survival and reproduction. Marketers have for long used these primary drivers with no need of neuroscience to prove them effective (figure 5.2).

Secondary stimuli are those that are learned; learned emotional stimuli are tricky because they depend upon the experience of the individual. After years building a relationship with a brand, an emotional response is elicited by a representation of brand. A brand can become a secondary emotional stimulus, positive or negative depending on the individual's experience with the brand. This is why it is important to know the target consumer and the consumer's experience with the brand so the communication is tailored to the consumer's needs. It has been claimed that our brain's reaction to marketing communication is similar across cultures; however, the consumer reaction to products and brands, as well as to their representations, depends on our experience with the brand. This is why population screening (and consumer insights) are very important to answer your market research question, in order to reach the portion of the population that is relevant to your business.

2. *Moving objects.* Brains show preference for moving objects. From an evolutionary perspective, humans have to react quickly to moving objects as they might be potential threats (predators, cars approaching, etc.). It has been shown that advertising on a moving object (e.g., ads on a bus) is more effective in terms of recall and noticeability. However, its effect on purchasing behavior is yet to be proven. It can be relatively easy to leverage this preference by inserting some movement around the product or brand you are advertising on any medium, in order to increase the chances of being, at the very least, spotted.

3. *Unexpected events.* As discussed earlier, an unexpected event contains more information than an expected one and therefore deserves to be evaluated more

Our brain's reaction to marketing communication is similar across cultures; however, the consumer reaction to products and brands, as well as to their representations, depends on our experience with the brand.

Advertising on a moving object (e.g., ads on a bus) is more effective in terms of recall and noticeability.

Look what happened! One dreamy moonlight night in a gondola, Jim said he really loves me."Never let any other man kiss your darling hands,"he said."They're mine now."

And-Oh. how soft I'll keep my hands for him. I'll always use Jergens Lotion.

Lucky for you there's Jergens — more effective than ever today. Due to recent research, your hands are even softer now, deliciously smoother with Jergens Lotion care. Protects longer, too.

Doctors' wisdom. Many doctors use 2 special ingredients for skin-beautifying; both those fine ingredients are in your Jergens Lotion today.

Movie Stars, too—what's their experience? The Stars, 7 to 1, use Jergens Lotion.

Be just as clever—use today's even-finer Jergens Lotion. Still 10¢ to $1.00 (plus tax). And lovely to use—never oily; no stickiness.

USED BY MORE WOMEN THAN ANY OTHER HAND CARE IN ALL THE WORLD

FIGURE 5.2
Emotional cues have long been used in advertising as a way to capture the consumer attention. Primary emotional stimuli, such as food or sex-related content, present an instinctive advantage in our attention system to bring us in, given these cues are naturally meant to promote survival. This advert displays a couple in a clear sexual mood. Advertisers have known for a long time that "sex sells," and now, we know why.

carefully. Our brain shows preference for unexpected events as they might contain relevant information. Any stimulus mismatching expectation will automatically use more attention resources. This can be a useful tool for advertisers (figure 5.3).

5.4 THE EFFECT OF THE CONTEXT ON BOTTOM-UP ATTENTION

Even early stages of bottom-up attention processing are not independent of the context. The amount of attention resources left will differ whether the individual is performing a demanding task or leaning back and watching television. Studies have shown that the amount of cognitive resources allocated in the unexpected stimulus will also depend on the level of difficulty of the task you are performing (or your working memory load; San Miguel, Corral, and Escera 2008). This means that when your brain is working hard, the level of distraction will be lower than when your brain is at rest. Again, let's keep in mind that our brain is constantly trying to keep a balance between allocating enough resources to process the target of focus, while at the same time monitoring the environment for potential relevant events. When the task on focus is more demanding, less resources will be available to monitor the surroundings; in that case, advertisers will need to try harder to attract the user's attention.

> The amount of cognitive resources allocated in the unexpected stimulus will also depend on the level of difficulty of the task you are performing.

Capitalizing on the audio in a television advertising campaign can be an effective way to bring the viewer's attention back to the screen. Biometrics studies have shown that the audio of an ad campaign can potentially be more engaging than just the video or the full audiovisual experience (Moses 2015). Capitalizing on the audio and being aware of the context might help advertisers generate awareness and maximize ad impact. Also, capitalizing on synchronized cross-platform campaigns could give the advertisers more control over both the content and the context. While the second screen might be viewed as a distraction, it can increase engagement with the campaign if the content of the multiple screens is related.

There are more elements about the context that can influence the amount of resources we allocate in the event during bottom-up attention. What would happen if the event occurs during an emotionally arousing moment? We have already learned than when the event is emotionally salient, the amount of attentional resources allocated to the distracting event would be larger given the potential relevance of the stimulus to promote survival. But what if the event is not emotionally salient but the context is? Researchers have shown that the amount of time and resources allocated in processing that event is larger when this event occurs in an emotionally arousing environment. Both EEG and brain imaging studies have shown the brain indicator of the amount of cognitive resources allocated on a stimulus is larger, as well as the activation of brain areas, such as the superior temporal gyrus, related to the shifting of attention (San Miguel, Corral and Escera 2008).

FIGURE 5.3
Unexpected events contain more information than expected ones; thus, our brain will instinctively monitor the surroundings for items that mismatch expectations and process these further, moving our attention focus towards these unexpected elements. This adverts displays a human-sized parrot screaming at a lady, a scenario clearly mismatching expectations, and therefore activating bottom-up attention.

Given the effect of an arousing environment (Dominguez-Borras, Garcia-Garcia, and Escera 2008), it would be advisable to take advantage of an arousing context to place your campaign and maximize ad impact. However, would it be effective to place a product during a horror movie to make it stand out? A major concern would be creating an association between the negative emotion and your product, especially given that during arousing environments, memory encoding, both implicit and explicit, is stronger.

5.5   LOW-INVOLVEMENT THEORY

While most researchers would agree that attention is a necessary ingredient in an effective advertising campaign, some voices go in a different direction. Robert Heath's research has challenged the traditional rational view of brand choice and offers a radical new model of how the consumer is influenced by advertising.

The understanding of how our brain works has brought to consumer research the notion of implicit processing, in which rather than drawing explicit verbal conclusions, we process and store data through implicit associations, often without even realizing it. More than high ad awareness, these implicit associations are the key to successful brands. Moreover, if consumers have never needed to process brand values at a high involvement, they probably have not bothered. This would explain why some advertising campaigns that are known to be brilliant tested poorly on articulated surveys (Heath and Muzinger 2008).

According to Heath's theory (Heath 2012), consumers are able to connect perceptions to semantic memory during exposure to advertising even at low levels of attention. This would explain how advertising could be highly effective also when it does not require high involvement and is displayed in a passive platform like television or radio. He argues that some emotional elements of advertising can elude the defense mechanisms we use to filter ads out and consciously redirect our attention toward something else. These elements would influence our brand perception in an automatic and subconscious way.

In fact, he talks about two important ways in which advertising is able to influence our behavior at a subconscious level:

1. Subconscious associative conditioning: this occurs when something in an ad triggers an emotive reaction and over time subconsciously transfers that emotive reaction to the brand.

2. Subconscious relationship manipulation: this occurs when the creativity in an ad subconsciously influences the way you feel about an ad.

> We process and store data through implicit associations, often without even realizing it.

5.6   VISUAL SALIENCE BIAS AND ATTENTIONAL BLINDNESS

The visual system is a portion of the central nervous system that interprets information from visual stimuli to create an overall analysis. The visual system plays a large role in attention compared to that of the other senses, given that individuals are constantly receiving important information from visual stimuli.

The time consumers spend on cluttered advertisements is as low as 1.73 seconds (Pieters and Wedel 2004). In this context, visual attention acquires special

> The visual system plays a large role in attention compared to that of the other senses, given that individuals are constantly receiving important information from visual stimuli.

relevance. With regard to vision, two cortical pathways are involved (where—dorsal pathway; and what—ventral pathway). Understanding these pathways, we are able to take a visual image and break it down into categories to understand or mimic how the brain would scan through the image (analyzing color, intensity, and orientation within the image). Our understanding of people's bottom-up attention, which is fully governed by mechanisms in the brain that are not accessible to us (like the parts of the brain that process colors, intensity, orientation, and more), allows us to format and alter content in the world to guarantee that audiences will notice it fast and early, with nearly no ability to control their shift of gaze. We can generate ads, commercials, and movies that recruit much of your immediate attention and determine what you will see first. Some fantastic photographers and directors have this ability without even being aware of the science of attention underlying it, and they make use of these techniques to capture the audience fully. It happens due to your unconscious rendering of the environment.

Using a simile from Janiszewski, Kuo, and Tavassoli (2012), when we think about visual attention, we can think of a collection of paintbrushes that are trying to paint stimuli in the environment. However, the amount of paintbrushes is limited, so if the environment is complex, the entire scene can be roughly painted or some specific locations can be finely painted while some others are not. The fact that attentional "paintbrushes" are limited is a factor that should be taken into account by advertisers who would not wish to fall victim to *attentional blindness*, a perceptual phenomenon by which people fail to see relevant information when attending to competing information in the same scene.

The reason paintbrushes are limited is that the visual cortex has limits in the amount of information it can process. The enhancement and inhibition of neural firing that controls the focus of attention (how finely a stimulus is painted in the environment) is an evolutionary mechanism that helps ensure attention is directed to the information that is most relevant to ongoing behavior—and to promote survival. There are three sources that influence attentional focus: experience (whether it has been seen before), top-down goal directedness (relevant items), and bottom-up environmental cues (salient items). One these patterns have been established for a specific stimulus, they will be retained in the future. This is a reason why keeping consistency in your brand cues is key to get you the attention of consumers.

A large amount of research has focused on *the visual salience bias*. This is the bias by which the most visually salient images are most likely to be processed in the brain. Visual salience bias is present especially under common fast or pressured decisions such as impulse buying (Milosavljevic et al. 2012).

Milosavljevic and colleagues (2012) shed some light on the fact that during rapid decisions, visual saliency influences choices more than preferences do. But what makes a stimulus (for instance, your product or brand) salient in the marketplace?

> Our understanding of people's bottom-up attention, which is fully governed by mechanisms in the brain that are not accessible to us (like the parts of the brain that process colors, intensity, orientation, and more), allows us to format and alter content in the world to guarantee that audiences will notice it fast and early.

> During rapid decisions, visual saliency influence choices more than preferences.

> The value assigned to stimuli at the time of choice will depend on the amount of attention they receive during the decision-making process.

Understanding saliency can make advertisers take advantage of the biases that our brains have due to the limited capacity for processing information. Eye-tracking research has already shown that visual attributes like brightness or color can definitely affect location and duration of fixations during exposure to complex displays (like a vending machine or a supermarket shelf). And the value assigned to stimuli at the time of choice will depend on the amount of attention they receive during the decision-making process (Armel, Beaumel, and Rangel 2008).

The value of a product for the consumer is an obvious key factor. Parts of the visual system and working memory are much more active when the choices contained the consumer's favorite brand in comparison to another brand (Deppe et al. 2005).

The context is also relevant for the visual salience bias. This visual bias toward salient objects is more applicable when there are fewer cognitive resources available. In these moments, our cognitive systems have to rely on these biases or fast-tracks to make decisions, and the visual salience bias will have a larger effect. In fact, Milosavljevic and colleagues demonstrated that it is longer-lasting and relatively stronger when the cognitive load is larger. The great question to test are the factors (maybe creative factors) that trigger these visual salience biases.

Research has shown that repeatedly allocating attention to a product and away from other products influences choices (Janiszewski, Kuo, and Tavassoli 2012). This means that if attention is allocated in a product prior to the moment of selection, that is, during advertising or even package testing, this will increase the likelihood of choosing that product over the competitors. These findings highlight the importance of evaluating attention in an advertising piece before placing the creative in the media or a product (or package) in the marketplace.

5.7   MEASURING ATTENTION IN THE BRAIN

5.7.1   EYE TRACKING

Eye tracking is the main tool to measure visual attention. As stated in previous chapters, the eye-tracker measures the point of gaze and the motion of the eye relative to the head. Eye-tracking data are typically collected by using a head-mounted eye-tracker that is connected to a computer; however, nowadays many mobile eye-tracking devices are available by mounting the hardware on glasses. It is also becoming popular to collect eye-tracking data through the webcam of a computer or mobile device.

Among all nonconscious measurement methods, eye tracking is the one that had already become most mainstream, due to its simplicity, low cost, and high value. The top consumer goods companies are now using eye tracking to help optimize product packaging and retail shelf design by making the packaging more appealing or attention-grabbing to customers. Agencies are starting to introduce

If attention is allocated in a product prior to the moment of selection, that is, during advertising or even package testing, this will increase the likelihood of choosing that product over the competitors.

this technology for website design as well as user experience in online applications. Eye tracking is also widely used in combination with any major biometric or neuroscience measure in the marketplace in order to establish a visual correlate to the body or brain reaction. While eye-tracking analyses are very helpful to define visual attention in multiple applications, it is mandatory to determine what a peak in engagement or attention is linked to within the marketing communication.

5.7.2 Electroencephalography

Electroencephalography is a safe and noninvasive technique that works by receiving input from a number of electrodes to the human scalp by using a head cap. Each electrode is typically covered in salted gel using a needle, in order to help conduct the brain signals. These electrodes can trace electrical signals that are generated in the brain and transmit these signals to the computer. The electroencephalograph (EEG) can receive these signals within milliseconds of when the processing occurred in the brain. In fact, one of the big advantages of the EEG is its very high temporal precision, which allows us to understand cognitive processes in real time and on a moment-by-moment basis. One potential drawback of the EEG is the lack of spatial precision. However, in order to evaluate marketing, high time precision is definitely most relevant.

Relative to attention, focus and concentration are very popular processes to be measured or even trained by means of an EEG. The synchronization and magnitude of alpha brain waves in the frontal location is a clear indication of concentration and attentional focus and easily detectable with electrodes on the forehead. This has been used for decades to train patients with attention disorders by sending them audiovisual signals (sometimes in the form of a brain-controlled video game) when their brain has achieved the desired level of concentration. With the development of the EEG technology and the appraisal of wireless devices, this application has moved into games where players control the movement of a ball via their brain waves and mobile devices that teach users how to concentrate through a smartphone app.

Despite the very high level of noise of the EEG, the signal is relatively easy to obtain, and it is used by many consumer neuroscience suppliers to determine the levels of *attention* elicited by the piece of marketing communication they want to evaluate. It is widely used by some suppliers in video ad testing, packaging, print ad testing, and even product user experience. However, the EEG requires some level of specialization that might not be necessary for more simple techniques like eye-trackers or biometrics, and that makes it also harder to understand and socialize.

5.7.3 Biometrics

Biometrics refer to metrics related to human characteristics. While some of them are stable and used for identification (fingerprints, DNA, etc.), changing metrics related to the state of the human body can give us a way into the inner emotional state of the individual. The most popular body metrics used to evaluate consumers' reactions are heart rate, respiration rate, galvanic skin response (GSR) or electrodermal activity (EDA), and pupil dilation. Most of these metrics are controlled by the sympathetic nervous system, which is the system that prepares your body to confront a potentially relevant situation with an emotional component. It is the system that makes your body ready to *fight or fly* by increasing blood flow in your body. Therefore, these popular biometrics are indicative of *arousal*.

The most popular biometric used to infer emotional excitement or arousal during the evaluation of marketing communication is EDA because of its higher precision, sensitivity, and temporal granularity. However, they are all often used together. While there is a component of alertness in these markers, we cannot really talk about attention per se being measured by biometrics. But while attention does not necessarily drive arousal, arousal does drive attention, so it can be assumed that these markers indicate an increase in level of attention, especially the bottom-up type.

The pupillary response is also controlled by the sympathetic nervous system. However, pupil dilation can be a reaction to different conditions, such as exposure to light, sexual stimulation, or it also may indicate interest in the subject of attention. So by maintaining constant lighting, it may be used to indicate interest and evaluate components of marketing communication that elicit interest in the consumer.

5.7.4 BRAIN IMAGING

Another popular technique in consumer neuroscience used to determine the level of *attention* elicited by a piece of marketing communication is functional magnetic resonance imaging (fMRI). fMRI works by measuring the amount of oxygenated hemoglobin throughout the brain. A more active part of the brain will require a higher content of oxygen and will have a higher content of oxygenated hemoglobin. Using fMRI technology, researchers can observe a consumer's brain activations in reaction to marketing subjects.

While fMRI allows for a very spatial precision, temporal granularity is a major drawback that limits its application to the evaluation of marketing communication. The most efficient use of this technique consists in testing a piece for activation of the reward system, proven to fire in the expectation of a reward.

However, in terms of testing attention, different frontal and parietal brain regions, including the frontal eye field, activate in response to attentional load. Given the lack of temporal granularity, the information provided by the fMRI while testing an ad or a package would let us know *how much processing* is going on while exposed to the stimulus, but not which elements are being more or less effective in grabbing the consumer's attention.

5.8 Conclusion

In sum, attention capture—or bottom-up—is both influenced by the stimulus (in our case the marketing communication) and the context (advertising platform, shopping environment, etc.). Stimuli that are emotionally relevant, unexpected, or moving have a preference for our brain to move our cognitive resources toward them. An emotionally arousing context will make our brain pay special attention toward the stimuli, while a cognitively demanding context will facilitate fast-track processing and decision making.

Testing an ad campaign (in the proper context) will help optimize marketing communication to ensure it will be noticed, capture the attention of consumers, and be processed in the first place. Different techniques provide a range of levels of sophistication that allow us to know whether the ad has been spotted, processed, and to what depth.

Box 5.1
What Is the Right Positioning for a Mainstream Beer in Romania?

General Description

The Romanian beer market is the eighth largest market in Europe, benefiting the presence of all major global players. The market is characterized by an intense competition on each of its price levels with the global players being active with at least one brand per segment. Recent years have been marked by a market size decrease as well as a skew of the market toward the lower-priced part of it. In this context, the lower-priced beer segment grew to the detriment of the mid-priced tier creating an extra competitive pressure on the brands active in the mid-priced/mainstream beer segment. We were called in to help with the efforts of one of the smaller mainstream brands to fine-tune its positioning in the segment. The challenge was both to check on the validity of the existing positioning used by the brand for the past years and to indicate a potential new territory.

Objectives

The project consisted of two stages. The first stage was meant to understand and rank the attributes that are important and drive the quality perception in the category both at the declarative level and the implicit level (attribute mapping and ranking for the beer category). The objective of the second phase was to identify the explicit rational and implicit emotional perceptions of the investigated brand among its users and non-users on the attributes ranked and qualified in phase 1.

Methodology

We used a combination of the classic design and a neuro-tool. The classic design aimed to measure the explicit ratings while the neuro-tool measured the implicit

Box 5.1
(continued)

ratings. The translation of the business objective stated above into research and measurement objectives was, for phase 1, to evaluate the strength of the relationship between the "a quality beer" statement and a set of attributes describing the beer category. In the second phase, we measured the strength of the association between the brand name and the prequalified attributes. Both studies consisted in an implicit association test (IAT) that took place in central locations in three different cities.

In the first study, we evaluated 60 attributes that belonged to the beer category, and we segmented the 244 participants in 3 categories (based on the price of the beer consumed): economy, mainstream, and premium.

In the second study, we looked at 20 attributes that performed well in the category study and belonged to the mainstream segment, and we tested their performance on users and non-users of our client's brand (180 participants in 3 cities).

Both studies were performed on the computer, and the participants were asked to read the claims on the screen as fast as they could and assess, on a 5-point Likert scale, whether they agreed with them or not.

The associations (between beer and the tested attributes in the first study and the brands and the attributes in the second) were measured on the declarative level, through the Likert scale, and on the nonconscious level, by the speed with which people clicked the answers. The implicit score was computed only for the answers in the "Top 2 boxes" (T2B). The faster the reaction (choosing one answer on the Likert scale), the stronger the implicit association, and the other way around. We further analyzed and compared the declarative state with the implicit, nonconscious state.

INTERPRETING THE RESULTS

The declarative results were reported as percentage of the total population (e.g., 96% of the respondents believed that the ideal beer is refreshing). The next level of analysis looked at the implicit associations and identified the attributes that had the strongest connections. Then, by correlating the two types of results, we ended up having four attribute categories, as shown in the figure.

The attributes that scored in the middle (both declarative and implicit scores) are considered neutral, and they have a low impact on the tested category or brand, as people neither believe nor reject them.

The attributes that have the highest potential are those from the third category— low declarative and high implicit score, because people believe those claims but they might not be aware of them, therefore the associations did not become overt yet. And that's where the potential comes from—these attributes are like "hidden gems" that the competition is not aware of, so "finders keepers." If they belong to your brand, meaning that people associate them with your brand also, apart from the category, then these attributes should be included in your communication because they provide a differentiating basis that is relevant for consumers.

Box 5.1
(continued)

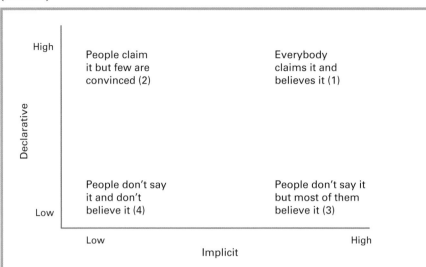

Declarative and implicit classification (the numbers represent attribute categories).

The attributes in the first category (high declarative and high implicit) are the ones that everybody is claiming and fighting on. Some of them are mandatory in the category, so everybody has them, therefore they cannot be used as differentiators. The attributes in the second and last categories are not important, as people do not really believe them, even if they claim the opposite.

In our first study, the beer category, we found eight attributes that scored above 90% on the declarative level, but only three of them were important at the nonconscious level. If we were to look only at the declarative results, we would have been misled by the other five attributes that people claimed but were not convinced about. On the implicit level, we found 12 attributes that were relevant, and four of them were in the third category, meaning they had the highest potential. We included them in the second study, to assess whether they belonged to a certain brand (our client's or the competition) or were free and could be claimed.

Almost half of the tested attributes scored in the second and last categories—low on the implicit level, meaning that people were not convinced about them or did not believe them, even if they claimed that they did. We advised our client not to use those attributes in communication, as they did not bring any added value.

We then looked at the beer category results segmented by the three categories: economic, mainstream, and premium. Based on the attributes that ranked the best at the nonconscious level, we came up with the blueprint of the ideal beer for each segment in the category. For the economy segment, for example, the ideal beer was cheap, traditional, and for hard-working people. Participants in the premium segment, in contrast, strongly rejected the "hard-working people" claim and were more

Box 5.1
(continued)

interested in a beer that was associated with parties, special occasions, and that was for real men. Mainstream beer was traditional and real, with a strong taste and associated with parties and soccer. The attribute "good quality" was not important for any segment at the implicit level, although it got a good declarative score.

The second study evaluated the "ownership" of the 20 attributes that were the most important in the category and also for our client. The attributes were plotted against three brands, the one belonging to our client and two competitor brands—the market leader and a follower. Each attribute was tested on all three brands.

We came up with some interesting findings:

- 64% of the respondents said that they would buy our client's brand but they were not strongly convinced about that. The same occurred for the follower brand. But when it came to the market leader, 78% of the respondents would buy it and they meant it.

- 61% would declaratively recommend both our client and the follower brands, but only for our client's brand did people really mean it. What's more interesting is that when it came to the leader, even if more people would recommend it on a declarative level, they did not actually believe it when they said it (it had the lowest implicit score among the brands).

- Regarding the "worth its price" attribute, although declaratively all brands scored well, people were only convinced about that for the market leader.

We went deeper and looked at the user/non-user evaluations of the three brands. The user/non-user target segments referred to our client's brand. We found out that the core users of the investigated brand were very loyal to their beer, therefore they rated it very high (on both declarative and implicit levels): 93% of users rated it as trustworthy, 91% said that they would buy and recommend it, and all of them were convinced about their claims.

The brand also had a good image among non-users that perceived it as trustworthy and authentic (more than 50% of non-users, with a strong implicit connection), and with balanced taste, thus being considered a good replacement for their favorite beer. This aspect is very important, as it shows that non-users are open to our client's communication and could be persuaded with targeted messages. The user segment was not so open toward the other brands, which is again a measure of their loyalty toward their favorite beer.

RECOMMENDATIONS
The results of the study helped the company to slightly reposition the brand. As a first step, this repositioning was reflected in the brand strategic document: the brand manifesto. Subsequently, the brand manifesto constituted the base on which to brief the development of a new communication strategy and the derived executions in through the line activation of the brand and its in-store presence. It also informed the fine-tuning of the packaging and product lineup as well.

Key Takeaways

- Attention can be thought of as top-down (voluntary goal-driven attention) and bottom-up (involuntary stimulus-driven attention).

- Emotionally relevant elements, unexpected events, and moving objects present an advantage to capture the attention of consumers.

- Context influences attention: while an emotionally arousing context enhances processing of the incoming event, a highly demanding situation facilitates low-involvement processing.

- According to the low-involvement theory, ad campaigns that elicit low involvement can be very effective by subconsciously generating associative memories.

- Techniques such as eye tracking, electroencephalography, and biometrics can be very effective to test the capacity of some marketing communications to capture the attention of consumers and elicit processing and to optimize a communication to achieve those goals.

Discussion Questions

1. Identify a campaign that successfully meets the criteria to capture the attention of consumers and elicit processing.

2. List the technique or techniques you would use in order to:

   a. Test whether a digital banner is being spotted on a website.

   b. Evaluate moment-by-moment the levels of attention elicited by a television ad.

   c. Test whether a product is noticed on a retail shelf.

   d. Measure the levels of processing elicited by a mobile app user-experience design.

   e. Identify the amount of cognitive load elicited by each of three versions of a long form of a print marketing communication.

3. Your company's department is developing a cross-platform campaign and asks for advice.

a. Choose three platforms.

b. Apply the learned principles on attention capture and context to start developing the creative for the different platforms.

c. Describe how you would test the creative to optimize the campaign before launch and secure its success.

REFERENCES

Armel, K. C., A. Beaumel, and A. Rangel. 2008. Biasing simple choices by manipulating relative visual attention. *Judgment and Decision Making* 3 (5): 396–403.

Deppe, M., W. Schwindt, H. Kugel, H. Plassmann, and P. Kenning. 2005. Nonlinear responses within the medial prefrontal cortex reveal when specific implicit information influences economic decision making. *Journal of Neuroimaging* 15 (2): 171–182.

Dominguez-Borras, J., M. Garcia-Garcia, and C. Escera. 2008. Emotional context enhances auditory novelty processing: Behavioral and electrophysiological evidence. *European Journal of Neuroscience* 28 (6): 1199–1206.

Escera, C., and M. J. Corral. 2007. Role of mismatch negativity and novelty-P3 in involuntary auditory attention. *Journal of Psychophysiology* 21 (3): 251–264.

Fischer, C., D. Morlet, and M. Giard. 2000. Mismatch negativity and N100 in comatose patients. *Audiology & Neuro-Otology* 5 (3–4): 192–197.

Heath, R. 2012. *Seducing the subconscious: The psychology of emotional influence in advertising.* Hoboken, NJ: Wiley-Blackwell.

Heath, R., and U. Muzinger. 2008. *How consumers process brand information—new insights for more effective brand communication.* Brand Equity and Advertising Research.

Janiszewski, C., A. Kuo, and N. T. Tavassoli. 2012. The influence of selective attention and inattention to products on subsequent choice. *Journal of Consumer Research* 39 (6): 1258–1274.

Knudsen, E. I. 2007. Fundamental components of attention. *Annual Review of Neuroscience* 30:57–78.

Milosavljevic, M. M., V. Navalpakkam, C. Koch, and A. Rangel. 2012. Relative visual saliency differences induce sizable bias in consumer choice. *Journal of Consumer Psychology* 22 (1): 67–74.

Moses, E. 2015. Sound or Sight? Wearable biometrics & facial coding solve engagement. Re! *Think (London, England,* 2015.

Pieters, R., and M. Wedel. 2004. Attention capture and transfer in advertising: Brand, pictorial and text-size effects. *Journal of Marketing* 68 (20): 36–50.

Riche, N., M. Mancas, D. Culibrk, V. Crnojevic, B. Gosselin, and T. Dutoit. 2012. *Dynamic saliency models and human attention: A comparative study on videos.* Asian Conference on Computer Videos.

San Miguel, I., M. J. Corral, and C. Escera. 2008. When loading working memory reduces distraction: Behavioral and electrophysiological evidence from an auditory-visual distraction paradigm. *Journal of Cognitive Neuroscience* 20 (7): 1131–1145.

Schreij, D., C. Owens, and J. Theeuwes. 2008. Abrupt onsets capture attention independent of top-down control settings. *Perception & Psychophysics* 72:672–682.

Theeuwes, J. 2010. Top-down and bottom-up control of visual selection. *Acta Psychologica* 135 (2): 77–99.

Wilson, M. 2002. Six views of embodied cognition. *Psychonomic Bulletin & Review* 9 (4): 625–636.

5.9 APPENDIX: USE OF NEUROIMAGING IN THE EVALUATION OF TELEVISION COMMERCIALS

Giovanni Vecchiato, Patrizia Cherubino, Arianna Trettel, and Fabio Babiloni

CASE STUDY: TWO DIFFERENT STYLES TO ADVERTISE PERFUMES
THE CARTIER AND PRADA TELEVISION COMMERCIALS

In a study conducted by BrainSigns, one of the leading consumer neuroscience companies, 28 subjects (12 women) observed a 20-minute-long documentary in which BrainSigns inserted two commercial breaks at 5 and 15 minutes after the beginning of the movie, respectively. Each interruption was formed by six commercial video-clips, each video clip 30 seconds in length. The television commercials used here in the case study were unknown to the subjects, and each was shown only once during the experiment. The television commercials were selected in order to define six commercial categories: *perfume, consumption, banks, sport, telephone*, and *clothing*. Randomization of the occurrence of all the commercial videos within the documentary was done to remove the sequence factor as a possible confounding effect in the following analysis.

Two specific advertisements belonged to the perfume category and were aired by Cartier and Prada. The plots of both advertisements have as main characters two lovers dancing on a floor. To inspect the cerebral activity in particular frame segments of the two commercials, the commercials were properly segmented to define the following scenes: *intro, dance, final, product*, and *brand*, as illustrated in figures 5A.1 and 5A.2.

The television commercials can be observed at the following URLs: Cartier: http://www.youtube.com/watch?v=D9yVNKEYlDU; Prada: http://www.youtube.com/watch?v=S_7fBn9enDE.

The cerebral activity was computed and compared in and between the defined frame segments of the two television commercials.

BEHAVIORAL RESULTS

The recording of the neurometric response included the detection of the electroencephalographic (EEG) signals and heart rate (HR) and galvanic skin response (GSR) parameters on a sample of 28 subjects (22 ± 1.7 years; 12 female), as illustrated in previous publications (Vecchiato et al. 2010, 2012; Vecchiato, Cherubino, et al. 2014). The experimental group was divided and analyzed by gender. Particularly, we took into account the groups of *women* (21 ± 1.7 years) and *men* (21.67 ± 1.61 years). The *z*-score values of percentage of spontaneous recalls and appreciation were computed for each subject and television commercial and averaged into the six categories of analysis. Figure 5A.3 shows the difference of *z*-score between women and men for spontaneous recall and appreciation.

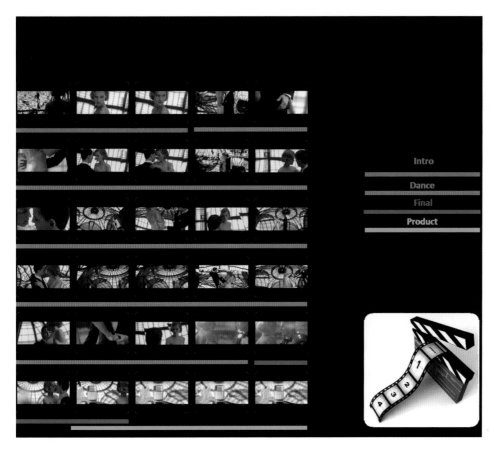

FIGURE 5A.1
Frame sequence of the Cartier commercial for each second of the video clip. The underlying colors highlight the different scenes in which it is possible to divide the advertisement, as the legend on the right shows. In such segments, the average z-score values for the estimated indices were computed.

The picture shows the differences related to the percentages of spontaneous recall and appreciation between the groups of women and men. Values are represented as z-score. From the bar graph, we can notice that the largest difference between the two genders is related to the observation of television commercials belonging to the perfume category, both for spontaneous recalls and appreciation. Particularly, the result is a higher percentage for women for both spontaneous recalls and appreciation in this category (spontaneous recall: $z_{women} = 0.31$, $z_{men} = -1.54$; appreciation: $z_{women} = 0.42$, $z_{men} = -1.49$).

In the following, we will analyze the cerebral variables related to the memorization, interest, and emotion for the perfume category and for the two commercial videos composing it, Cartier and Prada, by performing a comparison between gender and between video clips, respectively.

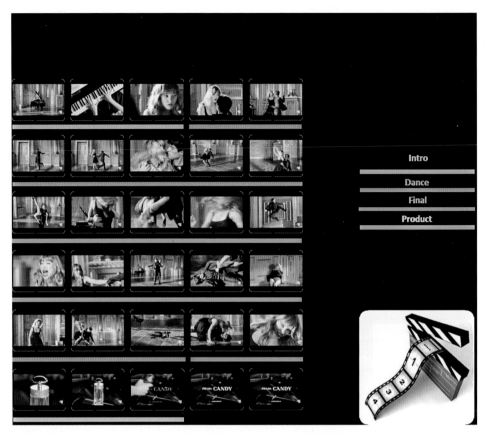

FIGURE 5A.2
Frame sequence of the Prada commercial for each second of the video clip. The underlying colors highlight the different scenes in which it is possible to divide the advertisement, as the legend on the right shows. In such segments, the average z-score values for the estimated indices were computed.

CEREBRAL INDICES

By analyzing the cerebral indices of *memorization, interest*, and *emotion* (Vecchiato et al. 2011; Vecchiato, Maglione, et al. 2014) for the two commercial advertisements, Cartier and Prada, belonging to the perfume category, we observed a different pattern of activation between the two experimental groups, as reported in figure 5A.4. In particular, the average values for memorization between women and men do not present high difference, both being negative and close to −1, but there were different results for emotion and interest. In fact, men show negative values for both emotion and interest, whereas the cerebral activity of women is characterized by positive values for both emotion and interest.

To more deeply investigate the gender difference during the observation of commercial spots related to perfumes, we will show a between-gender z-score

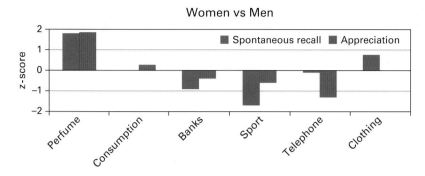

FIGURE 5A.3
The bar graph shows the difference of average *z*-score values of percentage of spontaneous recalls (blue) and appreciation (red) between women and men in the six commercial categories of analysis. Positive (negative) values indicate higher (lower) spontaneous recall and appreciation for women (men).

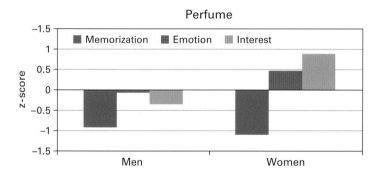

FIGURE 5A.4
Average *z*-score values related to the cerebral variables of memorization (blue), emotion (red), and interest (purple) for both groups of men (left) and women (right). The average z-score values refer to the observation of the two television commercials, Cartier and Prada, belonging to the perfume category.

analysis for Cartier and Prada video clips and a between-spot z-score comparison for the two genders. All the cerebral variables of memorization, emotion, and interest have been taken into account.

GENDER ANALYSIS

By analyzing the variations of the cerebral indices for the two commercials separately, we can observe that the two groups react differently to observation of the video clips. Specifically, women present higher values for all the cerebral variables for the Cartier television spot compared to men. The results are illustrated in figure 5A.5. The highest difference relates to emotion ($z_{women} = 1.91$, $z_{men} = -0.06$). The

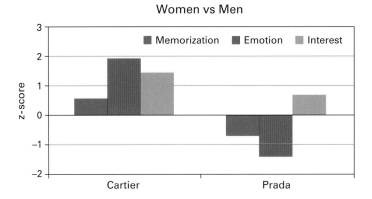

FIGURE 5A.5

Differences of average z-score values between women and men for the cerebral indices of memorization (blue), emotion (red), and interest (purple) for the two television commercials, Cartier (left) and Prada (right). Positive (negative) values indicate higher (lower) values of cerebral indices for women (men).

second television spot, Prada, returned higher values for memorization and emotion for men, although the values for interest were still higher for women.

Because the presented values relate to observation of the entire video clips, in the following figures we present the values of the cerebral variables within several scenes of interest. Vertical axes are fixed across figures in order to highlight differences of variations among memorization, emotion, and interest.

Figure 5A.6 illustrates the average z-score values for memorization for women and men for both Cartier and Prada television commercials. By analyzing the television spot by Cartier, we can observe that men show a decrease for memorization for the scenes related to the intro and dance ($z_{intro\_men} = -2.36$, $z_{dance\_men} = -2.28$). Conversely, women present low values of z-scores, in all scene segments of interest, closer to zero. Overall, for both men and women, the Cartier spot elicited values for memorization that were negative or very close to zero. Instead, Prada returned high values for memorization for men in the final scene ($z_{final\_men} = 2.11$), whereas women show a decrease for memorization in the intro ($z_{intro\_women} = -3.29$).

Figure 5A.7 illustrates the average z-score values for interest for women and men for both the Cartier and Prada television commercials. By analyzing Cartier, the value for interest for women across the whole commercial is positive and higher than for men. However, there are particular scenes for women in which interest is negative and lower than for men, such as product and brand exposition ($z_{product\_women} = -2.17$, $z_{brand\_women} = -2.61$). By comparing women and men segment values within the Cartier clip, we can observe that there are several segments in which the value for interest is lower for women compared to men, such as intro, product, and brand ($z_{diff\_intro} = -2.49$, $z_{diff\_product} = -2.19$, $z_{diff\_brand} = -2.84$), whereas it is higher during

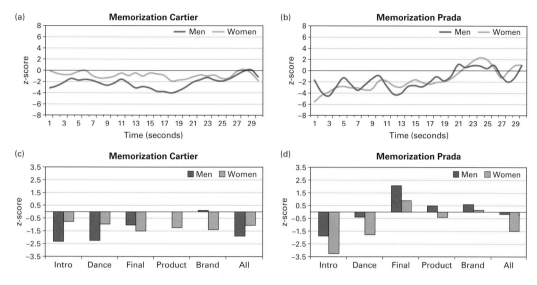

FIGURE 5A.6
Representation of the variations of the memorization index for Cartier and Prada television commercials for women and men. Top row: Time course of the average z-score memorization index for women (light blue) and men (dark blue) for the whole Cartier (a) and Prada (b) TV commercials. Bottom row: Average z-score values of the memorization index for the scenes of interest for women (light blue) and men (dark blue) for Cartier (c) and Prada (d) television commercials.

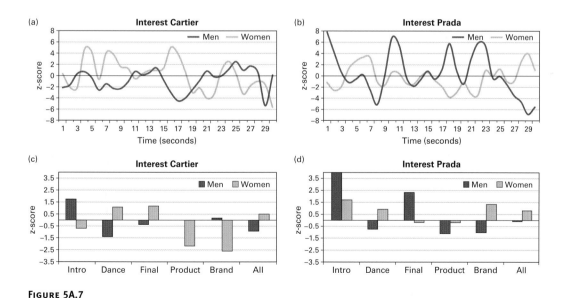

FIGURE 5A.7
Representation of the variations of the interest index for Cartier and Prada television commercials for women and men. Upper row: Time course of the average z-score approach/withdrawal index for women (light purple) and men (dark purple) for the whole Cartier (a) and Prada (b) television commercials. Bottom row: Average z-score values of the approach/withdrawal index for the scenes of interest for women (light purple) and men (dark purple) for Cartier (c) and Prada (d) television commercials.

dance ($z_{\text{diff\_dance}}$ = 2.52). For Prada, men present high values for interest for intro and final ($z_{\text{intro\_men}}$ = 4.24, $z_{\text{final\_men}}$ = 2.37), whereas women returned values for interest close to zero. By comparing the values of the segments between the two genders, we find that interest is higher for men in intro and final ($z_{\text{diff\_intro}}$ = −2.53, $z_{\text{diff\_final}}$ = −2.57), whereas it is higher for women in brand ($z_{\text{diff\_brand}}$ = 2.43).

Figure 5A.8 illustrates the average z-score values for emotion for women and men for both Cartier and Prada television commercials. For Cartier, the emotion value for women is higher during intro ($z_{\text{intro\_women}}$ = 2.29), whereas there is no emergence of any increase or decrease in fluctuation for emotion for men. In addition, by comparing the values for emotion between the two groups, we find that women present higher values for emotion, with respect to men, for the segments intro and dance ($z_{\text{diff\_intro}}$ = 2.84, $z_{\text{diff\_dance}}$ = 2.12). For Prada, all values for emotion are negative or close to zero both for women and men. In particular, women show a decrease of emotion during the intro ($z_{\text{intro\_women}}$ = −2.04), whereas there is no variation among scenes for men. However, by comparing emotion among segments, we found that women present lower values during the dance segment ($z_{\text{diff\_dance}}$ = −1.96).

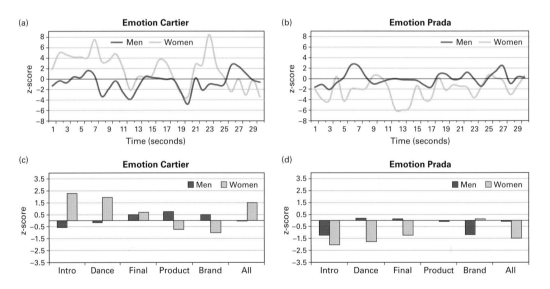

FIGURE 5A.8

Representation of the variations of the emotion index for the Cartier and Prada television commercials for women and men. Top row: Time course of the average z-score emotion index for women (light red) and men (dark red) for the whole Cartier (a) and Prada (b) television commercials. Bottom row: Average z-score values of the emotion index for the scenes of interest for women (light red) and men (dark red) for Cartier (c) and Prada (d) television commercials.

COMPARISON OF THE TWO VIDEO CLIPS

In figure 5A.9, we present the difference of average z-score values for memorization, interest, and emotion for both women and men between Cartier and Prada. In particular, panel (a) presents differences of cerebral variables between Cartier and Prada for both women and men. For this bar graph, it is possible to observe that Cartier elicited a higher level for emotion for women (EmoWomen: $z_{\text{Cartier}} - z_{\text{Prada}}$ = 3.39), whereas there is no deviation from zero for men in all variables. Additional panels highlight differences in the cerebral variables in the specific scenes of the two television commercials. For memorization (panel b), Prada elicited high values for both women and men in the final scene ($z_{\text{final\_women}} = -2.48$, $z_{\text{final\_men}} = -3.18$), while the intro returned a high value for Cartier only for women ($z_{\text{intro\_women}} = 2.491$). For interest (panel c), we can observe that the intro by Prada is characterized by higher values for both women and men ($z_{\text{intro\_men}} = -2.47$, $z_{\text{intro\_women}} = -2.44$), whereas the same commercial returns a higher value for women during product and brand ($z_{\text{product\_women}} = -1.97$, $z_{\text{brand\_women}} = -3.97$) and for men during the final scene ($z_{\text{final\_men}} = -2.75$). There is no increment for interest for Cartier with respect to Prada. For emotion (panel d), Cartier elicited higher values for women during the intro, dance, and across the whole video clip ($z_{\text{intro\_women}} = 4.33$, $z_{\text{dance\_women}} =$

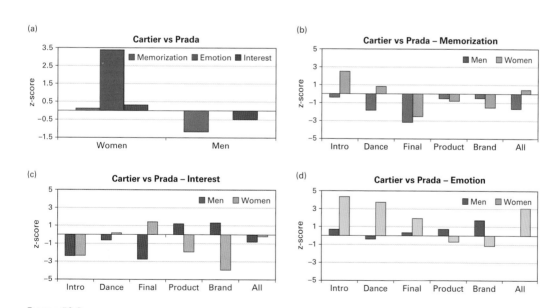

FIGURE 5A.9
(a) Difference of average z-score values for the cerebral indices of memorization (blue), emotion (red), and interest (purple) between Cartier and Prada television commercials for both men (right) and women (left). (b, c, d) Differences of memorization, interest, and emotion across scenes of interest for women (light colors) and men (dark colors).

3.72, $z_{\text{all\_women}}$ = 3.05). There was no deviation from zero for men between the two commercials.

DISCUSSION

Behavioral data in terms of spontaneous recall and appreciation showed that the highest difference between women and men is related to the observation of two television advertisements belonging to the category of perfume. In particular, women exhibit a higher percentage of spontaneous recall and level of appreciation compared to men.

The level of memorization of the two television commercials analyzed is low for both women and men, and there is no variation between the two groups. The values for memorization for Cartier and Prada are lower than those of the other commercial categories. For emotion, we observed that women are more engaged during some introductory scenes of the spot by Cartier but less for Prada. In particular, the Cartier dance scene gives more emotion for women while the Prada dance scene gives more emotion for men. The cerebral variable related to interest presents a variegated pattern because there are different catching scenes both for women and men depending on the television commercial. By comparing the cerebral variables between the two commercials, we observed that there are no differences of emotion between the two commercials for men, whereas women were more engaged during the observation of the Cartier video clip. Conversely, the advertisement by Prada returned higher values for memorization and interest for both women and men.

Overall, the biometric EEG, HR, and GSR recordings returned neurometric indices linked to the variation of the memorization, interest, and emotional involvement of the two experimental groups. Variation of such indices along the adopted time segments returned information about perception of the ads, scene by scene, on the total sample of recorded subjects and on subsamples of the group. This information may be analyzed by observing interesting indications about the efficacy of the different frame sequences or developing original insights related to cognitive and emotional variables. Also, these tools could provide a rational schema useful to guide a reduction of the times of the ads, which is often implemented in advertising campaigns after the first detailed creative production, by pointing out the best (least) performing scenes, which could be preserved (cut) by a possible time-frame reduction. Such time reduction could be specifically performed and differently adapted to men and women.

Nowadays, marketers are excited about the use of brain imaging for marketing purposes. First, they hope that neuroimaging may help to refine the possibilities of marketing research to improve an efficient trade-off between costs and benefits. This hope is based on the assumptions that people cannot fully articulate their preferences when asked to express them explicitly, and that consumers' brains contain hidden information about their true preferences. Such hidden information could, respecting the more recent neuroscience theory, be used to better understand their buying behavior and meet their needs. Thus, the cost of performing neuroimaging studies would be outweighed by the benefit of improved product design and increased sales. In theory, at least, brain imaging could illuminate not only what people like, but also what they will buy. Thus far, the presented approach to neuromarketing has focused on this post-design application, in particular on measuring the effectiveness of advertising campaigns. Particularly, we showed that there are results suggesting that it is possible to differentiate the communication according to the gender of the analyzed population. Properly designing and broadcasting two different versions of a marketing communication will help to enhance the efficacy and the quality of the message. Moreover, an objective method for reducing the time length of the television commercial will help the video-makers to have a rational basis for cutting ineffective scenes and, hopefully, to create new, more appealing television commercials. Thus, while the emotional and cerebral "engagement" of the video clip is preserved, the cost of airing the video clip could be reduced, saving some money by getting the same efficacy (or even more) as in the 30-second version.

Moreover, neuromarketing research can be implemented even before a product exists, because the assumption that neuroimaging data would give a more accurate indication of the underlying preferences than standard market research studies may be really useful to avoid expensive mistakes. If this is indeed the case, product concepts could be tested rapidly, and those that are not promising could be eliminated early in the process. This would allow more efficient allocation of resources to develop only promising products.

REFERENCES

Vecchiato, Giovanni, Laura Astolfi, Fallani Fabrizio De Vico, Febo Cincotti, Donatella Mattia, Serenella Salinari, Ramon Soranzo, and Fabio Babiloni. 2010. Changes in brain activity during the observation of TV commercials by using EEG, GSR and HR measurements. *Brain Topography* 23 (2): 165–179. doi:10.1007/s10548-009-0127-0.

Vecchiato, Giovanni, Patrizia Cherubino, Anton Giulio Maglione, Herrera Ezquierro Maria Trinidad, Franco Marinozzi, Fabiano Bini, Arianna Trettel, and Fabio Babiloni. 2014. How to measure cerebral correlates of emotions in marketing relevant tasks. *Cognitive Computation* 6 (4): 856–871. doi:10.1007/s12559-014-9304-x.

Vecchiato, Giovanni, Wanzeng Kong, Anton Giulio Maglione, and Daming Wei. 2012. Understanding the impact of TV commercials: Electrical neuroimaging. *IEEE Pulse* 3 (3): 42–47. doi:10.1109/MPUL.2012.2189171.

Vecchiato, Giovanni, Anton Giulio Maglione, Patrizia Cherubino, Barbara Wasikowska, Agata Wawrzyniak, Anna Latuszynska, Malgorzata Latuszynska, et al. 2014. Neurophysiological tools to investigate consumer's gender differences during the observation of TV commercials. *Computational and Mathematical Methods in Medicine* 2014 (July): e912981. doi:10.1155/2014/912981.

Vecchiato, Giovanni, Jlenia Toppi, Laura Astolfi, Fallani Fabrizio De Vico, Febo Cincotti, Donatella Mattia, Francesco Bez, and Fabio Babiloni. 2011. Spectral EEG frontal asymmetries correlate with the experienced pleasantness of TV commercial advertisements. *Medical & Biological Engineering & Computing* 49 (5): 579–583. doi:10.1007/s11517-011-0747-x.

CHAPTER 6

MEMORY

INGRID L. C. NIEUWENHUIS

How much information is stored in your brain? Just try to make a rough estimate of the amount of words, faces, television series, melodies, lyrics, books, or places you know or how many events, anecdotes, or thoughts you can remember. The brain is able to store an incredible amount of information. People can recognize thousands of faces, tens of thousands of words. Our ability to recognize images is almost limitless; in an experiment where subjects saw 10,000 pictures, they were able to correctly recognize more than 80% a few days later (Standing 1973). Feel the urge to procrastinate? Go to YouTube and find out how many television commercials, television tunes, or video games you remember from your childhood.

Although it is a fun pastime, the function of storing all these memories is not to enable us to reminisce about our past. Memory is essential to survive in the complex environment we live in. Remembering the location of, for instance, food or danger is vital for any organism. And we do not just store information; the brain is continually extracting patterns and regularities in the encountered data to prepare us for future events and decisions to be made. Although we might think we experience the world around us objectively, all these stored memories and extracted patterns constantly color everything we perceive and do. Therefore, it is essential to understand how new memories are created in the consumer's brain. Which information is stored in the first place, how are long-lasting associations formed, what type of memories are liable to decay, how do stored patterns influence every marketing effort consumers are exposed to, and how can we measure it all?

Our ability to recognize images is almost limitless; in an experiment where subjects saw 10,000 pictures, they were able to correctly recognize more than 80% a few days later.

6.1   Brain Areas Supporting Memory

The two most important brain areas for memory are the hippocampus and the neocortex (figure 6.1). The neocortex is the outer layer of the brain, which increased in size the most over mammalian evolution. It progressed to a surface size of about four sheets of paper, wrinkled up to fit the human skull. The hippocampus lays hidden deep inside the brain.

6.1.1   The Hippocampus

The hippocampus is one of the most interconnected areas of the brain; input from all other neocortical areas converges onto the hippocampus, and its output diverges onto the whole neocortex again. In 1950s, it became painfully clear that the hippocampus is essential for the formation of new memory traces. A surgeon at that time removed the hippocampus in a patient that was severely suffering from epilepsy. In this patient, the hippocampus was identified as the source of the seizures, and removing the source can cure patients from their seizures. The surgery was successful in controlling the patient's epilepsy; however, after the surgery, he could not form new long-lasting memories anymore. This patient has been thoroughly

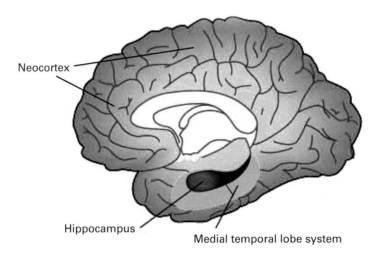

Figure 6.1

Brain areas involved in memory. Memories are initially stored in the hippocampus. Over time, information gets integrated and stored in the neocortical representational areas. The hippocampus is densely interconnected with the neocortex through the cortical areas surrounding the hippocampus in the medial temporal lobe.

assessed and was described in many scientific papers, called by his initials "H.M."
(Scoville and Milner 1957).

On first sight, H.M. would behave quite normally; his intelligence was fully
intact, he could still hold a conversation, read, or fill out crossword puzzles. But
after reading a few pages in a book, he could not remember what he just read. He
could not recognize people he newly met after the surgery. He could not even
recognize the doctor in whose company he had spent thousands of hours performing tests during the years after the procedure; she had to reintroduce herself every
time they met. Notably, he could learn new motor skills, like tracing a shape while
looking in a mirror. This was one of the tests they performed on him after the
surgery. Each time, the doctors had to explain what they wanted him to do—trace
a shape, for instance a star, while looking at the star and his hands in a mirror only.
(Try it yourself, draw a star on a piece of paper, and then trace the star while looking
at it through a mirror. This is actually quite hard, and you will be slow and make
many mistakes.) H.M. got better at it with the same rate normal people get better
at this task. But even while performing this task for the hundredth time, he did
not remember doing it ever before, and he was surprised how good he was at it.
So in summary, the hippocampus is important for encoding new *declarative memories* (memories for facts and events), but not for *procedural memories* (like motor
memory).

The hippocampus has to write away the memories as they happen, in real
time. Therefore, it is hard to do any thorough organization of the incoming information. You can picture the impossibility of this task by imagining someone sitting
in a mail room. There is a continual inflow of sheets of paper with information
that have to be filed in the right category, but there is no time to read what's on
them. Also, there might be information on the papers showing that a new category
has to be created or two existing categories have to be merged. Thus, organizing
the incoming information in real time on the basis of content is not an option.
Therefore, the hippocampus organizes the information mainly on the basis of
"where" something happened. You might have experienced the following that
illustrates this: You had a thought at some location (your desk, the kitchen) about
having to do something. Then you walk away to do it, and you cannot remember
what it was. When you go back to the place where you had the initial thought, it
suddenly comes back. The place where you created the memory works as a cue for
the hippocampus to retrieve the content of the memory.

6.1.2 THE NEOCORTICAL REPRESENTATIONAL AREAS

The hippocampus is not the end stage for memory content. With time, a transfer
of information takes place from hippocampus to neocortex (Marr 1971). Memories
are eventually stored in associative memory networks in the neocortex. This
also became evident from observations of patient H.M. and other patients with
hippocampal lesions. Besides not being able to encode new memories, they also

> The hippocampus is important for encoding new declarative memories (memories for facts and events).

> Memories are eventually stored in associative memory networks in the neocortex.

show *temporally-graded retrograde amnesia*; this means that older memories, encoded a long time before the hippocampus lesion occurred, were less disrupted, while newer memories that were still dependent on the hippocampus were disrupted by the lesion.

The networks supporting memory representations are widely distributed over the neocortex. The brain areas involved in memory overlap with the areas involved in perception and action (Martin 2007). The memory representation of a hammer, for instance, includes visual areas involved in shape and color perception, the temporal areas representing the meaning of the word *hammer* and the sound that hammering makes as well as the sound of the word *hammer*, combined with motor areas involved in executing the motor program of hammering. Thus, many areas in the neocortex are involved in memory representations, and these areas are strongly interconnected with the hippocampus.

Memories are not just copied over from the hippocampus to the neocortex; the two brain areas have a fundamentally different way of storing the information (McClelland, McNaughton, and Randall 1995). The difference lies in the way the information is organized. In contrast to the hippocampus, the organization of information in the neocortex is content-structured and stored in so-called *associative memory networks* (figure 6.2). That means neurons that are, for instance, involved in the representation of an apple are also involved in, or strongly connected to, neurons responsible for the representation of a pear, or a circle, or an iPhone. When a memory representation is activated, this results in the activation spreading along the nodes of the memory networks to related items, thereby increasing their chance of retrieval. So if you see an iPhone, it will be easier to retrieve the word *Apple*; in a way the brain prepares for the possibility of talking or thinking about things that are related to the concept "iPhone."

6.2 FORGETTING AND THE IMPORTANCE OF RETRIEVAL CUES

Not all information becomes incorporated into the associative memory networks of the neocortex. Only the important parts of the newly acquired information are integrated into the larger existing body of knowledge. The capacity of the hippocampus is limited, and many of the original *episodic memories* are overwritten. Pieces of information that do not fit in, are weak, or otherwise regarded as unimportant disappear.

Immediately after encoding, memories already start to decay. Memory decay follows a curve that is very steep immediately after learning and levels off over time. This curve was first mapped out in the late nineteenth century by the German

When a memory representation is activated, this results in the activation spreading along the nodes of the memory networks to related items.

Within the first hour after learning, already 50% of the learned information was lost.

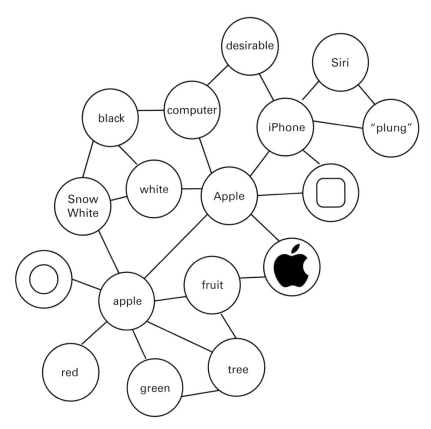

FIGURE 6.2
Associative memory network. The cortex stores information associatively. Related concepts are connected in memory networks. Activation can spread through connections; thinking of one thing can activate related information.

psychologist Hermann Ebbinghaus (Ebbinghaus 1964). Over the course of more than a year, he diligently performed a large series of experiments on himself. Every day he learned a list of nonmeaningful syllables (like BOK or YAT) up to the point where he could recall the whole list perfectly. Subsequently, he would test his recall at different times after learning and mapped out how his performance declined with time (figure 6.3).

The curve of figure 6.3 shows that within the first hour after learning, already 50% of the learned information was lost. Most of the forgetting took place in the first 24 hours after learning; after that, the forgetting rate leveled off. This curve describes the forgetting rate of meaningless neutral information, which is the hardest to retain (and learn) because it has no links to existing information stored in the brain. Forgetting is slower for meaningful information, but the rough shape

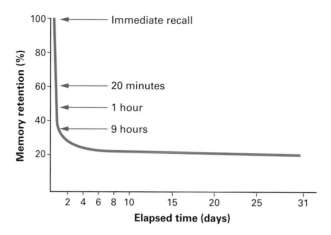

FIGURE 6.3

Forgetting curve. Information starts decaying from the moment it is encoded. Most forgetting takes place in the first 24 hours after learning. The rate of decay levels off later in time. The steepness of the curve depends on the type of material learned. This curve depicts the forgetting rate of Ebbinghaus's experiment in which he memorized nonsense syllables.

Relearning an old list that was almost fully "forgotten" was much faster the second time.

Showing a package or a store environment in a television commercial enables them to serve as a recognition cue. When consumers are later in the store and see the package, this may reactivate the memory of what the ad was communicating.

of the curve is the same with most forgetting taking place in the first 24 hours, leveling off after that.

Ebbinghaus also showed that the information is not fully gone if it cannot be recalled anymore. He found out that relearning an old list that was almost fully "forgotten" was much faster the second time. This illustrates that at least part of the information had to be still present in the brain in some form, but it could not be reached successfully. To recall information successfully, *retrieval cues* are essential. For instance, going back to the location where a memory was encoded can make the memory reemerge. The location in that case works as a cue, an "in" for the brain, enabling the reactivation of the full memory. In the 1970s, a classic experiment was performed illustrating that the location in which learning takes place is a powerful retrieval cue (Godden and Baddeley 1975). In this experiment, divers learned a list of words underwater. Recall of the list was much better when the test took place underwater as well. At the time of encoding, the memory trace representing the list of words gets linked to the memory trace of the underwater environment. If a part of the memory reactivates (the underwater environment), the activity can flow along the nodes of the network and reactivate the rest of the memory (the learned words). So, successful recall is dependent on providing the right cues to the brain to reactivate the memory.

The importance of retrieval cues for successful recall has significant implications for marketing communications. Linking this information to things that can serve as a recognition cue will increase the chance that consumers will reactivate the communicated information. For instance, showing a package or a store environment in a television commercial enables them to serve as a recognition cue. When consumers are later in the store and see the package, this may reactivate the memory of what the ad was communicating. First airing a full 30-second television commercial and later airing a 15-second version of the spot can be very effective. The 15-second version can generate the reactivation of the full 30-second spot. Creating recall cues may also be an explanation for the finding that seeing an ad on multiple devices (television, mobile, tablet) is more impactful than seeing the ad the same amount of times on only one device. An ad shown on multiple devices will be connected with more environments, and will thus have more "ins" for retrieval.

6.3   IMPLICIT MEMORY AND THE MERE EXPOSURE EFFECT

Even when no recall of information can be achieved, the information can still have made an *implicit* expression. Importantly, implicit unconscious impressions can have an effect on preference and behavior as well. It has been shown consistently that people develop a preference for things merely because they are familiar with them. This effect was first discovered by Robert Zajonc and has been dubbed the *mere exposure effect*. This phenomenon is for instance illustrated by an experiment in which the researchers published Turkish words in a neutral style in two campus newspapers in Michigan. Some words were published many times, some words only once or twice within a 25-day period. Later, students were asked to guess the meaning of words as being something positive or negative. The researchers found that the words that were published more often were rated more positively, even though many people did not have a conscious recollection of ever having seen any of the words (Zajonc and Rajecki 1969). This effect is not just observed for words, but also for symbols, pictures, and faces (Zajonc 1980). Moreover, even when stimuli were presented so briefly that subjects did not consciously perceive them (subliminal presentation), this mere exposure effect was still present (Bornstein, Leone, and Galley 1987). There is even research suggesting that unconscious processing is more effective in creating an increased liking by mere exposure.

The scientific explanation for the mere exposure effect is that the more often something is presented, the easier it becomes to mentally process; processing becomes more *fluent*. And it has been shown in numerous experiments that things that are processed more fluently are better liked (other examples are that a message written in a more legible font is rated more positively, and bands with an easier-to-pronounce name are liked better). Things that are unfamiliar and not fluent are unpredictable and potentially dangerous. The positive effect of mere exposure is largest for new stimuli. The effect typically reaches its maximum within 10 to 20 presentations.

> The more often something is presented, the easier it becomes to mentally process; processing becomes more fluent. And it has been shown in numerous experiments that things that are processed more fluently are better liked.

Thus, if consumers are not able to recall an ad, this does not mean that the information in the ad is not still stored in the brain somehow. Mere exposure to brands or products can increase fluency and thereby liking, and it does not matter if exposure is consciously noticed or not. The mere exposure effect has often been linked to the effectiveness of banner ads; regardless of measured click-through rates, banner ads may still create a positive attitude toward the brand (Fang, Singh, and Ahluwalia 2007). It's most effective for less familiar or new brands or products, as the increase in fluency is largest for the first exposures. Mere exposure removes the initial hesitation the brain shows toward everything new and unfamiliar. A recent study investigated the effect of Internet pop-ups showing a brand logo and a product for a fictitious brand that were viewed at a low level of attention (Courbet et al., 2014). The researchers observed whether there were any effects measurable after repeated brief exposure in subjects that had forgotten seeing the ads. Their memory was thus implicit. After 7 days, the (forgotten) exposure had changed the subjects' attitude toward the brand as well as the (verbally expressed) purchase intent of the brand. Their attitude had shifted from mainly negative among nonexposed subjects to mainly positive among people that were exposed. This effect was still noticeable even after a delay of 3 months.

6.4 PRINCIPLES ENABLING THE FORMATION OF LONG-LASTING MEMORY

For marketing communications to be effective, the information in these communications has to make it across two stages: First, the information needs to be encoded into the hippocampus, but that is just the start. To be able to make a long-lasting impression, the information subsequently needs to be integrated in the associative memory networks in the neocortex, and there shape the neural representation of the brand. Not all information makes that second stage; the brain needs to "decide" that the information is important enough. The brain uses several principles in that process of deciding which memories will make it into the neocortex.

6.4.1 REPETITION

Every memory has some small chance to make it into the neocortical memory networks. So if you see the same thing over and over again, the chance that it will be integrated increases. It's not a coincidence that the things we tend to remember from our childhood are television theme tunes, commercials, and computer games; these are all things that have been repeated numerous times. There is a basic law in neuroscience: cells that fire together wire together (Hebb 1949). You can interpret that as things that are presented together, or happen at the same time, become connected in the memory networks of the brain. It's how we learn from a very young age. For instance, how we learn a language; we see something and hear a sound. By consistently hearing the same sound paired with the same image, our brains automatically figure out that the sound describes the image, and a word is learned. This is totally automatic: just the consistent pairing of two items in the environment creates a link between the items in our mental representations.

It makes sense from an evolutionary point of view that things that repeatedly happen have a higher chance to be consolidated. It's important for the survival of any organism to be able to predict what is likely going to happen in its environment. Repetition signals importance, because things that repeat allude to regularity in the environment. Capturing these regularities enables better prediction of the future and thereby better decision making.

What does this mean for marketing and branding? Because it takes a lot of repetition to create long-lasting connections, it's important for brands to be consistent. Things that are consistently paired to a brand can become *iconic brand assets*; they are integrated into the neural representation of a brand. These brand assets can subsequently be used in marketing communications as very effective branding cues. A tagline that changes every campaign has less chance to be incorporated into long-lasting memory than a tagline that is consistently used for decades. "Just do it," "Melts in your mouth, not in your hands," or "Think different" are just some examples that will undoubtedly have automatically activated their associated brands in your memory after reading them. Also more abstract things such as colors, fonts, or package shapes can become associated to brands with consistent use. Private-label brands often deliberately try to mimic these assets to be able to tag along on the created equity the original brands built.

> **Because it takes a lot of repetition to create long-lasting connections, it's important for brands to be consistent. Things that are consistently paired to a brand can become iconic brand assets; they are integrated into the neural representation of a brand.**

6.4.2 EMOTION

Not all memories are created equally. Memories that are paired with emotions are much more likely to stick. There are numerous studies showing that emotional words are more easily recalled and emotional pictures are better recognized later (Adelman and Estes 2013). This holds true for both positive and negative emotions (Hamann et al. 1999). Emotions work as a label in the brain, signaling importance, like a little tag saying "keep". Many of our oldest childhood memories are of emotional events; getting lost in a department store, receiving a yearned-for birthday present, or that special pie your grandma used to bake of which you can still vividly recall the delicious taste and smell.

Holding on to emotional memories is a smart survival strategy; you need to remember a situation that has put you in danger to be able to avoid getting into a similar dangerous situation later in time. Many people that have experienced a near accident or got pulled over somewhere will have a vivid memory of the event. Moreover, this memory is automatically reactivated every time they drive by that location later. Just seeing the location will work as an automatic retrieval cue resulting in an increased level of vigilance. Also, positive emotions are relevant for

> **Emotions work as a label in the brain, signaling importance, like a little tag saying "keep".**

survival; if you found something rewarding, you need to know where and how to have a better chance of finding something similar again later. The events leading up to a dangerous or rewarding situation are better remembered as well, because whatever happened just before that situation needs to be recognized later to be avoided or sought out.

For marketers, this means that emotions are powerful tools; humor, slapstick kind of "ouch" moments, or goosebumps-drawing scenes or songs can protect marketing communications against decay. It's important though that the brand is sufficiently integrated into the emotion-evoking content, otherwise the ad is remembered, but people have no clue about (or worse, misattribute) the brand. Some of the best remembered ads are so sticky because of the emotions they evoke. Do you remember, for instance, the "Diet Coke break" (perfect integration of the brand by the way), or Dove's "Real Beauty Sketches" global ad campaign? Finally, it's important to realize that emotions are not only evoked by puppies and babies; also, more functional things like appetizing food shots, clearly resonating benefits, or a highly desired product can trigger reward signals in the brain and thereby increase the memorability of a television commercial or print ad.

6.4.3 EXISTING MEMORIES

Memories that fit well with the information we already know are better encoded and less vulnerable to decay (Alba and Hasher 1983). This is because during encoding, the new information works as a retrieval cue for related existing knowledge in the brain. This associated existing knowledge automatically becomes reactivated, and the new memory trace that is encoded in real time will contain both the new information and also some of the existing knowledge that came to mind when receiving that information. Imagine a physics student and an arts student both attending the same talk on the topic of quantum mechanics. Even though they received the exact same information, the physics student will likely have many more memories encoded immediately after the talk than the arts student. And this difference will only increase with time. This pattern would obviously be reversed if both attended a talk on the topic of the evolution of avant-garde art.

In a study using rats, it was shown that if newly learned information can be incorporated into preexisting knowledge structures (or *schemas*), it becomes integrated much faster into the neocortex and thus independent of the hippocampus (Tse et al. 2007). The rats learned to associate six locations on a grid to six flavors, so-called flavor-place associations. Subsequently, the rats were much faster in learning two additional flavor-place associations that fitted onto the same grid. Even when the hippocampus was taken out 48 hours later, the rats could still recall the two freshly learned flavor-place associations. However, if the flavor-place associations were not consistent (the same place would be paired to different flavors over time), the rats were much slower to learn two new flavor-place associations, and when the hippocampus was removed after the animals finally learned the two new associations, the newly formed memories were gone.

For marketers, this means that tying new information to existing memories can be very effective. This makes the communication easier to store and generates extra cues (the existing memories) for memory retrieval. For instance, when a celebrity is used in an ad, it builds onto the positive associations that are already tied to the celebrity, and people subsequently like and remember the product better (Klucharev, Smidts, and Fernández 2008). Another example is using a well-known song. Some brands successfully use the same ad strategy consistently, building every new ad on the foundation of the existing ads creating a rich interconnected representation in the brain. For instance, the MasterCard "Priceless" campaign has run since 1997 in more than 200 countries: "There are some things money cannot buy. For everything else, there's MasterCard." Also, when iconic brand assets are created by repetition (see section 6.4.1), these work as existing memories that ease the processing of every new marketing communication using them.

Existing memories can also hinder the formation of equity. If certain associations already exist that are incongruent with the newly presented message, the brain will have a harder time storing this information, and the information may not be integrated into the long-lasting memory networks. This is why companies sometimes create multiple brands when the equity is not fully congruent: one brand positioned for high efficacy, another brand for the use of ecologically friendly ingredients; one brand positioned as healthy, another brand as taste focused, and a third economical version for price seekers.

Existing associations can also create situations in which advertisement for one brand effectively results in a stronger implicit activation of a competitor brand. This can for instance happen when the competitor is the market leader. Showing a usage situation of a product of brand A can then trigger the market leader brand B, because usage of brand B has created a link in the consumer's minds between the usage situation and brand B. This can also happen when a brand shows benefits or equity that is already linked to a competitor brand. Communicating competitor-owned equity as a new feature of a target brand can result in strong implicit activation of the competitor, despite using clear branding cues for the target brand like the logo or brand name. In situations in which the co-activation of competitor brands is likely, unique brand assets for the target brand can be utilized to boost target brand activation above the competition. It is very important to be aware of existing memories and associations. If a competitor is for instance strongly positioned as natural, and the target brand incidentally uses a lot of green in an ad, this could accidently boost the memory activation of the competitor.

Communicating competitor-owned equity as a new feature of a target brand can result in strong implicit activation of the competitor, despite using clear branding cues of the target brand like the logo or brand name.

6.5   MEASURING MEMORY

In consumer neuroscience, there are several ways to measure whether memory formation has taken place after, for instance, watching a television commercial. The easiest way is just asking consumers in a survey if they remember seeing it. It is, however, important *when* the survey takes place—to know how much time has passed between exposure to the ad and testing. A big difference can be expected in the recall rate between a survey that takes place soon after viewing and a survey that takes place the next day, as most forgetting happens within the first 24 hours after creating a memory. If a memory is still present 24 hours later, that is a good indication that a longer-lasting memory representation has been created.

It's also important *how* people are asked about their memories. There is a big difference in memory performance between free recall (which ads have you seen yesterday) or cued recall. In the latter, memory is triggered with some sort of cue, which could be a description of the ad or frames from the ad that have to be recognized. It could be that people do not remember the ad if probed as free recall but do remember seeing it when probed with a question. Also, the way a question is phrased can influence whether people will successfully remember the ad, and how many specifics they can recall, because some descriptions will serve as a better recall cue than others. To interpret the results, it's important to understand the exact way the survey was executed. And, importantly, surveys probing memories are not able to pick up on implicit memory formation.

It could be that people do not remember the ad if probed as free recall but do remember seeing it when probed with a question.

It is also possible to measure the brain activity related to memory using functional magnetic resonance imaging (fMRI). In these experiments, participants go through a study phase in which they are exposed to a series of stimuli that have to be remembered and a test phase in which previously shown (old) items are shown intermixed with new ones. What successful *encoding* looks like in the brain is revealed when the brain activity for items that were later remembered is contrasted with the brain activity for items that were later forgotten. Researchers call this the *subsequent memory effect* (Wagner et al., 1998; Klucharev, Smidts, and Fernández 2008). Successful *recognition* can be shown by contrasting brain activity seen during recognition of old items versus correct rejection of new items in the test phase: this is called the *old-new effect*. Both during successful encoding and successful recognition, the hippocampus shows increased activity (Henson 2005). And the older memories are, the more the neocortical representational areas become active while the activity of the hippocampus decreases over time (Takashima et al. 2009).

An fMRI study revealed the importance of existing memories in rating the taste of Coke versus Pepsi (McClure et al. 2004). Participants in this study performed blind and brand-cued taste tests of Coke in the scanner. The researchers compared the brain activity and preferences of drinking unlabeled Coke versus Coke labeled as Coke. People liked the taste of the same drink (Coke) better when this drink was labeled as Coke. This shows that the presence of a brand cue can modify the perception of taste; meaning that the (probably positive) existing memories and associations to Coke made the drink taste better. In line with this, the fMRI during the branded taste test demonstrated more activity in memory-related brain areas such as the hippocampus.

The activation of memory systems also shows a reliable pattern in the brain waves measured by electroencephalography (EEG). The EEG signal can be decomposed into activity in different frequency bands. The different frequency bands are associated with different brain systems and cognitive tasks. By zooming in on the right frequencies, activity in the memory system can be monitored in real time. There are numerous studies showing higher power in the so-called theta and gamma frequency ranges during both successful encoding (subsequent memory effect) and successful retrieval (old-new effect) (Osipova et al. 2006; Jensen, Kaiser, and Lachaux 2007). A study using magnetoencephalography (MEG), which is a technique very similar to EEG, revealed that over time a spontaneous reorganization takes place in the brain areas supporting memory. When time passes, brain areas start to become involved that are important for the integration of information (Nieuwenhuis et al. 2012).

Finally, existing memory associations can be measured by a task called a *lexical decision task* (McNamara 2005). In this task, a participant sees a word (like "table") or a nonword (like "bluck"), and the participant has to classify them as fast as possible by pressing a button; one button for a nonword, another button for a word. If a related word is flashed briefly just before a word is presented, people are faster in classifying the second word as being a word. So when you flash the word "chair," the reaction time for classifying "table" is shorter than when you flash the word "car" before showing "table." This happens because the mental representation of the flashed word is activated in the brain, which spreads to associated words. This increased activation decreases the time needed to process the second word thereby shortening the reaction time. This is called a *priming effect*. Priming can take place between words, but also between a picture and a word, or between pictures. This priming effect can be used to quantify brand-equity associations. If the reaction time for classifying an equity word ("premium") decreases when primed with a brand name or logo, this means that the brand is linked to that equity in the consumer's mind.

KEY TAKEAWAYS

By quickly storing incoming information in the hippocampus, and gradually filing away the important pieces in the organized neocortex, the brain is capable of storing an incredible amount of information in an efficient and structured way. Which parts of the memory are considered to be important depends on the strength of the memory trace, the consistency of the new information with the existing knowledge, and also its emotional valence, or how gratifying the content was during acquisition. Marketers that are aware of the principles the brain uses to decide which information stays or goes can be much more effective in creating strong advertising material that has a long-lasting impact on the memory representations in the minds of consumers. In addition, it's wise to use a combination of tools to test the formation of both explicit and implicit memories, to ensure that the right memories are created and linked to the target brand.

DISCUSSION QUESTION (CASE STUDY)

RISING ABOVE THE CATEGORY

A brand has a product in a market in which its competitors are dominating. The brand developed a television commercial to promote its product aiming to increase market share. The commercial displayed a classic problem situation in which the product is needed, and the branded product featured prominently in the ad accomplishing the desired outcome while the product benefits were stated. It ended with a branding sequence showcasing the product, brand logo, and the brand's iconic brand character. The commercial had been tested on consumers before airing using a survey approach testing immediate memory for the brand and the main communicated benefits. Consumers displayed above-average brand and benefit recognition.

The commercial aired for several months and got sufficient quantity and quality of air time necessary for making an impact. However, no increase in market share was observed for the brand at all. Subsequently, the brand tested the commercial using a neuromarketing approach. Twenty-four consumers watched the commercial while their brain activity was measured with EEG, and eye tracking was performed. Additionally, the strength with which the commercial activated the target and competitor brands on an implicit level (the implicit brand resonance) was measured.

The test revealed high emotional engagement and memory activation during the scene in which the problem was displayed, signifying that consumers recognized and related to the depicted problem. Memory activation during the problem-solving part of the ad featuring the product was also strong. However, eye-tracking heat maps revealed that although consumers did look at the product, the part of the package receiving the most significant gaze had features that were common across the product category as a whole. The label of the package, displaying the brand logo, attracted little eye gaze. Memory activation during the final branding sequence was moderate, and cognitive load was high, suggesting an overload of information preventing optimal processing of all information.

Finally, testing revealed that implicit brand resonance with the ad as a whole was higher for the competitor brands than for the target brand! This may sound surprising because consumers had shown clear brand recognition in the pretesting that was performed. Thus, consumers consciously knew the ad they just saw was for the target brand, while at the same time, the competitor brands became strongly activated in their mind as well (see figure 6.4). This pattern can be explained by existing memories in the minds of the consumers. Because the competitor brands had a large market share, most consumers had more experience using the competitor products in the depicted problem situation than the target brand. By repeated use of a competitor product in the problem situation, the problem situation was linked to the competitor brands in the consumers' associative memory networks. Displaying the engaging problem situation in the ad, and by showcasing the product in a manner where consumers mostly noticed the category-specific elements of the package, resulted in strong coactivation of the competitor brands.

Suggest a few recommendations for the brand to increase its memorability.

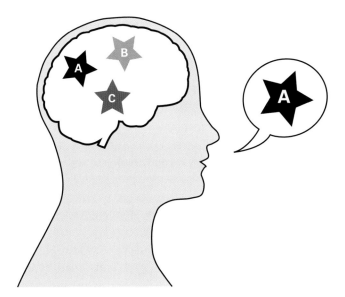

FIGURE 6.4
Explicit versus implicit brand resonance. Viewers of an ad can explicitly state that an ad is for the target brand, while at the same time competitor brands are activated in their brain. Strong subconscious coactivation of competitor brands should be avoided because this can result in the formation of associations between the communicated benefits to the competitors.

Answer

The following actions can be taken to produce a commercial resulting in a distinct branding profile:

- Try finding a more unique problem situation that is not tied to the competitors.

- Use the iconic brand character from the start of the commercial. Consider creating a story line in which the brand character plays a prominent role.

- Showcase the product in a way that emphasizes the label of the package instead of the general category elements.

- Be mindful in color, shape, and sound use. Avoid elements that are tied to the competition, and use elements that are unique to the target brand. Consider investing in building more iconic brand assets that can be leveraged in future campaigns.

- Simplify the final branding sequence for optimal processing.

References

Adelman, James S., and Zachary Estes. 2013. Emotion and memory: A recognition advantage for positive and negative words independent of arousal. *Cognition* 129 (3): 530–535.

Alba, Joseph W., and Lynn Hasher. 1983. Is memory schematic? *Psychological Bulletin* 93 (2): 203.

Bornstein, Robert F., Dean R. Leone, and Donna J. Galley. 1987. The generalizability of subliminal mere exposure effects: Influence of stimuli perceived without awareness on social behavior. *Journal of Personality and Social Psychology* 53 (6): 1070.

Courbet, Didier, Marie-Pierre Fourquet-Courbet, Roland Kazan, and Julien Intartaglia. 2014. The long-term effects of e-advertising: The influence of Internet pop-ups viewed at a low level of attention in implicit memory. *Journal of Computer-Mediated Communication* 19 (2): 274–293.

Ebbinghaus, Hermann. 1964. *Memory: A contribution to experimental psychology.* (H. A. Ruger & C. E. Bussenius, Trans.). New York: Dover. (Originally published 1885)

Fang, Xiang, Surendra Singh, and Rohini Ahluwalia. 2007. An examination of different explanations for the mere exposure effect. *Journal of Consumer Research* 34 (1): 97–103.

Godden, Duncan R., and Alan D. Baddeley. 1975. Context-dependent memory in two natural environments: On land and underwater. *British Journal of Psychology* 66 (3): 325–331.

Hamann, Stephan B., Timothy D. Ely, Scott T. Grafton, and Clinton D. Kilts. 1999. Amygdala activity related to enhanced memory for pleasant and aversive stimuli. *Nature Neuroscience* 2 (3): 289–293.

Hebb, Donald Olding. 1949. *The organization of behavior: A neuropsychological approach.* New York: John Wiley & Sons.

Henson, Richard. 2005. A mini-review of fMRI studies of human medial temporal lobe activity associated with recognition memory. *Quarterly Journal of Experimental Psychology Section B* 58 (3–4): 340–360.

Jensen, Ole, Jochen Kaiser, and Jean-Philippe Lachaux. 2007. Human gamma-frequency oscillations associated with attention and memory. *Trends in Neurosciences* 30 (7): 317–324.

Klucharev, Vasily, Ale Smidts, and Guillén Fernández. 2008. Brain mechanisms of persuasion: How 'expert power' modulates memory and attitudes. *Social Cognitive and Affective Neuroscience* 3 (4): 353–366.

Marr, D. 1971. Simple memory: A theory for archicortex. *Royal Society of London Philosophical Transactions Series B* 262:23–81.

Martin, Alex. 2007. The representation of object concepts in the brain. *Annual Review of Psychology* 58:25–45.

McClelland, James L., Bruce L. McNaughton, and Randall C. O'Reilly. 1995. Why there are complementary learning systems in the hippocampus and neocortex: Insights from the successes and failures of connectionist models of learning and memory. *Psychological Review* 102 (3): 419.

McClure, Samuel M., Jian Li, Damon Tomlin, Kim S. Cypert, Latané M. Montague, and P. Read Montague. 2004. Neural correlates of behavioral preference for culturally familiar drinks. *Neuron* 44 (2): 379–387.

McNamara, Timothy P. 2005. *Semantic priming: Perspectives from memory and word recognition.* Hove, UK: Psychology Press.

Nieuwenhuis, Ingrid L. C., Atsuko Takashima, Robert Oostenveld, Bruce L. McNaughton, Guillén Fernández, and Ole Jensen. 2012. The neocortical network representing associative memory reorganizes with time in a process engaging the anterior temporal lobe. *Cerebral Cortex* 22 (11): 2622–2633.

Osipova, Daria, Atsuko Takashima, Robert Oostenveld, Guillén Fernández, Eric Maris, and Ole Jensen. 2006. Theta and gamma oscillations predict encoding and retrieval of declarative memory. *Journal of Neuroscience* 26 (28): 7523–7531.

Scoville, William Beecher, and Brenda Milner. 1957. Loss of recent memory after bilateral hippocampal lesions. *Journal of Neurology, Neurosurgery, and Psychiatry* 20 (1): 11.

Standing, Lionel. 1973. Learning 10000 pictures. *Quarterly Journal of Experimental Psychology* 25 (2): 207–222.

Takashima, Atsuko, Ingrid L. C. Nieuwenhuis, Ole Jensen, Lucia M. Talamini, Mark Rijpkema, and Guillén Fernández. 2009. Shift from hippocampal to neocortical centered retrieval network with consolidation. *Journal of Neuroscience* 29 (32): 10087–10093.

Tse, Dorothy, Rosamund F. Langston, Masaki Kakeyama, Ingrid Bethus, Patrick A. Spooner, Emma R. Wood, Menno P. Witter, and R.G. Morris. 2007. Schemas and memory consolidation. *Science* 316 (5821): 76–82.

Wagner, Anthony D., Daniel L. Schacter, Michael Rotte, Wilma Koutstaal, Anat Maril, Anders M. Dale, Bruce R. Rosen, and Randy L. Buckner. 1998. Building memories: Remembering and forgetting of verbal experiences as predicted by brain activity. *Science* 281 (5380): 1188–1191.

Zajonc, Robert B. 1980. Feeling and thinking: Preferences need no inferences. *American Psychologist* 35 (2): 151.

Zajonc, Robert B., and Donald W. Rajecki. 1969. Exposure and affect: A field experiment. *Psychonomic Science* 17 (4): 216–217.

CHAPTER **7**

EMOTIONS
CARL MARCI AND
BRENDAN MURRAY

7.1 INTRODUCTION

The importance of emotion in advertising is well established (e.g., Binet and Field 2009). However, despite major advances in the modern neuroscience of emotion over the past few decades, there is still debate about the fundamental mechanisms that give rise to emotional experiences. In particular, the relationship between the brain and bodily responses and how these lead to the phenomenological experience of "emotion" is an area of active academic investigation. The goals of this chapter are to review contemporary models of emotion, along with their relevant basic neurobiology for marketers, and to review how to measure emotion with tools related to consumer neuroscience.

7.2 WHAT IS AN EMOTION?

What defines *emotion* (or *affect* as it is typically referred to in emotion science) has historically been, and continues to be, a topic of some debate in modern psychology and emotion science (for a review, see Barrett and Bliss-Moreau 2009). One commonly accepted definition comes from Davidson, Scherer, and Goldsmith (2002), the editors of the *Handbook of Affective Sciences*, which states, "Emotion refers to a relatively brief episode of coordinated brain, autonomic, and behavioral changes that facilitate a response to an external or internal event of significance for the organism" (p. xiii). Note that the term *feelings* is more narrowly defined by emotion experts specifically to reflect the subjective and conscious representation of some emotional experiences. The term *affect* here is used broadly to describe any state in which an emotional response is present, regardless of whether the emotional response is experienced on a conscious level or not. The term *autonomic* here refers to the autonomic nervous system, a branch of the human nervous system that transmits information from the brain to the body, largely without conscious awareness.

Emotional responses are typically relatively fast (milliseconds to seconds at onset) and relatively brief responses to an internal or external event, while the term *mood* is applied to longer-lasting, lower-intensity, and more diffuse emotional responses over time (such as minutes, hours, or days). Wilhelm Wundt, one of the first modern emotion theorists, has suggested that individuals are never in a completely "neutral" state, but rather are always experiencing some underlying state of emotional response (Wundt 1897/1998).

Although the details of what exactly defines an emotion or emotional state are still an open topic of debate in the scientific community, market researchers will typically use the term *emotion* as shorthand to describe a fast and relatively brief response to an external stimulus, such as a marketing communication or advertisement. Although an individual's *mood* (or other underlying internal emotional or social factor like temperament, sense of self, or situational context) can certainly influence in-the-moment responses such as purchasing decisions (Coleman and Williams 2013), these internal factors are typically outside of the control of marketers and advertisers. Marketers and advertisers seek to influence an individual's fast, in-the-moment emotional response to external marketing-related events and stimuli. As we will discuss, these in-the-moment emotional responses are critical, on a neurobiological and practical level, for influencing future behaviors and forming brand-building associations in the brains of consumers.

> "Emotion refers to a relatively brief episode of coordinated brain, autonomic, and behavioral changes that facilitate a response to an external or internal event of significance for the organism."

7.3   HOW ARE EMOTIONS MADE?

In practice, emotional responses can be understood in many ways. Although there exist many different theories for defining how emotions arise (for a review, see Gross and Barrett 2011), the two most popular theories for operationalizing emotions are the *basic emotion theory* (e.g., MacDougall 1908/1921; Ekman 1972; Davis 1992; Panksepp 1998; LeDoux 2000) and the *psychological construction theory* (e.g., Wundt 1897/1998; Schacter and Singer 1962; Russell 1980, 2003; Barrett 2009). Many of the tools used in consumer neuroscience are grounded in research from one or both of these two theories.

The basic emotion theory posits that there is a discrete set of biologically basic emotions (e.g., fear, sadness, anger, happiness) that are universal across individuals and cultures, are the building blocks of mental states, and cannot be deconstructed beyond the emotion itself (Ekman 1972). Under this theory, a stimulus (such as a brand communication) elicits one of the "basic emotions" by activating a dedicated neural circuit, much like executing a computer program, which leads to an acute feeling state and associated bodily response (figure 7.1, top panel). By its strictest definition, basic emotion theory suggests that each individual emotional experience is consistent from one elicitation to the next, leaving little room for flexibility across experiences and individuals (e.g., one person's "fear" is biologically identical to another individual's "fear," and an individual's "fear" at one point in time is identical to that same individual's "fear" at a later point in time) (Panksepp 1998).

In contrast, the psychological construction theory uses a multidimensional scaling approach to parse emotional responses into two orthogonal dimensions upon which emotions are constructed: arousal and valence (Russell 1980, 2003). In this framework, arousal is broadly defined as a range of responses from calm to excited, while valence is a dimension that varies from unpleasant (negative) to pleasant (positive; figure 7.2). Psychological construction theory uses this two-dimensional space, wherein the valence and arousal responses are the "ingredients" that give rise to the physiologic and phenomenological experience of an emotion (rather than prescribing specific circuitry for discrete emotions). Emotion words in the form of language-based symbols or verbal utterances of subjective feeling states can be assigned to an emotional response on the basis of where it falls in the two-dimensional axis, but these emotion words do not necessarily adhere to strict neurobiological circuits or universal bodily states.

The basic emotion theory posits that there is a discrete set of biologically basic emotions (e.g., fear, sadness, anger, happiness) that are universal across individuals and cultures.

7.4 THE BIOLOGY OF EMOTION: WHAT ABOUT THE BRAIN?

For the purposes of marketing executives and researchers interested in consumer neuroscience, these two major theoretical emotion models can be considered in terms of their neurobiological implications, and thereby the methods with which to measure emotion in a market research setting. Broadly speaking, the basic emotion theory is considered to be a "location-based" account of emotion, which assumes a strict biological and genetic basis of emotion with universal characteristics of body, brain, and facial patterns underlying discrete emotional states (e.g., fear, sadness, anger, happiness). The psychological construction model, in contrast, assumes that emotional experiences emerge or are "constructed" out of a basic set of physiologic and psychological responses that are not specific to any one discrete emotional experience (e.g., fear, sadness, anger, happiness) but rather emerge from a "domain-specific" set of neural networks. These neural-based responses produce psychological events on the basis of the specific context of the experience and draw on past experiences (i.e., memories) of the person having the experience. Both

The psychological construction theory uses a multidimensional scaling approach to parse emotional responses into two orthogonal dimensions upon which emotions are constructed: arousal and valence.

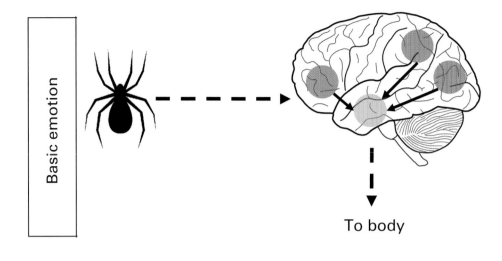

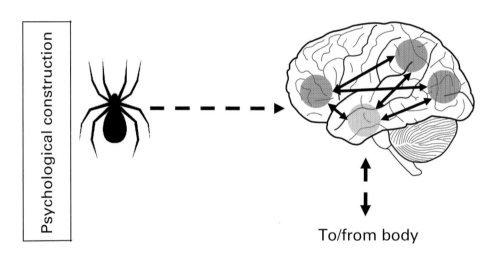

FIGURE 7.1

Two different ways of conceptualizing emotion generation, each based on a different theory of emotion. Note that the circles are for illustrative purposes only and make no claim about specific brain regions or networks implicated in emotion generation. Top: According to basic emotion theory, a stimulus elicits a distinct set of neural processes that are specific to the emotion being generated. Bottom: According to psychological construction theory, a stimulus elicits a coordinated set of brain-body interactions that will vary on the basis of situational and individual contexts.

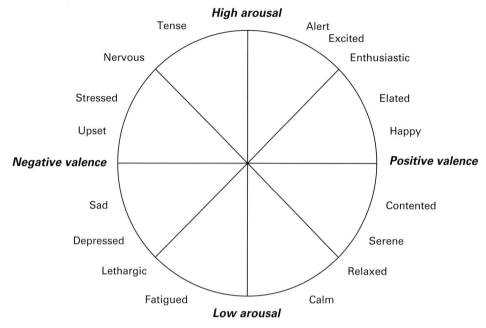

FIGURE 7.2

Representation of the affective circumplex model (Russell 1980), in which the experience of emotion is operationalized along two orthogonal axes: emotional arousal (vertical axis) and emotional valence (horizontal axis). Labels for emotions (e.g., "alert," "fatigued," etc.) represent potential communicative labels for emotional states, dependent on the state's valence and arousal. Note that under psychological construction theory, different emotions (e.g., "alert") can vary in their phenomenological experience from one individual to the next and from one instantiation to the next.

models are grounded in academic work and have a neurobiological framework worth understanding at a basic level for marketing.

As discussed, the basic emotion model assumes distinct categories of emotion and suggests that there is a single "mode" or biologically distinct network of neurons that have a specific "location" in the brain for each discrete emotion. In this model, emotions have certain universal characteristics with a corresponding physiologic, facial, and bodily mapping. While the model allows for some developmental and cultural influences (e.g., reduced facial expression in certain Eastern cultures), at a first order of approximation, emotional responses are "hardwired" into the self from an early age (Lindquist et al. 2012).

Thus, in the basic emotion model, there is an assumption of a one-to-one brain-emotion correspondence. One classic example in support of this location-based model is the role of the amygdala in fear responses. Originally described by Klüver and Bucy (1939), the amygdala is a well-studied and reported brain region that has long been assumed to play a role in emotion (Aggleton 1992; Gallagher and Chiba 1996; Cahill and McGaugh 1995; though see Feinstein et al., 2013, for a discussion of emotional responses in individuals with bilateral amygdala lesions). The location-based model suggests that a fear response in humans would preferentially and consistently trigger activation of the amygdala (whereas disgust, for example, might preferentially trigger the insula; see the meta-analysis by Vytal and Hamann 2010).

In the basic emotion model, there is an assumption of a one-to-one brain-emotion correspondence.

This model makes sense when considering data related to the amygdala as a brain locus for fear. This amygdala-fear hypothesis was advanced considerably by animal models of fear that showed rats freezing or having a startle response (an arousing event) to auditory cues that were paired with a shock, as in a classical conditioning paradigm (Adolphs and Tranel 2000; Davis et al. 2010). Data in humans came in the form of patients with damage in all or portions of their amygdala (on one or both sides). These patients had dampened skin conductance responses, a measure of emotional arousal (LaBar et al. 1995), or had difficulty perceiving fear cues in laboratory settings (Bechara et al. 1995; Adolphs et al. 1999). Other studies reported patients with amygdala damage failing to report a fear response when they were in close proximity to stimuli that would be expected to generate fear (e.g., snakes, spiders, or when they were startled unexpectedly; Feinstein et al. 2010).

However, in order for the basic emotion model to be complete, studies that induce emotions other than fear should, in theory, not trigger activity in the amygdala. In other words, as just described, this location-based model suggests a one-to-one and unique role of the amygdala (and potentially other brain regions) in fear. This turns out not to be the case, as studies showed that the amygdala likely plays a broader role in generating emotional responses. For example, other research shows that the amygdala is active when the brain is faced with an unclear or ambiguous situation or stimulus (i.e., the target stimulus is ambivalent or only partly noticeable) or when a situation is unresolved (Camerer, Loewenstein, and Prelec 2005). Other studies showed that the amygdala plays a broader role in emotional intensity or arousal in emotions other than fear (e.g., Sabatinelli et al. 2005).

The construct-based model suggests that emotions are "constructed" through a process.

This and other research led some investigators to develop the *construct-based model* of emotions. Based on psychological construction theory, the less anatomically specific construct-based model is fundamentally different from the location-based model in that it does not require or conceive of a one-to-one relationship between distinct emotional responses (e.g., fear, anger, joy) and distinct networks of neurons or specific regions in the brain. Rather, the construct-based model suggests that emotions are "constructed" through a process that, like the location-based model, also begins with an embodied response to a stimulus. However, it differentiates from the basic emotion model in that all emotional responses fundamentally follow a similar process and involve similar networks of neurons or regions in the brain. The main difference is how the brain conceptualizes the response that leads to what we think of as an emotional experience.

In support of basic emotion theory, evidence from brain imaging research has suggested that there may, indeed, be dedicated neural circuits for discrete emotional responses. In a recent meta-analysis by Vytal and Hamann (2010), the authors showed that dissociable neural circuits have been found for the discrete, basic emotions of happiness, fear, anger, disgust, and sadness. However, as noted by Lindquist and Barrett (2012), those authors do not demonstrate a consistent and specific relationship between any one brain region or network and the perception of any one discrete emotion (e.g., happiness or anger). This lack of specificity is consistent with previous findings from a variety of other studies (see Lindquist and Barrett 2012, box 2). Moreover, the authors of the meta-analysis indicate that their findings are *not* inconsistent with psychological construction theory, but rather may provide evidence in favor of *both* the basic emotion and psychological construction theories (Vytal and Hamann 2010).

Broadly speaking, the psychological construction model essentially has four steps and engages a similar network of neurons and brain regions regardless of which emotion is ultimately experienced. Step 1, as noted above, happens when an embodied response is triggered after information is received through one of the five sensory modalities (i.e., sight, sound, touch, taste, smell). This embodied experience, sometimes referred to as core affect, is manifested by some combination of bodily changes that are often somatosensory, kinesthetic, proprioceptive, and/or neurochemical in nature. Step 1 is similar in both models. These bodily responses are mapped onto the brain leading to the next step of the construct-based model.

Step 2 is a conceptualization step, which refers to a psychological situation–specific mental process that links the core affect generated in the body to meaningful interpretations of the experienced stimulus or situation. Importantly, the construct-based approach creates the meaning of the experience in part on the basis of the stimulus (either externally or internally generated) and prior relevant experience (i.e., memories from past experience). The conceptualization is done automatically, nonconsciously, and without noticeable effort. Conceptualization can be based on a direct physical experience (e.g., "my head hurts"), a non-discrete feeling state, (e.g., "I feel tired and blah"), a discrete feeling state, (e.g., "I feel sad"), or a projection onto an object (e.g., "That sunset is beautiful").

In tandem or immediately after conceptualization is step 3, directing executive attention. Executive attention is the directing of attentional resources in response to core affect and the immediate conceptualization of the experience toward motivationally salient and relevant interpretations (and ultimately to behavioral responses). This is evolutionarily and practically important to marketers as at any given time, the brain is inundated with information about the internal and external world. Executive attention plays a role in amplifying some experiences and ignoring others. One goal of marketing is to amplify the experience of a brand communication.

In support of basic emotion theory, evidence from brain imaging research has suggested that there may, indeed, be dedicated neural circuits for discrete emotional responses.

Finally, step 4 completes the full experience of emotion in the construct-based model with the association to or expression of emotion words. In this model, emotion words act as anchors for abstract emotion categories that are often largely socially constructed and, as noted above, underlie feeling states. The emotion words, rooted in language, allow us to communicate (albeit sometimes inaccurately or incompletely) internal emotional experiences. Note that not all emotional experiences reach step 4 as not all embodied experiences of core affect lead to an emotion word, and, in fact, core affect is happening all the time to some degree while the conscious awareness of emotion is a relatively rare event by comparison (as first suggested by Wundt 1897/1998; Barrett and Bliss-Moreau 2009). This is an important consideration when evaluating tools for measuring emotions in advertising, whether on a nonconscious or conscious basis.

7.5   THE BIOLOGY OF EMOTION: WHAT ABOUT THE BODY?

It is important also to note that both the basic emotion and psychological construction models assume that the experience of emotion involves some form of sensory input from the body, variously described as raw somatic, visceral, vascular, or neurochemical of varying degrees (Lindquist et al., 2012). Bodily states are a primary ingredient in the mental experience of emotion and likely critical to consciousness and a consistent sense of self-identity (Damasio 2010). Changes in bodily states (i.e., the embodied response or core affect) represent an evaluation of whether objects or experiences in the environment are relevant and valuable (or not) in a given context.

When considering the role of bodily states and emotional processes in consumer decision-making, it is worth considering the somatic marker hypothesis (*soma* meaning "body") posited by the influential neurologist and emotion neuroscientist Antonio Damasio (1994). Very simply, the underlying tenet of the somatic marker hypothesis is that ultimately, decision making and choice rely on both nonconscious emotion processing (as described above) and a largely separate and distinct, deliberate, conscious cognitive process. Many decisions (including purchase decisions) are difficult to make by relying solely on deliberative, conscious, cognitive processes, and therefore lean heavily on nonconscious emotion processing as an aid in decision making (e.g., Kahneman 2011). When an individual is confronted with a stimulus that elicits an emotional response, information about that response is manifested in the body and is stored as a "somatic marker" in the prefrontal cortex (and likely other areas) of the brain (figure 7.3). When an individual is later confronted with a future, similar decision, relevant prior somatic markers are accessed and provide nonconscious feedback to help inform the decision (Bechara et al. 1994; Damasio 1994; Damasio, Everitt, and Bishop 1996).

When an individual is confronted with a stimulus that elicits an emotional response, information about that response is manifested in the body and is stored as a "somatic marker."

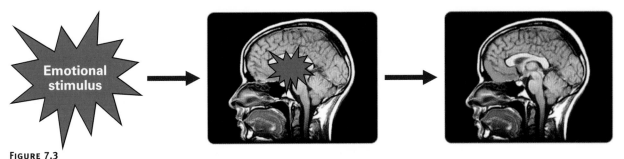

FIGURE 7.3
Representation of the formation of a "somatic marker." A stimulus (far left) elicits an emotional response in the perceiver (middle), and information about that experience is stored as a "somatic marker" in the brain (far right, shown here as being "stored" in the ventromedial prefrontal cortex).

In both models, the fundamental role of emotion is to lead people (or consumers) to attend to certain features, information sources, events or stimuli and simultaneously ignore other features, information sources, events or stimuli in their environment, all toward some motivationally relevant goal (Schwarz and Clore 1983; Damasio, 1994; Cosmides and Tooby 2000). This process is fundamental to marketing, as the categorizing of stimuli in the environment with an emotion process is critically important for determining meaning and allowing inferences and judgments to be made about subsequent behaviors. In marketing, the goal of communications is to leverage emotional responses to create and amplify "meaning" and trigger "approach" (as opposed to "ignore" or "avoid") behaviors in consumers. The outcome is the same regardless of the associated emotion word or subjective feeling state generated, leading toward the end goal of a creating positive sentiment toward, endorsement or purchase of a brand, product, or service.

7.6   TECHNIQUES FOR MEASUREMENT

There are multiple ways of measuring conscious and nonconscious emotional responses in market research. Conscious measures include traditional measures of self-report, such as surveys and focus groups. Emotions, in this context, are evaluated based on the emotion words and associated language used by the participant. In some cases, the two dimensions of emotion (valence and arousal) described above are mapped through direct questions. For example, "Did you find the commercial you just saw exciting?" or "On a scale from 1 to 5, with 1 representing low and 5 representing high, how exciting did you find the commercial you just saw?" This line of questioning can be followed with valence questions on a similar scalar dimension (e.g., "How good do you feel about the commercial you just saw?" or

"How much did you like the commercial you just saw?), but more focused on whether the experience was more positive or negative and to what degree.

The challenge with relying on self-report or conscious measures of emotion in market research is twofold. First, the reporting is done after the experience of the target stimulus (in the case of market research, this is often some form of market communication related to the brand). This introduces certain well-known biases that can interfere with the accuracy of the research (Mick 1996; Aaker, Kumar, and Day 2007). Second, as described above, both the basic emotion and psychological construction models strongly suggest that much of emotion processing is happening below the level of conscious awareness, and not all emotional responses reach a state where an emotion word or subjective feeling state is consciously experienced. Thus, measures that rely entirely on self-report or conscious response will, by definition, be incomplete.

Much of emotion processing is happening below the level of conscious awareness, and not all emotional responses reach a state where an emotion word or subjective feeling state is consciously experienced.

Starting in the mid-2000s, a new style of market research company began to emerge that introduced tools, techniques, and technologies that for the first time allowed market researchers to measure nonconscious processes at affordable prices.[1] These companies introduced market-ready measures with proprietary algorithms to collect and analyze nonconscious responses, many of which were focused on capturing the early steps of the emotional process outlined above. The technologies used include biometrics (which includes traditional psychophysiologic measures like skin conductance response, heart rate, and respiration), electroencephalography (EEG), facial coding, implicit measures, and functional magnetic resonance imaging (fMRI). All of these measures allow for the noninvasive measurement of some aspect of nonconscious emotional response and often draw on both models in order to provide valuable insights for marketers.

Biometrics refers to a variety of measures of the autonomic branch of the peripheral nervous system that indirectly reflect brain responses but directly measure the embodied response and components of core affect. As core affect represents the very earliest of the steps in emotion generation, one advantage of biometrics is the ability to capture "upstream" emotional reactions, even when these emotional experiences are not experienced on a conscious level. Biometric measures are also among the best techniques for capturing information related to the formation of somatic markers, which, as mentioned above, have a critical role in the formation of emotional experiences and memories (e.g., Bechara et al. 1997). Another advantage of biometric techniques is relatively low price and portability of the equipment used to collect data. The two most common biometric measures in market research are skin conductance and heart rate.

1. There were companies that existed prior to the year 2000 that used fMRI and variants of EEG, but most of them failed to achieve a meaningful level of market penetration, and many of them failed as a result of high costs and the limitations of computational power at that time.

The measure of skin conductance response (also known as galvanic skin response or electrodermal response) is one of the oldest and most efficient and minimally invasive measures of emotional arousal (Damasio, Tranel, and Damasio 1991; Buchel et al. 1998; Damasio 1994). The skin momentarily becomes a better conductor of electricity when either internal or external stimuli are experienced as arousing. These responses are communicated from the brain via sympathetic fibers of the autonomic nervous system and have been linked to certain brain regions related to emotion processing, including the amygdala and anterior cingulate cortex (Mangina and Beuzeron-Mangina 1996; Buchel et al. 1998; Gentil et al. 2009). Skin conductance is relatively easy and inexpensive to collect but can pose challenges in terms of signal processing, as many internal and external stimuli generate a skin conductance response. Because of the signal strength generated, the palmar surface of the hands or proximal areas of the fingers are common sites for measurement (Fowles et al. 1981). The signals have relatively good temporal resolution (i.e., timing of onset) but have a known lag in the response profile that limits the timing accuracy to within a few seconds (Kotses and Glaus 1977).

Another biometric measure is heart rate, which can be collected with electrocardiology (ECG) equipment or using a pulse transducer. ECG measures are significantly more accurate, and, like skin conductance, heart rate measures are relatively inexpensive and easy to collect. Also similar to skin conductance, a significant amount of post-data collection processing is needed to make sure the readings are accurate, and interpretations of the fluctuations in heart rate need to be made with care. While connections to emotion and emotion centers of the brain have been well documented (Lang, Bradley, and Cuthbert 1998; Kuniecki et al. 2003), in contrast to skin conductance response, heart rate variability is influenced by both sympathetic and parasympathetic fibers of the autonomic nervous system, and thus much care must be taken when using heart rate as a measure of emotional response (Marci et al. 2007).

Electroencephalography (EEG) is another time-tested and popular measure in neuroscience and consumer neuroscience (see the case study in box 7.1) and reflects the direct electrical activity in neurons in the upper cortex of the brain as cells become active to convey information (Niedermeyer and da Silva 2004).

The measure of skin conductance response (also known as galvanic skin response or electrodermal response) is one of the oldest and most efficient and minimally invasive measures of emotional arousal.

Box 7.1
The Shelter Pet Project

GENERAL DESCRIPTION

As viewers have more choice than ever and more screens to distract them from television commercials, the bar for engagement is higher than ever. For nonprofits with big ambitions and small budgets, maximizing each television ad is critical. Effective television advertising needs to communicate its main message, generate an emotional response with its audience and make a memorable impression. Nielsen Consumer Neuroscience and the Ad Council, the oldest and largest producers of public service announcements in the United States, used neuroscience tools to create an effective ad for The Shelter Pet Project. Shelter Pet is a nonprofit with the goal of making pet shelters the first place potential adopters turn to when they're looking for a new pet.

Box 7.1
(continued)

Business Issue and Methodology

The Shelter Pet Project already had a relatively strong-performing ad. The ad's star, Jules the dog, earned an initial version of their public service announcement (PSA) a score of 6.8 out of 10 for overall effectiveness based on initial electroencephalograph (EEG) results. This score ranks the initial ad in the top 40 percent of Nielsen-tested ads. But there was room to improve and increase the emotional engagement with the ad.

Using EEG and eye tracking technology, Nielsen graphed how people's brains responded emotionally and visually consumed the ad to help the creative team identify, second-by-second, which scenes did and did not resonate with the target audience. In addition to overall scores that can be compared to a database, EEG generates subcomponents including attention processing, emotional motivation and memory activation scores. Eye tracking is used diagnostically and allows for a detailed assessment of where an audience is looking throughout the ad.

Results

The results also showed that when Jules was off screen, attention and emotional levels dropped. They also determined that showing Jules along with key messaging, including the logo and the website URL at the end of the ad, competed for viewers' visual attention—causing confusion and lowering the potential impact of the message and call to action. So the team needed to eliminate that confusion and refocus the audience on the PSA's message, final branding, and call to visit their website.

To capitalize on the findings, the team re-edited the PSA to shorten Jules's off-screen moments, enhance messaging and sharpen the ending. When the team tested the re-edited and updated version of the PSA, viewers were found to be more consistently emotionally engaged and the ad scores improved. The updated ad also held viewers' visual attention better and suggested that the ad could be recalled more clearly than the earlier version.

By combining EEG and eye-tracking measurements to determine the impact the ad had on viewers, the team effectively quantified the power of Jules, the dog. It did so by confirming previous research suggesting that showing emotional faces on screen—including a dog's—boosts viewers' emotional engagement.

Win-Win Outcome

In the first three months after the February PSA launch, traffic to ShelterPetProject. org increased 133 percent, and the average monthly traffic increased from 74,000 to 174,000 visitors—a change that may have real life or death implications for shelter pets. By keeping the powerful presence of Jules and clarifying the main message and call to action, The Shelter Pet Project improved its ad while preserving the main storyline leading to a powerful return on investment for the Ad Council. "Sometimes people aren't able to tell you their real reactions, sometimes they don't want to tell you, and you circumvent all of that with this methodology," stated the Vice President and Research Director for the Ad Council. "Nielsen helps us grow our business by insuring that our creative is the best that it can be."

High-quality EEG is typically more intrusive than biometric measures (requiring up to 64 wet scalp electrodes), but as a direct measure of brain activity it has been demonstrated to be one of the best measures of emotion motivation (i.e., approach vs. avoid response) on a nonconscious level using a derivative of the EEG signal referred to as frontal asymmetry (Davidson et al. 1990; Coan and Allen 2004; Harmon-Jones, Gable, and Peterson 2010). Derivatives of EEG also include evoked potentials, which have been used to evaluate the response to brands and brand attributes. While there are limitations to EEG in terms of understanding the precise brain regions that are active, the signals have superior temporal resolution and allow marketers to understand the onset of a brain response to within a few hundred milliseconds of accuracy (Niedermeyer and da Silva 2004).

Other tools, such as software programs for coding facial expressions, are used to further categorize the emotional responses of a target audience to a marketing communication (e.g., a video ad or digital experience). Facial coding is a relatively new tool with strong explanatory power and the ability to collect data from web-based cameras in the home over the Internet (McDuff et al. 2014). Facial coding draws more heavily on the basic model than other techniques. However, it must be kept in mind that facial expressions evolved to communicate our feeling states in a social context and therefore occur at relatively low levels in the context of the passive media upon which the vast majority of marketing communications occur (i.e., television, Internet, out-of-home signage), and there is some evidence that an expressed emotion does not necessarily reflect accurate information about the individual's actual internal emotional state (Fridlund 1994; Russell and Fernandez-Dols 1997). Most software-based techniques are based on the facial action coding system (Ekman and Friesen 1978). Facial coding records video of an individual's face while he or she is exposed to some content (e.g., a television advertisement). Facial landmarks and features (e.g., the mouth corners, bridge of the nose, etc.) are identified in the recorded videos through automated software, and small changes in facial musculature are identified on the basis of deviations from the identified landmarks. In this way, the software can identify when an individual is expressing a smile, a frown, a disgust face, or several other discrete facial expressions. Facial coding can be a useful diagnostic tool to understand whether a stimulus has elicited a specific facial expression (e.g., a smile) and is increasingly used to evaluate ad effectiveness (Teixeira, Picard, and Kaliouby 2014).

Implicit testing is another technique that can be used to try and understand information—specifically, semantic associations or "feeling states"—that individuals are unable or unwilling to verbalize. Any stimulus, such as a brand or product name, is connected to some number of semantic word associates that will influence how an individual perceives that stimulus. A wide range of implicit tasks are employed by market researchers, many of which are either directly taken from academic literature or derived from existing academic techniques. These include the implicit association test (Greenwald, McGhee, and Schwartz 1998), semantic

Coding of facial expressions is used to further categorize the emotional responses of a target audience to a marketing communication (e.g., a video ad or digital experience).

priming techniques (e.g., Meyer and Schvaneveldt 1971), the Stroop test (Stroop 1935), the affective misattribution procedure (Payne et al. 2005), and other proprietary or novel techniques, and, like automated facial expressions, data can be collected online. These tests typically rely on either reaction time–based measures or priming tasks to try and indirectly assess how positively or negatively individuals feel about a brand, or what semantic word associations they hold for that brand, without asking direct questions about the brand itself (Dimofte 2010). These measures tend to require large sample sizes because the effects are often small, and the data can be difficult to interpret in the absence of a careful study design and methodology (Greenwald, Nosek, and Banaji 2003).

The last major technique to discuss in relation to emotion measurement in consumer neuroscience is functional magnetic resonance imaging (fMRI). The use of fMRI as a brain imaging technique is based on two principles. First, neurons in the brain need oxygenated blood to fire, and a constituent of oxygenated and deoxygenated blood (oxyhemoglobin and deoxyhemoglobin) has magnetic properties and acts as a natural contrast for the magnets used in fMRI (Ogawa et al. 1990). When a region of the brain is active during a task, the neurons in that region send signals that increase oxygenated blood to the area of activation. This blood oxygen level–dependent (BOLD) response can be measured by the fMRI scanner, revealing areas of the brain that receive relatively increased levels of oxygenated blood. Functional MRI introduces a task-based element to the measures of conventional MRI. Individuals lie in the fMRI scanner and can complete cognitive tasks or watch marketing content (e.g., a television ad) while the fMRI scan takes place. Because there is constant non-task-related activity in the brain, fMRI is based on subtractive logic. Activity during the task of interest (e.g., watching an ad) is subtracted by activity during some independent baseline task (e.g., looking at a fixation dot). Brain activity that remains after the subtraction is assumed to be uniquely related to the target task and not to the filler task.

Although the BOLD response is an indirect measure of neural activity, a landmark study by Logothetis and colleagues (2001) measured BOLD response in the visual cortex of monkeys while simultaneously taking single-unit recordings (in which an electrode is implanted directly into brain tissue to measure local neuronal activity). The study revealed that the BOLD response was, in fact, an accurate measure of local neural activity. Functional MRI has excellent spatial resolution, is able to record brain activity in areas as small as a square millimeter, and can therefore localize activity in very small or in deep-brain structures. However, because the BOLD response is dependent on the flow rate of oxygenated blood, the temporal resolution of fMRI is relatively poor (with approximately 5–8 seconds of biological lag) compared to a technology like EEG (Kim, Richter, and Ugurbil 1997). In addition, because fMRI is dependent on subtractive logic, the test and control conditions must be very well-defined and theoretically motivated. Because there is non-task-related brain activity, fMRI studies are very sensitive to "fishing expedition" type studies; differences will almost *always* be found between two task conditions, and therefore those conditions must be very carefully specified and hypotheses made ahead of time about what regions the researchers expect to see activate differentially. While fMRI use has been linked to predicting sales performance with market communications (Venkatraman et al. 2015), these considerations (coupled with the facts that fMRI is an extremely costly technology to implement and requires participants to lie still in a loud imaging scanner) tend to suggest care must be taken with the technology's application in market research (Weber, Mangus, and Huskey 2015).

7.7   HOW DO EMOTIONS IMPACT MARKETING?

While there have been many studies on the role of emotion in advertising, one of the largest and most comprehensive was reported by Binet and Field (2009). The unusually large data set spanned multiple large brand advertisers across multiple categories. The analyses included 880 advertising campaign "case studies" submitted to the Institute of Practitioners in Advertising (IPA) in the United Kingdom, all of which had clearly stated business objectives and "hard" business outcomes reported (e.g., sales, market share, price sensitivity, profit). One question the review set out to address was the role of "emotional" versus "rational" focus in advertising in business outcome. For some time, marketers have increasingly been open to emotional appeals, but the conventional wisdom was that both were needed in some sort of perceived "balance" for success.

The results of the Binet and Field (2009) report suggested otherwise. The data clearly suggested that the more emotions were at the center of the campaign, the bigger the business impact. Importantly, the authors found that the most effective advertising campaigns were those with little or no rational content at all (the only exception was direct-response advertising, which required some rational appeal to be effective). How can this be?

Although there is no "catch-all" for what *types* of emotional responses an advertiser might want to elicit, it is critical to understand that the elicitation of an emotional response can have important implications for the attention and retention of information as well as on an individual's future behavior based on that information. Emotional information benefits from priority processing in the brain through rapid orientation and increased attention to emotional stimuli over non-emotional stimuli (Öhman, Flykt, and Esteves 2001). Other research suggests that emotional information is typically processed more fluently and faster than non-emotional information (Kityama 1990), even when attention is limited or divided (Kensinger and Corkin 2004; Talmi et al. 2007; Talmi et al. 2008). Moreover, the impact of emotional responses can come at the expense of attention to other concurrent or proximal non-emotional information (Murray and Kensinger 2012; Mickley-Steinmetz and Kensinger 2013; Murray and Kensinger 2014). Importantly, when an event or stimulus is emotional in nature, research shows that it typically receives a benefit in memory processing and retention relative to non-emotional stimuli (Brown and Kulik 1977; LaBar and Cabeza 2006; Murray and Kensinger 2014; see reviews by Hamann 2001 and Kensinger 2009).

This impact of emotional response on attention and memory is not limited to the brain. As discussed above, the embodiment of emotion is a critical step in emotion processing and is the basis for some consumer neuroscience measures (e.g., biometric measures). For example, medications that selectively reduce heart rate (e.g., beta-adrenergic antagonists, such as propranolol), when given prior to encoding novel information, have been shown to reduce the long-term retention advantage associated with emotionally arousing stimuli relative to neutral stimuli (Cahill et al. 1994). This effect appears to be dependent on the medication crossing the blood-brain barrier, suggesting that the effect is not solely due to the heart rate decreases (i.e., decreased arousal) but may also be in response to neuroreceptor response in the brain (van Stegeran et al. 1998).

Thus, it is critical for marketers to consider emotion when creating their products and advertisements and to understand the consequences of not leveraging emotion to "stand out" from the clutter in the modern media and marketing landscape. Regardless of which theory of emotion generation is ultimately proven correct (and it may be aspects of both), using emotional messaging, imagery, or other creative content designed to elicit an affective response literally in the "hearts" and "minds" of consumers is critical to getting a brand or product noticed, remembered, and selected over competitors.

7.8 CONSUMER NEUROSCIENCE MEASURES RELATIONSHIP TO MARKETING AND SALES

There have been a number of studies that show the relationship between various nonconscious consumer neuroscience measures of emotional response and behaviors relevant to marketers. These behaviors cross the spectrum and include correlations between various neurometrics of emotion and what consumers will watch, say, and purchase. Given the importance of video-based and television advertising in generating an emotional response (Treutler, Levine, and Marci, 2010), this review will predominantly focus on video-based and television advertising.

One example of research into what consumers will watch in terms of television advertising comes from research conducted by Innerscope Research[2] and TiVo (MediaPost 2009). The research investigated 40 participants that were biometrically monitored (using a combination of skin conductance and heart rate) in a central

Sidebar (left margin):

Although there is no "catch-all" for what types of emotional responses an advertiser might want to elicit, it is critical to understand that the elicitation of an emotional response can have important implications for the attention and retention of information as well as on an individual's future behavior based on that information.

Medications that selectively reduce heart rate (e.g., beta-adrenergic antagonists, such as propranolol), when given prior to encoding novel information, have been shown to reduce the long-term retention advantage associated with emotionally arousing stimuli relative to neutral stimuli.

2. *Innerscope Research is now part of the Nielsen Consumer Neuroscience business unit of the Nielsen Company.*

location while watching a live, 1-hour cable television program that included 55 advertisements. The levels of emotional arousal to the ads were compared with data from TiVo's database of 100,000 in-home viewers to see if there was a relationship between the levels of emotional response to the advertising and the probability of the ad being watched in its entirety. The results showed that ads with low emotional response based on the biometrics were 25% more likely to be skipped (either via fast-forwarding or channel changing) compared with ads with high emotional response.

While watching (i.e., not skipping) television ads is important, the next important behavior is getting consumers to comment about marketing communications. One proxy for measuring what consumers will say is to use the number of online Twitter "Tweets" (which include comments by viewers) per minute during a program episode. Nielsen neuroscientists recently reported a study of EEG activity and Twitter volume (Nielsen 2015). The study included more than 300 participants monitored in a central location watching nine television programs and found a positive relationship between an EEG-derived metric, an important component of which includes emotional response in the brain, and the number of comments on Twitter. While focused more on television programming than advertising, the study builds on prior research reported in the academic literature using EEG and fMRI to predict Twitter commenting activity (e.g., Dmochowski et al., 2014).

Another proxy for what consumers will say is to look at the number of views and comments for advertising online after the Super Bowl. In a 2009 study, a biometric measure of emotional engagement including skin conductance and heart rate collected live during the big game by Innerscope Research showed a significant and positive correlation to the number of views and comments for the national advertisements over the course of 9 months after the game (Seifert et al. 2009). Importantly, the results showed that the biometric response was better than traditional, conscious measures using dial-turning and self-report of emotion (i.e., stated liking).

Other behaviors related to advertising have been studied by academics using neuroscience tools including predicting population call volume in response to antismoking campaigns (Falk, Berkman, and Lieberman 2012). In this study, researchers investigated the brain activations in smokers using fMRI as they viewed three different television campaigns promoting the National Cancer Institute's telephone hotline as an aid to help smokers quit their habit. The number of phone calls to 1–800-QUIT-NOW was used as a behavioral response to the television advertisements. The results showed that a region in the brain known as the lower region of the medial prefrontal cortex that is also implicated in emotion processing predicted call volume better than the same participants' self-reports of the effectiveness of the campaign.

While predicting television advertising viewership, consumer expressions online, and call volume are important for marketers, the ultimate goal of marketing is to produce sales behavior. One of the first nonacademic studies to do so came

It is critical for marketers to consider emotion when creating their products and advertisements and to understand the consequences of not leveraging emotion to "stand out" from the clutter in the modern media and marketing landscape.

Ads with low emotional response based on the biometrics were 25% more likely to be skipped.

from Innerscope Research, which partnered with Mimoco, the manufacturer of Mimobots, a personalized USB digital storage device. Mimoco was interested in understanding which of its hundreds of designs—the company's primary marketing tool—would drive online sales behavior. Using biometric responses that combined skin conductance and heart rate accelerations plus state-of-the-art eye-tracking technology (a measure of visual attention), Innerscope analyzed the physiologic responses of 30 participants in a laboratory-based research protocol. The participants were exposed to more than 30 different designs in a randomized fashion (to control for order effects) while simultaneously collecting the nonconscious measures. The results of the analyses were combined with sales data from Mimoco and showed a significant positive correlation between the emotional response from the biometrics and the sales volume of the designs tested. When the biometric response was combined with one of the eye-tracking measures (fixation count), the correlation increased (Dooley 2012).

In addition to the sales correlation analyses, the Mimoco designs were reviewed by human coders to identify any similarities or differences between the top-selling and the weaker-selling items. This independent review revealed that the top performers tended to have certain qualities. The Mimobot design features a stylized figurine, and top performers tended to have more prominent eyes and other facial features as well as brighter colors (figure 7.4). The results were used

FIGURE 7.4
Results from a 2009 Innerscope Research study for Mimoco. Top-performing designs, based on a combination of biometrics and eye tracking, were colorful and had prominent facial features visible. The designs that shared these features performed well on the combined biometric and eye-tracking analysis and ended up being the highest sellers (with the exception of no. 26, which was emotionally arousing—likely due to the depiction of a scantily clad female—but did not sell well).

for several years to guide creative and sales-strategy decisions. "Our hit rate of producing good and great selling Mimobot designs has improved as a result of Innerscope's design recommendations," noted a Mimoco executive.

This research was followed by another Innerscope study that also used biometric responses to predict a sales-related index. In this case, the outcome was opening weekend box office sales and the levels of emotional response to movie trailers (Randall 2013). The study included 40 movie trailers for different films collected in more than 1,000 participants over the course of 2 years. The analyses used an index of biometric reactivity to measure the overall emotional response of the participants to the movie trailer. The results suggested that in addition to an overall correlation to ticket sales, a failure to reach a particular level of emotional response to a movie advertisement predicted a very poor performance in market (less than $10 million generated in the opening weekend). Importantly, the results also gave recommendations to film marketers on how the keys to success are based on the moment-to-moment emotional response (table 7.1). The outcome results were supported by a separate academic study that used EEG to also show a relationship between EEG activity in response to video-based movie trailers in a small sample correlated with movie sales in the general population (Boksem and Smidts 2015).

Finally, one of the clear trends in both academic and business applications of consumer neuroscience is to move beyond single measures and to combine multiple measures for comparison and for new predictive power. In one of the largest comparison studies to date, researchers at Temple University collaborated with the Advertising Research Foundation (ARF) in a study sponsored by large consumer package goods brands to investigate the relationship between a wide variety of neurometrics and in-market sales (Venkatraman et al. 2015). The results showed that for predicting the variance in sales elasticities (a measure of sales in

> A failure to reach a particular level of emotional response to a movie advertisement predicted a very poor performance in market (less than $10 million generated in the opening weekend).

TABLE 7.1
Five keys to box office sales success based on nonconscious biometric responses

1. Grab the audience early. Do not let the popcorn distract them. (See: *The Avengers*; *The Amazing Spider-Man*.)

2. Take them on an emotional journey. The classic hero's journey story line works in trailers, too. (See: *Kung Fu Panda 2*; *Flight*.)

3. Hold back some pivotal moments. Leave them wanting to see the movie for the full experience. (See: *Super 8*; *The Dark Knight Rises*.)

4. Watch out for attention vampires. Use special effects to support the story, not distract from it. (See: *Harry Potter and the Deathly Hallows*; *The Hunger Games*.)

5. Star power, action sequences, and cool music help, but ... great stories with compelling characters are what ultimately drive emotional response. (See: *Pirates of the Caribbean: On Stranger Tides*.)

relationship to the amount spent on media), fMRI was the best. In this study, an area of the brain called the ventral striatum (typically associated with emotional or behavioral reward) was the strongest predictor of real-world, market-level response to the advertising tested. The team at Temple University also partnered with Innerscope Research on a Super Bowl study that combined biometric responses (again, a combination of skin conductance and heart rate) with fMRI results (Lausch 2014). The results showed that ads that had very high levels of emotional response also showed increased activity in the ventral striatum and in other important emotional and memory centers including the amygdala and hippocampus.

The studies described in brief above cut across a range of technologies. They demonstrate their ability to capture emotional responses below conscious levels using the tools of consumer neuroscience and their relationship to relevant consumer behaviors. As alluded to above, the power of consumer neuroscience tools goes beyond correlating to important consumer behaviors. There is very strong explanatory power in consumer neuroscience, and the majority of the business applications focus on the diagnostic power of these nonconscious measures increasingly used by marketers of major companies around the world to improve their marketing communications. Future academic work will strive to resolve the remaining conflicts in models of emotion, and business applications will continue to show relationships between biological and brain responses and consumer behavior and continue to demonstrate the importance of measuring nonconscious processing of emotional response to advertising for market research.

KEY TAKEAWAYS

- Emotions—which are understood to be brief episodes of brain, autonomic, and behavioral changes—tag information as "relevant" and help guide future behavior.

- It is critical for marketers to consider emotion when creating products and advertisements, because emotional messaging or imagery can trigger brain-based responses that prioritize the brand's messaging for notice, long-term memory encoding, and attitude formation.

- Consumers are limited in their ability to fully articulate their thoughts, feelings, and beliefs or may be unwilling to share their truthful thoughts. Consumer neuroscience employs nonconscious measurement to create a more holistic picture of consumers' responses to stimuli.

- Consumer neuroscience techniques (such as EEG, biometrics, and eye tracking) are best used *in conjunction* with one another: each methodology has its own unique strengths and weaknesses, and the combination of measures can provide the most comprehensive insights.

• It has been demonstrated via in-market case studies that consumer neuroscience techniques can be significantly predictive of sales, online buzz, channel-changing, and other real-world behaviors.

DISCUSSION QUESTIONS

1. What neuroscience techniques would be the most appropriate for each of the following client business questions, and why? Note that more than one technique may be appropriate for testing some of these.

   • How do I know if individuals are noticing our branding in our latest advertising campaign?

   • Are the final 10 seconds of my advertising connecting with consumers on an emotional level?

   • What is the network of brain regions that is more active when consumers are viewing a series of successful in-market advertisements, relative to viewing a series of unsuccessful in-market advertisements?

2. What are the advantages and drawbacks of each of the following consumer neuroscience techniques?

   • Electroencephalography

   • Biometrics

   • Functional magnetic resonance imaging

   • Facial coding

3. You are an advertiser that is planning to launch a coordinated, cross-platform campaign. You will be running advertisements on television, along with video ads on social media sites such as YouTube and Facebook.
   • How would you pretest consumer responses to your campaign using consumer neuroscience techniques?

     ▪ What tools would you use?

     ▪ Why might some neuroscience tools not be appropriate for testing these types of content?

   • What conclusions would you draw or what actions might you take if you found that one of your advertisements was found to engage consumers on television, but *not* on social media sites?

REFERENCES

Aaker, D. A., Kumar, V., & Day, G. S. (2007). *Marketing research*. Hoboken, NJ: Wiley.

Adolphs, R., & Tranel, D. (2000). Emotion recognition and the human amygdala. In J. P. Aggleton (Ed.), *The amygdala* (pp. 587–630). New York: Oxford University Press.

Adolphs, R., Tranel, D., Hamann, S., Young, A. W., Calder, A. J., Phelps, E. A., et al. (1999). Recognition of facial emotion in nine individuals with bilateral amygdala damage. *Neuropsychologia*, 37, 1111–1117.

Aggleton, J. P. (1992). The contribution of the amygdala to normal and abnormal emotional states. *Trends in Neurosciences*, 16, 328–333.

Barrett, L. F. (2009). The future of psychology: Connecting mind to brain. *Perspectives on Psychological Science*, 4, 326–339.

Barrett, L. F., & Bliss-Moreau, E. (2009). Affective as a psychological primitive. *Advances in Experimental Social Psychology*, 41, 167–218.

Bechara, A., Tranel, D., Damasio, H., Adolphs, R., Rockland, C., & Damasio, A. R. (1995). Double dissociation of conditioning and declarative knowledge relative to the amygdala and hippocampus in humans. *Science*, 269, 1115–1118.

Bechara, A., Damasio, A. R., Damasio, H., & Anderson, S. W. (1994). Insensitivity to future consequences following damage to human prefrontal cortex. *Cognition*, 50, 7–15.

Bechara, A., Damasio, H., Tranel, D., & Damasio, A. R. (1997). Deciding advantageously before knowing the advantageous strategy. *Science*, 305, 599.

Binet, L., & Field, P. (2009). Empirical generalizations about advertising campaign success. *Journal of Advertising Research*, 49(2), 113–114.

Boksem, M., & Smidts, A. (2015). Brain responses to movie trailers predict individual preferences for movies and their population-wide commercial success. *JMR, Journal of Marketing Research*, 52, 482–492.

Brown, R., & Kulik, J. (1977). Flashbulb memories. *Cognition*, 5, 73–99.

Buchel, C., Morris, J., Dolan, R., & Friston, K. (1998). Brain systems mediating aversive conditioning: An event-related fMRI study. *Neuron*, 20, 947–957.

Cahill, L., & McGaugh, J. L. (1995). A novel demonstration of enhanced memory associated with emotional arousal. *Consciousness and Cognition*, 4, 410–421.

Cahill, L., Prins, B., Weber, M., & McGaugh, J. L. (1994). ß-Adrenergic activation and memory for emotional events. *Nature*, 371, 702–704.

Camerer, C., Loewenstein, G., & Prelec, D. (2005). Neuroeconomics: How neuroscience can inform economics. *Journal of Economic Literature*, 43, 9–64.

Coan, J. A., & Allen, J. J. B. (2004). Frontal EEG asymmetry as a moderator and mediator of emotion. *Biological Psychology*, 67, 7–49.

Coleman, N. V., & Williams, P. (2013). Feeling like my self: Emotion profiles and social identity. *Journal of Consumer Research*, 40, 203–222.

Cosmides, L., & Tooby, J. (2000). Evolutionary psychology and the emotions. In M. Lewis & J. M. Haviland-Jones (Eds.), *Handbook of emotions* (2nd ed., pp. 91–115). New York: Guilford Press.

Damasio, A. (1994). *Descartes' error: Emotion, reason, and the human brain*. New York: Putnam Berkeley Group.

Damasio, A. (2010). *Self comes to mind: Constructing the conscious brain*. New York: Pantheon Books.

Damasio, A. R., Everitt, B. J., & Bishop, D. (1996). The somatic marker hypothesis and the possible functions of the prefrontal cortex. *Philosophical Transactions of the Royal Society of London. Series B, Biological Sciences*, 351, 1413–1420.

Damasio, A. R., Tranel, D., & Damasio, H. C. (1991). Somatic markers and the guidance of behavior: Theory and preliminary testing. In H. S. Levin, H. M. Eisenberg, & L. B. Benton (Eds.), *Frontal lobe function and dysfunction* (pp. 217–229). New York: Oxford University Press.

Davidson, R. J., Scherer, K. R., & Goldsmith, H. H. (Eds.). (2002). *Handbook of affective sciences.* New York: Oxford University Press.

Davidson, R. J., Ekman, P., Saron, C. D., Senulis, J. A., & Friesen, W. V. (1990). Approach-withdrawal and cerebral asymmetry: Emotional expression and brain physiology. *Journal of Personality and Social Psychology*, 58, 330–341.

Davis, M. (1992). The role of the amygdala in fear and anxiety. *Annual Review of Neuroscience*, 15, 353–375.

Davis, M., Walker, D. L., Miles, L., & Grillon, C. (2010). Phasic vs sustained fear in rates and humans: Role of the extended amygdala in fear vs anxiety. *Neuropsychopharmacology*, 35, 105–135.

Dimofte, C. V. (2010). Implicit measures of consumer cognition: A review. *Psychology and Marketing*, 27, 921–937.

Dmochowski, J. P., Bezdak, M. A., Abelson, B. P., Johnson, J. S., Schumacher, E. H., & Parra, L. C. (2014). Audience preferences are predicted by temporal reliability of neural processing. *Nature Communications*, 5, 1–9.

Dooley, R. 2012. The neuromarketing challenge: First response [blog post]. Available at www.neurosciencemarketing.com/blog/articles/challenge-innerscope.htm

Ekman, P. (1972). Universal and cultural differences in facial expressions of emotions. In J. K. Cole (Ed.), *Nebraska symposium on motivation, 1971* (pp. 207–283). Lincoln: University of Nebraska Press.

Ekman, P., & Friesen, W. (1978). *Facial action coding system: A technique for the measurement of facial movement.* Palo Alto, CA: Consulting Psychologists Press.

Falk, E. B., Berkman, E. T., & Lieberman, M. D. (2012). From neural responses to population behavior: Neural focus group predicts population-level media effects. *Psychological Science*, 23, 439–445.

Feinstein, J. S., Adolphs, R., Damasio, A. R., & Tranel, D. (2010). The human amygdala and the induction and experience of fear. *Current Biology*, 21, 34–38.

Feinstein, J. S., Buzza, C., Hurlemann, R., Follmer, R. L., Dahdaleh, N. S., Coryell, W. H., et al. (2013). Fear and panic in humans with bilateral amygdala damage. *Nature Neuroscience*, 16, 270–272.

Fowles, D. C., Christie, M. J., Edelberg, R., Grings, W. W., Lykken, D. T., & Venables, P. H. (1981). Publication recommendations for electrodermal measurements. *Psychophysiology*, 18, 232–239.

Fridlund, A. (1994). *Human facial expression: An evolutionary view.* San Diego: Academic Press.

Gallagher, M., & Chiba, A. A. (1996). The amygdala and emotion. *Current Opinion in Neurobiology*, 6, 221–227.

Gentil, A. F., Eskandar, E. N., Marci, C. D., Evans, K. C., & Dougherty, D. D. (2009). Physiological responses to brain stimulation during limbic surgery: Further evidence of anterior cingulate modulation of autonomic arousal. *Neuron*, 66, 695–701.

Greenwald, A. G., McGhee, D. E., & Schwartz, J. L. K. (1998). Measuring individual differences in implicit cognition: The implicit association test. *Journal of Personality and Social Psychology*, 74, 1464–1480.

Greenwald, A. G., Nosek, B. A., & Banaji, M. R. (2003). Understanding and using the implicit association test: An improved scoring algorithm. *Journal of Personality and Social Psychology*, 85, 197–216.

Gross, J. J., & Barrett, L. F. (2011). Emotion generation and emotion regulation: One or two depends on your point of view. *Emotion Review*, 3, 8–16.

Hamann, S. (2001). Cognitive and neural mechanisms of emotional memory. *Trends in Cognitive Sciences*, 5, 394–400.

Harmon-Jones, E., Gable, P. A., & Peterson, C. K. (2010). The role of frontal cortical activity in emotion-related phenomena: A review and update. *Biological Psychology*, 84, 451–462.

Kahneman, D. (2011). *Thinking, fast and slow*. New York: Farrar, Straus and Giroux.

Kensinger, E. A. (2009). Remembering the details: Effects of emotion. *Emotion Review*, 1, 99–113.

Kensinger, E. A., & Corkin, S. (2004). Two routes to emotional memory: Distinct neural processes for valence and arousal. *Proceedings of the National Academy of Sciences of the United States of America*, 101, 3310–3315.

Kim, S.-G., Richter, W., & Ugurbil, K. (1997). Limitations of temporal resolution in functional MRI. *Magnetic Resonance in Medicine*, 37, 631–636.

Kityama, S. (1990). Interaction between affect and cognition in word perception. *Journal of Personality and Social Psychology*, 58, 209–217.

Klüver, H., & Bucy, P. C. (1939). Preliminary analysis of functions of the temporal lobes in monkeys. *Archives of Neurology and Psychiatry*, 42, 979–1000.

Kotses, H., & Glaus, K. D. (1977). Latency of multiple skin conductance responses in differential classical conditioning. *Biological Psychology*, 5, 1–6.

Kuniecki, M., Urbanik, A., Sobiecka, B., Kozub, J., & Binder, M. (2003). Central control of heart rate changes during visual affective processing as revealed by fMRI. *Acta Neurobiologiae Experimentalis*, 63, 39–48.

LaBar, K. S., & Cabeza, R. (2006). Cognitive neuroscience of emotional memory. *Nature Neuroscience Reviews*, 7, 54–64.

LaBar, K. S., LeDoux, J. E., Spencer, D. D., & Phelps, E. A. (1995). Impaired fear conditioning following unilateral temporal lobectomy in humans. *Journal of Neuroscience*, 15, 6846–6855.

Lang, P. J., Bradley, M. M., & Cuthbert, B. N. (1998). Emotion, motivation, and anxiety: Brain mechanisms and psychophysiology. *Biological Psychiatry*, 44, 1248–1263.

Lausch, B. 2014. Cutting edge research combines fMRI and biometric results to reveal key elements in Super Bowl ad success [online press release]. Available at www.fox.temple.edu/posts/2014/02/cutting-edge-research-combines-fmri-biometric-results-reveal-key-elements-super-bowl-ad-success/

LeDoux, J. E. (2000). Emotion circuits in the brain. *Annual Review of Neuroscience*, 23, 155–184.

Lindquist, K. A., & Barrett, L. F. (2012). A functional architecture of the human brain: Emerging insights from the science of emotion. *Trends in Cognitive Sciences*, 16, 533–540.

Lindquist, K. A., Wager, T. D., Kober, H., Bliss-Moreau, E., & Barrett, L. F. (2012). The brain basis of emotion: A meta-analytic review. *Behavioral and Brain Sciences*, 35, 121–202.

Logothetis, N. K., Pauls, J., Augath, M., Trinath, T., & Oeltermann, A. (2001). Neurophysiological investigation of the basis of the fMRI signal. *Nature*, 412, 150–157.

MacDougall, W. (1908/1921). *An introduction to social psychology*. Boston: John W. Luce.

Mangina, C. A., & Beuzeron-Mangina, J. H. (1996). Direct electrical stimulation of specific human brain structures and bilateral electrodermal activity. *International Journal of Psychophysiology*, 22, 1–8.

Marci, C. D., Glick, D. M., Low, R., & Dougherty, D. D. (2007). Autonomic and prefrontal cortex responses to autobiographical recall of emotions. *Cognitive, Affective & Behavioral Neuroscience*, 7, 243–250.

McDuff, D., Kaliouby, R. E., Senechal, T., Demirdjian, D., & Picard, R. (2014). Automatic measurement of ad preferences from facial responses gathered over the internet. *Image and Vision Computing*, 32, 630–640.

MediaPost. 2009. TiVo: Viewers don't skip engaging ads. Available at www.mediapost.com/publications/article/103233/tivo-viewers-dont-skip-engaging-ads.html.

Meyer, D. E., & Schvaneveldt, R. W. (1971). Facilitation in recognizing pairs of words: Evidence of a dependence between retrieval operations. *Journal of Experimental Psychology*, 90, 227–234.

Mick, D. G. (1996). Are studies of dark side variables confounded by socially desirable responding? The case of materialism. *Journal of Consumer Research*, 23, 106–119.

Mickley Steinmetz, K. R., & Kensinger, E. A. (2013). The emotion-induced memory trade-off: More than an effect of overt attention? *Memory & Cognition*, 41, 69–81.

Murray, B. D., & Kensinger, E. A. (2012). The effects of emotion and encoding strategy on associative memory. *Memory & Cognition*, 40, 1056–1069.

Murray, B. D., & Kensinger, E. A. (2014). The route to an integrative associative memory is influenced by emotion. *PLoS One*, 9, 1–8.

Niedermeyer, E., & da Silva, F. L. (2004). *Electroencephalography: Basic principles, clinical applications, and related fields*. Philadelphia: Lippincott, Williams & Wilkins.

Nielsen. 2015. Brain activity predicts social, T. V. engagement [white paper online]. Available at www.nielsen.com/content/dam/nielsenglobal/co/docs/Reports/2015/Nielsen%20Neuro%20Report%20 April%202015.pdf.

Ogawa, S., Lee, T. M., Kay, A. R., & Tank, D. W. (1990). Brain magnetic resonance imaging with contrast dependent on blood oxygenation. *Proceedings of the National Academy of Sciences of the United States of America*, 87, 9868–9872.

Öhman, A., Flykt, A., & Esteves, F. (2001). Emotion drives attention: Detecting the snake in the grass. *Journal of Experimental Psychology. General*, 130, 466–478.

Panksepp, J. (1998). *Affective neuroscience: The foundations of human and animal emotions*. New York: Oxford University Press.

Payne, B. K., Cheng, C. M., Govorun, O., & Stewart, B. D. (2005). An inkblot for attitudes: Affect misattribution as implicit measurement. *Journal of Personality and Social Psychology*, 89, 277–293.

Randall, K. 2013. How your brain can predict blockbusters. Available at https://www.fastcompany.com/3006186/how-your-brain-can-predict-blockbusters.

Russell, J. A. (1980). A circumplex model of affect. *Journal of Personality and Social Psychology*, 39, 1161–1178.

Russell, J. A. (2003). Core affect and the psychological construction of emotion. *Psychological Review*, 110, 145–172.

Russell, J. A., & Fernandez-Dols, J. M. (1997). *The psychology of facial expression*. New York: Cambridge University Press.

Sabatinelli, D., Bradley, M. M., Fitzsimmons, J. R., & Lang, P. J. (2005). Parallel amygdala and inferotemporal activation reflect emotional intensity and fear relevance. *NeuroImage*, 24, 1265–1270.

Schacter, S., & Singer, J. E. (1962). Cognitive, social, and physiological determinants of emotional state. *Psychological Review*, 69, 379–399.

Schwarz, N., & Clore, G. L. (1983). Mood, misattribution, and judgments of well-being: Informative and directive functions of affective states. *Journal of Personality and Social Psychology*, 45, 513–523.

Seifert, C. J., Kothuri, R., Jacobs, D., Levine, B., Plummer, J., & Marci, C. D. (2009). Winning the Super Bowl buzz: How biometrically-based emotional engagement correlates with online views and comments for Super Bowl advertisements. *Journal of Advertising Research*, 49, 293–303.

Stroop, J. R. (1935). Studies of interference in serial verbal reactions. *Journal of Experimental Psychology*, 18, 643–662.

Talmi, D., Luk, B. T. C., McGarry, L. M., & Moscovitch, M. (2007). The contribution of relatedness and distinctiveness to emotionally-enhanced memory. *Journal of Memory and Language*, 56, 555–574.

Talmi, D., Anderson, A. K., Riggs, L., Caplan, J. B., & Moscovitch, M. (2008). Immediate memory consequences of the effect of emotion on attention to pictures. *Learning & Memory (Cold Spring Harbor, N.Y.)*, 15, 172–182.

Teixeira, T., Picard, R., & Kaliouby, R. (2014). Why, when and how much to entertain consumers in advertisements? A web based facial tracking field study. *Marketing Science*, 33, 809–827.

Treutler, T., Levine, B., & Marci, C. D. (2010). Biometrics and multi-platform messaging: The medium matters. *Journal of Advertising Research*, 50, 243–249.

van Stegeran, A. H., Everaerd, W., Cahill, L., McGaugh, J. L., & Gooren, L. J. (1998). Memory for emotional events: Differential effects of centrally versus peripherally acting beta-blocking agents. *Psychopharmacology*, 138, 305–310.

Venkatraman, V., Dimoka, A., Pavlou, P., Vo, K., Hampton, W., Bollinger, B., et al. (2015). Predicting advertising success beyond traditional measures: New insights from neurophysiological methods and marketing response modeling. *JMR, Journal of Marketing Research*, 52, 436–452.

Vytal, K., & Hamann, S. (2010). Neuroimaging support for discrete neural correlates of basic emotions: A voxel-based meta-analysis. *Journal of Cognitive Neuroscience*, 22, 2864–2885.

Weber, R., Mangus, M. J., & Huskey, R. (2015). Brain imaging in communication research: A practical guide to understanding and evaluating fMRI studies. *Communication Methods and Measures*, 9, 5–29.

Wundt, W. (1897/1998). *Outlines of psychology* (C. H. Judd, Trans.). Bristol, UK: Thoemmes Press.

CHAPTER 8

DECISION MAKING

MORAN CERF

"Would you tell me, please, which way I ought to go from here?"
"That depends a good deal on where you want to get to," said the Cat.
"I don't much care where—" said Alice.
"Then it doesn't matter which way you go," said the Cat.
"So long as I get SOMEWHERE," Alice added as an explanation.
"Oh, you're sure to do that," said the Cat, "if you only walk long enough."
—Lewis Carroll, *Alice in Wonderland*

8.1 INTRODUCTION

Decision science has exploded as a research topic in the past decade, and because so many of our decisions are economic, decision science incorporates the fields of behavioral economics and cognitive neuroscience as well as studies of irrational behavior. Why should the field of marketing care about decision-making processes then? So much of consumer behavior depends on making a choice: which product to buy when, where, and for how much. Which products and promotions will appeal to which consumers? Do customers really relate to brands as they do to people? Consumer neuroscience can answer these questions and more.

The more we understand human decision-making processes, the more likely we are to make consumers choose what we want and help them make more satisfying choices. Marketers need to understand what goes through the mind when we make a choice, and neuroscience is essential to this understanding. Brain imaging studies allow us to see what participants are unable to report. People are not always

> The more we understand human decision-making processes, the more likely we are to make consumers choose what we want and help them make more satisfying choices.

able to articulate their choices and may tell themselves a story about their choice that is not necessarily true. For example, a woman may reason that buying a too-small dress is okay because she will soon lose enough weight to fit in it. Other people are unwilling to explain their choices and are uncomfortable with answering certain questions. For example, if you polled the public about their porn-viewing behavior, would you expect to receive accurate responses?

That being said, choice is a fundamental human behavior, and we love having choices. Burger King's slogan for many years was "Have it your way." Similarly, Starbucks offers thousands of beverage customization options. The United States is known as the "land of opportunities," and Americans are encouraged to explore all alternatives for everything from potato chip flavors to which college to attend. We also believe that we express ourselves via our choices and that our "likes" define us. What book are you reading? What did you have for breakfast? How do these decisions set you apart from others? We believe that our choices are ours alone and that we can explain how and why we made each choice. In this chapter, we will show that this is not necessarily true.

8.2   WHO REALLY DECIDES?

Science often deals with simple choices such as A or B, left or right, red pill versus blue pill. This choice format is called 2-alternative-forced-choice, or 2AFC. However, most choices in life are not binary and are more complex than the "pill in the *Matrix*." Outside of the lab, the full set of options for a decision is not always clear, and the options do not always present themselves at the same time. The probability of a purchase decision is thought to depend on brand awareness first then brand consideration second. In a marketing context, a *consideration set* is defined as the group of brands a consumer evaluates when making a purchase, given awareness of those brands (Roberts 1989). This differs from the *choice set* presented in most empirical studies, which may involve hypothetical or disguised products.

Consumer choices are also influenced by which items a retailer decides to carry. For example, your local drugstore may stock only four or five kinds of toothpaste instead of every toothpaste available on the market. In this way, the drugstore biases your decision by narrowing your set of options.

While there are many ways to explain the mechanisms by which a choice happens, ranging from the influence of the options on the decision to the set of parameters that manipulate a choice, we focus here on the building blocks of the decision process in the brain. Although decision-making processes reside in our brain, the process by which we make a decision is not entirely accessible to us. Multiple studies in neuroscience and psychology have shown that although we arrive at an outcome every time we make a decision, the narrative or explanation of the path that led to that specific decision is often beyond our grasp. Simply put, our decisions are so complex and obscure that we are not able to articulate entirely the process by which a choice was determined. Between the moment our brain arrived at the decision and the time we are asked to articulate it are a number of steps that obscure the decision parameters, change them, and even reverse them entirely.

To demonstrate, Johansson and colleagues (2005) investigated the relation between intention, choice, and self-reflection. Participants were shown pairs of faces and asked to choose the more attractive face. Seemingly, this is an easy choice and one that does not require much thinking or elaborative processing. We just look at the alternatives and can easily select the most attractive face without the need for much deliberation. In these studies, a participant is usually presented with two cards, each showing a face, and asked to point to the one he or she finds more attractive. Then they receive the card they selected and are asked to explain why they preferred that face. However, in this experiment, the researchers manipulated the outcomes so that participants received, at times, the alternative card—the face they did not choose. Most participants failed to notice the manipulation and proceeded to give explanations for their "choice," unaware that they were reflecting on the wrong preference. The researchers call this obliviousness to past decisions *choice blindness*. We are, surprisingly, unable to recognize and interpret our own decisions.

There is much room for neuroscience research to explain who decides and how they do it by peeking inside the brain of a subject to see both the part of the brain that makes the original choice and the part of the brain that explains the choice and by following the flow of information to show that the deciding and explaining parts of the brain are independent. Whereas we think our decisions are set and fixed and explicable, it turns out that we tend to explain things in the present on the basis of evidence from the past that resides in our brain. However, we do not really have access to the past self that made the choice. Therefore, if I change your choice and convince you that this was your decision, you will tell *yourself* a story that convinces you that the choice is yours. If you make a choice at time $t = 0$, and store it in your memory, and at a later time the choice is changed without your knowledge, you may likely accept the new outcome as the result of your prior decision. You will not only *not* question it, but also you will proceed into the future explaining to yourself and others the wrong choice, thinking it was always yours. Imagine what this means for marketing: I can change the things you thought you wanted, and you will *help me* by justifying why you wanted them all along.

Many of the models of decision making make an explicit distinction between the processes that give rise to intuitive judgments and those responsible for more deliberate reasoning. Collectively, these processes tend to be referred to as two

Although decision-making processes reside in our brain, the process by which we make a decision is not entirely accessible to us.

Participants failed to notice the manipulation and proceeded to give explanations for their "choice," unaware that they were reflecting on the wrong preference.

If I change your choice and convince you that this was your decision, you will tell yourself a story that convinces you that the choice is yours.

TABLE 8.1
Features of the two systems governing "thinking" in our brain

System 1	System 2
Automatic processes that lead to "intuitive" judgments	"Reflective" processes that lead to reasoned judgments
Fast	Slow
Automatic	Controlled
Associative and heuristics-based	Rule-based and analytical
High capacity	Low capacity
Context dependent	Context independent
Concrete reasoning only	Capable of abstract reasoning
Parallel processes	Serial processes
Evolutionarily old	Evolutionarily recent

"systems" (popularized in recent publications such as Kahneman's *Thinking, Fast and Slow*) with separate and contrasting characteristics (table 8.1): System 1 processes have more influence on our choices than we often assume. We tend to characterize "thought" as involving only the rational, effortful, slow-thinking System 2–type processes, and therefore we assume these System 2 processes must be responsible for all of our decisions. In reality, we often overstate their importance in motivating us to do things, and the "fast thinking" of System 1 often influences our decisions more than we imagine.

8.2.1 SYSTEM 1 PROCESSES PROVIDE DIRECT SHORTCUTS FOR THE BRAIN TO USE FOR DECISIONS

The information from these automatic processes is often sufficient for the brain to make a decision without needing to engage our slower, deliberate thought systems very much, and when we can get away with basing our decisions primarily on the easy automatic processes, we will.

As Erik du Plessis discusses in his book *The Advertised Mind,* one of the benefits of this kind of decision making is the speed with which it allows us to act in circumstances where delay could present great danger. Referencing the work of Prof. Joseph LeDoux (1998) on fear and the brain's response to potentially dangerous stimuli, he describes encountering a twig shaped like a snake while out on a hike in an area where encountering a snake would not be uncommon:

> Immediately, involuntarily you are afraid. This produces a physical reaction: you will freeze, and your heart rate will increase. Then, with luck, you will realise that the twig really is only a twig. Slowly your body will return to its normal state, and you go happily on with your hike.

The reaction we have to the potential danger posed by the twig is the product of a purely System 1–based judgment. We have not had time to process the stimulus fully and decide on a considered course of action (or else we would have noticed it was only a stick and needed no special response), but the automatic responses evoked by the "rough and dirty" visual processing have been enough to alert the brain to the potential danger and prepare the body for fight or flight (box 8.1).

Box 8.1
Milward Brown on how System 1 Is Involved with Choices

GRAHAM PAGE AND SARAH WALKER

A recent Millward Brown study looking at people's instinctive, System 1 responses to snakes showed a strong link between people's involuntary reactions and their reported fear. Using what they call the "emotional priming paradigm" (based on the principles of the implicit association task pioneered by Anthony Greenwald and colleagues at Harvard), they measured inherent positivity or negativity toward an object, concept, or brand.

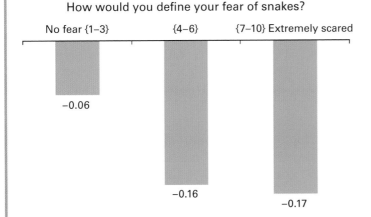

How would you define your fear of snakes?

They see that people who express a fear of snakes have much stronger automatic negative reactions to them than those without fear (see figure), which likely results from the same involuntary processes that cause us to be afraid of the twig. Notably, those who admitted only a moderate fear of snakes actually exhibited almost as strong a response as those who admitted being extremely scared. Whether these people are just unwilling to admit a stronger fear or whether they have developed coping strategies to lessen the impact of their instinctive responses on their mood or mental state,

Box 8.1
(continued)

> we do not know. But the stronger our intuitive System 1 responses in a situation, the more likely we will be to make a System 1–suggested decision.
>
> For brands, these shortcuts will have less to do with fear or survival and more to do with pointing us toward safe or reliable choices with minimal effort. In most cases, the System 1 response to a brand will be less strong than to a snake, but often no less influential. In many situations involving purchase or product choice, the ability to decide quickly is far more important to us than the feeling of confidence and certainty that might arise from deliberate consideration. Consequently, many brand decisions are made predominantly on the basis of System 1 judgments that rely on the same kind of mental shortcuts as those that prepare us to respond to danger. These might include picking the option that evokes the strongest positive emotional response, feels the most familiar, or even reminds us of a situation in which it worked before. Using any of these as heuristics to make a decision allows us to make that decision far more quickly and with less effort than if we considered and fully thought through each decision.

8.2.2   SYSTEM 1 RESPONSES ALSO FRAME ANY SYSTEM 2 THINKING THAT DOES OCCUR

Because they are rapid and automatically activated, System 1 processes are "always on," and any outputs are always available to the brain before the slower System 2 thinking is initiated. One of the consequences of this is that these automatic outputs provide the backdrop for any analytical processing that does occur and will inevitably "frame" this thinking.Because they are rapid and automatically activated, System 1 processes are "always on," and any outputs are always available to the brain before the slower System 2 thinking is initiated.

The most widely known description of this kind of framing comes from Damasio's work on emotions and their roles in decision making. He describes events and memories as having "somatic markers" that influence the way they are processed by the brain. Damasio characterizes a somatic marker as an emotional "tag" that gets ascribed to the mental representation of a situation, object, or place. The tag then acts as a signal to the brain whenever it encounters or considers that thing and sets the scene for interpretation or consideration of other things we think or hear about it.

Damasio's work with brain-damaged patients demonstrates the importance of these emotional markers to our ability to make decisions. He demonstrates that without the ability to generate the relevant emotional backdrop to rational thinking, patients with damage to the frontal lobes (particularly the ventromedial prefrontal cortex) make poorer, less-optimal decisions. Damasio posits that the reason behind these impaired decisions is that the damage results in an inability to use emotions

(sidebar) Because they are rapid and automatically activated, System 1 processes are "always on," and any outputs are always available to the brain before the slower System 2 thinking is initiated.

from past experience to highlight potential appropriate responses in future decisions, which forces these patients to rely on slow and laborious cost-benefit analyses (System 2) for every given choice.

He does not suggest that the role of this emotional tag is to become the sole basis for decision-making itself, without needing any conscious thought (as many often misinterpret), but that these emotional markers create a rapidly occurring "soma," which provides the backdrop against which subsequent cognition or deliberate "thinking" occurs. Damasio does not suggest that emotion drives all of our decisions directly; rather, these emotional tags help set the relevant context for the decision in order for it to be made more easily and quickly. Damasio is saying emotion has a foot on the accelerator, not that it is holding the steering wheel.

Consider this situation: I am in the market for buying a new car. I go to a dealership and see that two possible models fit my broad criteria and price bracket, car A and car B. Instinctively, I like car A better (an intuitive process), and find it the more attractive option—the clear winner if I were to rely on my System 1 response. However, because it is an important decision, I am motivated to start considering some of the facts about performance, and so forth—engaging System 2—to weigh up the two options and make a more "rational" choice.

But it is impossible to make this "rational" analysis in isolation—I am not able to block out my original preference for car A, and so even if I choose not to decide on this basis, I ca not help but be aware of my preference, which affects how easy it is for me to make a "rational" choice. If the information that I'm rationally considering *supports* this preference, it will be a much easier decision than if I have to use the analytical reasoning to overcome and disregard my inherent preference and choose car B.

8.2.3 SYSTEM 1 CAN BE OVERRULED WHEN IT NEEDS TO BE

While important, our instinctive response is not the only thing that governs our behavior, and we are able to override it if we want to or if the situation demands it. Take as example the process of recognizing a person in the street: I am not in control of whether I choose to recognize him or remember his name, but I can choose not to stop and speak to him if I am in a rush, even if I might want to.

This ability to override our instincts is evolutionarily quite recent and is certainly more developed in humans than in other species that survive predominantly on System 1 responses. It is also something that develops over the course of our lifetimes. As children, we are guided largely by our instinctive responses to things and often have difficulty overriding our desire to act on them. As we grow up and learn to cooperate in groups and on tasks, we develop better abilities to suppress the responses suggested by our intuitive systems and exert more control over our choice of actions. This explains why a 3-year-old left alone in a room with sweets is usually unable to resist eating them even when told not to, while a 9-year-old can.

This ability to override our instincts is evolutionarily quite recent and is certainly more developed in humans than in other species that survive predominantly on System 1.

In humans, System 1 processes signal to the brain potentially important intuitive responses that might be useful for a given decision. The brain, however, does not *have* to act on them. System 2 is virtually always able to overrule System 1's response if it needs to—as long as it has the time, capacity, and motivation to do so.

8.2.4 DIFFERENT SYSTEMS DOMINATE IN DIFFERENT CONTEXTS

Engaging our System 2 processes to deliberately consider decisions takes time and effort, so we need to be motivated to do it—otherwise we will default to our intuitive reactions or even avoid making any decision altogether. However, when we do choose to make a decision—particularly one that involves spending money—we are usually motivated to want to make the right choice, even if it involves a certain degree of effort.

But it is not always easy. The extent to which System 2 can and will override System 1 depends on the context in which the decision is being made, and whether these contextual factors cue the brain to rely on one system over the other.

In any decision, almost the first thing our brains have to decide is which route is the best way of getting to that decision: the fast, easy one that relies predominantly on System 1 processes or the slower and more effortful approach that engages more System 2 processes to provide more rigor at the expense of speed and resource conservation (figure 8.1).

The context in which the decision is being made has a big impact on which route is taken. Our brain's default is to try to use System 1 processes wherever possible, because it is quick, easy, and requires far less mental capacity. However, there are situations that require the more deliberate thought of slower System 2. The brain must assess which risk is worse: the risk of being wrong or the risk of being slow (figure 8.2)?

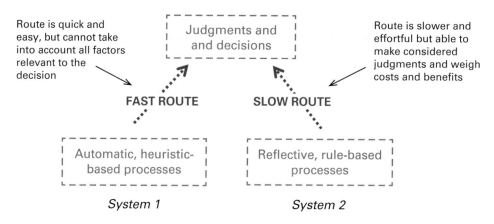

FIGURE 8.1
System 1 and System 2.

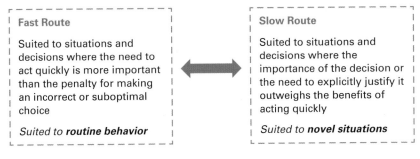

FIGURE 8.2
Fast route and slow route.

As well as influencing the type of processing or route that is favored by the brain, context can also affect how able each of these routes is to proceed, depending on what information we have (what we know), our mental state and cognitive capacity (how we are feeling, etc.), and what else we are trying to do at the time (figure 8.3).

It is clear just from the length of the two lists that there are many more contextual factors that bias us toward relying predominantly on System 1's "fast thinking," even in cases where we are motivated to expend the effort making the right decision. Consequently, we see the influences of these System 1 processes in many situations, and understanding their influence is vital when trying to make sense of how people make decisions in reality.

8.3 WHEN DO WE DECIDE?

For a while now, scientists have been exploring the processes that drive our decisions "behind our back," specifically addressing the question, "How earlier *before* I make a decision can one know what I am about to choose?" Researchers are finding ways to identify a choice before it happens and see the interplay between various brain mechanisms prior to the subject's awareness of his or her own choice (i.e., the gap between the moment our brain makes a choice and the moment we are aware of it). Central to this research is the discovery that we can locate single neurons in the brain that code the decision to act. Fried, Mukamel, and Kreiman (2011), replicating the work of Benjamin Libet, recorded the activity of neurons in the medial frontal lobe while participants watched a revolving clock, deciding to stop the clock at a certain time. After stopping the clock, the participants were asked to identify the moment where they felt the urge to act—the moment they felt the will to press the button that stops the clock. Subjects reported their intention to act fractions of a second before they pressed the button. While motor neurons

Factors favoring
SYSTEM 1

Factors favoring
SYSTEM 2

STRENGTH OF THE INPUTS

How much do our brains know about the options?

How easily is this knowledge accessed?

How strong is our instinctive emotional response to the options?

The stronger the input, the stronger the System 1 responses will be.

COMPLEXITY OF DECISION

How complex is the decision?

Does it require abstract reasoning?

Decisions that require complex or hypothetical reasoning need involvement from System 2. System 1 cannot solve these problems on its own.

SYSTEM 2 CAPACITY

How many other things are we trying to think about at the same time?

How many other things are vying for our attention?

How much hard thinking have we had to do already?

We only have limited System 2 resources, so if they are already occupied or depleted by previous hard thought, then they are less able to override System 1.

IMPORTANCE

How important is it to get the answer correct?

Will we need to justify our decisions?

More important decisions will increase our motivation to engage System 2.

MENTAL STATE

How tired are we?

Tiredness decreases our ability to overide our System 1 responses, increasing our reliance on our instincts.

TIME PRESSURE

How important is it to decide quickly?

The need for quick decisions favors a reliance on System 1 responses.

FIGURE 8.3
Factors favoring System 1 and System 2.

were actively "planning" the button press a short time before the instruction to press the button, other neurons in the medial temporal lobe fired even earlier than the decision and before the moment the subjects identified as the first time they felt the urge to stop the clock (at 1.5 seconds before the reported urge to press the button and 2 seconds before the actual press). This means that neural activity precedes the experience of free will (also called *volition*) and can predict when volition will occur.

In a similar study, Perez and colleagues (2015) examined the neural processes behind decisions such as route and turn selection while driving a virtual car. The researchers recorded electrical brain activity in patients making turn decisions (right vs. left) in a computer-based driving simulator and found that activity in the premotor cortex preceded subjects' reported time of decisions. This allowed the researchers to accurately predict the content of the subjects' decisions.

Cerf and Mackay (2011) were also able to anticipate subjects' decisions in the lab. They put electrodes in subjects' brains and gave them two buttons to press (right or left; figure 8.4). Subjects were told to press the button of their choice at will but to not touch a button when it was lit up. The researchers found cells in each subject's brain that coded the decision to press the button, and the researchers used this information to turn on the intended button before the subject had a chance to press it. The subjects never realized that their brain activity was triggering the buttons to light up (Cerf 2015).

Together, these studies show that decisions happen in our brain seconds before they are accessible to us. Free will happens earlier than we think, and that the idea of "I decided" is only partially right. We do not arrive at our decisions independently. As a marketer, this means that I can learn your preferences and start catering to those preferences early in the purchasing process, eventually driving your behavior in a certain direction. For example, if I discover that you are drawn to the color blue, I can show you more blue items and influence you to buy blue before you realize that is what you want.

> Neural activity precedes the experience of free will (also called volition) and can predict when volition will occur.

> I can learn your preferences and start catering to those preferences early in the purchasing process, eventually driving your behavior in a certain direction.

8.4   WHAT FACTORS AFFECT OUR DECISIONS?

If marketing managers understand the parameters of decision making, they can better understand and influence consumer choices. The many factors that affect our decisions include emotions, cognitive load, aspects of the physical environment, culture, the availability of options, and memories. We will discuss these factors in the following subsections.

8.4.1   EMOTION

Emotion is one of the primary drivers of our decisions. Perceived as *gut feelings* or intuitions, emotions allow us to make split-second decisions and predictions

(a)

(b)

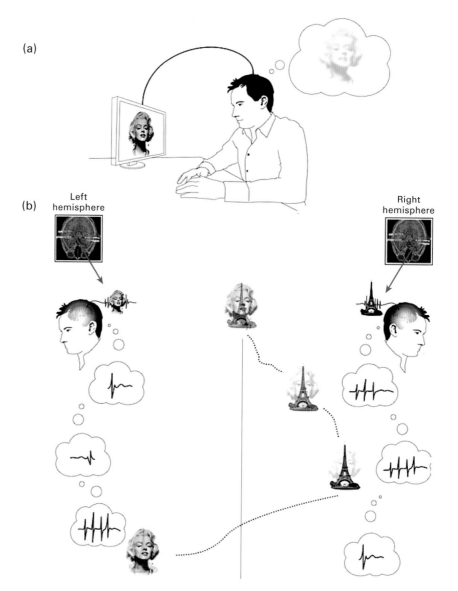

FIGURE 8.4

(a) Recording from intracranial electrodes, neurons are identified that respond to a specific concept. In this instance, a cell responsive to the image of Marilyn Monroe was found. This cell increases its firing rate to the image or thought of Monroe. (b) This cell is then pitted against one found to represent the Eiffel Tower. The two images are superimposed, and the subject is asked to bring the image of Monroe to maximum visibility. The visibility of the image is controlled by real-time decoding of the activity of each neuron relative to the other neuron and its own baseline. In this example, we show a case where the subject initially begins to fail the experiment—the firing of the Eiffel neuron increases and the visibility of the tower increases, creating negative feedback. However, the subject is able to exert control and, by concentrating on the internal thought of Monroe, is able to override this sensory input and increase the firing rate of the Monroe neuron and decrease that of the Eiffel neuron, bringing the image of Monroe to visibility. The scans show the location of the respective electrodes within the brain. Credit: Moran Cerf.

with little mental effort. Yuval Harari (2015) defines emotions as biochemical algorithms that developed over millions of years of natural selection to streamline the brain's cognitive processes. For example, if we see a lion approaching us, we feel afraid, and that fear compels us to run away. We do not waste time or risk our life deciding what to do—we just run. Today, some of these algorithms may be out of date or maladaptive. For example, we may choose a romantic partner based purely on physical appearance even though a less attractive partner may be a better choice, because humans evolved to favor attractive partners in mating.

Accordingly, one can suggest that, in the future, machines may actually come to know what is best for us. We already feed search engines massive amounts of data on our preferences and habits. Eventually, these engines could develop algorithms that are more accurate than our own, because they are free of human cognitive biases.

Nonconscious biases can be very beneficial, though, in helping us navigate risk. The *Iowa gambling task* was developed to measure risk aversion, or to what extent someone avoids taking a risk (Bechara et al. 1994). In this task, players are shown four decks of cards and told to choose one card at a time to try to win the most amount of money. Two of the decks contain larger rewards than the others but also larger penalties; they are "bad decks." Most players learn to avoid these decks after a certain number of losses, but patients with damage to the ventromedial prefrontal cortex keep drawing from the bad decks, oblivious to the penalties. The researchers also found that healthy participants "know" which decks are bad before they can consciously report this knowledge. In the Bechara et al. (1997) study, healthy participants showed skin conductance responses (an indicator of stress) in anticipation of drawing from the risky decks, and, although not fully aware of it at the time, participants changed their strategy to make better choices. Emotions served as a nonconscious bias to guide behavior to a more advantageous outcome.

8.4.2 COGNITIVE LOAD

According to Shiv and Fedorikhin (1999), there are two types of decision-making processes: affective and cognitive. The affective, or emotional, process is fairly automatic, whereas the cognitive process is more controlled. When the cognitive process is activated, we consciously think about the consequences of our actions, and those thoughts impact our choice. We are more likely to engage in this process when mental resources, such as energy and attention, are available. When resources are low, our decisions tend to be automatic and impulsive. Shiv and Fedorikhin manipulated availability of resources in participants by giving them a chore: half had to memorize a seven-digit number and the other half a two-digit number. Participants were then faced with two alternatives for a snack: chocolate cake or fruit salad. As predicted, those who had to memorize the seven-digit number were more likely to choose the cake over the fruit salad. The *cognitive load* required for the memory chore deceased their willpower. However, this effect was only seen in

> In the future, machines may actually come to know what is best for us. We already feed search engines massive amounts of data on our preferences and habits. Eventually, these engines could develop algorithms that are more accurate than our own, because they are free of human cognitive biases.

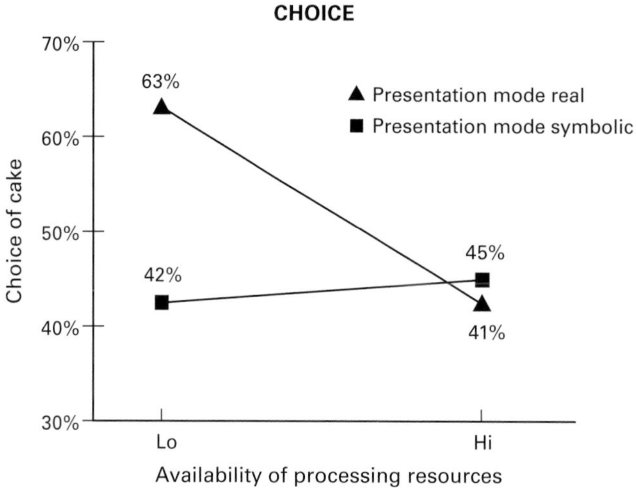

CHOICE

FIGURE 8.5
Choice and decision basis as a function of processing resources and presentation mode.

When resources are low, our decisions tend to be automatic and impulsive.

Marketers who want to increase impulsive purchasing behavior would benefit from actions designed to increase cognitive load in the shopping environment.

participants who were presented with the actual foods rather than symbols (i.e., photographs) of the foods. When they saw photos, lack of willpower did not affect their snack choice (figure 8.5). Participants high in impulsivity were particularly susceptible to choosing the cake when processing resources were low.

On the basis of these findings, marketers who want to increase impulsive purchasing behavior would benefit from actions designed to increase cognitive load in the shopping environment. For example, retailers could play music to distract shoppers or they could display trivia questions to keep shoppers' minds occupied while browsing. Retailers could also reduce checkout time so consumers have less chance to mull over what is in their carts and a greater chance of leaving the store with an impulse purchase.

Even when deciding between the same brands to fulfill the same need, the mental context can make a big difference. A 2013 global study by LivePerson showed consumers were far more likely to "impulse buy" when in a store environment than when shopping for the same products online. Undoubtedly, part of this effect is being driven by stronger System 1 responses that arise from the greater array of brand and purchase cues in-store: rather than just the text and images available online, in-store decisions will be influenced by physical interaction with products, visual displays, audio cues—even fragrances. The social pressure of the in-store environment also means that people are less likely to pull out of a purchase once it has been started, whereas the absence of this in an online context means basket abandonment is a huge challenge for e-commerce (figure 8.6).

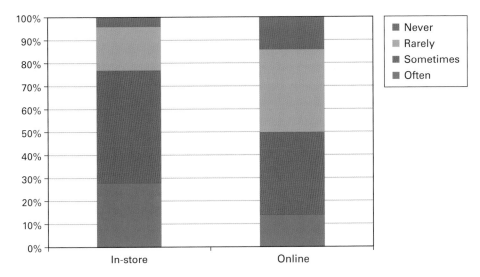

FIGURE 8.6
Frequency of impulse shopping online versus in-store. Data source: *The Connecting with Customers Report*, LivePerson (2013).

Even in-store, the local context can have a big impact. The effects of point-of-sale marketing are well documented, but even the presence of different competitors on the shelf can have a big influence on whether any brand is bought or not.

Some brands have used the influence of context to their benefit. Nespresso famously "re-framed" the value that people assigned to their 60-cents-per-cup price point by positioning themselves not as an alternative to other in-home coffees (it would take $150 worth of Nespresso capsules to get the same amount of brew you would get from a single jar of ordinary coffee!), but to the far more inflated prices of big coffee chains.

There is also evidence that making people think harder while making a purchase can actively deter people from purchasing. Though increasing choice in a decision increases the potential options for people and can motivate them more to make a selection than when there is very limited choice, a study by Iyengar and Lepper (2000) demonstrated that these effects get reversed when respondents experience what they term "choice overload."

Iyengar and Lepper compared the subsequent purchase rates of jams that were part of a tasting display in a grocery store for which respondents were given a $1-off coupon. When the choice of jams in the tasting display was relatively limited (six to choose from), about 30% of respondents that stopped to taste jams subsequently used their discount coupon to purchase one of the jams. When the tasting display included 24 jams, however, though more people stopped at the booth initially, on

Consumers were far more likely to "impulse buy" when in a store environment than when shopping for the same products online.

average, people sampled the same number of jams as they had in the limited display, and subsequent purchase rates fell to just 3%. Respondents visiting the 24-jam booth reported finding the choices more difficult, more frustrating, and ultimately less satisfying than those who had been given the more limited choice. Too much choice meant respondents had to think harder to differentiate between the options—a process we humans try to avoid, and one that can have hugely detrimental consequences on decision motivation.

To fully understand how consumers make decisions, brands and marketers must recognize the importance of context and framing on the processes involved and the roles that brands and their communications can play as cues to shape them. The influence of context is clearly important in a purchase situation, so it has obvious implications for things like retail and point of sale. But context is also something we need to bear in mind when researching brands. The influence of an ad on responses in a pretest will not translate directly into sales, because that actual decision will be made in a different context with other influences. This does not mean those survey responses are "wrong"—we just need to be mindful that showing an ad or asking about a brand in a simple category context cannot replicate the variations in context that will play a big role in any individual purchase decision.

8.4.3 THE ENVIRONMENT

Cognition is not strictly confined to the mind. Thoughts can be influenced by physical sensations, a phenomenon known as embodied cognition. Imagine that you are conducting an important business negotiation. Would you rather sit in a high chair, towering over everyone else in the room, or sit in a low chair, with everyone looking down upon you? You would probably prefer the high chair, just as a king or queen prefers to sit upon a throne. The height of the chair affects how grandiose we feel and how confident we act, because we associate height with status. Likewise, the weight of a notebook can affect the depth of the thoughts we write in it, because we think of importance as heavy. Williams and Bargh (2008) found empirical support for embodied cognition in their study of the effect of temperature on judgments of personality. Participants who held a warm cup of coffee were more likely to rate a target person as "warm" compared to participants who held a cup of iced coffee. The researchers concluded that the physical experience of warmth influenced feelings and perceptions of interpersonal warmth, without the participant being aware of such influences.

Hunger and fatigue can have a tremendous effect on decision-making processes. Imagine that you are a judge in charge of granting parole. Would you think that time of day could affect your ruling decisions? Probably not. However, Danziger, Levav, and Avnaim-Pesso (2011) found that judges in Israel were more likely to grant parole at the beginning of the day or right after taking a break compared to later in the day or right before lunch, presumably because they were more tired and hungry before a break (figure 8.7).

> Too much choice meant respondents had to think harder to differentiate between the options—a process we humans try to avoid, and one that can have hugely detrimental consequences on decision motivation.

> Judges in Israel were more likely to grant parole at the beginning of the day or right after taking a break compared to later in the day or right before lunch, presumably because they were more tired and hungry before a break.

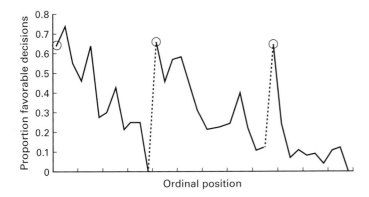

FIGURE 8.7
Proportion of decision where prisoners were granted parole throughout the day. In the early part of the day (leftmost) the chances of getting parole are high and they decrease as the day progresses. The line gets to zero after a few hours just before the lunch break, marked with a dashed line. After the break the parole decisions again spike and again are decreasing as the day progresses before the afternoon break. Source: Adapted from S. Danziger, J. Levav, and L. Avnaim-Pesso (2011). Extraneous factors in judicial decisions. *Proceedings of the National Academy of Sciences of the United States of America*, 108(17):6889–6892. doi: 10.1073/pnas.1018033108.

Previously, Gailliot and colleagues (2007) found that glucose level affects decision making. Across multiple studies of self-control and social behavior, participants showed less willpower and more prejudice when their glucose levels were low and when their mental resources were depleted.

Further research examined the effect of physical constraints on value judgments. Gross, Woelbert, and Strobel (2015) tested whether the anticipated effort required to obtain a good influenced participants' evaluation of it. Participants were fitted with wrist-bands containing either 10 lb of weight or no weight at all and asked what they would pay for a particular food item. Although participants never had to reach for the food, those wearing weights reported that they would be willing to pay less for it than those not wearing weights. In other words, when reaching would have been difficult, participants perceived the item to be less valuable. This study confirms that consumers are more likely to make an impulse purchase or to overeat if the item is easy to reach.

8.4.4 CULTURE

Although many of the parameters that affect decision making are universal, important cultural differences exist in choice behavior. For example, the average American prefers to make his or her own decisions as an individual, but people in other cultures may prefer to defer decision making to a person they trust. To illustrate, Iyengar (2010) compared Anglo-American and Asian-American children in San Francisco. The first group of children was allowed to pick out their own materials

Consumers are more likely to make an impulse purchase or to overeat if the item is easy to reach.

for a puzzle task. The second group received the same materials but was told that the materials were chosen by their mother. A third group was told that the materials were chosen by the experimenter. The Anglo-American children performed best on the task when they were allowed to choose their own materials, and the Asian-American children did best when they were told that their mother chose for them. Iyengar explains that Americans view choice as a way to define and assert "the self," whereas collectivist cultures view choice as a way to maintain group harmony.

8.4.5 THE OPTIONS

As we suggested earlier, many in the Western world believe that having more options is better. Walmart.com sells more than 4 million products, and Amazon.com offers more than 350 million—an unfathomable selection of goods. But in some cultures, unlimited choice can be overwhelming and stressful, and therefore undesirable. When Iyengar asked Eastern Europeans about the introduction of choice in their consumer marketplace, many remarked that there were too many options and that they could not tell the difference between similar products. The study by Iyengar and Lepper (2000) confirmed the idea that more choice is not necessarily better.

Anyone who has used an online dating site has experienced this feeling of choice overload. With millions of members on Match.com or Tinder, it seems certain that users will find "the perfect match." But with all these options come more opportunities to choose unwisely and to regret our decisions. Once we see a quirk or flaw in a date, we think surely there must be someone better out there for us, if we could only find him or her. Schwartz (2005) refers to this phenomenon as the paradox of choice. With choice comes freedom but also disappointment because we form such high expectations for each choice. Thus, marketers should be careful not to overload consumers with too many choices. Marketers can also help costumers feel more satisfied with their choices by increasing the overall value of the consumer experience. Choice alone may not be satisfying, but other aspects of the consumer experience can be optimized to ensure customer satisfaction and enjoyment.

8.4.5.1 DEFAULTS

Options have a huge impact on our choices. We often think we have made a choice independent of outside influence when in fact the number or type of available options drove us in one direction. Take, for example, the decision whether or not to donate your organs after death. This is a personal and profound decision, one that you would think would only be influenced by personal or cultural values. However, residents of certain European countries are much less likely than residents of other countries to sign up as organ donors, and what differentiates these countries is not culture or religion but simply the design of the form that residents fill out at the department of motor vehicles. Forms on which respondents are asked to check a box to opt *in* to the organ donation program yield a lower sign-up rate

The Anglo-American children performed best on the task when they were allowed to choose their own materials, and the Asian-American children did best when they were told that their mother chose for them.

When faced with more choices, we feel more responsible for our decisions, and we worry about making the wrong choice. This cognitive burden may lead us to bow out of the decision-making process entirely.

than forms on which respondents are asked to check a box to opt out of the organ donation program. Thus, the designated default option ends up determining the outcome of a very important decision for many people.

8.4.5.2 Inferior Third Option Effect

The fact that options exert such an influence on our thinking calls the rationality of our decisions into question. Consider the following scenario from Ariely (2008): If you give a person the option of an all-expenses-paid trip to either Rome or Paris, they will probably have trouble deciding between the locales, because they are equally desirable. But if you add the option of Rome without coffee, Rome with coffee suddenly becomes the superior option, even more appealing than Paris. In other words, you can boost the value of an option in a choice set just by adding a closely related yet slightly inferior option. For marketers, this could mean making adjustments to a choice set to steer consumers to the desired target. For example, given three bottles of wine, consumers will often choose the middle-priced bottle. Therefore, if retailers want customers to choose a $20 bottle of wine instead of a $10 bottle, they could simply add a $40 bottle to the display to increase the appeal of the $20 wine.

8.4.6 Memory

Internal as well as external forces shape our purchasing decisions, and implicit processes such as memory impact which brands we favor. Deppe and colleagues (2005) used functional magnetic resonance imaging (fMRI) to investigate implicit processes in a simulated buying task. They asked participants to choose between different brands of either coffee or beer that were indistinguishable. When the target brand was the participant's favorite, participants showed reduced activation in brain areas associated with working memory and reasoning (i.e., the dorsolateral prefrontal, posterior parietal, and occipital cortices and the left premotor area), while activity was increased in areas involved in emotional processing and self-reflection (i.e., the inferior precuneus and posterior cingulate, the right superior frontal gyrus, the right supramarginal gyrus, and especially the ventromedial pre-frontal cortex). From a marketing standpoint, this means that once a brand is chosen as a favorite, it is continually selected in a "winner-take-all" fashion, even when indistinguishable from other brands. Once a consumer identifies with a brand, it's difficult to override this preference.

As the research shows, most choices happen in our brain without our aware-ness, and we cannot explain them entirely. Neuropsychologists refer to these processes as nonconscious or *preconscious*. In his book *How We Decide*, Jonah Lehrer (2009) illustrates preconscious choice by breaking down the game-winning play of football quarterback Tom Brady in the 2002 Super Bowl. With great skill, Brady executed a series of split-second passing decisions and commands to navi-gate his team through the chaos on the field. Years of experience allowed Brady to

Residents of certain European countries are much less likely than residents of other countries to sign up as organ donors, and what differentiates these countries is not culture or religion but simply the design of the form that residents fill out.

Given three bottles of wine, consumers will often choose the middle-priced bottle.

make accurate predictions by assimilating new information about each player's location and intention in an instant. Lehrer explains, "Each pass is really a guess, a hypothesis launched into the air, but the best quarterbacks find ways to make better guesses." Lehrer argues that Brady's skills are not rooted in logic or reasoning but in intuition and emotion. When a potential play does not feel right—when it feels too risky—a quarterback will consider a different target.

Such gut feelings guide many of our decisions. And now that we know what precedes a choice, we can predict choices before they occur. Levy and colleagues (2011) did just that in a study when they showed images of consumer goods to participants inside an fMRI scanner. Later, outside of the scanner, the participants were asked to choose between pairs of the same goods. Activation in the striatum and medial prefrontal cortex predicted participants' subsequent choices, suggesting that these brain areas are involved in assigning value to an object. For marketers, this means that consumers form opinions about products even when they are not actively shopping for them.

Consumers form opinions about products even when they are not actively shopping for them.

8.5 MATHEMATICAL MODELS OF DECISION MAKING

With such a large body of information, researchers in the fields of neuroeconomics and consumer neuroscience have created various models for purchasing decisions. One such model is the attentional drift diffusion model (DDM). This model is based on findings that the comparison process between two or more stimuli is guided by eye movements back and forth between the stimuli. As we look at an item, we accumulate evidence toward or away from selecting that item (figure 8.8). Krajbich and colleagues (2012) found that the model was reasonably accurate in describing the relationship between visual fixations and value-based choices. They also found that participants in a buying task looked longer at products than they did at prices. Therefore, sellers with an inferior product would benefit from restricting the amount of time potential buyers can see it. Looking longer at a product will not help a customer choose it if they know it's an inferior option.

Marketing managers should consider how the above information regarding decision-making processes can be applied to business strategy. Within the 3 C's model (company, customer, and competition), it is important to think about how customers make purchasing decisions, how they view and interact with the company, and how they size up the competition. Plassmann, Kenning, and Ahlert (2007) examined the neural correlates of customer loyalty and found that loyal customers actually have emotional bonds to a store brand, as shown by increased activation in the striatum, the ventromedial prefrontal cortex, and the anterior cingulated cortex. Accordingly, the authors recommend that managers focus less on developing price promotions and more on creating positive affective bonds between the customers and the company.

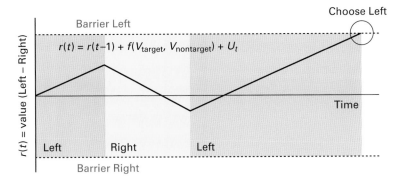

$$r(t) = r(t-1) + f(V_{target}, V_{nontarget}) + U_t$$

FIGURE 8.8

Drift diffusion model illustration. Imagine a drunken man walking on a bridge with no edges. He stumbles to the left, stumbles to the right, left again, right again ... until ultimately he reaches the very edge and maybe falls off the bridge. Drift diffusion model suggests that a decision, at times, can be modeled by this process whereby our threshold for a choice is the edge, and when we cross that threshold we commit to a decision. Say you have to decide whether to have the salad or the steak for lunch. You may start with a bias (preference) toward steak to begin with, making the choice not start at the 50/50 mark. You think in your mind about the options and in doing so add information to your likelihood of choosing steak/salad. Your brain moves in this space between the options by assessing features of the two options and seeing how the weighted decision affects the desire for each of them, until enough evidence for one option is accumulated and the brain commits to one choice by crossing the boundary. The time it takes for the choice to happen, the number of pieces of evidence needed for each choice, and the amount by which each piece of evidence moves us closer to the edge are all part of the DDM.

In a prior study, Plassmann and colleagues (2006) investigated the interplay of emotion and cognition in consumer decision-making. Participants were asked to choose between two different brands of the same type of product. A participant's first-choice brand activated the affect heuristic in the brain, whereas a lower-rated brand did not. This suggests that when customers are faced with their favorite brand, they base their buying decisions on emotions and other implicit information, rather than on analytical reasoning.

8.6   APPLICATIONS OF DECISION MAKING TO IMPROVE MARKETING MIX MODELS

Neuroscientific research and insights into decision making can also be applied to the 4 P's of marketing: price, product, promotion, and place.

8.6.1   PRICE

Regarding price tactics, Plassmann and colleagues (2008) found that how a product is labeled affects consumer experience. They conducted an fMRI study of marketing

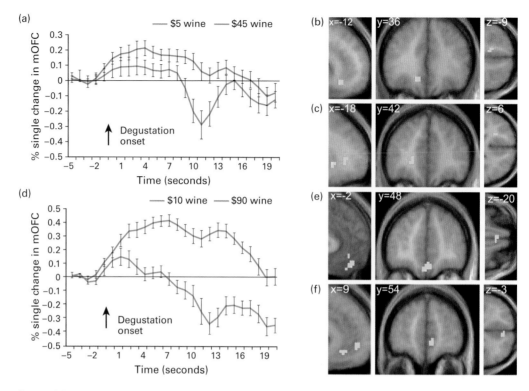

FIGURE 8.9
The effect of price on each wine. mOFC, medial orbitofrontal cortex. Source: Adapted from H. Plassmann, J. O'Doherty, B. Shiv, and A. Rangel (2008). Marketing actions can modulate neural representations of experienced pleasantness. *Proceedings of the National Academy of Sciences of the United States of America*, 105(3):1050–1054. doi: 10.1073/pnas.0706929105.

actions on the neural mechanisms of pleasantness. Participants tasted several wines that they believed were sold at different prices, when in reality the $5 and $45 wine were the same, and the $10 and $90 wine were the same. Not surprisingly, participants reported that the wines labeled with a higher price tasted more pleasant (figure 8.9). Researchers also found increased activity in the medial orbitofrontal cortex, an area of the brain related to experienced pleasantness, when the participants tasted the supposedly "higher priced" wines. (Many more pricing strategies influenced by consumer neuroscience can be found in chapter 11.)

8.6.2 PRODUCT

If consumers form emotional bonds to brands, does that mean that we think of brands as human? An fMRI study by Yoon and colleagues (2006) explored whether we judge products the same way we judge people. The results suggest that we do not. Judgments about persons are processed in the medial prefrontal cortex regions, whereas judgments about products are processed in the left inferior prefrontal cortex, an area known for object processing. Although we often describe brands as having personalities, our brain processes these characterizations differently than human personalities.

8.6.2.1 BRANDS

Additional research examined one of the most well-known brand rivalries: Coke versus Pepsi. McClure and colleagues (2004) conducted an fMRI study in which participants were given sugary soft drinks, either labeled with a brand or with the brand kept anonymous. In the labeled conditions, brand knowledge had a dramatic impact on both behavioral preferences and brain responses, at least for Coke. The participants enjoyed a soda more if they believed they were drinking Coke. In a similar fMRI study, participants viewed logos of car manufacturers and then imagined using the companies' cars (Schaefer et al. 2006). Results showed that the logos of the familiar but not unfamiliar brands elicited activation in a single region in the medial prefrontal cortex, which is an area associated with self-reflection. Preferred brands seem to be part of our identity, and these preferences impact our enjoyment.

Philiastides and Ratcliff (2013) provided further insight into the influence of branding on customer preference. Participants completed a binary decision task for clothing items in the presence and absence of branding information. Results showed that as participants compared the values of the two items, they accumulated evidence toward a decision for the selected item. Furthermore, brand information biased the comparison process by leading participants to assign more value or weight toward to the preferred brand. This suggests that the brain combines brand information and personal preference into a single piece of evidence in the decision-making process. For marketers, this means that attracting consumers with low prices or fancy updates is not enough. Companies should also emphasize brand relationships and awareness.

8.6.3 PROMOTION

Research has confirmed the effectiveness of advertising and promotion that targets emotions via involvement of the amygdala. In one study (Grabenhorst et al. 2013), researchers paired foods that were identical except for a label that emphasized either taste benefits or potential health costs. Participants had to evaluate the foods and choose one while undergoing brain imaging. For labels emphasizing taste, activity in the amygdala was related to subjective ratings of taste pleasantness. For labels emphasizing health, amygdala activity was related to perceived healthiness of the food. These results suggest that the amygdala encodes key variables when we evaluate food choices and that labels affect decision-making by engaging the brain's emotional system.

Judgments about persons are processed in the medial prefrontal cortex regions, whereas judgments about products are processed in the left inferior prefrontal cortex, an area known for object processing.

The brain combines brand information and personal preference into a single piece of evidence in the decision-making process.

An imaging study showed that the brain implicitly registers consumer products even when not actively attending to them, and this affects later choices.

Another imaging study showed that the brain implicitly registers consumer products even when not actively attending to them, and this affects later choices. Tusche, Bode, and Haynes (2010) measured brain responses to images of cars in two separate groups. Group 1 was told to pay close attention to the cars and to rate their attractiveness, while group 2 was distracted from the images with a fixation task. Participants later reported their willingness to buy each car. Activation patterns in the insula and the medial prefrontal cortex were found to reliably predict participant choices in both the low- and high-attention groups, which suggests that product evaluation and decision making are not dependent on attention. Automatic processes can guide consumer decisions. From a marketing standpoint, future research should examine whether "willingness to buy" is associated with actual intent to purchase when consumers are exposed to subtle advertising.

How does physical presence of a product or good, compared to a photo or text description of it, affect consumer decision-making? As a restaurant goer, would you be more tempted to purchase a side of guacamole if the server brought a sample to your table or if you simply read about it on the menu? Evidence suggests that actual presence of a good is more tempting because it activates preprogrammed processes of consumption. In one experiment, Bushong and colleagues (2010) set up an auction with three different conditions: text displays, image displays, and displays of the actual item. When participants saw the actual item, they were willing to pay 40% to 61% more. This result held true for both food and small trinkets, eliminating the smell of food as a possible factor. The researchers concluded that Pavlovian consummatory processes triggered by the item's presence might be responsible for the effect. With this in mind, companies should aim to find the right packaging and displays for their products and to showcase real products whenever possible. Allowing more sensory interactions, for example, test-driving cars that have a "new car smell," could substantially increase consumer's willingness to purchase.

8.6.3.1 Advertising Works in a Variety of Ways

There are many different ways in which advertising can have influence, so it is important to measure many different aspects of campaign performance. The enhanced understanding of decision making that has emerged from the cognitive sciences gives greater insight into these processes and helps us to better understand some of the effects that we have seen in our research.

Broadly speaking, advertising has two routes to influence:

- Filling the brand "iceberg"
- Shaping decision heuristics

Advertising influences can occur at multiple points in the decision cycle, which means focusing on just one point of impact or one approach to advertising is likely to underrepresent the power of campaigns. Similarly, a single campaign can work via a number of mechanisms all at once—and the most powerful campaigns do exactly that.

FILLING THE BRAND "ICEBERG" AND SHAPING DECISION HEURISTICS

The biggest challenge for brands is generating some meaning beyond the basic functional traits of what it is, what it does, and how we can recognize it. Those basic associations are crucial, but can be quickly discerned while shopping or browsing. Marketing campaigns, especially for established brands, need to create meaning and make those associations salient and accessible so that people can think "fast" and use them easily in decision making.

Advertising can affect brand associations, and so influence decisions, in several ways:

1. By *improving overall salience*. Advertising affects how easily the brand springs to mind by repeatedly activating the brand networks. The more we think about a memory, the more readily it can be activated again, so the more advertising activates brand networks, the more likely they are to be activated again later. This biases people toward the brand in scenarios where it is necessary to spontaneously think of brand options (e.g., many service sectors, such as telephone directory enquiry services), but also by affecting the *availability* heuristic. This is a powerful shortcut wherein the ease with which something comes to mind affects its perceived frequency of occurrence—so a brand that easily springs to mind is more likely to be seen as a popular and appropriate choice to meet a given need.

2. By *impacting perceived familiarity*. The familiarity heuristic, and the underlying mere exposure effect, is a well-documented and hugely powerful skew in people's decision making: a familiar item, even one that has simply been seen before but with no other information attached, automatically feels like a safer choice and tends to be preferred. General brand size has a big effect on this, as bigger brands simply tend to be seen in stores and homes more often, but advertising can also impact familiarity by making people encounter the brand more frequently and across a wider range of contexts. More salient brands—those that spring to mind more easily—are also likely to benefit from this effect.

3. By *conditioning emotional responses*. Associating the brand with positive emotional experiences can make it a positive signifier, giving it an automatic, "fast" positive emotional tag as "good" thing, which will in turn give a brand an immediate advantage when people are not thinking hard about their choice. This is not a conscious process where viewers smile, laugh, or feel inspired, and then "decide" that the brand is something they like as a result. Simply the co-experience of the

Marketing campaigns, especially for established brands, need to create meaning and make those associations salient and accessible so that people can think "fast" and use them easily in decision making.

brand in the context of a positive experience will help it become associated with positive feelings in the brain, through a process called *associative conditioning*. Therefore ads (or other experiences) that are emotionally positive will generate these effects, provided that the brand is a prominent part of the experience. If the brand is not clearly part of the positive experience, then any association of the brand with such positive feelings is unlikely or will require enormous numbers of repetitions to occur.

4. By *associating the brand with specific ideas*. Repetition and/or distinctive illustration of the brand delivering, or simply being associated with, a specific idea can lead to the association of the brand with that concept. While this can be a direct message about the brand delivering on that benefit or concept, it can also simply work via simple associative conditioning, in the same way that emotional responses to brands can be generated (see above). This association can then influence consumers' choices in a number of ways:

a. Association with a particular functional benefit can skew people toward the brand when functional performance is a key criteria and can influence perception of brand performance during later experience.

b. Association with personally relevant values can skew people toward the brand when functional criteria are equally met or deemed less important.

c. Association with anything—be it a specific device, image, sound, or phrase—can provide a trigger for choice when many brands (or none) meet other criteria. Given that brand decisions are often not thought through, any non-negative associations are better than nothing, as they can provide the point of difference necessary to tip the balance. Advertising can be a rich source of these points of differentiation, though again, it is crucial that the brand is associated with them for the effect to become apparent.

These associations can come from the creative treatment of the campaign, which has a huge impact on the success of the campaign in generating these associations, but they can also come from implicit associations generated by the media and context in which the campaign is encountered. Mass media such as television can carry implications of stature and safety for the brand (imagine seeing a local beer brand suddenly advertised on national television), viral campaigns can help establish a sense of contemporary relevance, direct marketing may imply a degree of aggression if done badly, and experiential marketing may convey a strong sense of personal interest. Likewise, the context in which the campaigns are encountered may also bring associations that help or hinder the intent of the campaign—lots of daytime television may not help with premium associations, and placement of online campaigns on irrelevant sites my dilute the message.

8.6.4 PLACE

Finally, regarding place, do consumers decide differently when shopping online versus in a brick-and-mortar store? Online sites offer decision aids, customization tools, and search capabilities not available offline. Häubl and Trifts (2000) simulated an online shopping experience to determine how recommendation agents and comparison matrices affect the quality and efficiency of buying decisions. Results showed that recommendation agents reduced the effort required to search for product information and boosted the quality (while decreasing the size) of consideration sets. Comparison matrices also decreased the size and increased the quality of consideration sets. Both tools improved the quality of consumers' purchase decisions. These findings suggest that interactive decision aides are excellent marketing tools for helping consumers make better decisions with less effort.

Clearly, consumer neuroscience research can help marketers with every facet of the 4 P's and 3 C's business models, from branding to price setting. Implicit processes such as emotion play a crucial role in consumer decisions and value judgments, and thus, the most successful marketing strategies are those that take these automatic processes into account.

> Recommendation agents reduced the effort required to search for product information and boosted the quality (while decreasing the size) of consideration sets.

8.7   CONCLUSION

The brain is incredible at finding meaning in the noise of the world. Our brain translates input from millions of sensors and out of the chaos creates cohesive, conscious experience. Much of this experience involves choice behavior. The more we understand how we decide, the better we will be at making smarter, more rational decisions. We can also become more accurate in knowing what we want and how to get it. This is important for both consumers and marketing managers, and insights into the brain are guiding this process.

To revisit the quote from *Alice in Wonderland*, if you do not care where you end up, then every choice you make will get you there. But we do indeed care about reaching specific goals, whether it is to enjoy a refreshing soft drink or ensure a successful product launch. Therefore, we must attend to our choices and to their various internal and external correlates.

KEY TAKEAWAYS

- Decisions are a complex interplay of conscious and unconscious processes. While we are aware of some of the mechanisms that drive our decision making, much of it is driven by things that are beyond our cognition. Our biology, the environment, and things outside of our control have a larger effect on outcomes than we foresee.

- Some of our decisions are made using cognitive mechanisms in our brain, whereas others use more internal emotional mechanisms. Distinguishing between the two allows us to predict some aspects of a choice as well as understand how they are shaped.

- Some decisions can be decoded in our brain milliseconds (and sometimes even seconds) before we act on them or even are aware of them.

- Abundance of choices, while often desired by people, at times lead to less joy from the ultimate preference or even paralysis when it comes to the actual process of deciding.

- Interplay between the reward system, emotional control, emotional regulation, and rational decision-making are key to the formation of a decision in the brain. Measuring the neural activity in those regions can give us an understanding about the probabilities each option carries and, at times, allow us to assign numeric value to items.

- Decision-making processes are often broken down to a set of binary options one selects from. Thus, we can actually model some of the choices using a mathematical simulation. One popular such model is the drift diffusion model.

DISCUSSION QUESTIONS

1. Imagine a person is standing in front of a shelf in a convenience store and making a choice between two items (say, two cereal boxes). Name a few environmental elements that could affect his decision-making process.

2. You are trying to help a company think of ways to increase the sales of a new camera in a big electronics retail company. Describe how the marketing mix could be thought of in the context of decision making and how one can affect the consumer experience to increase the likelihood of a specific camera being selected.

3. On the shelf in a supermarket are three bottles of wine. On the left: a cheap one at $5. In the middle: a $10 one. On the right: an expensive $20 one. Decision-making theories suggest that customers are more likely to purchase the middle one. Explain why? If you were to add a fourth option—say a $50 bottle on the right—what do you think would happen to the sales of the $5 one or the $20 one?

REFERENCES

Ariely, D. 2008. Are we in control of our own decisions? [video file.] Available at https://www.ted.com/talks/dan_ariely_asks_are_we_in_control_of_our_own_decisions?language=en#t-497984.

Bechara, A., Damasio, A. R., Damasio, H., & Anderson, S. W. (1994). Insensitivity to future consequences following damage to human prefrontal cortex. *Cognition*, 50(1–3), 7–15.

Bechara, A., Damasio, H., Tranel, D., & Damasio, A. R. (1997). Deciding advantageously before knowing the advantageous strategy. *Science*, 275(5304), 1293–1295.

Bushong, B., King, L. M., Camerer, C. F., & Rangel, A. (2010). Pavlovian processes in consumer choice: The physical presence of a good increases willingness-to-pay. *American Economic Review*, 100, 1–18.

Cerf, M. 2015. Free won't [video file]. Available at https://www.youtube.com/watch?v=6dqNiSGo9yU.

Cerf, M., & Mackay, M. (2011). Studying consciousness using direct recordings from single neurons in the human brain. In S. Dehaene & R. Christen (Eds.), *Characterizing consciousness: From cognition to the clinic? Research and perspectives in neurosciences* (pp. 133–146). Berlin: Springer-Verlag.

Danziger, S., Levav, J., & Avnaim-Pesso, L. (2011). Extraneous factors in judicial decisions. *Proceedings of the National Academy of Sciences of the United States of America*, 108(17), 6889–6892.

Deppe, M., Schwindt, W., Kugel, H., Plassmann, H., & Kenning, P. (2005). Nonlinear responses within the medial prefrontal cortex reveal when specific implicit information influences economic decision making. *Journal of Neuroimaging*, 15(2), 171–182.

Fried, I., Mukamel, R., & Kreiman, G. (2011). Internally generated preactivation of single neurons in human medial frontal cortex predicts volition. *Neuron*, 69(3), 548–562.

Gailliot, M. T., Baumeister, R. F., DeWall, C. N., Maner, J. K., Plant, E. A., Tice, D. M., et al. (2007). Self-control relies on glucose as a limited energy source: Willpower is more than a metaphor. *Journal of Personality and Social Psychology*, 92(2), 325–336.

Grabenhorst, F., Schulte, F. P., Maderwald, S., & Brand, M. (2013). Food labels promote healthy choices by a decision bias in the amygdala. *NeuroImage*, 74, 152–163.

Gross, J., Woelbert, E., & Strobel, M. (2015). The fox and the grapes—How physical constraints affect value based decision making. *PLoS One*, 10(6), e0127619.

Harari, Y. 2015. Techno religions and silicon prophets [video file]. Available at https://www.youtube.com/watch?v=g6BK5Q_Dblo

Häubl, G., & Trifts, V. (2000). Consumer decision making in online shopping environments: The effects of interactive decision aids. *Marketing Science*, 19(1), 4–21.

Iyengar, S. 2010. The art of choosing [video file]. Available at www.ted.com/talks/sheena_iyengar_on_the_art_of_choosing?language=en

Iyengar, S., & Lepper, M. (2000). When choice is demotivating: Can one desire too much of a good thing? *Journal of Personality and Social Psychology*, 79(6), 995–1006.

Johansson, P., Hall, L., Sikström, S., & Olsson, A. (2005). Failure to detect mismatches between intention and outcome in a simple decision task. *Science*, 310(5745), 116–119.

Krajbich, I., Lu, D., Camerer, C., & Rangel, A. (2012). The attentional drift-diffusion model extends to simple purchasing decisions. *Frontiers in Psychology: Cognitive Science*, 3(193), 1–18.

LeDoux, J. (1998). *The emotional brain: The mysterious underpinnings of emotional life*. Chicago: Simon and Schuster.

Lehrer, J. (2009). *How we decide*. Boston: Houghton Mifflin Harcourt.

Levy, I., Lazzaro, S. C., Rutledge, R. B., & Glimcher, P. W. (2011). Choice from non-choice: Predicting consumer preferences from blood oxygenation level-dependent signals obtained during passive viewing. *Journal of Neuroscience*, 31(1), 118–125.

LivePerson. 2013. The connecting with customers report: A global study of the drivers of a successful online experience. Available at http://info.liveperson.com/rs/liveperson/images/Online_Engagement _Report_final.pdf.

McClure, S. M., Li, J., Tomlin, D., Cypert, K. S., Montague, L. M., & Montague, P. R. (2004). Neural correlates of behavioral preferences for culturally familiar drinks. *Neuron*, 44, 379–387.

Perez, O., Mukamel, R., Tankus, A., Rosenblatt, J. D., Yeshurun, Y., & Fried, I. (2015). Preconscious prediction of a driver's decision using intracranial recordings. *Journal of Cognitive Neuroscience*, 27(8), 1492–1502.

Philiastides, M. G., & Ratcliff, R. (2013). Influence of branding on preference-based decision making. *Psychological Science*, 24(7), 1208–01215.

Plassmann, H., Kenning, P., & Ahlert, D. (2007). Why companies should make their customers happy: The neural correlates of customer loyalty. In G. Fitzsimons & V. Morwitz (Eds.), *NA—Advances in Consumer Research* (Vol. 34, pp. 735–739). Duluth, MN: Association for Consumer Research.

Plassmann, H., Kenning, P., Deppe, M., Kugel, H., Schwindt, W., & Ahlert, D. 2006. *How brands twist heart and mind: neural correlates of the affect heuristic during brand choice.* Unpublished manuscript, University of Muenster, Germany.

Plassmann, H., O'Doherty, J., Shiv, B., & Rangel, A. (2008). Marketing actions can modulate neural representations of experienced pleasantness. *Proceedings of the National Academy of Sciences of the United States of America*, 105(3), 1050–1054.

Roberts, J. (1989). A grounded model of consideration set size and composition. In T. K. Srull (Ed.), *NA—Advances in Consumer Research* (Vol. 16, pp. 749–757). Provo, UT: Association for Consumer Research.

Schaefer, M., Berens, H., Heinze, H.-J., & Rotte, M. (2006). Neural correlates of culturally familiar brands of car manufacturers. *NeuroImage*, 31, 861–865.

Schwartz, B. 2005. The paradox of choice [video file]. Available at https://www.ted.com/talks/barry _schwartz_on_the_paradox_of_choice?language=en.

Shiv, B., & Fedorikhin, A. (1999). Heart and mind in conflict: The interplay of affect and cognition in consumer decision making. *Journal of Consumer Research*, 26(3), 278–292.

Tusche, A., Bode, S., & Haynes, J.-D. (2010). Neural responses to unattended products predict later consumer choices. *Journal of Neuroscience*, 30(23), 8024–8031.

Williams, L. E., & Bargh, J. A. (2008). Experiencing physical warmth promotes interpersonal warmth. *Science*, 322(5901), 606–607.

Yoon, C., Gutchess, A. H., Feinberg, F., & Polk, T. A. (2006). A functional magnetic resonance imaging study of neural dissociations between brand and person judgments. *Journal of Consumer Research*, 33(1), 31–40.

CHAPTER 9

REWARD SYSTEM

NEAL J. ROESE, HANS MELO, THALIA VRANTSIDIS, AND WILLIAM A. CUNNINGHAM

A young man casually walks into a medical research center and volunteers to have electrodes implanted in his brain for the specific purpose of being able to self-deliver electrical jolts to his brain's "pleasure center." The man is described as young with long hair, and he tells a doctor that he had read in a magazine article that "one jolt of electricity was like a dozen orgasms. It sounded really terrific" (Crichton 1972, p. 87). The various physicians who later learn of this encounter marvel at the possibility of electrical addiction—addiction to the pleasure elicited by electrical stimulation of specific brain regions. This fictional scene, from the 1972 novel *The Terminal Man* by *Jurassic Park* author Michael Crichton, is rooted to historical fact and hints both at the possibilities and folly of harnessing the human brain's reward network. The historical fact is the landmark discovery in 1954 by James Olds and Peter Milner that rats would self-stimulate when an electrode was placed within (and delivered electrical stimulation to) a specific region of their brain, assumed at that time to be a "pleasure center" (Olds and Milner 1954). The possibilities involve the ability to control and optimize the experience of pleasure itself, and, for marketers in particular, they include the ability to verify directly from brain-based data which products or services achieve maximal pleasure. The folly is that human pleasure is not so easily reduced to a single location in the brain that, when electrically stimulated, produces the same feeling state as that engendered by chocolate, companionship, or triumph.

The goal of this chapter to provide an overview of the current state of knowledge regarding reward, which we define as a physiologic event that is experienced subjectively as pleasure, and which increases the likelihood of engaging in acts that in the past were followed by such pleasure. In marketing terms, our key

> Rats would self-stimulate when an electrode was placed within (and delivered electrical stimulation to) a specific region of their brain, assumed at that time to be a "pleasure center." The possibilities involve the ability to control and optimize the experience of pleasure itself.

interest is in predicting initial trial and repeat purchase. We first lay a conceptual foundation by considering what reward is, then trace the anatomic and chemical underpinnings of reward, draw a key distinction between wanting and liking, and throughout consider the current capabilities and future prospects of consumer neuroscience as it pertains to measuring reward responses.

9.1   What Is Reward?

Eat a piece of a chocolate, and the immediate experience is pleasure. It is a powerful experience, yet fleeting: in a moment it is over. This subjective feeling forms the core of the concept of reward, but a contemporary definition further embraces the economic concept of utility, by which we mean a general internal calculation of value for the individual.

In terms of the impact on behavior, reward is the carrot whereas punishment is the stick. If chocolate brings pleasure, it also brings repeat consumption. Termed the "law of effect" (Thorndike 1898), the most basic behavioral pattern involving pleasure and pain is its effect on learning, and in particular the tendency for animals to continue doing whatever brings pleasure and cease doing whatever brings pain. In classic animal experiments (especially mice, rats, and pigeons), simple behaviors such as running a maze or pecking at bull's-eye targets tend to increase in frequency when their performance is immediately followed by a reinforcer (i.e., an external event that elicits a psychological response, such as pain or pleasure). (Negative reinforcement, sometimes confused with punishment, involves a behavior change after pain is removed.) This so-called *instrumental learning* forms the basis of animal training. In people, feelings of enjoyment with movies, music, cuisine, fashion, and so forth motivate continued consumption and exploration of related product lines. Food, water, and sex are primary rewards because they connect to basic biological imperatives. Consumer products, and money itself, are secondary rewards, yet both primary and secondary are converted by the brain to a common currency of utility, and so are easily compared and prioritized.

Whereas early conceptions of experienced utility involved reference to pleasure and pain, more contemporary economic conceptions center on preferences inferred from observed behavioral choices, formalized in expected utility theory and the tenet of maximizing expected utility. This latter conception is sometimes termed *decision utility* and is proposed to represent the utility signal used at the moment of making a decision. Connecting these ideas to neuroscience, the pivotal aspect of anticipation versus experience assumes center stage, and on this stage a network of brain region—the mesolimbic dopaminergic system—plays a central role (Haber and Knutson 2010; Ikemoto 2010; Berridge and Kringelbach 2015). We return to these ideas subsequently.

Food, water, and sex are primary rewards because they connect to basic biological imperatives. Consumer products, and money itself, are secondary rewards.

9.2 HOW MARKETERS BENEFIT FROM NEUROSCIENCE IN MEASURING REWARD

At the end of the day, marketers want to sell more, and neuroscience assessment of reward offers a tool for doing this, in at least three ways: (1) new product design (i.e., which elements within a product to include or leave out); (2) product testing (i.e., which among several prototypes to launch and promote); and (3) concept testing (i.e., which of several forms of messaging, including verbiage and imagery, to use to support a product). The goal in all of these ways is to capture a "gut-level" reward responses, because this will predict future market demand (Ariely and Berns 2010; Reimann et al. 2010).

Similar to the description in chapter 8, marketers have distinguished between more immediate reward reactions versus more elaborated and reflective product attitudes. For the sake of convenience, we use the standard terminology of System 1 and System 2 (Kahneman 2011). System 1–like responses are more immediate "gut-reaction" evaluative responses. A friend surprises you with a cupcake, and there is an immediate and automatic categorization of cupcake as a delicious sweet food, memories of previous surprises and friendly moments, and salivation in anticipation of its sugary goodness. Yet, our initial impression is not our final impression. With more time, more information can be considered, transforming this initial impulse into what is often called a System 2 evaluation. For these evaluations, a greater number of concerns can be considered to shape one's response. Are genetically modified foods such a bad idea? Are electric cars like the Tesla a good way to protect the environment? Opinions toward such issues depend more on careful consideration. Although the System 1 versus System 2 distinction is widely used, we note that this is a distinction that is made for convenience in chunking a highly dynamic and interactive set of processes rather than two completely independent systems (see Cunningham and Zelazo 2007). Thus, for the marketer, it is important to remember that a "System 1" gut feeling often evolves over time into a System 2 attitude, much like a snowball might grow from pebble-size to boulder-size. The snowball may look entirely different, but the initial conditions (the original snowball) directly determine, at least in part, the size and shape of the final snowball (Van Bavel, Xiao and Cunningham 2012).

That said, marketers often rely on the distinction between System 1 versus System 2 because this conceptualization allows for the prediction of different kinds of purchasing behavior. System 1 connects to impulsive shopping behavior. The placement of magazines, candies, batteries, and lighters at the end caps of grocery store checkouts are an obvious example of a choice set optimized for impulsive purchase. The consumer likely had no preexisting intent to buy any of these items, but upon seeing them at the moment of purchase, there is an immediate, gut-level reward response of "I like candy," and a subsequent "what the hell" behavior of purchasing a Snickers bar. By contrast, System 2 connects to more elaborative, deliberative purchase, as when a consumer checks Yelp reviews, compares multiple items on Amazon, and expends effort so as to fortify the purchase decision with facts. To summarize, System 1 connects to impulsive purchase, whereas System 2 connects to deliberative purchase.

A fundamental challenge is that System 1 responses are hard to verbalize. Traditional questionnaires and focus groups capture System 2 responses. System 1 responses may evolve into System 2 responses (like a snowball). For example, a "love at first sight" reaction for a new Ford Mustang might evolve into a more considered preference for the Ford product on the basis of detailed comparison shopping. In this case, the traditional questionnaires will probably give the same result as a neuroscience metric. However, sometimes people have System 1 liking that does not translate into a preference that is easily measured in a questionnaire. For example, sometimes people feel an initial liking but do not share it with others because it is socially sensitive (e.g., attitudes toward drugs or pornography). In this case, the consumer might say one thing but buy something else. Another case is where a consumer simply does not know, or cannot verbalize, his or her implicit, System 1 preference. One promise of a neuroscience approach is the ability to capture these System 1 impulses that cannot be captured with questionnaires or focus groups, thus gaining critical market intelligence that can guide marketing decisions.

The fundamental challenge boils down to whether a neuroscience method can provide market intelligence that offers value above and beyond that of a traditional questionnaire method. In statistical terms, the question is whether a neuroscience method explains unique variance in market behavior (i.e., purchasing) above and beyond that explained using questionnaire responses. We briefly describe three studies that have tackled this challenge, and we also point out that rather few such studies exist, and so there remains a great need for further research to (1) refine the methods and statistical tools that will provide the optimal market intelligence and (2) determine which product and service categories might represent the greatest opportunity for a neuroscience method to shine above a questionnaire method.

The pivotal early study used functional magnetic resonance imaging (fMRI) to predict purchase behavior, as implemented within by a computer-presented shopping task (selecting items from a virtual catalog) that was undertaken during scanning (Knutson et al. 2007). Three brain regions predicted purchase action and did so above and beyond the role of self-reported shopping preferences. Nucleus accumbens activation, along with medial prefrontal cortex and insula activation, were found to correspond to particular time points within the unfolding choice. When participants first encountered a desirable product (such as Godiva chocolate), nucleus accumbens activation was noted, which may connect with desire of the product. When the price appeared, insula activation was noted, which may connect with the pain of having to pay. Finally, as the final decision to buy or not buy is reached, medial prefrontal activation was noted, which perhaps reflects the summary computation of utility (for a similar result, see McClure et al. 2004). These early results were exciting, yet the incremental validity (or increase in predictive power of choice by neuroimaging over and above self-reports) was modest.

Berns and Moore (2012) used fMRI to predict pop music sales. The research was striking in that unlike most neuroimaging research, the brain measure and the outcome behavior were not tracked within the same individuals; rather, a small sample of respondents was used to predict a wider market outcome. A small sample of teenagers listened to song snippets while being scanned, and, in addition to brain imaging, the teenagers provided explicit questionnaire ratings of the songs (which came from new bands who had uploaded the music to a social media website). Subsequently, Nielsen SoundScan data constituted the index of market performance. The result was that activation in the nucleus accumbens in response to hearing a song provided a meaningful predictor of subsequent sales tracked over about 4 years. By contrast, questionnaire ratings did not predict sales. The magic here, then, is a tool to predict aesthetic reactions—intangible preferences to objects or art, fashion, design, or culture—that people cannot put into words. Direct access to the brain provides a way for marketers to pick winners and to know which products to back with enhanced marketing spend. It is plausible that the product category, involving aesthetic judgment, is more deeply rooted to System 1 and is more difficult to verbalize, contributing to the clear superiority of fMRI as a predictor over and above that of questionnaire ratings (a similar result of better prediction of market behavior by fMRI over questionnaire data appeared in Falk, Berkman, and Lieberman 2012).

A recent research demonstration was a comprehensive "horse race" among key neuroscience metrics, including fMRI, electroencephalography (EEG), eye tracking, and biometrics (heart rate and galvanic skin response), assessed alongside a traditional questionnaire (Venkatraman et al., 2015). The metrics all assessed responses to the same set of 30-second television ads; the metrics were then pitted against one another as predictors of market outcome, indexed via the relevant company's estimates of advertising elasticity (i.e., the ratio of proportional change in sales per proportional change in advertising spend). Focusing only on neuroscience metrics, fMRI was the winner. Nucleus accumbens activation indexed by fMRI was the only neuroscience metric to explain variance in market outcome over and above the traditional questionnaire metric. Importantly, however, questionnaires provided the best overall predictive capability. Although EEG did reliably predict market outcome, it added nothing above and beyond that of the questionnaire. These research examples underscore two conclusions and one lingering question. First, simple questionnaires are still the best bet as the first go-to method: they are cheaper than neuroscience methods, and they get the job done. Second, fMRI holds the crown for the most effective tool to gain new market intelligence above and

Three brain regions predicted purchase action and did so above and beyond the role of self-reported shopping preferences. Nucleus accumbens activation, along with medial prefrontal cortex and insula activation, were found to correspond to particular time points within the unfolding choice.

Activation in the nucleus accumbens in response to hearing a song provided a meaningful predictor of subsequent sales tracked over about 4 years.

beyond questionnaires. The lingering question is which product and service categories afford the greatest opportunity for neuroscience to provide a competitive advantage. Will it be hedonic products, like desserts and beverages that embody biologically based reward anticipation? Will it be new technology, the benefits of which people have trouble imagining? Will it be for socially sensitive products, such as those involving the sex industry or the emerging legal marijuana industry? These important questions require hard answers from basic research before managers can make informed choices as to which, if any, neuroscience research methods to deploy in the service of market intelligence.

Simple questionnaires are still the best bet as the first go-to method: they are cheaper than neuroscience methods, and they get the job done. Second, fMRI holds the crown for the most effective tool to gain new market intelligence above and beyond questionnaires.

9.3 WANTING AND LIKING

Wanting and liking for most people seem indistinguishable. We want a particular polo shirt because we like that polo shirt. Nevertheless, our current understanding of reward suggests that these two processes rest on separate neural systems and may sometimes be uncoupled (Dai, Brendl, and Ariely 2010; Kringlebach and Berridge 2012). For the marketer, this means that neuroscience methods that capture wanting will be useful for assessing consumer anticipation of a new product experience (which connects to trial), whereas methods that capture liking will be useful for assessing pure enjoyment and hence repeat purchase (loyalty).

In terms of brain anatomy, the "wanting" system involves a network of neurons that bridge the two important regions (in general terms, the prefrontal cortex and the limbic system). The ventral tegmental area comprises the largest number of dopamine neurons, and these form connections to the prefrontal cortex by way of a bridge called the mesocortical pathway and to the limbic system (especially the nucleus accumbens) by way of another bridge called the mesolimbic pathway (Smith and Berridge 2007; Smith et al. 2010). This "wanting" system is akin to a subway line that connects the most "human" part of the brain (specializing in considering and planning) with the most "animal" part of the brain (specializing in raw feeling). Dopamine is a chemical that plays an important role in this "wanting" system, and in the next section, we explain what exactly dopamine is. The experience of pleasure involves the "liking" system, which includes pathways from the ventral pallidum over to the nucleus accumbens (a different part of the nucleus accumbens than is involved in "wanting").

The experience of pleasure involves the "liking" system, which includes pathways from the ventral pallidum over to the nucleus accumbens (a different part of the nucleus accumbens than is involved in "wanting").

9.4 THE ROLE OF DOPAMINE

The specific chemicals involved in the wanting versus liking reward pathways are of lesser importance for marketers, in the same way that a deep knowledge of the materials science underlying carbon fiber is not necessary to sell cars. However, because the word *dopamine* is often used in popular culture, we take a moment to give some brief background details.

Dopamine is a neurotransmitter. Neurotransmitters are chemical messengers that pass between the junction separating two neurons. The brain comprises about 100 billion neurons arranged in a network, and the constant interplay of signals that pass between neurons composes the basic substrate of the mind. Signals are both electrical and chemical; the electrical aspect sits within each neuron, whereas chemical messengers—neurotransmitters—continue the signal between neurons. For the most part, each neuron is specialized at releasing one type of neurotransmitter. At least a hundred neurotransmitters have been identified, the most famous being dopamine, serotonin, and epinephrine, and these differ by way of their chemical structure. A wide range of drugs operate by either facilitating or blocking the action of particular neurotransmitters. For example, Prozac works by facilitating the action of serotonin, resulting in a general mood-enhancing effect. By the same token, drugs that activate the reward network, and so produce feelings of bliss or euphoria (such as cocaine, nicotine, and cannabis), do so by facilitating the effect of dopamine. On the flip side, drugs such as Thorazine and Valium block dopamine with a resulting antipsychotic and anti-anxiety effect, respectively. Several dopamine networks operate in the brain, and they are not exclusive to reward. Further, dopamine is not the only chemical messenger involved in reward; opioids are another.

Both dopaminergic and opioid neurons make up the nucleus accumbens, and it should be obvious that opiate drugs (such as morphine and heroin) produce pleasurable experiences by way of mimicking the action of naturally occurring opioids (such as encephalin). Naloxone and naltrexone are drugs that can treat opiate (and also alcohol) addiction, doing so by blocking the action of opioid neurons (and having the subjective effect of eliminating the pleasurable aspect of opiates and alcohol). At present, imaging methods such as fMRI cannot distinguish between activation of dopamine and opioid pathways. In the future, when this becomes possible, it will prove especially useful to marketers, as the dopamine network connects more to anticipations of reward, whereas the opioid network connects more to the reward experience itself. Accordingly, future marketers would be able to distinguish how much consumers want a new product on the basis of marketing communications (which gives an indication of trial) from how much consumers enjoy the product (which gives an indication of repeat sales, i.e., loyalty).

To summarize, the particular specifics of anatomy and chemistry that underlie the dopamine reward and opioid networks are of smaller importance to marketers in the current era. These specifics are "under-the-hood" details that can be safely left out of the managerial decision process.

Drugs that activate the reward network, and so produce feelings of bliss or euphoria (such as cocaine, nicotine, and cannabis), do so by facilitating the effect of dopamine.

Future marketers would be able to distinguish how much consumers want a new product on the basis of marketing communications (which gives an indication of trial) from how much consumers enjoy the product (which gives an indication of repeat sales, i.e., loyalty).

9.5   Anticipating versus Experiencing Rewards, and What This Means for Customer Loyalty

Functionally, the neural systems involved in reward allow for people to make predictions to guide decisions. Because people want to have the most accurate predictions, the system is designed to update its representations with experience. A currently accepted framework suggests that there are three processes at work to optimize the relationship between environmental reinforcers and behavior (Sutton and Barto 1990, 1998, building from earlier ideas in Rescorla and Wagner 1972). The first is the evaluation function that provides the organism with its best guess about the rewarding or punishing properties of a particular stimulus. This information is used to generate policies for action (which can be conceptualized as an "actor"). After prediction and then subsequent reinforcement, a "critic" function computes a prediction error to update value representations for the next iteration of behavior. In other words, individuals compare the actual reward received to what they expected and use the difference to update their expected future reward, which then feeds into a subsequent choice. For marketers, these ideas are similar to the standard view of customer satisfaction, which is greater when products and services exceed expectations (Churchill and Surprenant 1982; Oliver 2010). Critically, dopamine is believed to encode the prediction error signal in the midbrain and ventral striatum, with larger prediction errors eliciting a stronger dopamine signal (for a review, see O'Doherty 2004).

Individuals compare the actual reward received to what they expected and use the difference to update their expected future reward, which then feeds into a subsequent choice.

Thus, when considering the dynamics of reward processing, it is useful to consider three relatively discrete phases of reward—the anticipatory phase when people infer the likely reward that they will obtain if they make a particular choice ("how will this chocolate bar taste?"), the consummatory phase when people have direct experience with the consequences of their choice ("this chocolate bar is pretty good"), and an updating phase when the system uses the discrepancies between what was predicted and experienced to influence future predictions ("this chocolate bar was not as delicious as expected, and so I expect similar products from this brand to be about the same as this one"). Although dopamine is linked to greater anticipation of rewarding outcomes, increased bursts of dopaminergic neurons have been shown to fire only after unexpected rewards or when rewards are larger than expected (Schultz, Dayan, and Montague 1997; Wickens 1997; Schultz 2002; Bayer and Glimcher 2005). In other words, in the moment of reward, dopamine may only represent greater than expected rewards. What is important here is that although anticipated reward is likely to drive behavior in any given instance, repeated behavior (e.g., brand loyalty) is going to be driven by the updated reward signals that develop over time through learning—and these signals are only updated when there are discrepancies between what is expected versus what is experienced.

Information regarding expected outcomes is passed from limbic areas (e.g., the nucleus accumbens) to the orbitofrontal cortex, where it is evaluated with respect to current status, for example, with regard to current goal attainment. Whereas subcortical structures such as the nucleus accumbens provide information regarding predicted outcomes after the perception of a stimulus, the orbitofrontal cortex represents the current (or anticipated) affective experience as a result of those outcomes. Specifically, the orbitofrontal cortex is responsible for the subjective pleasure associated with receiving (or displeasure associated with not receiving) an expected outcome or the anticipation of a likely outcome. Because the orbitofrontal cortex receives input from multiple sensory modalities (eyes, ears, tongue, etc.), it likely constitutes the key platform of a common currency for representing and comparing different aspects of evaluative information, including the evaluative connotations of self-generated mental representations (Peters and Büchel 2010). Neuroscientists have observed orbitofrontal activity following the same dynamics in response to primary rewards (e.g., food) as well as secondary rewards (e.g., money).

To the extent that brain areas such as the nucleus accumbens provide a low-resolution estimate of expected outcomes after the perception of a stimulus, and the orbitofrontal cortex represents the current (reward) state of the organism, the dense reciprocal connections between these regions allow for a comparison of expected rewards and punishments with current experience.

These ideas converge on several key conclusions for the marketer. First, of the currently available technology, only positron emission tomography (PET) and fMRI offer tools for distinguishing activation in the nucleus accumbens, which is a deep brain structure that is largely invisible to EEG. Second, it is overly simplistic to think of the nucleus accumbens as a "pleasure center" that gets "turned on" by rewarding experiences. Rather, the interplay between nucleus accumbens and orbitofrontal activation gives an indication of the extent to which a product, service, or marketing communication delivers a rewarding experience that is better than expected. Third, measuring anticipation (wanting) versus reward (liking) with currently available technology is not feasible, and so the marketer is left with a mixed message from neuroscience techniques. Fourth, a driving idea of current neuromarketing is that reward signals can be measured as predictors of market behavior, but this leaves out a crucial part of the equation. If fMRI and EEG are tracking System 1 responses, these are certainly not the only inputs into a final purchase decision. When passing a table of free chocolate samples at a grocery store, the impulse is to try one, and yet for some people there is a goal to avoid excess calories, possibly operating with more reflection, that thwarts the initial impulse. Without taking into account these goal-based trade-offs that most people make, measures aimed purely at System 1 will fail to predict market activity.

Information regarding expected outcomes is passed from limbic areas (e.g., the nucleus accumbens) to the orbitofrontal cortex, where it is evaluated with respect to current status.

The interplay between nucleus accumbens and orbitofrontal activation gives an indication of the extent to which a product, service, or marketing communication delivers a rewarding experience that is better than expected.

9.6   The Future

Alena Graedon's (2014) novel *The Word Exchange* describes a near future in which breakthrough wearable technology is capable of instantly capturing a consumer insight, in the moment where it matters the most. Imagine working at the office, and feeling the desire for a latte, but before the desire becomes a fully realized purchase intention, a freshly steaming cup arrives at your desk. In effect, the tech "read" your desire, connected to a vendor, made the purchase against your own account, and delivered the product to you ... before you consciously realized you wanted it. Contrast this to the more limited tech vision in Steven Spielberg's 2002 film, *Minority Report*, in which the Tom Cruise character enters a Gap store, is personally identified by a retinal scan, has his identity linked into a "big data" database containing his prior purchase history, and then is offered a promotion uniquely suited to particular preferences. The two visions are similar (personalization amplified!), but the first one exemplifies the pitfalls of using neuroscience methods to capture System 1 reward responses. In short, if future neuroscience becomes so accurate at reading reward responses, what happens if our smallest whims are easily attainable? Will we overindulge? And what happens if the act of choosing itself is usurped by a piece of technology? What we like is not always what we want, because of the many trade-offs necessitated by the complexity of modern life (for discussion, see Wilson, Gaines, and Hill 2008). If we imagine further that technology will one day make smart choices for us, and balance these trade-offs for us, the technology would be so fantastically advanced as to constitute essentially a second brain.

That said, we believe the future may afford exciting opportunities for marketing with greater precision and personalization by way of neuroscience methods if the following two breakthroughs are achieved. First, the computational model that specifies the dynamic interplay of activation in specific brain regions will need to be vastly more complex than that currently used (for discussion, see Breiter et al. 2015). In essence, this is the filter through which raw neural signals pass on the way to usable market intelligence, and a great deal more basic research is needed to establish and validate such a computational model. Second, the spatial resolution of current neuro methods needs to be increased substantially. Although fMRI trumps EEG in spatial resolution, fMRI remains unable to discriminate fine brain structures that may carry pivotal signals in terms of anticipated versus experienced reward value.

Key Takeaways

- Neuroscience can inform and guide marketers in product design and testing and predict future market demand.

- Distinguishing between "wanting" and "liking" can help to assess a consumer's anticipation of a new product and enjoyment of a product, leading to repeated purchase.

- Dopamine is more directly related to motivation and anticipation of rewards, whereas opioids are more directly related to the experience of pleasure itself.

- The interplay between nucleus accumbens and orbitofrontal activation gives an indication of the extent to which a product delivers a rewarding experience.

Discussion Questions

1. How are "liking" and "wanting" different, and how can that distinction be exploited in marketing?

2. How can neuroimaging methods help us differentiate between anticipated and experienced rewards? And what are their limitations?

3. As technology continues to develop, what implications will this bring for choice behavior? Will these developments help us make better choices or make us slaves to our vices?

References

Ariely, D., & Berns, G. S. (2010). Neuromarketing: The hope and hype of neuroimaging in business. *Nature*, 11, 284–292.

Bayer, H. M., & Glimcher, P. W. (2005). Midbrain dopamine neurons encode a quantitative reward prediction error signal. *Neuron*, 47, 129–141.

Berns, G. S., & Moore, S. E. (2012). A neural predictor of cultural popularity. *Journal of Consumer Psychology*, 22, 154–160.

Berridge, K. C., & Kringelbach, M. L. (2015). Pleasure systems in the brain. *Neuron*, 86(6), 646–664.

Breiter, H., Block, M., Blood, A., Calder, B., Chamberlain, L., Lee, N., et al. (2015). Redefining neuromarketing as an integrated science of influence. *Frontiers in Human Neuroscience*, 8, 1–7. doi:10.3389/fnhum.2014.01073.

Churchill, G. A., Jr., & Surprenant, C. (1982). An investigation into the determinants of customer satisfaction. *JMR, Journal of Marketing Research*, 19(4), 491–504.

Crichton, M. (1972). *The terminal man.* New York: Knopf.

Cunningham, W. A., & Zelazo, P. D. (2007). Attitudes and evaluations: A social cognitive neuroscience perspective. *Trends in Cognitive Sciences*, 11, 97–104.

Dai, X., Brendl, C. M., & Ariely, D. (2010). Wanting, liking, and preference construction. *Emotion (Washington, D.C.)*, 20(June), 324–334.

Falk, E. B., Berkman, E. T., & Lieberman, M. D. (2012). From neural responses to population behavior: Neural focus group predicts population-level media effects. *Psychological Science*, 23(5), 439–445. doi:10.1177/0956797611434964.

Graedon, A. (2014). *The word exchange.* New York: Doubleday.

Haber, S., & Knutson, B. (2010). The reward circuit: Linking primate anatomy and human imaging. *Neuropsychopharmacology Reviews*, 35, 4–26.

Ikemoto, S. (2010). Brain reward circuitry beyond the mesolimbic dopamine system: A neurobiological theory. *Neuroscience and Biobehavioral Reviews*, 35, 129–150. doi:10.1016/j.neubiorev.2010.02.001.

Kahneman, D. (2011). *Thinking, Fast and Slow.* New York: Macmillan.

Knutson, B., Rick, S., Wimmer, G. E., Prelec, D., & Loewenstein, G. (2007). Neural predictors of purchase. *Neuron*, 53, 147–156.

Kringelbach, M. L., & Berridge, K. C. (2012). The joyful mind. *Scientific American*, 307, 40–45.

McClure, S. M., Li, J., Tomlin, D., Cypert, K. S., Montague, L. M., & Montague, P. R. (2004). Neural correlates of behavioral preference for culturally familiar drinks. *Neuron*, 44, 379–387.

O'Doherty, J. P. (2004). Reward representations and reward-related learning in the human brain: Insights from neuroimaging. *Current Opinion in Neurobiology*, 14, 769–776.

Olds, J., & Milner, P. (1954). Positive reinforcement produced by electrical stimulation of septal area and other regions of rat brain. *Journal of Comparative and Physiological Psychology*, 47(6), 419–427.

Oliver, R. L. (2010). *Satisfaction: A behavioral perspective on the consumer.* New York: M. E. Sharpe.

Peters, J., & Büchel, C. (2010). Neural representations of subjective reward value. *Behavioural Brain Research*, 213, 135–141. doi:10.1016/j.bbr.2010.04.031.

Reimann, M., Zaichkowsky, J., Neuhaus, C., Bender, T., & Weber, B. (2010). Aesthetic package design: A behavioral, neural, and psychological investigation. *Journal of Consumer Psychology*, 20, 431–441. doi:10.1016/j.jcps.2010.06.009.

Rescorla, R. A., & Wagner, A. R. (1972). A theory of Pavlovian conditioning: Variations in the effectiveness of reinforcement and nonreinforcement. In A. H. Black & W. F. Prokasy (Eds.), *Classical Conditioning II: Current research and theory* (pp. 64–99). New York: Appleton-Century-Crofts.

Schultz, W. (2002). Getting formal with dopamine and reward. *Neuron*, 36, 241–263.

Schultz, W., Dayan, P., & Montague, P. R. (1997). A neural substrate of prediction and reward. *Science*, 275, 1593–1599.

Smith, K. S., & Berridge, K. C. (2007). Opioid limbic circuit for reward: Interaction between hedonic hotspots of nucleus accumbens and ventral pallidum. *Journal of Neuroscience*, 27, 1594–1605.

Smith, K. S., Mahler, S. V., Pecina, S., & Berridge, K. C. (2010). Hedonic hotspots: Generating sensory pleasure in the brain. In M. L. Kringelbach & K. C. Berridge (Eds.), *Pleasures of the Brain* (pp. 27–49). New York: Oxford University Press.

Sutton, R. S., & Barto, A. G. (1990). Time-derivative models of Pavlovian reinforcement. In M. Gabriel & J. Moore (Eds.), *Learning and computational neuroscience: Foundations of adaptive networks* (pp. 497–537). Cambridge: MIT press.

Sutton, R. S., & Barto, A. G. (1998). *Reinforcement Learning: An Introduction.* Cambridge: MIT Press.

Thorndike, E. L. (1898). Animal intelligence: An experimental study of the associative processes in animals. *Psychological Review Monograph*, (Suppl. 2), 1–109.

Van Bavel, J. J., Xiao, Y. J., & Cunningham, W. A. (2012). Evaluation is a dynamic process: Moving beyond dual system models. *Social and Personality Psychology Compass*, 6, 438–454.

Venkatraman, V., Dimoka, A., Pavlou, P. A., Vo, K., Hampton, W., Bollinger, B., et al. (2015). Predicting advertising success beyond traditional measures: New insights from neurophysiological methods and market response modeling. *JMR, Journal of Marketing Research*, 52(4), 436–452.

Wickens, J. (1997). Basal ganglia: Structure and computations. *Network (Bristol, England)*, 8, R77–R109.

Wilson, R., Gaines, J., & Hill, R. (2008). Neuromarketing and consumer free will. *Journal of Consumer Affairs*, 42, 389–410.

9.7 APPENDIX: NEURO-AESTHETICS: THE ROLE OF DOPAMINERGIC REWARD IN PROCESSING AESTHETICALLY APPEALING PACKAGE DESIGN

Martin Reimann

Why are consumers oftentimes drawn to aesthetic package design? Some research claims that beauty elicits the notion of "If it is beautiful, then it must be good" (Dion, Berscheid, and Walster 1972). Following the idea of a beautiful-is-good stereotype, consumers would be expected to infer higher product quality from more aesthetic package designs. Other research argues that beauty can also give rise to a good mood (Norman 2004) in the sense that viewing a beautiful package design simply puts consumers in a positive affective state.

While these psychological processes and states are likely to arise from being exposed to aesthetically appealing packages, a third process has received attention more recently: dopaminergic reward. Some of my own research together with Judy Zaichkowsky, Carolin Neuhaus, Thomas Bender, and Bernd Weber has argued and provided initial evidence that aesthetically appealing packages can automatically activate areas of the brain to which the neurochemical dopamine is projected and which are associated with reward and "wanting" (Reimann et al. 2010). Specifically, one of our functional magnetic resonance imaging (fMRI) experiments found that anticipating the choice of aesthetically appealing packages (compared to standardized packages) is associated with increased activation in the striatum, specifically the nucleus accumbens, as well as the ventromedial prefrontal cortex (see figure 9A.1). These spikes in activation indicate that dopamine was released

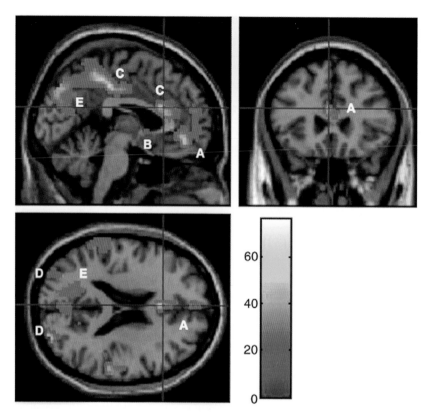

FIGURE 9A.1
Aesthetic package design triggers activation in the striatum and the ventromedial prefrontal cortex. Note the increased activations in the ventromedial prefrontal cortex (A), nucleus accumbens (B), cingulate cortex (C), visual cortices (D), and precuneus (E) during presentation of aesthetic package design. Credit: Reprinted with permission from the *Journal of Consumer Psychology*.

(D'Ardenne et al. 2008; Schott et al. 2008) and imply that a reward response (also referred to as "wanting" response; Berridge and Robinson 2003) triggered downstream preferences, judgments, and choices (Reimann et al. 2010).

Despite the facts that (1) dopamine release can only be indirectly measured using fMRI (Schott et al. 2008) and (2) inferring psychological function from fMRI data can sometimes be speculative (Poldrack 2006), support for our claim of the involvement of a reward or "wanting" response in aesthetics is found in observations of consumers describing beautiful objects using terms such as "passionate," "lustful," or "seductive" (Norman 2004). Highly aesthetic stimuli may also be intrinsically desirable because they can fulfill a vital, hard-wired human need (Maslow 1967, 1971). Observations of the need to be surrounded with aesthetics can be found in consumers who actively yearn for aesthetics in their environment and experience a state akin to sickness if encircled by ugliness and can only be "cured" through the exposure to beautiful objects. Our claim that reward responses are associated with aesthetic packages is also coherent with the notion of "drive" states such as yearning for food, sex, or alcohol (Loewenstein 1996). Drive states triggered by aesthetic packages can thus prompt consumers to temporarily deactivate all previously set goals and concentrate solely on the goal of acquiring the aesthetic object of desire. Taken together, aesthetics in package design can be a powerful propellant of consumers' judgments and choices and should, therefore, be considered as an additional product differentiator in any competitive marketplace.

REFERENCES

Berridge, K. C., & Robinson, T. E. (2003). Parsing reward. *Trends in Neurosciences*, 26(9), 507–513.

D'Ardenne, K., McClure, S. M., Nystrom, L. E., & Cohen, J. D. (2008). BOLD responses reflecting dopaminergic signals in the human ventral tegmental area. *Science*, 319(5867), 1264–1267.

Dion, K., Berscheid, E., & Walster, E. (1972). What is beautiful is good. *Journal of Personality and Social Psychology*, 24(3), 285–290.

Loewenstein, G. (1996). Out of control: Visceral influences on behavior. *Organizational Behavior and Human Decision Processes*, 65(3), 272–292.

Maslow, A. (1967). A theory of metamotivation: The biological rooting of the value-life. *Journal of Humanistic Psychology*, 7(93), 93–127.

Maslow, A. (1971). *The farther reaches of human nature*. New York: Viking Press.

Norman, D. A. (2004). *Emotional design: Why we love (or hate) everyday things*. New York: Basic Books.

Poldrack, R. A. (2006). Can cognitive processes be inferred from neuroimaging data? *Trends in Cognitive Sciences*, 10(2), 59–63.

Reimann, M., Zaichkowsky, J., Neuhaus, C., Bender, T., & Weber, B. (2010). Aesthetic package design: A behavioral, neural, and psychological investigation. *Journal of Consumer Psychology*, 20(4), 431–441.

Schott, B. H., Minuzzi, L., Krebs, R. M., Elmenhorst, D., Lang, M., Winz, O. H., et al. (2008). Mesolimbic functional magnetic resonance imaging activations during reward anticipation correlate with reward-related ventral striatal dopamine release. *Journal of Neuroscience*, 28(52), 14311–14319.

CHAPTER 10

BRAND EQUITY

MING HSU

10.1 INTRODUCTION

Marketers have long appreciated the role of branding in guiding managerial decision making (Gardner and Levy 1955; Keller 1993; Aaker 2009). An understanding of how consumers feel and think about brands, for example, provides valuable guidance to development of marketing strategy in areas including advertising, pricing, and channel strategies (Rust, Zeithaml, and Lemon 2004; Aaker 2009). At the same time, however, consumer researchers have noted increasing dissatisfaction on the part of practitioners due to shortcomings in existing methods of measuring the impact of brand-building activities (Feldwick 1996; Ambler and Barwise 1998; Berthon et al. 2001). As early as the 1990s, for example, researchers noted that advertising's share of the marketing budget had shifted downward from more than 60% to less than one third (Shocker, Srivastava, and Ruekert 1994).

In particular, compared to marketing actions that yield more direct and immediate effects, the ability of marketers to measure returns on brand investment have lagged in key metrics such as revenue and profitability (Kamakura and Russell 1993; Knox and Walker 2001; Rust, Lemon, and Zeithaml 2004). Thus, although brands are often seen as one of the most valuable assets for firms, brand managers nevertheless face significant challenges to justify the impact of their spending. Moreover, existing theories of brand equity have tended to be largely based on folk psychological concepts such as image, loyalty, and value. In some cases, they are built on psychological models that have been superseded by more scientifically rigorous models that are based on our knowledge of the underlying neurobiology (figure 10.1).

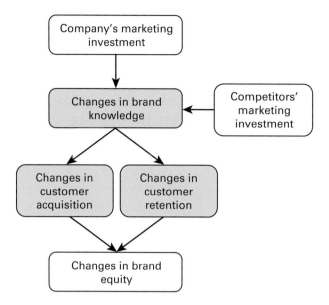

Figure 10.1
Brand knowledge and brand equity through a customer lifetime valuation (CLV) framework. Source: Adapted from Rust, Lemon, and Zeithami (2004).

These challenges have only increased in recent years as branding has grown to focus more on abstract and intangible considerations, and managers are increasingly seeking to understand aspects of brands unrelated to the actual physical product or service specifications (Aaker 2009; Keller 2012). It is perhaps not surprising that some scholars have even called into question the validity and managerial usefulness of the brand equity concept itself (Berthon et al. 2001).

This chapter describes how recent developments in cognitive and behavioral neuroscience of consumer decision-making can help to address these issues and organize the fragmented literature on brand equity. Importantly, a neuroscientific perspective has the potential to provide a rigorous scientific foundation toward understanding the core components of brand equity, how they are generated, and how they can be influence by marketing actions (Yoon et al. 2006; Plassmann, Ramsøy, and Milosavljevic 2012). Much like the way that classification of species by modern genetic methods is often consistent with that using more qualitative methods (Archibald 2009), this new science has thus far validated a number of the hard-won insights about brand equity, but at the same time organizes them more rigorously and makes clear how the marketing action inputs ultimately translate to consumer response outputs.

First, a framework is put forward conceptualizing brand equity as the product of (1) the knowledge that customers possess regarding a particular brand and (2) the actions that this knowledge leads to, which affect key metrics such as revenue and profitability. Second, neuroscientific evidence shows that brand knowledge consists of multiple forms of memories that are encoded in the brain, which correspond to well-established forms of memory associated with semantic (facts and concepts), episodic (experiences and feelings), and instrumental (rewards and habits) types of memory. Third, this knowledge is associated with different forms of behavioral systems, including a goal-directed system that captures valence of attitudes and preference for a brand and a habit system that captures previously learned values but no longer reflects ongoing preferences. Finally, the chapter concludes by providing a new brain-based framework of brand equity and a discussion of the outstanding questions and possible future directions.

10.2 DEFINING BRAND EQUITY

Despite its intuitive nature, the definition of *brand equity* is surprisingly contentious. In particular, two perspectives on brand equity must be distinguished—firm-based and consumer-based (Feldwick 1996; Baker, Nancarrow, and Tinson 2005; Christodoulides and de Chernatony 2010). Under the former, brand equity is defined according the financial benefits that a brand brings to a firm (Kamakura and Russell 1993; Reynolds and Phillips 2005). This could include price premium, net discounted cash flow brand, market share, and others that are attributable to the brand.

In keeping with a customer-centered perspective of modern marketing theory and practice (Keller 1993; Keller and Lehmann 2006), a customer-based definition of brand equity is used. Here, brand equity is defined as the added value, from the perspective of the customer, endowed by the brand to the product (Keller 1993; Rust, Lemon, and Zeithaml 2004; Christodoulides and de Chernatony 2010). This is done for two reasons. First, in contrast to firm-based brand equity, which tends to be well defined, there remains substantial conceptual and methodological controversy regarding customer-based brand equity, which may particularly benefit from recent insights from consumer neuroscience (Keller 1993; Rust, Zeithaml, and Lemon 2004).

Second and more important, a customer orientation provides a natural way to link these two concepts that define customer-based equity using models of customer lifetime valuation (CLV) (Rust, Lemon, and Zeithaml 2004; Reynolds and Phillips 2005; Aaker 2009). These models view firms' marketing efforts as competitive investments that attempt to shape customer perceptions, which then result in effects on customer acquisition and retention, leading to increased CLV (Srivastava, Shervani, and Fahey 1998; Rust, Lemon, and Zeithaml 2004). Return on marketing investment can then be calculated simply by subtracting the cost of marketing investment.

Conceptualizing brand equity in this way has provided a powerful framework for marketers to measure returns on brand investment, particularly in an age where customer acquisition and retention are increasingly observable. However, there remains little consensus regarding the middle ground between marketing actions and observed consumer responses. This essentially includes everything that is not under direct observation or control of the firm. In particular, there is poor agreement regarding (1) what are the constituent parts underlying consumer brand knowledge, and (2) how this knowledge is ultimately translated into consumer responses. This lack of consensus is in part reflected in the sheer number of frameworks that have been proposed for customer-based brand equity (table 10.1). Although they all correspond to some intuitive notions of "knowledge" and "value," they also differ in important ways from each other and could conceivably provide contradictory recommendations to a brand manager. One potential contribution of a neuroscientific approach to these issues is thus simply to ground these concepts in well-established scientific facts about how the brain stores information and make use of such information in decisions.

TABLE 10.1
Different conceptualizations of customer-based brand equity in the academic literature

Study	Dimensions of customer-based brand equity
Aaker (1991, 1996)	Brand awareness
	Brand associations
	Perceived quality
	Brand loyalty
Blackston (1992)	Brand relationship
	(trust, customer satisfaction with the brand)
Keller (1993)	Brand knowledge
	(brand awareness, brand associations)
Sharp (1995)	Company/brand awareness
	Brand image
	Relationships with customers/existing customer franchise
Berry (2000)	Brand awareness
	Brand meaning
Burmann et al. (2009)	Brand benefit clarity
	Perceived brand quality
	Brand benefit uniqueness
	Brand sympathy
	Brand trust

Source: Christodoulides and de Chernatony (2010).

10.3   BRAND KNOWLEDGE

Beginning with the seminal works of Aaker (2009) and Keller (1993), conceptualizations of brand knowledge and their constituent parts have largely been based on ideas from cognitive psychology. In particular, drawing upon models of human memory developed in the 1970s and 1980s, these authors conceptualize brand knowledge as a collection of thoughts, images, feelings, and experiences that consumers associate with brands and store in associative memory.

10.3.1   BRAND KNOWLEDGE AS ASSOCIATIVE MEMORY NETWORKS

In associative network models, information is stored in a set of nodes and connected by links that vary in strength. Information retrieval is then conducted via a "spreading activation" process where activation of one node can spread to other linked nodes in memory. When the activation of another node exceeds some threshold level, the information contained in that node is recalled (Collins and Loftus 1975; Keller 1993).

Such models have been highly useful at generating novel and sophisticated theories of mental processes and explain a number of important facts about brand associations and managerial implications, such as brand extension. Hutchinson, Raman, and Mantrala (1994) showed that consumers' brand and product name recall to the cue "beverage" is highly consistent with an associative memory model. In the particular example given in figure 10.2, the consumer recalls first Coke, followed by a number of other sodas, before moving on to related product categories such as beer. Note also that in most cases, the brands and products used more frequently appeared to be "top of mind" more quickly than those that were used less frequently.

However, associative models have difficulty explaining noncognitive phenomena, such as the effects of emotion and motivation, on memory. Mood effects on memory, for example, have been an important area of study for consumer researchers (Bettman 1970; Bettman, Johnson, and Payne 1991). This has potentially important implications for understanding how vehicles of advertising, such as television, can influence memory for the advertisements themselves. In addition, studies of so-called implicit memories have shown that memory traces are possible even without conscious recall. In advertising, for example, implicit memories have been shown to be important in cases of high distraction, such that respondents do not possess explicit memories of advertising claims. Most important, a unitary model of consumer memory ignored the growing consensus in cognitive neuroscience that memory is not a monolithic faculty, but rather a collection of relatively independent systems characterized by different patterns of learning, unlearning, and biases (figure 10.3) (Milner, Squire, and Kandel 1998; Squire and Wixted 2011).

These authors conceptualize brand knowledge as a collection of thoughts, images, feelings, and experiences that consumers associate with brands and store in associative memory.

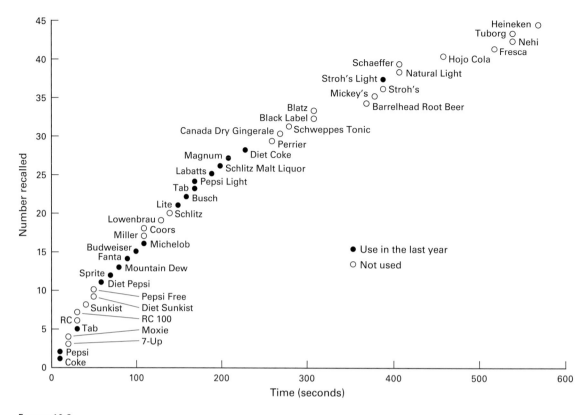

FIGURE 10.2
Clustering in brand name recall for a typical subject. In addition to influencing the recall of particular alternatives, the categorical structure of memory is likely to influence which brands co-occur in the consideration set. Brand names tend to be recalled in categorical clusters. Source: Adapted from Hutchinson Raman, and Mantrala (1984).

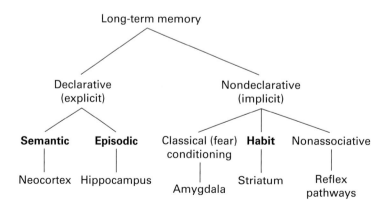

FIGURE 10.3
Multiple memory systems model of human long-term memory. Source: Adapted from Milner, Squire, and Kandel (1998)

10.3.2 BRAND KNOWLEDGE: A MULTIPLE MEMORY SYSTEMS VIEW

Modern research on memory systems was inspired in part by neurologic studies of amnesic patients, such as the famous patient H.M. (Milner, Squire, and Kandel 1998; Schacter 1999). After temporal lobe resection to treat his epilepsy, H.M. lost the ability to form new episodic memories but retained other forms of memory, such as existing factual knowledge and motor skills. Over the next decades, researchers using a variety of neuroscientific techniques, including brain imaging, lesion studies, and animal models, have confirmed and clarified the brain basis of these different forms of memory (table 10.2).

More broadly, that multiple memory systems underlie brand knowledge is important for three reasons. First, substantial neuroscientific evidence suggests that these systems are associated with different patterns of learning and unlearning. These have important implications for behavioral expression. Episodic memory, for example, is fast forming and context dependent. In contrast to episodic and semantic systems, however, Pavlovian systems, likely underpinned by reinforcement mechanisms, are slow in acquisition as well as extinction (Milner, Squire, and Kandel 1998).

Second, different memory systems are subject to different forms of biases and distortions (Schacter and Slotnick 2004). For example, episodic memory is a recently evolved, late-developing, and early-deteriorating past-oriented memory system, more vulnerable than other memory systems to neuronal dysfunction, and probably unique to humans (Tulving 2002; Schacter and Slotnick 2004). In contrast, semantic memory appears widely distributed and robust with respect to brain damage. Finally, habits and procedural memory appear to be robust even in late stages of Alzheimer's disease (Wood and Neal 2007). In the case of episodic memory, in particular, there has been much focus on the creation of "false memories" (Schacter 1999; Schacter and Slotnick 2004). There is now substantial evidence that each retrieval of an episode, in particular those that are highly memory charged, alters the memory in some significant way (Nader, Schafe, and LeDoux

TABLE 10.2
Memory systems of particular importance for consumer decision-making

Memory system	Memory type	Learning rate	Neural substrates
Semantic	Knowledge and facts	Slow	Neocortex, highly distributed
Episodic	Events and experiences	Fast	Hippocampus, localized
Instrumental	Rewards, habits	Fast for reward associations, slow for habits	Basal ganglia, orbitofrontal cortex, localized

2000). Such mechanisms have now been exploited to "erase" debilitating fear associations, which are central to disorders such as PTSD (Schiller et al. 2010).

Finally, these systems are known to interact, alternatively compensating and competing under different conditions, and are differentially modulated by emotional processes and contextual factors (Milner, Squire, and Kandel 1998). Compensatory effects, for example, have been witnessed in the case of amnesic individuals who use habit systems to "remember" to take their medication (Squire and Zola 1996; Squire and Wixted 2011).

10.3.3 MULTIPLE MEMORY SYSTEMS FOR BRAND KNOWLEDGE

In terms of brand knowledge, there are two lines of evidence suggesting that consumer brand knowledge engages multiple memory systems. The first is indirect and comes from theoretical and empirical studies that attempted to decompose brand knowledge into its component parts. Aaker (1997), for example, provided a psychometrically validated scale to measure the set of human-like traits that consumers associate with brands. For example, Apple is often described as cool and imaginative, whereas Gucci is described as glamorous and feminine.

Other studies have sought to capture more experiential aspects of consumers' interactions with brands. The brand experience scale, for example, attempts to capture the degree to which brands engage consumers at the sensory, affective, intellectual, or behavioral dimensions (Brakus, Schmitt, and Zarantonello 2009). Keller (1993) also distinguished the included experiential benefits for users and the tangible product attributes in his brand equity framework. Notably, because Keller relies on a single associative memory system, the organization of brand knowledge reflects much more of how a marketer might organize brand knowledge for managerial purposes than how it is reflected in the mind of the consumer.

The second came from more recent neuroscientific studies of consumer brand processing. This is important given the possibility that previous evidence only reflects surface similarities between the relevant concepts; for example, brand experience and episodic memory, or brand associations and semantic memory. The addition of neuroscientific evidence thus promises to benefit consumer psychology models of brand knowledge in much the same way as it did for basic memory research.

In an early study modeled after the Pepsi Challenge, McClure et al. (2004) found that when consumers knew that they were consuming Coke, a set of regions including the hippocampus and dorsolateral prefrontal cortex was activated compared to when they did not know it was Coke. Because the actual consumption experience was identical in both cases with the exception of the knowledge of the brand, the study was able to isolate the set of associations that Coke triggered. Notably, Pepsi did not elicit significant responses in these regions and behaviorally elicited significantly lower preference ratings than Coke. In subsequent studies,

> When consumers knew that they were consuming Coke, a set of regions including the hippocampus and dorsolateral prefrontal cortex was activated compared to when they did not know it was Coke.

similar effects were found when stimuli included automobiles and luxury products (Erk et al. 2002; Schaefer and Rotte 2007). Comparing a wider set of brands, Esch et al. (2012) found a similar activation in the hippocampus when comparing strong brands versus unfamiliar brands. In addition, a number of other cortical regions were activated with respect to brand strength and familiarity, including the lateral prefrontal cortex and insula.

However, an important potential shortcoming of these above studies is that they rely on localization approaches that may fail to capture representations and processes that are not contained in any single set of brain regions, but rather emerge from the correlated activity across a network of brain areas (Kriegeskorte, Goebel, and Bandettini 2006; Mitchell et al. 2008). That complex constructs such as conceptual knowledge emerge out of a distributed system has a long and distinguished history dating back at least to Lashley's search for engrams (Lashley 1950) and connectionist models of learning systems (Hinton, McClelland, and Rumelhart 1986; McClelland and Rogers 2003).

Recently, Chen, Nelson, and Hsu (2015) took an important step toward addressing the possibility that brand knowledge is in fact distributed widely across the brain. Specifically, using newly developed machine learning approaches that have become increasingly popular in studies of basic perceptual and cognitive processes (Formisano et al. 2008; Kay et al. 2008), the authors used cross-validation techniques to consider what type of knowledge is contained in a distributed set or "pattern" of brain activity, possibly distributed across many regions. They found that, consistent with distributed accounts of semantic knowledge, a widely distributed set of brain regions appeared to contain information regarding brand associations as hypothesized in the Aaker (1997) brand personality framework (figure 10.4). In contrast, consistent with models of episodic memory, brand experience appears to be contained in a far more restricted set of hippocampal regions (unpublished data).

10.4   CUSTOMER RESPONSE: TRANSLATING KNOWLEDGE INTO ACTION

Given the eventual goal of every marketing program is to increase sales, no account of brand equity is complete without an understanding of how the influence of consumer perception ultimately translates into consumer responses (Kamakura and Russell 1993; Aaker 2009). Whereas traditional marketing theories take it for granted that more favorable associations stored in consumer memory will result in increased customer acquisition and retention (Keller 1993), advances in decision and consumer neuroscience have provided a more nuanced understanding of conditions under which memory influences decisions.

Consistent with distributed accounts of semantic knowledge, a widely distributed set of brain regions appeared to contain information regarding brand associations.

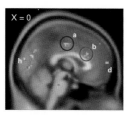 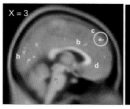 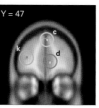 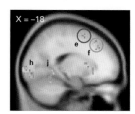

Feature	z	Prob.
(a) anterior cingulate	7.78	0.74
experiencing	5.81	0.85
empathic	3.25	0.79
(b) middle cingulate	5.29	0.87
autobiographical memory	5.29	0.87
perspective	4.83	0.81

Feature	z	Prob.
(c) dorsomedial prefrontal	6.92	0.87
personality traits	4.42	0.85
social	4.57	0.72
(d) medial prefrontal	7.60	0.80
person	4.83	0.79
autobiographical memory	4.74	0.87

Feature	z	Prob.
(e) abstract	4.56	0.81
imitation	4.12	0.86
imagery	3.56	0.77
(f) familiarity	4.61	0.83
thinking	4.48	0.86
recollection	4.03	0.82

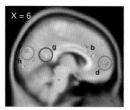 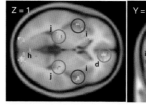 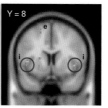 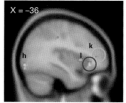

Feature	z	Prob.
(g) posterior cingulate	8.85	0.81
autobiographical	8.69	0.89
memories	4.55	0.79
(h) primary visual	4.85	0.84
mental imagery	4.00	0.86
visual cortex	3.93	0.72

Feature	z	Prob.
(i) insula	10.91	0.79
sensation	4.32	0.80
affective	3.28	0.64
(j) hippocampus	11.04	0.85
thoughts	4.17	0.86
memory	5.53	0.71

Feature	z	Prob.
(k) lateral prefrontal	4.06	0.74
memory	4.27	0.65
(l) inferior frontal	5.55	0.67
semantic	6.30	0.72
words	4.74	0.68
emotion	3.94	0.66

FIGURE 10.4

Brain regions that contain information about brand associations in the Aaker (1997) brand personality framework. Each panel shows clusters of at least 10 contiguous significant voxels. To make inferences about cognitive processes subserved by these regions, the meta-analytic tool Neurosynth (Yarkoni et al. 2011) was used to generate the probability that a specific cognitive process is engaged given activation in a particular brain region. For example, given a specific voxel location of the observed activation in the dorsomedial prefrontal cortex (cluster c), there is a 0.85 probability that the term "personality traits" was used in a study given the presence of reported activation. Source: Adapted from Chen, Nelson, and Hsu (2015).

Of central importance here is the existence of the two interacting systems for decision making mentioned in chapter 8: the more evaluative, deliberative, goal-directed system, and the more automatic, reflexive, habit system (Yin and Knowlton 2006; Kahneman 2011). Similar to consumer memory, these systems likely evolved to address different adaptive demands in our evolutionary history. As anyone who has held a conversation while driving a car can attest to, the two systems can operate independently but can interact or interfere with potentially important consequences.

10.4.1   GOAL DIRECTED VERSUS HABITUAL DECISION-MAKING

First, the goal-directed system assigns values to actions by computing action-outcome associations and then evaluating the rewards that are associated with the different outcomes (Hsu et al. 2005; Rangel, Camerer, and Montague 2008). That is, using information stored in semantic and episodic memory systems, the goal-directed system makes decisions via a deliberative strategy. This system corresponds closely to the standard consumer decision-making models widely used in marketing (figure 10.5).

Human functional neuroimaging studies have shown that brain activity in the frontostriatal circuit, in particular the orbital frontal circuit (OFC), to be associated with behavioral measures of goals (Rangel et al. 2008; Sugrue et al. 2005; Schultz et al. 1997). Moreover, individuals with damage to the medial OFC are known to have a number of problems making consistent appetitive choices. In the context of branding, Koenigs and Tranel (2008) have shown that damage to this

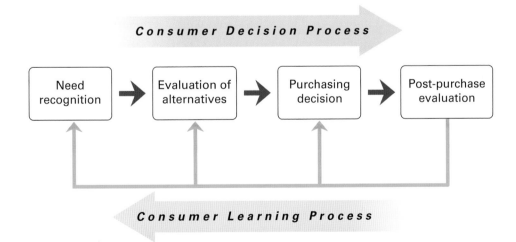

FIGURE 10.5
Typical consumer decision-making process. Source: Adapted from Kotler and Armstrong (2010).

area abolishes the influence of brand, specifically Coca-Cola, on behavioral preference, consistent with the view that this region receives and integrates value-relevant information that drive choice behavior.

In contrast to the goal-directed system, habits are prepotent responses that are quick to activate in memory over alternatives and that have a slow-to-modify memory trace (Yin and Knowlton 2006; Rangel, Camerer, and Montague 2008). For example, one study found that moviegoers who habitually eat popcorn in cinemas would eat even stale popcorn while satiated, but only in the context associated with past performance (Neal et al. 2011). Because of the low cognitive demand of such decisions, habit systems are likely evolutionarily ancient. Indeed, studies using a variety of rodent and non-human primate species suggest that the basal ganglia plays a crucial part in the control of habits. In particular, lesion studies using rodents have shown that damage to these regions disrupts the ability of rodents to establish and deploy habits (Yin, Knowlton, and Balleine 2004; Faure et al. 2005).

Thus, unlike semantic and episodic memories, habit systems specify actions in direct response to environmental contexts and are inseparable from habit memory. Because habits are acquired through trial-and-error learning, habit systems are believed to learn relatively slowly (see table 10.2). As a consequence, they might forecast the value of actions incorrectly, as anyone can attest after a home remodeling or a software user interface upgrade. Moreover, such actions can be highly specific, such as motor command programming when one is typing a password, but they can also be quite general, for example actions in approach or avoidance. Finally, habits are not immune to deliberative processes. Habits are learned largely as people pursue goals in daily life, and habits are broken through the strategic deployment of effortful self-control (Yin and Knowlton 2006; Wood and Neal 2007). This is an important growth area in decision and consumer neuroscience and is still not completely understood.

CLV calculations can be improved by incorporating information about development and breaking of consumer habits. For example, branding and marketing strategies that are ineffective may be so because they have not had sufficient time to break previous consumer habits.

In branding and marketing, the distinction between these two types of systems is rarely made but has a number of important implications. First, building consumer habits is critical for increasing customer retention. Consumers that develop the habit of purchasing a particular brand, product, or from a specific channel may be less likely to search for information for alternatives, to deliberate about competing products, or to delay purchasing for the future. Second, it makes clear that overt behavior such as customer loyalty may have multiple causes. A customer who makes repeated purchases might be doing so either because of the attractiveness of the offering or simply out of habit. Likewise, certain marketing strategies may have differential effects on these two systems, raising the possibility that marketers can optimize and target strategies for different goals or segments.

Finally, the presence of these two systems opens the possibility that CLV calculations can be improved by incorporating information about development and breaking of consumer habits. For example, branding and marketing strategies that are ineffective may be so because they have not had sufficient time to break previous consumer habits or because they are truly ineffective. Likewise, encouraging current retention statistics may belie weaknesses in future retention.

10.5 Conclusion

This chapter highlights two areas where insights from cognitive and behavioral neuroscience can help to improve and guide managerial decision-making of customer-based brand equity. First, it helps to ground conceptualizations of customer-based brand equity on a firmer scientific footing. This is particularly important in the development and validation of brand equity scales. In contrast to the myriad of systems proposed in previous academic literature summarized in table 10.1, a brain-based view of brand equity can be constructed by first distinguishing between memory and behavioral systems, with each containing subcomponents corresponding to different types of memory or behaviors (table 10.3). For example, the fact that episodic memory is fast forming but easily distorted and semantic memory is slow forming but resilient also has implications for when and how often brand managers should measure these components of brand knowledge and the types of brand-building activities necessary to consolidate these memories.

Second, the fact that memory is often inaccessible to conscious recall opens the door to neuroscientific and implicit measures to supplement self-report measures, including fMRI, EEG, and the implicit association test. This will be particularly important in cases where consumers are either unable, such as in the case of habits, or unwilling, such as personally sensitive information, to reveal information to the researcher.

Finally, this framework makes clear the need to link two very different traditions of measuring brand equity. On the one hand are brand managers that deal primarily with recognition, recall, and awareness related to brand knowledge, whereas on the other hand are those that focus on consumer responses such as acquisition and retention. A brain-based view of brand equity makes clear that each is incomplete by itself, as behavior depends on knowledge, but knowledge does

TABLE 10.3
Customer-based brand equity according to consumer neuroscience

Dimensions	Components	Correspondence to previous literature
Brand knowledge	Semantic	Brand associations
	Episodic	Brand experience, brand relationship
Customer response	Goal-directed	Perceived quality, brand benefit, brand trust
	Habit	Brand loyalty

not benefit the firm per se without it ultimately being translated into action. Although it is still far from clear how this relationship can be probed and measured at a scale necessary for practical use, even a small step forward is a significant advance given the importance of brand equity to firms and their stakeholders.

KEY TAKEAWAYS

- Customer-based brand equity derives from the differential effect of brand knowledge on consumer response to the marketing of the brand.

- Brand knowledge is composed of different forms of memories that operate on different timescales and are subject to different distortions.

- Consumer actions in response to brand knowledge are guided by at least two behavioral systems that differ in automaticity and cognitive processing intensity.

- Measuring customer-based brand equity requires capturing both brand knowledge and consumer responses to this knowledge.

DISCUSSION QUESTIONS

1. What was the scientific basis of the original models of brand knowledge? How has the foundational science underlying brand knowledge changed in the intervening years?

2. A CEO responds to a marketing budget request by stating, "Our CLV analysis can tell us everything we need to know about the health of our brand equity. Why are we allocating money to measure something we already know about?" How would you use neuroscientific research on habitual behavior to respond to the CEO's concern?

REFERENCES

Aaker, D. A. (1991). *Managing brand equity*. New York: Free Press.

Aaker, D. A. (1996). *Building strong brands*. New York: Free Press.

Aaker, J. (1997). Dimensions of brand personality. *JMR, Journal of Marketing Research*, 34(3), 347–356.

Aaker, D. A. (2009). *Managing brand equity*. New York: Simon & Schuster.

Ambler, T., & Barwise, P. (1998). The trouble with brand valuation. *Journal of Brand Management*, 5(5), 367–377.

Archibald, J. D. (2009). Edward Hitchcock's pre-Darwinian (1840) "tree of life. *Journal of the History of Biology*, 42(3), 561–592.

Baker, C., Nancarrow, C., & Tinson, J. (2005). The mind versus market share guide to brand equity. *International Journal of Market Research*, 47, 525–542.

Berry, L. (2000). Cultivating service brand equity. *Journal of the Academy of Marketing Science*, 28(1), 128–137.

Berthon, J. P., et al. 2001. Organizational and customer perspectives on brand equity: issues for managers and researchers. In *Proceedings of the ANZMAC Conference*. Citeseer.

Bettman, J. R. (1970). Information processing models of consumer behavior. *JMR, Journal of Marketing Research*, 7(3), 370–376.

Bettman, J. R., Johnson, E. J., & Payne, J. W. (1991). Consumer decision making. In T. S. Robertson & H. H. Kassarjian (Eds.), *Handbook of Consumer Behavior* (pp. 50–84). Englewood Cliffs, NJ: Prentice-Hall.

Blackston, M. (1992). Building brand equity by managing the brand's relationships. *Journal of Advertising Research*, 32(3), 79–83.

Brakus, J. J., Schmitt, B. H., & Zarantonello, L. (2009). Brand experience: What is it? How is it measured? Does it affect loyalty? *Journal of Marketing*, 73(3), 52–68.

Burmann, C., Jost-Benz, M., & Riley, N. (2009). Towards an identity-based brand equity model. *Journal of Business Research*, 62, 390–397.

Chen, Y., Nelson, L., & Hsu, M. (2015). From "where" to "what": Distributed representations of brand associations in the human brain. *JMR, Journal of Marketing Research*, 52, 453–466.

Christodoulides, G., & de Chernatony, L. (2010). Consumer-based brand equity conceptualisation and measurement: A literature review. *International Journal of Market Research*, 52(1), 43.

Collins, A. M., & Loftus, E. F. (1975). A spreading-activation theory of semantic processing. *Psychological Review*, 82(6), 407.

Erk, S., et al. (2002). Cultural objects modulate reward circuitry. *Neuroreport*, 13(18), 2499–2503.

Esch, F. R., et al. (2012). Brands on the brain: Do consumers use declarative information or experienced emotions to evaluate brands? *Journal of Consumer Psychology*, 22, 75–85.

Faure, A., et al. (2005). Lesion to the nigrostriatal dopamine system disrupts stimulus-response habit formation. *Journal of Neuroscience*, 25(11), 2771–2780.

Feldwick, P. (1996). What is brand equity anyway, and how do you measure it? *Journal of the Market Research Society*, 38(2), 85–104.

Formisano, E., et al. (2008). "Who" is saying "what"? Brain-based decoding of human voice and speech. *Science*, 322, 970–973.

Gardner, B. B., & Levy, S. J. (1955). The product and the brand. *Harvard Business Review*, 33, 33–39.

Glimcher, P. W., et al. (2009). *Neuroeconomics: Decision making and the brain*. Cambridge, MA: Academic Press.

Hinton, G. E., McClelland, J. L., & Rumelhart, D. E. 1986. Distributed representations. In *Parallel distributed processing*, 77–109. Cambridge, MA: MIT Press.

Hsu, M., et al. (2005). Neural systems responding to degrees of uncertainty in human decision-making. *Science*, 310(5754), 1680–1683.

Hutchinson, J. W., Raman, K., & Mantrala, M. K. (1994). Finding choice alternatives in memory: Probability models of brand name recall. *JMR, Journal of Marketing Research*, 31(4), 441–461.

Kahneman, D. (2011). *Thinking, fast and slow*. New York: Macmillan.

Kamakura, W. A., & Russell, G. J. (1993). Measuring brand value with scanner data. *International Journal of Research in Marketing*, 10(1), 9–22.

Kay, K. N., et al. (2008). Identifying natural images from human brain activity. *Nature*, 452(7185), 352–355.

Keller, K. L. (1993). Conceptualizing, measuring, and managing customer-based brand equity. *Journal of Marketing*, 57, 1–22.

Keller, K. L. (2012). Understanding the richness of brand relationships: Research dialogue on brands as intentional agents. *Journal of Consumer Psychology*, 22(2), 186–190.

Keller, K. L., & Lehmann, D. R. (2006). Brands and branding: Research findings and future priorities. *Marketing Science*, 25(6), 740.

Knox, S., & Walker, D. (2001). Measuring and managing brand loyalty. *Journal of Strategic Marketing*, 9(2), 111–128.

Koenigs, M., & Tranel, D. (2008). Prefrontal cortex damage abolishes brand-cued changes in cola preference. *Social Cognitive and Affective Neuroscience*, 3(1), 6.

Kotler, P., & Armstrong, G. (2010). *Principles of marketing*. Upper Saddle River, NJ: Pearson Education.

Kriegeskorte, N., Goebel, R., & Bandettini, P. (2006). Information-based functional brain mapping. *Proceedings of the National Academy of Sciences of the United States of America*, 103(10), 3863–3868.

Lashley, K. S. 1950. In search of the engram. In *Physiological mechanisms in animal behaviour*, Society for Experimental Biology (Great Britain), 454–482. New York: Academic Press.

McClelland, J. L., & Rogers, T. T. (2003). The parallel distributed processing approach to semantic cognition. *Nature Reviews. Neuroscience*, 4, 310–322.

McClure, S. M., et al. (2004). Neural correlates of behavioral preference for culturally familiar drinks. *Neuron*, 44(2), 379–387.

Milner, B., Squire, L. R., & Kandel, E. R. (1998). Cognitive neuroscience and the study of memory. *Neuron*, 20(3), 445–468.

Mitchell, T. M., et al. (2008). Predicting human brain activity associated with the meanings of nouns. *Science*, 320(5880), 1191–1195.

Nader, K., Schafe, G. E., & LeDoux, J. E. (2000). The labile nature of consolidation theory. *Nature Reviews. Neuroscience*, 1(3), 216–219.

Neal, D. T., et al. (2011). The pull of the past: When do habits persist despite conflict with motives? *Personality and Social Psychology Bulletin*, 37(11), 1428–1437.

Plassmann, H., Ramsøy, T. Z., & Milosavljevic, M. (2012). Branding the brain: A critical review and outlook. *Journal of Consumer Psychology*, 22(1), 18–36.

Rangel, A., Camerer, C., & Montague, P. R. (2008). A framework for studying the neurobiology of value-based decision making. *Nature Reviews. Neuroscience*, 9(7), 545–556.

Reynolds, T. J., & Phillips, C. B. (2005). In search of true brand equity metrics: All market share ain't created equal. *Journal of Advertising Research*, 45(02), 171–186.

Rust, R. T., Lemon, K. N., & Zeithaml, V. A. (2004). Return on marketing: Using customer equity to focus marketing strategy. *Journal of Marketing*, 68(1), 109–127.

Rust, R. T., Zeithaml, V. A., & Lemon, K. N. (2004). Customer-centered brand management. *Harvard Business Review*, 82(9), 110–120.

Schacter, D. L. (1999). The seven sins of memory. Insights from psychology and cognitive neuroscience. *American Psychologist*, 54, 182–203.

Schacter, D. L., & Slotnick, S. D. (2004). The cognitive neuroscience of memory distortion. *Neuron*, 44(1), 149–160.

Schaefer, M., & Rotte, M. (2007). Favorite brands as cultural objects modulate reward circuit. *Neuroreport*, 18(2), 141–145.

Schiller, D., et al. (2010). Preventing the return of fear in humans using reconsolidation update mechanisms. *Nature*, 463(7277), 49–53.

Schultz, W., Dayan, P., & Montague, P. R. (1997). A neural substrate of prediction and reward. *Science*, 275(5306), 1593–1599.

Sharp, B. (1995). Brand equity and market-based assets of professional service firms. *Journal of Professional Services Marketing*, 13(1), 3–13.

Shocker, A. D., Srivastava, R. K., & Ruekert, R. W. (1994). Challenges and opportunities facing brand management: An introduction to the special issue. *JMR, Journal of Marketing Research*, 31(2), 149–158.

Squire, L. R., & Wixted, J. T. (2011). The cognitive neuroscience of human memory since H.M. *Annual Review of Neuroscience*, 34, 259–288.

Squire, L. R., & Zola, S. M. (1996). Structure and function of declarative and nondeclarative memory systems. *Proceedings of the National Academy of Sciences of the United States of America*, 93(24), 13515–13522.

Srivastava, R. K., Shervani, T. A., & Fahey, L. (1998). Market-based assets and shareholder value: A framework for analysis. *Journal of Marketing*, 62, 2–18.

Sugrue, L. P., Corrado, G. S., & Newsome, W. T. (2005). Choosing the greater of two goods: Neural currencies for valuation and decision making. *Nature Reviews. Neuroscience*, 6(5), 363–375.

Tulving, E. (2002). Episodic memory: From mind to brain. *Annual Review of Psychology*, 53, 1–25.

Wood, W., & Neal, D. T. (2007). A new look at habits and the habit-goal interface. *Psychological Review*, 114(4), 843–863.

Yarkoni, T., Poldrack, R. A., Nichols, T. E., Van Essen, D. C., & Wager, T. D. (2011). Large-scale automated synthesis of human functional neuroimaging data. *Nature Methods*, 8(8), 665–760.

Yin, H. H., & Knowlton, B. (2006). The role of the basal ganglia in habit formation. *Nature Reviews. Neuroscience*, 7(6), 464–476.

Yin, H. H., Knowlton, B. J., & Balleine, B. W. (2004). Lesions of dorsolateral striatum preserve outcome expectancy but disrupt habit formation in instrumental learning. *European Journal of Neuroscience*, 19(1), 181–189.

Yoon, C., et al. (2006). A functional magnetic resonance imaging study of neural dissociations between brand and person judgments. *Journal of Consumer Research*, 33(1), 31–40.

CHAPTER 11

PRICING

HIRAK PARIKH,
DAVIDE BALDO, AND
KAI-MARKUS MÜLLER

After the first crunch into Lay's crispy, salty potato chips you cannot but agree with the tagline's undeniable truth: "No one can eat just one." PepsiCo's Lay's not only nailed the perfect product but also the perfect tagline. As authors of this chapter, we confess to feeling helpless and not being able to stop until our salty fingers feel the bottom of the bag.

While the tagline aims to create an outstanding product experience, the producer is interested in the bottom line. Other than indirect factors, such as marketing, advertising, and PR, price is a key factor that directly affects the bottom line (Monroe and Cox 2001).

So what should the price be for a product that captures customers from the first crunch? PepsiCo Turkey wanted to identify this key question together with the authors. Their main question was, "What is the willingness-to-pay for two different sizes of Lay's chips?" We use that real case to explain how prices are set in markets, how they are perceived in the brain, and how neuroscience can lead to better methods to determine prices. When dealing with price management and price psychology, many other questions keep surfacing in various contexts: How will customers react to a price change in an existing product? How do we price different packages? At what price point should we introduce a different size?

The customer, however, would want to get more crunch for the buck. In other words, pay as little as possible before he or she digs into the bag of crispy, potato goodness. And there is a price ceiling no matter how hungry one is or how appetizing the chips look. If the price is below that ceiling, one believes one is getting a great deal; ideally, obtaining more value than what one pays for the chips.

Somewhere in the middle is that sweet spot where the price feels just right—not too high and not too low.

The challenge of pricing is quite complicated for a company. There are myriads of consumers eating tons of potato chips in a large market such as Turkey, but the price is the same for all. So, in addition to understanding the sweet spot for a customer, it is mandatory to understand the statistics of all customers: How many customers will we lose when we raise our price? Is this price change going to increase profit?

Anyone who eats potato chips knows that the decision to bite into them is not always a rational one. If it was one, then the authors of this chapter would be eating something more healthful like broccoli instead of popping chips from time to time. As humans, we are part rational and part emotional; driven by reason and also impulse. Numerous experiments have shown the irrational and emotional nature of our decision making (Tversky and Kahneman 1974; Ariely 2008). The price of a product should resonate with us on an emotional and rational level for us to be persuaded to buy the product.

11.1   TRADITIONAL AND NON-BRAIN APPROACHES

The need to set prices is certainly as old as the invention of money, which supposedly appeared first in Mesopotamia circa 3000 B.C. Since then, sellers have tried to figure out the maximum acceptable price for a customer. Over the few thousand years since, methods to determine this have indeed become more sophisticated, but the question has not really changed much: How much is a customer willing to pay, and how to predict a customer's reaction to different prices?

> The need to set prices is certainly as old as the invention of money, which supposedly appeared first in Mesopotamia circa 3000 b.c.

Whether you are trying to sell papyrus in Mesopotamia in 3000 B.C. or an international food giant trying to estimate the appropriate price for a bag of chips today, there are several ways you could proceed:

1. Directly observe customer buying behavior in a real or replicated buying environment, known as the *observational approach*; or

2. Ask questions of potential customers, directly or indirectly, concerning what they would pay if they were going to buy the product, known as the *survey approach*.

3. A third approach has only become possible in very recent years: observe brain activity and derive willingness-to-pay for a product directly from the brain. We call this approach *neuropricing*.

11.1.1   THE OBSERVATIONAL APPROACH

During observational studies, prices of the product to be tested can be systematically varied over time, and a customer's reaction can be observed and measured

(Breidert, Hahsler, and Reutterer 2006). As real buying behavior is measured, such methods can indeed provide reliable results. However, the drawback is that these kinds of experiments are costly and highly time-consuming as they require a considerable amount of time for collection of data. They are also confined to relatively small test markets, because most companies simply cannot change prices permanently without losing credibility.

Another related approach is to figure this out, not by asking customers, but by analyzing their buying patterns from historical sales data. Today, faster and less expensive computers make it possible to analyze extremely vast amounts of information to look for patterns and trends—popularly called "big data." As such methods are based on real buying transactions, they are considered to be reliable in determining willingness-to-pay and predicting future demand. In order to identify the demand on the basis of models, it is necessary that the product has been sold at different price points in the market. In practice, this is often not the case, because companies shy away from frequent price changes for the same product.

11.1.2 THE SURVEY APPROACH

When historical sales data are not available and results are needed quickly, observational methods cannot be implemented. Therefore, several other survey-based approaches for estimating willingness-to-pay were developed. Survey-based methods ask a selected group of potential customers to state, directly or indirectly, how much they would be willing to pay for a specific product. As such tests are conducted with a relatively small number of participants, it is important that the group of tested customers accurately reflects the target population. Popular examples of these approaches are the Gabor-Granger method, the Van Westendorp price sensitivity meter, the conjoint survey method, discrete-choice experiment methods, and so forth. These methods are relatively easy to implement, and results can be achieved quickly. However, they heavily depend on explicit answers from respondents, which are not always reliable.

11.1.3 WHY NEUROPRICING?

While the standard methods have their merits, they often sidestep the fundamental question: What is really happening in my customer's mind as he experiences my product and sees the price?

The problem is that humans are bad at predicting their own behavior, which may or may not be intentional. Perhaps not always consciously, we often say one thing and do another. We want to believe one thing, yet want to give answers that sound "right" or are "what the surveyor might want to hear." We are all familiar with the feeling that we simply cannot or will not say in words what we really feel. Price is not just a number. It comes along with a rich set of associations that affect how we value and perceive a product and its worth.

Price is not just a number. It comes along with a rich set of associations that affect how we value and perceive a product and its worth.

Again, looking into thinking as a culmination of System 1 and System 2 (which were extensively described in chapter 8) allows us to link those to neuropricing. The goal of neuropricing is to use these brain metrics to tap into the mind of the customer directly and decipher willingness-to-pay. This particular price is a proxy for the "value" the customer really seeks when he exchanges money for the product. Neuropricing approaches the question of value by measuring as directly as possible where and when the computation is made—in the brains of customers. Before we dive into how we go about pricing a bag of chips, let's take a brief detour and discuss our current understanding of neural mechanisms of prices.

The goal of Neuropricing is to use these brain metrics to tap into the mind of the customer directly and decipher willingness-to-pay.

11.2 NEURAL MECHANISMS OF PRICE PERCEPTION

The price for a bag of chips is denoted by a number. This number in turn is an abstract feature of the product "bag of Lay's chips." Thus, relevant for the brain are four important steps: (1) product perception, (2) price perception, (3) integration of price as a product feature, and finally (4) evaluation and decision. Taking our bag of Lay's chips, let's see how the brain makes that decision to either "buy" or "not buy."

11.2.1 PRODUCT PERCEPTION

How do we perceive objects? Our current understanding suggests this sequence: Photons reach the retina, and then through a number of initial stations, the visual information is passed on to the lateral geniculate nucleus (LGN), a part of the thalamus. The LGN partially combines, computes, and processes visual information before relaying it to the primary visual cortex located in the occipital lobe at the back of the brain.

From the occipital lobe, processing of the visual information is split into two parallel paths: the dorsal and the ventral path, or simply, the "where?" and the "what?" path to the parietal and occipital lobes of the brain, respectively (Mishkin et al. 1983). Along the parietal lobe, the dorsal path encodes where in the external world the bag of chips lies: "Is it on the top shelf or is it on the bottom? To the left or the right?" As humans, we need our parietal lobe to locate the yummy snacks: people who have had an injury or a stroke in the parietal lobe have trouble finding things and orienting themselves in the supermarket. If the parietal lobe helps process the "where?" then the ventral path along the temporal lobe processes the "what?" The above-described patients once directed to the shelf are completely capable of recognizing the "bag of Lay's chips."

Among several different hypotheses on how an object becomes an "object in consciousness," one suggested idea is that there are highly specialized neurons in the ventral path encoding for specific objects or people. These "grandmother neurons" are always active when you perceive a certain object or a person, for example your grandmother (Cerf et al. 2010). If an object is close enough to resemble a bag of chips, then those neurons that encode "chips" become more activated than others and finally generate the emerging perception of a bag of chips. Others have proposed that the brain processes many features of an object, such as color, shape, or texture in separate areas, which need to be integrated before we perceive. This implies that perception is generated step-by-step from small pieces from the bottom to the top; for example, from dots or lines encoded in the primary visual cortex, to larger pieces such as angles and shapes in later areas of the ventral stream, culminating in the perception of an object further down in the inferotemporal cortex. However, Shaul Hochstein and Merav Ahissar (2002), two Israeli neuroscientists, proposed that late visual areas or even frontal cortex areas are involved in perception very early on and deliver a broad sense of the object even before the primary visual areas fill in the details. Many experiments support this idea that the brain "sees and feels" before actually "seeing all the details."

The details of human visual perception are still being worked out, but we do know that for perceiving a bag of chips, the brain needs to know "where" and "what" it is. The prefrontal cortex will later determine what needs to be done with the bag of chips. But before that—unless you are a scoundrel stealing potato chips—your brain still has to process the price.

11.2.2 Price Perception

While humans are the only animals that are known to do calculus and trigonometry, all animals have an elementary concept of number for making foraging or confrontation choices such as: "How many seeds?" "One lion or two?" When it comes to prices, humans do not simply rely on this rough sense of number. Our brains (being more evolved than a guinea pig's) need to understand and translate the abstract symbolic representation of a number into something meaningful. Lionel Naccache and Stanislas Dehaene (2001) have conducted functional magnetic resonance imaging (fMRI) studies showing that the intraparietal cortex is responsible for most of the number processing in the brain. The intraparietal cortex in the right hemisphere works out rough quantities while the intraparietal cortex of the left hemisphere performs the higher-level mathematical processes such as making calculations.

11.2.3 Integration of Price as a Feature of the Product

The classic perspective of visual attention has been strongly influenced by Anne Treisman and Garry Gelade, perceptual psychologists who suggested that features of a visual object are integrated into a coherent percept. For example, when the shopper looks at the bag of Lay's chips, he sees different features—the shiny

While humans are the only animals that are known to do calculus and trigonometry, all animals have an elementary concept of number.

packaging, a rectangular shape, an overall yellowish color, and the familiar swirling Lay's logo. According to Treisman and Gelade (19980), the brain integrates all these features into an object. The shopper also needs to integrate the price as one of the features of the product. Once price and product are integrated as one being a feature of the other, the brain is ready for the buying decision.

Once price and product are integrated as one being a feature of the other, the brain is ready for the buying decision.

11.2.4 THE BUYING DECISION

How does the brain buy? Both marketers and neuroeconomists would like to know how the brain takes all these various inputs and produces a "buy" or a "not buy" decision for the product. By designing smart experiments, scientists have managed to approximate real buying decisions in the laboratory while using modern imaging technology to see the brain in action.

In 2007, Brian Knutson and his colleagues performed an experiment to see the brain in action while people combined preference for a product and its price (Knutson et al. 2007). In a cleverly designed game, participants were given $20 to spend on a series of 80 different products whose prices ranged from $2 to $20. In each repetition (called *trial*), the participant could "choose to buy" or "decline to buy" the presented product. At the end of the study, only one of the trials would be randomly selected via lottery and the chosen outcome for that trial realized. For example, in a three-product sequence: Participant A chooses to buy a box of chocolates ($12) in trial 1 and the displayed cookies ($6) in trial 2 but declines to buy the CD ($15) in trial 3. If at the end of the game the lottery wheel decides to pick trial 1, then participant A gets the box of chocolates and keeps the $8 that remains; alternatively, if the lottery wheel had chosen trial 3 instead, then participant A would get to keep the $20. Because participants are using real money and choosing real products, this design forces them to make real buying decisions and respond truthfully. Nobody wants to get stuck with something that they do not really want if they can keep the twenty bucks instead.

While the participants were playing this game in the fMRI scanner, Knutson and his colleagues were intently looking at the brain in action. They found that when subjects liked the product and its price, their nucleus accumbens was activated. The nucleus accumbens is often activated when people are feeling good. Notably, drug and nicotine addicts experience alterations in brain pathways that cross the nucleus accumbens.

As mentioned in chapter 9, the relationship between a pleasurable experience and nucleus accumbens activation was shown much earlier in the 1950s by Canadian neurophysiologists James Olds and Peter Milner. They implanted rats with electrodes in brain areas that project to the nucleus accumbens. They connected a lever to an electrical circuit such that the rat could press the lever and stimulate its own brain. Rats kept hitting the levers stimulating their reward circuits until they were completely exhausted. During this task, they no longer showed any interest in food, water, or even sex!

What about when Knutson's study participants did not like the price for the product? The participants first saw the product and then subsequently saw the price. The researchers made the observation that when the prices were high, the insula of the subjects was active. The insula is a region that is active when experiencing various emotions, as well as pain. Obviously, there is no physical pain of paying; however, Knutson and his colleagues suggested that negative emotions associated with high prices correspond to some degree with insular activation. Additionally, they found that the difference between their willingness-to-pay and the price displayed was encoded by activity in the mesial prefrontal cortex. The mesial prefrontal cortex decreased its activity when people encountered prices that they did not like. The most fascinating observation was that solely on the basis of brain activity, Knutson and his colleagues were able to predict if a customer liked the product and price and whether she would buy the product or not!

11.3 USING NEUROPRICING TO FIND THE GOLDILOCKS PRICE

How do we tap into this decision making process in the brain to discover the willingness-to-pay for potato chips? Like the story of Goldilocks and the Three Bears, we are interested in finding a price that is neither too "high" nor too "low," but "just right"—the Goldilocks price.

To that end, we measure extent of a "match" or "mismatch" signal in the brain to the price being shown (for an analogy, see Garrido et al. 2009). If a product is overpriced, then the brain will detect the discrepancy between the product value and its price, and there will be a distinguishable mismatch signal. Notably, this is also the case if the product is underpriced compared to the perceived value. Starting from the nonmatching prices as a benchmark, we identify the Goldilocks price at which the brain's reaction indicates the best price-to-product fit.

11.4 CASE STUDY: PRICING PACKAGES OF POTATO CHIPS

The task is to price PepsiCo's Lay's chips in Turkey and determine what would happen when the price was changed. We chose a simple paradigm in which the subjects saw a picture of the particular package of Lay's chips followed by one of the set of prices (figure 11.1). Using a 64-channel electroencephalography (EEG) system, we recorded their brain waves as they were presented the test prices. For each presented price, they indicated if they found the price to be "cheap" or "expensive" by pressing a key on the computer (figure 11.2). For neuropricing, only

If a product is overpriced, then the brain will detect the discrepancy between the product value and its price, and there will be a distinguishable mismatch signal.

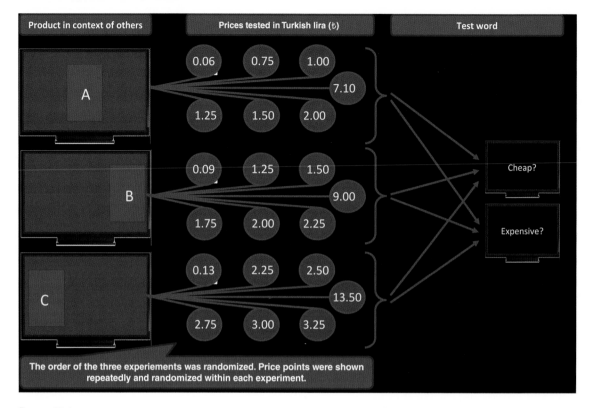

Product in context of others	Prices tested in Turkish lira (₺)	Test word

A: 0.06, 0.75, 1.00, 7.10, 1.25, 1.50, 2.00

B: 0.09, 1.25, 1.50, 9.00, 1.75, 2.00, 2.25

C: 0.13, 2.25, 2.50, 13.50, 2.75, 3.00, 3.25

Test word: Cheap? Expensive?

The order of the three experiments was randomized. Price points were shown repeatedly and randomized within each experiment.

Figure 11.1
Testing prices for packages of chips.

Figure 11.2
Collecting data for neuropricing.

the instantaneous brain reaction after the price is presented is of consequence. Our brains react very quickly to the price, earlier than we make any movement to indicate our choice. The only reason to include a behavioral response is to ensure that the participants are engaged in the task. Much better results are obtained when subjects have an active role in the experiment; else, they tend to get bored or fall asleep (see box 11.1).

11.4.1 HOW TO OBTAIN THE BRAIN SIGNALS?

Experiments done by our group and others (Bourgeois-Gironde, Tallon-Baudry, and Florent. 2011) have shown that the reaction to price is almost instantaneous, appearing in less than a second after the price is shown. We exclusively use EEG data to do pricing studies on account of the millisecond-by-millisecond resolution afforded by this method.

First, the neuropricing graph is determined indicating the "feel-good-price" with the highest match signal for price and product in the brain. Subsequently, the obtained graph is remodeled to predict demand for the product to know how customers would react to a price increase or decrease (shown in figure 11.3 for the medium-size package). In order to obtain the modeled revenues at each price, the x and y axes of the modeled demand curve are simply multiplied. Finally, in order to estimate profits, variable costs are subtracted from the revenues. These predictions at each price are crucial to figure out if profits will increase or decrease in response to a price change.

11.4.2 RELEVANCE AND VALIDATION

To validate and test the predictions from neuropricing, PepsiCo Turkey changed prices for the packages for 2 months in two of their largest markets. Their goal was not to simply find out the willingness-to-pay but also to find out how their revenue index (change from existing) changed as a function of price increase or decrease (i.e., how many customers would they lose or win as a fraction of current customers).

According to the neuropricing results, if the price for the medium-size package was increased to £1.75 from the then-existing price of £1.5, neuropricing predicted a decrease in revenues of 9.3%. Using the Gabor-Granger survey method, the predicted decrease was 33.1%. The real decrease measured in the field by PepsiCo was 7%. The prediction made by neuropricing was correct with a margin of 2.3%. Similarly, the price for the large-size package was increased to £2.75 from the then-existing price of £2.5. Neuropricing predicted the decrease in revenue to be 11%. The real decrease measured in the field was 7%. The prediction made by neuropricing was correct with a margin of error of 4%.

In general, there is some skepticism about consumer neuroscience, and one the chief criticisms leveled against this field is that because algorithms and techniques are not published or peer-reviewed, the validity of such methods is

Box 11.1
Anchoring

The "anchoring" effect, first theorized by Kahneman and Tversky during the 1970s, describes the human tendency to rely on available information and existing mental frameworks to make decisions. As prices are just numbers linked to products, they are relative and the brain is unable to categorize a product as truly cheap or expensive without comparing its price with others. It has been shown that it is possible to affect one's willingness-to-pay (WTP) by showing a high or low number before presenting the customer with the actual price.

We investigated the WTP for the well-known WhatsApp mobile app, which was priced at €0.89 per year. To quantify the anchoring effect, we measured WTP under two different conditions: in condition A ("low anchoring"), participants were primed by telling them that "Telegram" (a WhatsApp competitor) was available for free. In condition B ("high anchoring"), participants were told that SMS costs an average of €35 per year (see figure). Using EEG recordings, the brain response to the same set of prices was determined and used to investigate participants' WTP in both conditions. When subjects were "anchored low," their feel-good price was €0.49. However, when primed with the yearly cost for SMS, their WTP increased to €1.49. The higher anchor of €35 induced a threefold increase in apparent value!

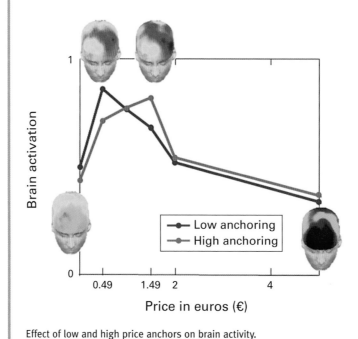

Effect of low and high price anchors on brain activity.

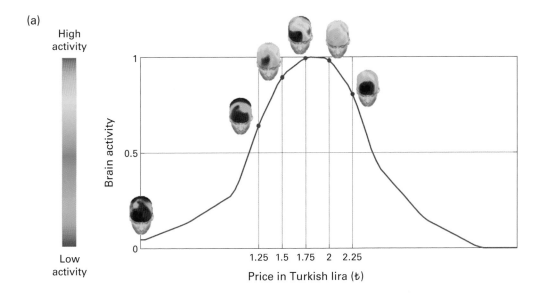

FIGURE 11.3

(a) Neuropricing curve and derived customer demand for the medium-size package of chips. Neuropricing curve showing the brain activity at the prices presented. Peak corresponds to the price that resonated the best with aggregate number of customers. (b) Derived customer demand from the neuropricing curve. Shows how what % of customers will buy at particular price.

questionable. It is understandable that for commercial reasons, algorithms and specific techniques are proprietary and hence results are presented via a black box. In our view, there is perhaps a way around both the scientific and proprietary concerns. The solution is to have independent validation of the recommendations on real customers in a real marketplace, similar to drug efficacy tests in the pharmaceutical industry. Because most questions in consumer neuroscience and pricing in particular arise from a need to solve a real-world problem, the results and recommendations can be immediately applied and tested in the marketplace.

In cases where the stakes are too high to change prices, then these recommendations can be applied to a select group of customers in the field or compared in A versus B tests for a brief period to gauge the improvement over other methods. Not only will it weed out bad approaches, but it will also serve to deliver useful results to customers and assure skeptics that these methods indeed make valid predictions.

KEY TAKEAWAYS

- Pricing is the key factor that determines the bottom line (i.e., profits of a company).

- Prices should resonate with us on both emotional and rational levels for consumers to be persuaded to buy a product.

- The right price can be set by using an observational survey or a neuropricing approach.

- Prior exposure or changing of the frame of reference, known as anchoring, changes the perception of prices.

- The intraparietal cortex in the right hemisphere works out rough number quantities while the intraparietal cortex of the left hemisphere performs the higher-level mathematical processes such as making calculations.

- When customers liked both the product and price, their nucleus accumbens was found to be active.

- Negative emotions associated with high prices correspond to some degree with insular activation.

- The extent of mismatch between customers' willingness-to-pay and the price was encoded by decreased activity in the mesial prefrontal cortex when they did not like the higher prices.

- Neuropricing allows accurate modeling of population demand from sample sizes of about 40 subjects.

- Neuromarketing algorithms are proprietary, but the results should be benchmarked and tested by an independent entity.

Discussion Questions

1. Discuss times when you felt an emotional or rational pull to buy a product based on the price and the eventual result.

2. Think of examples in the real world that exploit or could exploit the phenomenon of anchoring.

3. Does the WhatsApp study corroborate or contradict the hypothesis that neuropricing reveals perceived value? Why?

4. Why are studies in the laboratory in many cases better predictors of real-world behavior in the field than research studies conducted directly in the field?

5. What could be other approaches to validate or benchmark consumer neuroscience?

6. Where are places where neuropricing might be possibly the best approach?

References

Ariely, Dan. 2008. *Predictably irrational.* New York: HarperCollins.

Bourgeois-Gironde, S., C. Tallon-Baudry, and M. Florent. 2011. Fast and automatic activation of an abstract representation of money in the human ventral visual pathway. *PLoS One* 6 (11): 1–7.

Breidert, C., M. Hahsler, and T. Reutterer. 2006. A review of methods for measuring willingness-to-pay. *Innovative Marketing* 2 (4).

Cerf, M., N. Thiruvengadam, F. Mormann, A. Kraskov, R. Q. Quiroga, C. Koch, and I. Fried. 2010. On-line, voluntary control of human temporal lobe neurons. *Nature* 467 (7319): 1104–1108. doi:10.1038/nature09510.

Garrido, M. I., J. M. Kilner, K. E. Stephan, and K. J. Friston. 2009. The mismatch negativity: A review of underlying mechanisms. *Clinical Neurophysiology* 120 (3): 453–463. doi:10.1016/j.clinph.2008.11.029.

Hochstein, S., and M. Ahissar. 2002. View from the top: Hierarchies and reverse hierarchies in the visual system. *Neuron* 36 (5): 791–804.

Kahneman, D. 2011. *Thinking, fast and slow.* New York: Farrar, Straus and Giroux.

Knutson, B., S. Rick, G. E. Wimmer, D. Prelec, and G. Loewenstein. 2007. Neural predictors of purchases. *Neuron* 53 (1): 147–156. doi:10.1016/j.neuron.2006.11.010.

Mishkin, M., L. G. Ungerleider, and K. A. Macko. 1983. Object vision and spatial vision: Two cortical pathways. *Trends in Neurosciences* 6:414–417.

Monroe, K. B., and J. L. Cox. 2001. Pricing practices that endanger profits. *Marketing Management* 10 (3): 42.

Naccache, L., and S. Dehaene. 2001. The priming method: Imaging unconscious repetition priming reveals an abstract representation of number in the parietal lobes. *Cerebral Cortex* 11 (10): 966–974.

Treisman, A. M., and G. Gelade. 1980. A feature-integration theory of attention. *Cognitive Psychology* 12 (1): 97–136.

Tversky, A. and D. Kahneman. 1974. Judgment under uncertainty: Heuristics and biases. *Science* 185 (1974): 1124–1131.

CHAPTER 12

SOCIAL MARKETING

DANTE M. PIROUZ

While much of the current research in consumer neuroscience has focused on improving the efficiency and performance of marketing stimuli on consumers to benefit the bottom line of many companies, a number of researchers are using neuroscience tools and theories in order to understand how to enhance the overall well-being of consumers. This particular research perspective is focused on looking at ways to strengthen consumers' abilities to make intelligent consumption decisions and to ward off "bad" behaviors that sometimes bring unwanted, unhealthy, and unwise outcomes. This chapter will focus on the growing interest in social marketing and will also outline some of the ways that consumer neuroscience research might help to improve results for marketing campaigns that focus on helping consumers live better lives.

12.1 CREATING BETTER MARKETING AND A BETTER WORLD WITH CONSUMER NEUROSCIENCE AND SOCIAL MARKETING

For consumers, marketing cues and messages are a ubiquitous and pervasive part of everyday life. For the most part, marketers assume that consumers are cognitively adept enough to filter and process marketing cues in a sophisticated way. In fact, the neoclassical economic view of marketing is that it provides consumers with more information, allowing consumers to make informed and calculated choices (Nelson 1974). Thus, marketing cues such as advertising, retail displays. and packaging information should allow for wiser, more informed, happier consumers.

While many of these cues, such as advertisements, have sounds, visuals, and colors that are considered merely distractions by many consumers, for some people, these cues conspire to overload, overwhelm, or mislead consumers and make their day-to-day decision making much more difficult. This can lead many of us to eat too much, eat the wrong things, spend too much, put off retirement planning, mismanage debt, spend too much time watching television or surfing the Internet, and even buy and sell the wrong stocks. The costs to society are high when individuals lack the ability to self-regulate prudently. However, the benefits are enormous if we are able to limit short-term, impulsive choices and behaviors in favor of temperance and long-term well-being. This is where social marketing tries to make a difference.

> Benefits are enormous if we are able to limit short-term, impulsive choices and behaviors in favor of temperance and long-term well-being. This is where social marketing tries to make a difference.

12.2 WHAT IS SOCIAL MARKETING?

Social marketing is a term that has been used since the 1970s to describe the use of marketing to influence positive social behavior. Social marketing can come in many forms and formats including public service announcements (PSAs), social media awareness campaigns, school-based interventions, informational PR strategies, global initiatives, and even behavioral "nudges." From a strategic perspective, social marketing has been used to help shape a number of behavior domains including drug, alcohol, and cigarette use, overeating, responsible debt use, healthy eating, health screening recommendations, family planning, littering, and gambling. A wide array of institutions including for-profit companies in addition to nonprofits, charitable foundations, and governmental agencies have implemented social marketing campaigns with a variety of objectives.

The whole point of social marketing is to apply marketing principles to gain results for important societal issues rather than to increase profits and sales for corporations. Marketing messages can not only encourage consumers to accept and endorse desired social behaviors and attitudes such as eating more healthy fruits and vegetables or endorsing social tolerance but can also encourage people to modify or reject bad, undesirable, or potentially dangerous behaviors and attitudes such as drug use or texting while driving (Lee and Kotler 2011).

An early example of social marketing is the 1987 "This Is Your Brain on Drugs" antidrug television PSA launched by the nonprofit Partnership for a Drug-Free America (now the Partnership for Drug-Free Kids). This campaign was considered at the time to be a dramatic and creative characterization of the dangerous effect drug use can have on even casual users. The objective of the campaign was to shock, especially young people, into staying away from drugs whether they have never tried them or were currently using them. Since that time, there have been several versions of the campaign, and it has become well-known enough to even be parodied on YouTube (e.g., by Cartoon Network's Adult Swim television show *Robot Chicken*; https://www.youtube.com/watch?v=k4H517oi7pU).

Another more recent example is an ad and social media campaign sponsored by New York City's Health Department that ran from 2009 to 2015 as a way of informing consumers that obesity may be linked to their consumption of soda. This campaign also tried to communicate a message that would be surprising to most consumers. The hope was that, in terms of the persuasive effect of the ad, consumers would pay more attention to the message being communicated (that drinking soda is bad for your health) and that consumers would, as a result of seeing the ad, change their consumption habits.

These campaigns and other social marketing campaigns like them are criticized on the basis that there is conflicting evidence that the attention-grabbing creative elements in the ads really work as they are intended (Werb et al. 2011). There is skepticism that social marketing can work to dissuade people from engaging in risky or unhealthy behaviors or successfully encourage people to do good things for themselves and others (for an example of a recent critique of the "This Is Your Brain on Drugs" ad, see Blistein 2014). And if this is indeed the case, then the funding spent on social marketing campaigns like these are simply being wasted, and these resources could be expended elsewhere. This is why it has become increasingly important to understand how social marketing campaigns can be optimized in order to influence consumers' behaviors for the better. This is where consumer neuroscience can help.

Next, we will look at a few key findings from consumer neuroscience research that is leading to breakthroughs in how best to communicate social marketing, health, and consumption messages (such as antismoking, antidrug, and health PSA campaigns) to consumers.

> There is skepticism that social marketing can work to dissuade people from engaging in risky or unhealthy behaviors or successfully encourage people to do good things for themselves and others.

12.3 UNDERSTANDING ADDICTIVE CONSUMER BEHAVIORS

Consumers do not always do things that are healthy or smart. Public institutions, such as government departments, hospitals, and consumer advocacy groups, often struggle with how to best encourage people to behave in ways that will lead to better health, family, and societal outcomes. The benefit to individuals and their families can be a longer, happier, healthier life for everyone concerned. But society as a whole can also benefit. Tempering dangerous and risky behaviors such as cigarette smoking or drinking alcohol can lower the economic and social costs that all members of society bear. A report by the U.S. Surgeon General estimates that the economic loss due to drug, alcohol, and tobacco use in the United States is upward of $500 billion per year (National Institute on Drug Abuse 2008a). In addition, social marketing campaigns strive to encourage healthy behaviors like exercising more or saving more money for retirement.

12.3.1 ADDICTIVE CONSUMPTION

The personal and social costs of risky and addictive consumption behaviors are enormous. For example, in the United States, more than 45 million consumers smoke cigarettes; moreover, smoking causes 440,000 premature deaths and generates $75 billion in direct medical costs annually (for a review, see National Institute on Drug Abuse 2008b). While the marketing of addictive products is in some cases restricted, exposure to marketing cues promoting addictive products is still commonplace for many consumers. Surprisingly, despite restrictions, more than $13 billion is spent annually on the marketing and promotion of cigarettes, including $50 million on traditional print advertising (Federal Trade Commission 2007). More than $2 billion is spent annually on promoting alcohol products using traditional media-based advertising alone (Johns Hopkins Bloomberg School of Public Health 2007).

> While the marketing of addictive products is in some cases restricted, exposure to marketing cues promoting addictive products is still commonplace for many consumers.

Traditionally, the word *addiction* has been reserved for substances that interact with the biochemistry in the body to cause physical dependency such as drugs or tobacco. But increasingly, researchers are finding evidence that many consumption behaviors also qualify as potentially addictive and harmful (Grover et al. 2011; Martin et al. 2012). This can include compulsive shopping, technology use, hoarding, overeating, plastic surgery, use of pornography, kleptomania, dietary supplement use, religious convictions, and exercise. Marketing cues might help encourage such problematic consumption, including excessive credit card use (Feinberg 1986), gambling (Binde 2009), and unhealthy food consumption (Harris, Bargh, and Brownell 2009).

Despite the magnitude of addictive product use and promotion, surprisingly little attention has been paid to marketing cues for addictive products and to whether exposure to such marketing cues might instigate a generalized array of unintended behavioral effects not necessarily related to the product advertised (Litt, Pirouz, and Shiv 2011; Martin et al. 2012). Thus, there is a need for a better understanding of the underlying psychological and physiologic mechanisms that drive responses to marketing cues for addictive products.

There are many other types of addictive behavior being investigated using theories developed from neuroscientific techniques, with relevance for neuroeconomics and behavioral decision theory. Examples include pathologic gambling; substance abuse including nicotine, heroin, cocaine, and alcohol; and pathologic shopping, credit card use, and Internet use (Margolin and Kelly 1992; Robinson and Berridge 1993; Carter and Tiffany 1999; Warren and McDonough 1999; Due et al. 2002; Chambers, Taylor, and Potenza, 2003; Potenza et al. 2003a, 2003b; Spinella, Yang, and Lester 2004; Wilson, Sayette, and Fiez 2004).

Box 12.1
Concerns about the Use of Neuroscience Tools to Understand Consumer Behavior

Some have criticized the use of neuroscience for the benefit of marketers. There is a concern that consumers are often taken advantage of in the marketplace resulting in consumption habits that are ultimately harmful to individuals, families, and society as a whole. Consumer groups have criticized companies that have used consumer neuroscience in their marketing research as a ploy to find the "buy button" (Blakeslee 2004).

In addition, there is an ongoing debate as to whether consumers are able to regulate the cognitive and affective decision-making process that drives them to consume things that are not necessarily good for them. The use of neuroscience tools to analyze consumer behavior is especially sensitive. Some question whether consumer neuroscience will give marketers specific tactics that can be used to influence consumers without their consent or explicit awareness (Wilson, Gaines, and Hill 2008). This includes heavily marketed product categories such as alcohol, food, and pharmaceuticals—all of which can, for some consumers, become addictive, dangerous, and potentially lethal (for more on neuroethics, see chapter 15).

The theory of cue reactivity also might serve to explain why addiction levels remain high even though subjects self-report that they are striving to quit and they do not enjoy the consumption of their addictive substance (Carter and Tiffany 1999; Laibson 2001). In a functional magnetic resonance imaging (fMRI) study that analyzed neural response in adolescents to alcohol related imagery, researchers found that adolescents with even a short history of alcohol use had significantly higher blood oxygen response in areas of the brain associated with reward, desire, positive affect, and episodic recall (Tapert et al. 2003).

While traditionally, there has been a focus by researchers and clinicians on addictions to substances, there is a growing awareness that a wide array of consumer behaviors may exhibit neural activation patterns that overlap some of those found to be involved with substance addictions (box 12.1).

12.4 CREATING SOCIAL MARKETING CAMPAIGNS THAT WORK

Many PSAs are aimed at changing behavior. The key question is how to create PSAs that work. If we can understand how the brain responds to marketing cues of all types, we can become better informed as to how to help people be more productive, happier, and more cooperative. There is the opportunity to do this as

In a functional magnetic resonance imaging (fMRI) study that analyzed neural response in adolescents to alcohol related imagery, researchers found that adolescents with even a short history of alcohol use had significantly higher blood oxygen response in areas of the brain associated with reward, desire, positive affect, and episodic recall.

well using neuroscience methods. There seem to be some initial indications as to what works in making a social marketing campaign effective.

Some researchers have focused on how creative elements that elicit shock can increase attention to the primary message. For example, one set of researchers using fMRI looked at whether the sensation value of antismoking TV PSA ads made a difference (Langleben et al. 2009). Sensation value is defined as the intensity or attention-grabbing quality of the creative elements in the ad. Surprisingly, they found that antismoking ads that were low in message sensation value were easier to remember than those that were high in sensation value. They also reported greater brain activation in the prefrontal and temporal regions of the brain when participants were exposed to low- versus high-sensation ads. According to the researchers, this seems to indicate that the antismoking ads that were more low key can be effective because they allow for better cognitive processing of the ad content and do not overwhelm the viewer's processing capacity. It seems the bottom line is that a more shocking social marketing campaign does not automatically mean that the campaign will be more efficacious. These findings were confirmed in another study on health that found messages with low sensation value are actually remembered better than ones with high sensation value (Seelig et al. 2014).

But do these antismoking ads make people stop smoking? Researchers used fMRI to test whether antismoking PSAs could persuade smokers to smoke less (Wang et al. 2013). They found that if the ad showed a strong argument against smoking but did not detract from that argument with a high shock or sensation value, the ad worked better. There was increased activation in the dorsomedial prefrontal cortex, which indicates cognitive processing. More important, smokers smoked less a month after viewing those ads as measured by urine cotinine levels, which is an indicator of cigarette smoking. That's good news for organizations who want to use social marketing to help consumers and are concerned about getting their social marketing message right.

In addition, consumer neuroscience research might offer social marketers a better way to speak to specific target audiences. As discussed previously in this chapter, campaigns have traditionally focused on simple demographic categories such as age in order to target messages. However, more recent consumer neuroscience research has found that messages might need to be tailored on the basis of other psychographic traits as well. For example, there is evidence that personality traits, such as the need for cognition, can be linked to certain neural substrates (Plassmann and Weber 2015). According to Plassmann and Weber, this understanding may allow consumer groups and public policy institutions to create more powerful and effective PSAs and marketing campaigns to move consumer behavior in a positive direction (Kessler 2015).

However, negative affect is more effective in changing behavior than positive affect. The bottom line is that creative content that is emotionally engaging tends

Campaigns have traditionally focused on simple demographic categories such as age in order to target messages. However, more recent consumer neuroscience research has found that messages might need to be tailored on the basis of other psychographic traits.

to work the best. This was tested in a study that pitted a set of antidrug PSAs that were rated to be strongly convincing against antidrug PSAs that were rated to be weakly convincing and a set of nondrug control ads (Ramsay et al. 2013). The study sought to understand whether either affective or executive processing alone was enough to move behavior or whether there was an interplay of coactivation between regions related to both emotional affect and executive control. The findings showed that left lateralized inferior frontal gyri coactivated with the amygdala when participants viewed strong versus weak antidrug PSAs. These findings indicate that it is critical for both executive frontal and socioemotional regions of the brain to be activated when exposed to social marketing persuasive messages.

> **It is critical for both executive frontal and socioemotional regions of the brain to be activated when exposed to social marketing persuasive messages.**

Another fMRI study looked at whether actual consumer behavior changes (not just attitude toward the ad) could be predicted from brain activation patterns in the domain of health communications. Study participants were exposed to persuasive messages regarding the use of sunscreen as a way to protect against skin cancer (Falk 2010). The researchers found that neural activity in the medial prefrontal cortex was related to behavior change 2 weeks after exposure to the persuasive messages. Remarkably, the brain imaging data from the study were able to predict even more accurately than the self-reported intentions and attitudes of the study participants whether or not the participants would use sunscreen after seeing the persuasive messages. A subsequent study using a measure of exhaled carbon monoxide instead of urine cotinine supported the findings (Falk 2010). Findings like these substantiate the value of using consumer neuroscience brain imaging methods for better understanding how and why social marketing stimuli work to change consumer behavior.

Persuasion theory tells us that salience is also an important element in social marketing effectiveness (Hale, Householder, and Greene 2002). This was tested in the context of antismoking messages aimed at current smokers (Chua et al. 2009). They found that when the antismoking message was tailored specifically to the type of smoking behaviors the study participants actually engaged in (smokes while talking on the phone vs. smokes while doing other things), there was differential activation in the medial prefrontal cortex and the precuneus/posterior cingulate, which the researchers attribute to increased self-related cognitive processing. This means that if social marketing can speak in a relevant way to a consumer's personal experience, this increased level of salience will engage processing related to the self. This should in turn increase the effectiveness of the message on changing behavior.

> **If social marketing can speak in a relevant way to a consumer's personal experience, this increased level of salience will engage processing related to the self. This should in turn increase the effectiveness of the message on changing behavior.**

A prime example of how insights from consumer neuroscience techniques have shaped social marketing campaigns is the Shelter Pet Project, an organization focused on encouraging adoptions of abandoned and homeless pets from animal shelters. The nonprofit worked with Nielsen and the Ad Council to enhance the performance of an existing ad featuring a dog named Jules. Study participant responses to the ad were tracked using electroencephalography (EEG) and eye tracking. Based on the academic literature on facial processing, it was hypothesized that faces, even those of an animal like Jules, would stimulate viewers' emotional engagement with the ad. The results of the study indeed showed that when Jules the dog was not onscreen, attention and emotional engagement were lower. In addition, at the end of the ad when the URL, logo, and Jules were onscreen at the same time, there was evidence of divided attention among the elements, which diminished the effectiveness of the ad. As a result of these findings, the ad was re-edited to increase Jule's onscreen time and to simplify the ending graphics. This resulted in a 133% increase in traffic to the ShelterPetProject.org website within 3 months of the campaign launch (Smith 2014).

12.5   FUTURE DIRECTIONS IN SOCIAL MARKETING

There is a great deal that has yet to be explored in creating marketing campaigns, cues, and environments that promote positive social and personal attitudes and behaviors versus negative ones. It is still not clear how addiction to consumer substances and behaviors can be reversed (Litt et al. 2011; Martin et al. 2012). How do consumers who want to stop smoking or eat less protect themselves from marketing messages that might sabotage their best intentions? How do marketers communicate effectively with consumer segments without confusing or enticing other consumer segments who do not process the information in the same way (box 12.2)? Can consumer neuroscience give us more clues as to how to best target and communicate to different consumer segments on the basis of their neural processing profiles?

Box 12.2
Protecting Special Populations

There are segments of the population that institutions have designated as needing particular protections from marketers. For example, particular age demographics have traditionally been viewed as segments that need to be shielded from undue and/or inappropriate influence. As one example, children are believed to be ill-equipped cognitively to discern whether marketing messages are truthful or not and to resist appeals that might drive them to want products. In addition, there is neurobiological evidence that adolescents, because they are undergoing significant changes in their neural development, may be more likely to seek out and engage in risky behaviors and are also vulnerable to influence from outside sources including marketers (Pechmann et al. 2005). The elderly are also a potentially vulnerable age group (Pechmann et al. 2011).

The other side of the coin is to look at how best to "nudge" smart consumer behavior (Thaler and Sunstein 2008). Behavioral nudges have been touted as a less punitive way to get people to do things that will help improve their lives. Nudges have been used to get consumers to buy insurance, eat more healthy foods, sign up for automatic retirement savings plans, get health screenings for cancer, and for other potentially beneficial choices. However, there has been very little work done incorporating consumer neuroscience and behavioral nudges to understand the mechanism by which default choices aid in directing long-term behavioral changes. These are all areas that warrant continuing examination of the neural underpinnings of healthy and wise decision making using consumer neuroscience tools and theories. The overarching promise of this deeper understanding of motivation, persuasion, and behavior change from social marketing efforts is a happier, healthier, and smarter consumer.

> There has been very little work done incorporating consumer neuroscience and behavioral nudges to understand the mechanism by which default choices aid in directing long-term behavioral changes.

KEY TAKEAWAYS

- Social marketing is the use of marketing tools to promote positive social behavior. For example, public service announcements have been used to advocate for topics such as healthier eating habits, responsible credit card use, and rejection of smoking and illicit drug use.

- Consumer neuroscience tools and techniques may be able to improve the effectiveness of social marketing campaigns.

DISCUSSION QUESTIONS

1. What do the findings in consumer neuroscience tell us about whether social marketing campaigns work or not?

2. What are the ethical implications of using neuroscience tools to investigate consumer behavior and social marketing?

3. How can companies and institutions prevent their marketing research findings from being misinterpreted and misused by others?

4. What questions still remain unanswered regarding creation of effective social marketing messages and campaigns?

5. According to the consumer neuroscience research findings thus far, what should an effective social marketing campaign have?

References

Binde, P. (2009). Exploring the impact of gambling advertising: An interview study of problem gamblers. *International Journal of Mental Health and Addiction*, 7(4), 541–554. doi:10.1007/s11469-008-9186-9.

Blakeslee, S. 2004. If you have a "buy button" in your brain, what pushes it? New York Times, October 19. Available at http://www.nytimes.com/2004/10/19/science/if-your-brain-has-a-buybutton-what-pushes-it .html?_r=0/.

Blistein, D. 2014. This is your brain on drugs. *Huffpost Health News*. Available at www.huffingtonpost.com/ david-blistein/this-is-your-brain-on-dru_1_b_4832929.html.

Carter, B. L., & Tiffany, S. T. (1999). Meta-analysis of cue-reactivity in addiction research. *Addiction (Abingdon, England)*, 94(3), 327–340.

Chambers, R. A., Taylor, J. R., & Potenza, M. N. (2003). Developmental neurocircuitry of motivation in adolescence: A critical period of addiction vulnerability. *American Journal of Psychiatry*, 160(6), 1041–1052.

Chua, H. F., Liberzon, I., Welsh, R. C., & Strecher, V. J. (2009). Neural correlates of message tailoring and self-relatedness in smoking cessation programming. *Biological Psychiatry*, 65(2), 165–168.

Due, D. L., Huettel, S. A., Hall, W. G., & Rubin, D. C. (2002). Activation in mesolimbic and visuospatial neural circuits elicited by smoking cues: Evidence from functional magnetic resonance imaging. *American Journal of Psychiatry*, 159(6), 954–960.

Falk, E. B. (2010). Communication neuroscience as a tool for health psychologists. *Health Psychology*, 29(4), 355–357.

Federal Trade Commission. (2007). *Federal Trade Commission cigarette report for 2004 and 2005*. Washington, DC: Federal Trade Commission.

Feinberg, R. A. (1986). Credit cards as spending facilitating stimuli: A conditioning interpretation. *Journal of Consumer Research*, 13(3), 348–356.

Grover, A., Kamins, M. A., Martins, I. M., Davis, S., Haws, K., Mirabito, A. M., et al. (2011). From use to abuse: When everyday consumption behaviours morph into addictive consumptive behaviours. *Journal of Research for Consumers*, 19, 1–6.

Hale, J. L., Householder, B. J., & Greene, K. L. (2002). The theory of reasoned action. In J. P. Dillard & M. Pfau (Eds.), *The persuasion handbook: Developments in theory and practice* (pp. 259–286). Thousand Oaks, CA: Sage.

Harris, J. L., Bargh, J. A., & Brownell, K. D. (2009). Priming effects of television food advertising on eating behavior. *Health Psychology*, 28(4), 404–413.

Johns Hopkins Bloomberg School of Public Health. (2007). *Fact sheet: Alcohol advertising and youth*. Baltimore, MD: Johns Hopkins.

Kessler, B. (Producer). 2015. Brain scans show what's wrong with conventional marketing. *Knowledge*, May 6. Available at http://knowledge.insead.edu/marketing-advertising/brain-scans-show-whats-wrong -with-conventional-marketing-3934.

Laibson, D. I. (2001). A cue theory of consumption. *Quarterly Journal of Economics*, 116(1), 81–120.

Langleben, D. D., Loughead, J. W., Ruparel, K., Hakun, J. G., Busch-Winokur, S., Holloway, M. B., et al. (2009). Reduced prefrontal and temporal processing and recall of high "sensation value" ads. *NeuroImage*, 46(1), 219–225.

Lee, N. R., & Kotler, P. A. (2011). *Social marketing: Influencing behaviors for good* (4th ed.). Thousand Oaks, CA: Sage Publications.

Litt, A., Pirouz, D. M., & Shiv, B. (2011). Neuroscience and addictive consumption. In D. G. Mick, S. Pettigrew, C. Pechmann, & J. L. Ozanne (Eds.), *Transformative consumer research for personal and collective well-being*. New York: Routledge.

Margolin, A., & Kelly, A. S. (1992). Cue reactivity and cocaine addiction. In T. Kosten & H. D. Kleber (Eds.), *Clinician's guide to cocaine addiction: Theory, research and treatment*. New York: Guilford.

Martin, I. M., Kamens, M., Pirouz, D. M., Grover, A., Davis, S. W., Haws, K. T., et al. (2012). On the road to addiction: The facilitative and preventative role of marketing cues. *Journal of Business Research*, 66(8), 1219–1226.

National Institute on Drug Abuse (Producer). 2008a. *Drug abuse costs the United States economy hundreds of billions of dollars in increased health care costs, crime, and lost productivity*. Available at https://www.drugabuse.gov/publications/addiction-science-molecules-to-managed-care/introduction/drug-abuse-costs-united-states-economy-hundreds-billions-dollars-in-increased-health.

National Institute on Drug Abuse. 2008b. *NIDA InfoFacts: Cigarettes and other nicotine products*. Available at https://www.drugabuse.gov/infofacts/tobacco.html.

Nelson, P. (1974). Advertising as information. *Journal of Political Economy*, 82(4), 729–754.

Pechmann, C., Levine, L. J., Loughlin, S., & Leslie, F. (2005). Impulsive and self-conscious: Adolescents' vulnerability to advertising and promotions. *Journal of Public Policy & Marketing*, 24, 202–221.

Pechmann, C. C., Moore, E., Andreasen, A., Connell, P. M., Freeman, D., Gardner, M., et al. (2011). Navigating the central tensions in research on consumers who are at risk: Challenges and opportunities. *Journal of Public Policy & Marketing*, 30(1), 23–30.

Plassmann, H., & Weber, B. (2015). Individual differences in marketing placebo effects: Evidence from brain imaging and behavioral experiments. *JMR, Journal of Marketing Research*, 52(4), 493–510.

Potenza, M. N., Leung, H.-C., Blumberg, H. P., Peterson, B. S., Fulbright, R. K., Lacadie, C. M., et al. (2003a). An fMRI Stroop task study of ventromedial prefrontal cortical function in pathological gamblers. *American Journal of Psychiatry*, 160(11), 1990–1994. doi:10.1176/appi.ajp.160.11.1990.

Potenza, M. N., Steinberg, M. A., Skudlarski, P., Fulbright, R. K., Lacadie, C. M., Wilber, M. K., et al. (2003b). Gambling urges in pathological gambling: A functional magnetic resonance imaging study. *Archives of General Psychiatry*, 60(8), 828–836.

Ramsay, I. S., Yzer, M. C., Luciana, M., Vohs, K. D., & MacDonald, A. W., III. (2013). Affective and executive network processing associated with persuasive antidrug messages. *Journal of Cognitive Neuroscience*, 25(7), 1136–1147.

Robinson, T. E., & Berridge, K. C. (1993). The neural basis of drug craving: An incentive-sensitization theory of addiction. *Brain Research. Brain Research Reviews*, 18, 247–291.

Seelig, D., Wang, A.-L., Jaganathan, K., Loughead, J. W., Blady, S. J., Childress, A. R., et al. (2014). Low message sensation health promotion videos are better remembered and activate areas of the brain associated with memory encoding. *PLoS One*, 9(11), e113256.

Smith, M. E. 2014. The brains behind better ads: Optimizing the cute and cuddly. *Nielsen Newswire*. Available at www.nielsen.com/us/en/insights/news/2014/the-brains-behind-better-ads-optimizing-the-cute-and-cuddly.html.

Spinella, M., Yang, B., & Lester, D. (2004). Prefrontal system dysfunction and credit card debt. *International Journal of Neuroscience*, 114(10), 1323–1332.

Tapert, S. F., Cheung, E. H., Brown, G. C., Lawrence, F. R., Paulus, M. P., Schweinsburg, A. D., et al. (2003). Neural response to alcohol stimuli in adolescents with alcohol use disorder. *Archives of General Psychiatry*, 60(7), 727–735.

Thaler, R. H., & Sunstein, C. R. (2008). *Nudge: Improving decisions about health, wealth, and happiness*. New Haven, CT: Yale University Press.

Wang, A.-L., Ruparel, K., Loughead, J. W., Strasser, A. A., Blady, S. J., Lynch, K. G., et al. (2013). Content matters: Neuroimaging investigation of brain and behavioral impact of televised anti-tobacco public service announcements. *Journal of Neuroscience*, 33(17), 7420–7427.

Warren, C. A., & McDonough, B. E. (1999). Event-related brain potentials as indicators of smoking cue-reactivity. *Clinical Neurophysiology*, 110(9), 1570–1584.

Werb, D., Mills, E. J., DeBeck, K., Kerr, T., Montaner, J. S., & Wood, E. (2011). The effectiveness of anti-illicit-drug public-service announcements: A systematic review and meta-analysis. *Journal of Epidemiology and Community Health*, 65(10), 834–840.

Wilson, R., Gaines, J., & Hill, R. P. (2008). Neuromarketing and consumer free will. *Journal of Consumer Affairs*, 42(3), 389–410.

Wilson, S. J., Sayette, M. A., & Fiez, J. A. (2004). Prefrontal responses to drug cues: A neurocognitive analysis. *Nature Neuroscience*, 7, 211–214.

USING KNOWLEDGE FROM NEUROSCIENCE TO MAKE BUSINESS PREDICTIONS

MORAN CERF

Predictions are very hard, especially about the future.
—Niels Bohr, Nobel Laureate in Physics

Prediction involves making estimations about the future on the basis of past events and new information from the present. Everyone uses predictions in their respective industries with varying degrees of success. Prediction is used in many areas, such as foreign monetary exchange, earthquakes, energy consumption, weather, business, and so forth. Predictions can be very hard at times, especially if there is not enough data present. In cases such as start-ups and new businesses, predictions can be hit or miss.

In the technical domain, prediction can be carried out on the basis of equations and mathematical evaluations. Some evaluations can be simple, typically using some forecasting method that fits the existing data with basic equations, while the others are affected by external stimulus and require complex learning mechanisms to find a complex equation that can be used to extrapolate the existing samples into future ones.

When a new business or start-up is considered, practitioners often use predictions in the attempt to accurately aim at a goal. Investors, venture capitalists, and employees want to have a path laid out on the road to success. They therefore need predictions. Specifically, marketing managers often want to know how their product will fare among the public. Will people buy it? Will they tell friends about it? How will it trend? Those are all important points in planning a successful marketing strategy.

Ultimately in marketing, predictions are what practitioners actually want. They do not care about knowing all the neural mechanics; they want a black box where you can feed something in and get a prediction: How well will my product do? How many people will buy it, like it, find it tasty, enjoy the movie, tell their friends about it, and so forth.

Most predicting companies tell you things such as "We looked at your brand and we think it scores X on emotionality, Y on memorability, Z on attention," etc., but this is useless for most marketing managers. They do not want the "data" or the "results"; they want the "meaning," or what do you predict will happen.

13.1   PREDICTION AND UNCERTAINTY

Uncertainty has been defined in many ways. It can be considered as a state in which the decision maker lacks the ability to make a decision because of lack of information. He or she is not clear about what the outcome would be and is therefore in a state of ambiguity about the probabilities. The aspect of uncertainty in predictions is considered as a state of *risk*. Neuroscientists and economists, accordingly, study this unique situation as a test of ambiguous information and probabilities. Accordingly, economists, psychologists, and neuroscientists have now studied different aspects of uncertainty in a prediction and how it can influence a decision. The common psychological response to uncertainty is a negative state with increased chances of anxiety. Simply put, most of us like to either not exist in states of risk or to at least have a feeling that it was a choice to enter one. Specifically, many of the works in these fields have focused on decision making and financial profits and losses.

One key assumption humans have when it comes to making decisions and using probabilities to estimate future decisions is the assumption that we actually have control over our outcomes: that the governing rules of the future are not deterministic and that probabilities indeed play a part in those. Specifically, that humans indeed have free will. Scientists have repeatedly challenged this assumption, suggesting that free will may merely be an illusion and nothing more than a mere biochemical phenomenon. While this remains unclear, what is certainly known by now is that the conscious moment of perceived decision is an illusion. Whether we are free in our decision making or not, decisions certainly occurred prior to our experience of them, and as an afterthought we merely assign the claim that they were chosen in the present. Simply put, when we exhibit our choice and feel we "made it," it is already long after it was made. This, ultimately, makes ancient philosophical notions raised by giants such as Kant and Descartes something that can now be tested by neuroscientists and translated into practical, actionable behavior that practitioners can employ. Similar to the change in the common perception that neuroscientists and philosophers do not see eye to eye and normally talk past each other, which has been refuted in the past few years—neuroscientists and philosophers now collaborate on projects—so will neuroscientists

---

Ultimately in marketing, predictions are what practitioners actually want. They do not care about knowing all the neural mechanics; they want a black box where you can feed something in and get a prediction: How well will my product do?

The conscious moment of perceived decision is an illusion. Whether we are free in our decision making or not, decisions certainly occurred prior to our experience of them.

and marketing managers collaborate in using the tools of the brain in making predictions to develop better marketing strategies.

13.2 Predictive Processing and the Brain

In an extremely expansive sense, predictive processing alludes to a handling that fuses or produces not only data about the past or the present but also probable conditions from the environment. Effectively, this is what our brain does all the time; that is, taking information and using it to decide how to act later. Some key states in our life are said to be even more specific and focused for this task. One such state, for example, is our dream state. One leading hypothesis about dreams is that this is a case where our guards and inhibitions are down, and our brain simulates the ultimate virtual reality where we are immersed in a situation and filter it through our value and belief systems so that it feels real. Then we use it to actually test a prediction about the future. How will it feel to live in Vermont? Do I want to be married to him? You basically live through the experience in your dreams—the ultimate prediction test—and see how it feels, before waking up with an understanding of the future potential. Such directedness toward the future has for quite some time been perceived as pertinent and advantageous for various parts of data.

Because the brain is the ultimate "big data" analytics tool, learning how it does its predictions is key to marketing predictions.

In spite of the fact that recommendations with respect to the significance of predictive components began with the early periods of both brain research and neuroscience, up to this point they have not been emphatically upheld by the neuroscience community at large. In fact, in many ways, the business world is a bigger client and proponent of those recommendations than the researchers. Part of the reason for the lack of acceptance of neural predictions is the run-of-the-mill approaches in depicting subjective procedures that hypothesize a fairly *serial* procedure, beginning with tactile, proceeding with cognitive and "higher" processing, and closing with plain behavior. Such thinking originates from the first behaviorist conceptualizations that accentuated the straight movement from tactile incitement to clear behavior, a perspective that was likewise present in early data-handling cognitivist speculations. This is not the thinking held in marketing or business. The focus on the very body-driven way of making predictions assumes that the integration of information by the brain is probabilistic merely because of the impossibly large data. However, this is a thinking that is derived from a world where data and the tools for handling it by computers were limited. Now, big data exists not only in the biological world, but also in the business world. And as such, analytics are used not only by our brain—in a fast processing—but also by computers and practitioners. Hence, the tools that are used by neuroscientists,

This is what our brain does all the time; that is, taking information and using it to decide how to act later.

neurobiologists, physicists, and essentially all analysts who try to make senses of large sets are the ones employed by marketing managers as well. The era of big data and analytics in marketing calls for using in the business world the same approaches our brain uses to make fast and accurate predictions from large data sets.

Therefore, we shall focus on the two classical methods by which the brain makes its predictions: correcting for prediction errors and using "learning" (which would be, in the context of marketing analytics, "machine learning") to improve the accuracy of future predictions.

13.2.1 Prediction Error

Human decision-making skills are guided by predictions regarding events in the future and comparing these events with actual results. These comparisons are employed in numerous models of learning in order to spot what needs to be learned further and what needs to be accelerated in the learning process.

As was already mentioned when discussing the reward system in chapter 9, prediction error occurs when the neuronal system recognizes a difference between the reward and its response. It is a fundamental concept for the brain to understand errors in order to correct future predictions. The brain expects a response based on prior experience. If there is a difference between the brain's prediction and the actual response, a "prediction error" is triggered.

Simply put, the brain has models that are built out of sensory inputs depending on the environment. On the basis of these models, the brain generates predictions about what would happen next (i.e., when I touch the table a specific sound will be heard, and a tactile response in my hand should emerge). The sensory system then expects those occurrences to take effect. A prediction is made. These predictions can occur on a concurrent timescale, leveling up all the way through the cortex. In this way, brain predicts sensory input on the basis of expectations of what might happen very soon and expectations of what might happen later.

As the brain generates expectation on the basis of the actual sensory input, perceptions are built. Prediction error is triggered when there is a difference between the outcome and the estimate. It is manifested by a set of neural activities that are amplified on the basis of the difference between the expected outcome and reality. Given a multitude of such prediction errors, the set of patterns that yielded the smaller error is fed forward into a learning mechanism that then feeds back into the sensory systems and adjusts the neural connections such that in a future occurrence, the likely outcome will be similar to the one we have just experienced. Essentially, we learn what the mistake was and update the probabilities such that next time it is less likely to happen. Importantly, the brain does not immediately change entirely to adapt to the last event, but rather nudges the probabilities a little in that direction. This way, not every error leads to new learnings, but rather to a challenge of the assumptions. This method allows for improved predictions over time, taking more information and changing, while allowing for multiple experiences to shape our future, rather than only recent ones.

13.2.2 MACHINE LEARNING AND PREDICTION

Neural networks, or machine learning, is a branch of computer science that combines the art of computational learning and pattern recognition. Through machine learning, algorithms can be constructed that allow systems to make predictions on the basis of available data. These algorithms build a model by following example inputs and result in outputs instead of simple static program instructions. Setting up an association with the purchaser is a basic component in the achievement of any business; yet, encouraging client communications cannot stop there.

One of the easiest examples of machine learning comes from an example of the type of learning it incorporates—in humans—a utilization in the poultry industry. In a rather gruesome type of education, newborn chicks are sorted by gender. The female chicks are raised to become hens that lay eggs and are used in the food business. The male chicks are simply shredded at birth. However, identifying the male from the female chicks is a tough task. The genitalia are rather small and nearly impossible to rapidly identify. However, there is a way to tell male from female that does not involve carefully looking at the genitalia with a microscope: the sound they make when they are squeezed. It turns out that pressing the little chick makes it yell in distress. The sound of male versus female chicks is uniquely different to the point that a trained expert can tell them apart. But how does one become an expert? Instead of teaching the rules, there is a different approach—a machine learning one. You sit the incoming chicks-trainee on a chair and have the trainee pick a single chick and guess, after listening to it screech, if it's a male or female. The trainee guesses and puts the baby chick in the male or female bucket. An expert standing behind the trainee's back knows the correct answer. If the trainee made a mistake—the expert taps on the trainee's shoulder, indicating the mistake and making the trainee correct it. No explanation. No real rule-based training. Simply a tap on the shoulder every time a mistake is made. Enough such examples make it so that the trainee, within about 7 hours of this process, becomes an expert herself, with more than 99% accuracy in telling male from female. Notably, the new expert rarely can explain and articulate the thing learned. He or she just knows the answer from having been exposed to enough examples "labeled" by an expert. This is essentially how machine learning works: a computer is given many examples that are labeled, and by generating clustering algorithms that separate those clusters, it essentially "learned" how to identify one type of data from another. This can then be used to tell male and female chicks apart, identify genes that match specific phenotypes, identify whether a customer is or is not interested in a product, or identify whether a product will fall into the "successful" or "unsuccessful" buckets. Additionally, this is potentially useful to tell something about our interest in content or our engagement with experiences by identifying customers'

Not every error leads to new learnings, but rather to a challenge of the assumptions.

responses to content by first learning how people respond to it, and later making predictions about future behaviors with it.

Machine learning is used to dissect customer conduct continually and perform prescient division to adjust corresponding experiences.

The prescient division and continual examination take into consideration the personalization of messages. Shopper engagement information (e.g., age, sex, area, and purchasing inclinations) is gathered from cell phones, computer, and televisions.

Ultimately, customized notices can be produced to best fit the particular needs or yearnings of an individual. For instance, a twenty-something living in an urban zone and looking for a new automobile may receive a new-vehicle-related coupon while he filters his choices. Machine learning can give advertisers and sponsors the chance to rapidly adjust to the continual advancement of customer engagement signals.

Numerous variables can influence shopper engagement. Ordinarily, the impacts on customer engagement are driven by current occasions or interim circumstances. The speedier the information is "learned" and broken down, the better. Machine learning takes into consideration a quick turnaround of big data investigation, which empowers advertisers to interface with the purchaser and convey customized promotions in an exceedingly opportune way, significantly expanding the viability of the commercial and driving online and in-store deals.

Machine learning is closely linked with computational statistics and mathematical optimization. There are different ways a model can be generated to predict results. There are three main models of machine learning: supervised, unsupervised, and reinforced.

Supervised models have input data, and a supervisory algorithm is present for corrections. In simpler words, a model is prepared and then put to the task of making predictions. If the system makes correct predictions, it is working perfectly. If it makes incorrect predictions, then the supervisory algorithm corrects the model and forces it to redefine its learning.

Unsupervised learning models have unlabeled input data and an unpredictable outcome. In this kind of learning, mathematical processes are applied to the data in case of wrong predictions in order to reduce redundancy.

What is important to note here is that the idea of machine learning is simply to mimic and replicate the way brain learns: without a supervising "authority" that sets the neural pathways and the connections at birth, we are merely given examples and experiences, using prediction errors to adjust the weights and ultimately use the labeled examples to derive future predictions that seem to minimize the error. At no point do we actually "know" the rules. They just exist intrinsically because we repeat the performance accurately. This means that in machine learning, we indeed can have computers fit a complex function and find meaning in data, but at no point can the algorithm actually indicate to us what are the rules

This is essentially how machine learning works: a computer is given many examples that are labeled, and by generating clustering algorithms that separate those clusters, it essentially "learned" how to identify one type of data from another.

Machine learning takes into consideration a quick turnaround of big data investigation, which empowers advertisers to interface with the purchaser and convey customized promotions in an exceedingly opportune way, significantly expanding the viability of the commercial and driving online and in-store deals.

that are used to solve a problem (i.e., to identify a clip of a cat in YouTube from many other clips or to know which customer is likely to buy a specific laundry detergent on the basis of prior shopping behavior).

13.3   NEUROSCIENCE AND MARKETING RESEARCH

In the past decade, the ways by which our brain makes predictions has been explored greatly. This exploration created a hopeful correlation between deeper neural mechanisms and marketing research. Detailed neuroscientific studies can help provide product insight for existing as well as nonexisting products. This can help provide information related to consumer preferences that might be unattainable if conventional methods are used.

The idea of machine learning is simply to mimic and replicate the way brain learns: without a supervising "authority" that sets the neural pathways and the connections at birth, we are merely given examples and experiences.

Because marketing strategies involve campaigns that target actual purchases, attitudes, and preferences of a consumer, the ability to predict choices and consumer preferences becomes extremely necessary. In such cases, a cost-effective tool that can predict the behavior of consumers in the future can be very beneficial in the long run. Every neuroscience academic paper is about prediction, because every statistical phenomenon that we understand can be later used to anticipate a behavior on the basis of the symptoms that occur along with it.

Two methods have been identified as avenues for incorporating marketing research with neuroscientific methods: functional magnetic resonance imaging (fMRI) and the electroencephalogram (EEG).

13.3.1   FUNCTIONAL MRI AND BEHAVIOR PREDICTION

Functional MRI, as mentioned in previous chapters, is used in refined neuroscientific experiments, allowing researchers to help understand the related brain activity while identifying the physical processes underneath when it comes to predictions. If neuroscientists manage to connect predictions with underlying brain activity, then the whole idea of free will is threatened. Free will, for example, and the ability to know how deterministic our behavior is and accordingly know how to predict it, was challenged by researchers not long ago. John-Dylan Haynes, a neuroscientist at the Bernstein Center for Computational Neuroscience, predicted the press of a button using fMRI in real time. The team discovered a pattern: as long as 7 seconds before the subjects made a decision, their brain had already decided for them (Soon et al. 2008). Haynes is not the first scientist to challenge the idea of free will. Benjamin Libet of the University of California studied unconscious decision-making in the 1980s (Libet et al. 1983). While Libet's study was controversial and critiques pointed out faults in his experiment, Haynes used a more modern approach (Smith 2011), although critics still claimed that Haynes's experiment was 60% accurate at best. Similar experiments were conducted by the author, using single electrodes, where a person's decision could be predicted 700 milliseconds before it occurred, with more than 80% accuracy (Fried, Mukamel, and Kreiman 2011). Another recent study by Dmochowski et al. (2014) subjected participating individuals to television broadcast content. They employed imaging techniques to test participants while they watched the content and discovered that similarity in brain activity, across individuals watching the same content, was higher when the content was engaging. Another group of scientists showed that fMRI measurements add a little more predictability to just asking people a question in surveys, which play a significant role in theory, research, and practice (Venkatraman et al., 2015).

As long as 7 seconds before the subjects made a decision, their brain had already decided.

A different study (Paulus and Stein 2006) measured the ability to use neuroscience to predict loss and preferences in advertising campaigns. Activation of the insula was shown to be correlated with self-reported negative arousal and loss prediction in the context of preferences. Following this work, Bryan Knutson and colleagues (Knutson et al. 2001) have shown, in a study that was mentioned in detail in chapter 11, that activation in the regions associated with anticipating gain (nucleus accumbens) correlates with product preferences, while loss (insula) correlates with excessive prices. This study, essentially showing a way to use neuroscience prediction to set pricing (as shown by Hirak Parikh and colleagues in chapter 11) allowed also for the predictions of future purchases. Specifically, activity in the insula showed decreased likelihood of future purchase of items shown in the experiment.

Similarly, a team of researchers asking "How does my product rank in the mind of the consumers after they see it for the first time?" measured neural activations in predefined brain areas while subjects viewed 20 different goods inside an fMRI scanner, without knowing that they had to make choices afterwards. The results showed that the activity in the medial prefrontal cortex and in the striatum, areas associated with value representations, can be used to predict later consumer choices in individual subjects (Levy et al. 2011).

These, of course, are just a few examples out of many, but they highlight the notion that is rising in the community of neuroscientists, and should propagate to the business community as well, that such brain research can be used to make behavioral predictions (oftentimes better than the ones we ourselves make when asked what we will choose/buy/do/like) and should be used as a new methodology in the service of marketing analytics.

13.3.2 USING EEG TO PREDICT CONSUMER BEHAVIOR

As alluded to earlier in this book, many companies have linked activity observed with EEG to consumer preferences. Given the hundreds of billions of neurons and synaptic connections present in the human brain, these neurons combine to form a neuronal circuitry. When the brain is subjected to a stimulus, these neurons fire electrical currents, which can be amplified and recorded. EEG serves this purpose. Many studies already exist on the use of EEG to study consumer behavior, advertisement responses, and media strategies. Recently, marketing researchers have started using the neural data to indeed highlight the possibility of doing just that. In a recent work, for example, scientists recorded intracranial EEG signals from six patients with respect to their automobile driving decisions (Perez et al. 2015). The reason for the study was to detect the predictive behavior of these patients. While driving, the brain makes a lot of conscious decisions, such as which route to take, which lane to switch to, and which turn to make. The researchers predicted the decisions of subjects up to 5.5 seconds before they made the decisions. This was done with an accuracy of 82.4%, highlighting the preconscious role of premotor cortices in early decision-making stages. These early stages can modify the real-life human choices and allow their forecast before they are consciously made by the subject.

Another recent study by Levy and colleagues also highlights the use of EEG for consumer behavior predictions (Telpaz, Webb, and Levy 2015). The team asked subjects to view individual consumer products while studying their neural activity through EEG. After viewing the products, the subjects were asked to choose between two products in a same-product pair. Their study found that they could accurately predict the choices of the consumers before they made them. This can be very beneficial in the future, because this prediction can help neuroscientists to conclude before a product launch whether the product will be well received or not.

> Researchers predicted the decisions of subjects up to 5.5 seconds before they made the decisions.

13.4   THE BRAIN AND PROACTIVITY

Humans do not interpret the world through simply analyzing information. They try to understand the incoming information through proactively linking with previous information. For example, when we see a new object, instead of perceiving it as "What is it?" we perceive it as "What is it like?" Once the brain forms an analogy on the basis of the question, it links it with previous related thoughts and starts a process that involves predictions accordingly. The brain can perceive these analogies on a number of levels including functional, semantic, conceptual, perceptual, and so forth. These analogies help the brain decide and predict the upcoming scenario. For example, if you have to pack for a vacation to Sydney and you have never been there before, your brain will predict Sydney's weather on the basis of your previous perceptions and the information you requested over the Internet.

Another important factor in brain proactivity is association, as the brain tries to link up new information with old analogies. All memories are stored in an associative manner. The brain creates a link with an analogy, and every time you come across that analogy, you are reminded of that specific memory.

The human brain is proactive and constantly uses past statistics and present information to make a probabilistic estimate of the future. For example, you are sitting in a train going to your destination and you pass a tree. On passing the tree, you start thinking about what would happen if a storm arrived and knocked down the tree. This lets your mind wander in imagination. During the imagination process, your brain predicts all the actions you would take in case that event was ever to happen. During the prediction, your brain also calculates the probability of the event happening and how effective your actions might be. In other words, letting your mind wander is also a way to let your brain train its predicting ability.

Interestingly, breaking the stream of timing in the brain can lead to false perception of cause and effect. An experiment where every button press on a keyboard led to a response with a slight (100 ms) delay, led subjects to believe—when the delay was removed—that their actions are actually happening before they pressed the button. The "clocks" that constantly compute time in our brain have the physics of "cause and effect" embedded into their built logic of the world. We expect actions to have reactions in real-time on many physical aspects of the world. If the reaction is intentionally delayed (but unbeknownst to us) we may shift our perspective of time and find it hard to recalibrate to real-time active/reactions. This may lead us to perceive time as speeding up or slowing down. All of this is to say that our perception of reality is bounded by the predictions and outcomes that we see and believe to be real. The narrative we call reality that our brain establishes is based on assumptions on how our predictions meet outcomes. Changes to the mechanics of those leads to a breakage of our ability to tie a cohesive narrative in our mind (Eagleman and Sejnowski 2009).

> During the imagination process, your brain predicts all the actions you would take in case that event was ever to happen. During the prediction, your brain also calculates the probability of the event happening and how effective your actions might be. In other words, letting your mind wander is also a way to let your brain train its predicting ability.

13.5   HOW CONSUMER-BASED NEUROSCIENCE COMPANIES CAN HELP

> Consumer neuroscience companies need to be better at providing actual predictions or telling their customers the truth about not having them if they do not.

Consumer neuroscience companies need to be better at providing actual predictions or telling their customers the truth about not having them if they do not. Making "predictions" without real ability to do them is a type of fraud and exploitation. The fact that "my ad is very memorable" does not matter if people remember but do not buy. We need to find ways to translate memorability, attention, emotion, rewards, interest, engagement, and so forth into something that predicts future behavior. Or, if we cannot, we should tell customers that we do not have this ability. But the current wishy-washy state is hurting the field of consumer neuroscience. Most marketing research companies, even those not in neuroscience, suffer from the same problem. They assess ads and content by surveys, focus groups, and so forth, and ultimately say things such as "People like your ad" or "People find your content engaging," but are wary of actually saying "We predict 82.5% of people who see the ad will make a call." This is because they do not do real experiments, just make some kinds of inaccurate statements about what they think. This way, you cannot hold them accountable when things do not work out and not pay them. That is why old marketing is now failing, because the companies (especially the

Googles, Amazons, Facebooks, and the ones run by engineers) are beginning to see that they are just getting "data" without predictions that can be tested from their marketing research companies, and accordingly are spending money or marketing research that cannot be tested. They therefore demand to get not just "data" but actual predictions—such that if the predictions fail, they can be compensated.

It is also true for pollsters: often we see polls predict election outcomes where the polls end up being dead wrong, but no one is doing anything about it—pollsters just keep using the same methods, and the polls are published on television as if they are accurate, ignoring the bad statistics behind them. This is a call to change that! All in all, either marketing companies need to be up front about their lack of predictability or we should agree that consumer neuroscience is essentially just another version of the old methods (i.e., focus groups) where we ask questions, get some answers, and have no way of knowing what people will actually do in the end (not what they currently promise). So ultimately, it's the job of consumer neuroscience to manage expectations and explain to customers when we can and cannot make predictions.

> Often we see polls predict election outcomes where the polls end up being dead wrong, but no one is doing anything about it—pollsters just keep using the same methods, and the polls are published on television as if they are accurate.

KEY TAKEAWAYS

- Prediction involves making estimations about the future on the basis of past events and new information from the present.

- The brain is the ultimate "big data" analytics tool. Hence, learning how it does its predictions is key to marketing predictions.

- There are two classical methods by which the brain makes its prediction: correcting for prediction errors and use of "learning" (which would be, in the context of marketing analytics, "machine learning") to improve the accuracy of future predictions.

- Prediction error occurs when the neuronal system recognizes a difference between the reward and its response. It is a fundamental concept for the brain to understand errors in order to correct future predictions. The brain expects a response based on prior experience. If there is a difference between the brain's prediction and the actual response, a "prediction error" is triggered.

- Neural networks, or machine learning, is a branch of computer science that combines the art of computational learning and pattern recognition. Through machine learning, algorithms can be constructed that allow systems to make predictions on the basis of available data.

- In the past decade, the ways by which our brain makes predictions has been explored greatly. This exploration created a hopeful correlation between deeper neural mechanisms and marketing research. Detailed neuroscientific studies can help provide product insight for existing as well as nonexisting products.

- Two methods have been identified as avenues for incorporating marketing research with neuroscientific methods. These methods include the use of functional magnetic resonance imaging (fMRI) and electroencephalogram (EEG).

- fMRI measurements add a little more predictability to just asking people a question in surveys, which play a significant role in theory, research, and practice.

- Our brain is a proactive decision maker. Using the elements of analogy and association, our brain has the ability to not only predict but also imagine, dream, and retrain its decision-making processes through learning.

- Many companies have linked activity observed with EEG to consumer preferences. Using EEG, researchers have been able to accurately predict the choices of consumers before they made them.

- Consumer neuroscience companies need to be better at providing actual predictions or telling their customers the truth about not having them if they do not.

DISCUSSION QUESTIONS

1. According to the theory of machine learning, one can learn how to solve a problem given a large number of examples, without being told how to actually solve it (the rules of solution). Can you think of two examples in your life when you learned something merely by being given examples and not by being told how exactly to do something?

2. Climate change is a situation where we have data about the weather for the past couple of decades, and this is being used to predict the trajectory of temperatures in the future. Can you think of examples of domains in marketing where we can use data from the past decades to predict actions in the future?

3. Many times when we think of predictions, we think of a simple linear trend. As in, if something grows every year by 50%, it will keep growing in the same fashion. However, many predictions use a more complex function

(exponential growth, logarithmic decay, or even nonlinear functions). Can you suggest a few domains where the growth was nonlinear?

REFERENCES

Dmochowski, J. P., Bezdek, M. A., Abelson, B. P., Johnson, J. S., Schumacher, E. H., & Parra, L. C. (2014). Audience preferences are predicted by temporal reliability of neural processing. *Nature Communications*, 5.

Eagleman, D. M., & Sejnowski, T. J. (2000). Motion integration and postdiction in visual awareness. *Science*, 287, 2036–2038.

Fried, I., Mukamel, R., & Kreiman, G. (2011). Internally generated preactivation of single neurons in human medial frontal cortex predicts volition. *Neuron*, 69(3), 548–562.

Knutson, B., Fong, G. W., Adams, C. M., Varner, J. L., & Hommer, D. (2001). Dissociation of reward anticipation and outcome with event related FMRI. *Neuroreport*, 12, 3683–3687.

Levy, I., Lazzaro, S. C., Rutledge, R. B., & Glimcher, P. W. (2011). Choice from non-choice: Predicting consumer preferences from blood oxygenation level-dependent signals obtained during passive viewing. *Journal of Neuroscience*, 31(1), 118–125.

Libet, B., Gleason, C. A., Wright, E. W., & Pearl, D. K. (1983). Time of conscious intention to act in relation to onset of cerebral activity (readiness-potential): The unconscious initiation of a freely voluntary act. *Brain*, 106, 623–642.

Paulus, M. P., & Stein, M. B. (2006). An insular view of anxiety. *Biological Psychiatry*, 60, 383–387.

Perez, O., Mukamel, R., Tankus, A., Rosenblatt, J. D., Yeshurun, Y., & Fried, I. (2015). Preconscious prediction of a driver's decision using intracranial recordings. *Journal of Cognitive Neuroscience*, 27(8), 1492–1502.

Smith, K. (2011). Neuroscience vs philosophy: Taking aim at free will. *Nature*, 477, 23–25.

Soon, C. S., Brass, M., Heinze, H.-J., & Haynes, J.-D. (2008). Unconscious determinants of free decisions in the human brain. Nature Neuroscience. *Brief Communications*, 11(5), 543–545.

Telpaz, A., Webb, R., & Levy, D. J. (2015). Using EEG to predict consumers' future choices. *JMR, Journal of Marketing Research*, 52, 511–529.

Venkatraman, V., Dimoka, A., Pavlou, P. A., Vo, K., Hampton, W., Bollinger, B., et al. (2015). Predicting advertising success beyond traditional measures: New insights from neurophysiological methods and market response modeling. *JMR, Journal of Marketing Research*, 52, 436–452.

CHAPTER 14

APPLICATIONS IN MARKET RESEARCH

DAVID BRANDT

The aim of marketing is to know and understand the customer so well the product or service fits him and sells itself.
—Peter Drucker

Marketing is the science and art of exploring, creating, and delivering value to satisfy the needs of a target market at a profit. Marketing identifies unfulfilled needs and desires. It defines, measures and quantifies the size of the identified market and the profit potential. It pinpoints which segments the company is capable of serving best and it designs and promotes the appropriate products and services.
—Philip Kotler

14.1   A BRIEF HISTORY OF MARKET RESEARCH

The essence of marketing comes down to identifying the wants and needs of the consumer and satisfying those needs with product, promotions, distribution, and pricing choices. This is true whether you are selling a laundry detergent or a new jetliner. The art and science of market research is an integral part of this process with the goal of identifying those needs and the best way to fill them.

Market research is an old practice, dating back to the end of the nineteenth century when N. W. Ayer first conducted custom research in an effort to win new business. In the 1920s, Daniel Starch launched his service to test recognition levels of advertising, the first organized effort to evaluate the effectiveness of advertising. In the 1930s, George Gallup began his political polling.

Procter & Gamble can be credited with bringing market research into widespread use within the business world. Neil McElroy, who introduced the idea of brand management in 1931, had a simple formula for success: "Find out what the consumer wants and give it to them."[1] Procter & Gamble followed up on this commitment by establishing a market research department under "Doc" Smelser (he had a PhD in economics from Johns Hopkins University). The company also made widespread use of the day after recall (DAR) technique to measure the success of their television advertising.

The industry continued to change through the 1900s with market research departments becoming common in both business-to-consumer and business-to-business companies and the responsibility for collecting and processing the data shifting from companies (Doc Smelser had his own field staff of young women going door to door to collect information—this unit was active up until the 1960s[2]) to independent research companies. By the end of the twentieth century, more than $30 billion was spent each year on market research.[3]

14.1.1   EARLY EXPERIENCE WITH THE "SUBCONSCIOUS": NEGATIVE PERCEPTIONS

The one common factor through all of this time was that there were only two ways to collect information from consumers: ask them questions or observe them. Nobody seriously questioned whether these were the best approaches or whether there really were any other options. Marketers were aware of studies on the subconscious; however, its role in marketing was often seen as nefarious. In 1957, Vance Packard published *The Hidden Persuaders*,[4] which focused on advertising. Packard felt that ads should focus on simple facts like price and effectiveness and was appalled by current-day advertising, believing that it preyed on psychological weaknesses of consumers; that it used psychological techniques to get them to buy products they did not want. Packard was a journalist, not a scientist and many of his observations on advertising's motivational techniques were based more on observation than science.

But one of the more sensational claims in the book was his report of a study conducted by James Vicary around the idea of "subliminal advertising." Vicary claimed to have conducted a study where subliminal commands ("Hungry? Eat popcorn") had been inserted during the movie *The Picnic* at a movie theater. The commands appeared and disappeared so quickly (he reported that they were shown for 1/3,000th of a second) that people were not aware that they had seen the words and thus were subconsciously manipulated. The same was said to be done with "Drink Coca-Cola." Vicary claimed that sales of popcorn and Coca-Cola had increased dramatically at the theater. Years later, Vicary recanted and admitted that the study was fraudulent.[5] But the damage had been done, and the perception that this is a true story exists today.

1. As quoted in Thomas K. McGraw, American Business, 1920–2000: How It Worked. *Harlan Davidson, 2000.*

2. *Ibid.*

3. *Source: ESOMAR. Global Market Research 2016*

4. *Vance Packard,* The hidden persuaders. *Random House, 1957.*

5. *Vicary exposed this in a television interview for* Advertising Age *with Fred Danzig in 1962. Fred Danzig, "Subliminal advertising—today it's just historic flashback for researcher Vicary."* Advertising Age, *September 17, 1962, pp. 72–73.*

In 1973, another book hit the market, titled *Subliminal Seduction*,[6] claiming that advertisers were inserting sexual images secretly into ads in order to entice consumers. The book, written by Wilson Bryan Key, insinuated that because consumers were not consciously aware of these images, they had no choice on whether to accept or reject them. Much like Vicary's claims, there are substantial questions surrounding the claims made in Key's books including documentation or any direct evidence that these insertions were done intentionally.

The issue of the power of subliminal messages was taken seriously enough though that subliminal advertising is banned in the United Kingdom (although there appear to be no cases where an advertiser was actually accused of doing so since the law was put in place). In the United States, the Federal Communications Commission (FCC) held hearings and proclaimed that subliminal advertising was "contrary to the public interest."[7] The FCC does not regulate advertising, so there was no legal ban. However, the Code of the National Association of Broadcasters does prohibit "Any technique whereby an attempt is made to convey information to the viewer by transmitting messages below the threshold of normal awareness."[8]

This stigma of manipulating the subconscious of consumers through "psychological techniques" remains even today and is still an objection of some advertisers to the use of neuroscience techniques.

14.1.2 OTHER BARRIERS TO USE OF NEUROSCIENCE

The ethical concerns, justified or not, were not the only barriers. Two others were prominent up until the mid-2000s. The first is the issue of cost and scale. Equipment was expensive, and it would be hard to recoup the costs without substantial volume. Also, most large research companies were global and would work with clients in many countries, which meant the techniques needed to be made available in many locations. This added to expense.

But the biggest issue was an ongoing belief that surveys provided everything the manager needed to know about his or her marketing efforts. This belief had two different underpinnings:

1. The belief that consumers were rational. Classic marketing theory is aligned with classic economic theory in the belief that humans are rational beings and call on available information, coupled with decision rules, to make their decisions. If you simply asked the consumer to profile brands along key dimensions, you could understand the relative value and strengths or weaknesses of a brand. Surveys could do all of this and had been for years.

2. Given this, emotions were often seen as a "higher-order benefit," an area a marketer could achieve once the functional benefits were well known. For example, the well-known qualitative technique of laddering is "used to develop an understanding of how consumers translate the attributes of products into meaningful associations with respect to self. ... It is these higher-order knowledge structures that we use to process information relative to solving problems."[9] Emotions (or

This stigma of manipulating the subconscious of consumers through "psychological techniques" remains even today and is still an objection of some advertisers to the use of neuroscience techniques.

6. *Wilson Bryan Key*, Subliminal seduction: Ad media's manipulation of a not so innocent America. *Signet, 1974.*

7. *Federal Communications Commission. Public Notice FCC 74–78 08055, "Broadcast of information by means of 'subliminal perception' techniques," 1974.*

8. *Ibid.*

9. *Thomas J. Reynolds and Jonathan Gutman, "Laddering theory, method, analysis and interpretation."* Journal of Advertising Research, *February/ March 1988, pp. 11–31.*

what they call values) emanate from product benefits. And even then, emotions could be measured by asking people how they felt. After all, people had been telling us if they liked a product for many years. And they could tell us if an ad was irritating, made them happy or sad, or if it was humorous. Emotions were fully accessible. Evidence of this can be seen in a well-cited 1999 article by Bagozzi, Gopinath, and Nyer[10] on the role of emotion in marketing. The article runs for 15 pages plus a 5-page bibliography reviewing research on emotions and marketing and never once mentions the use of neuroscience.

14.1.3 DISCUSSION

We have highlighted the barriers that have kept the marketing and market research industries from widespread adoption and application of neuroscience learning and techniques. There is a commonality across these issues:

- They assume that consumers have access to all the information and factors that impact their decisions.

- There is no clear and consistent road map to how emotions impact decisions.

These are areas where consumer neuroscience can and should disrupt the current approaches to market research. And the more important of these two may be the second point. While neuroscience techniques add value to sources of data and insight to the research process, they are of little use until the marketing community has a strong sense of *how* to use these insights. For example, knowing that an ad generates strong emotional engagement is of little use unless you understand how to incorporate this information into your analysis of the success of the ad.

The advertising testing market is a good example of this. As the talk about the importance of emotion in effective advertising has gained in volume, most companies have adapted by adding some form of emotional measurement to their ad testing service. This varies from systems that use pictures of faces expressing various emotional responses as a way of cueing the consumer to his or her own reaction to picture sorts to verbal descriptors. Some have also started using automated facial coding (which is a neuroscience-based technique).

But often these data are used as a diagnostic for other key metrics such as recall (ability to remember the ad) or persuasion (did the ad make you more likely to buy the product) than as a direct indicator of success. This is in contrast to many of the behavioral and decision models that originate in the neuroscience or psychology community (which are discussed elsewhere in this book) where emotions are often a direct driver of behavior and not just a mediator of conscious and rational behavior (figure 14.1). (For example, Damasio's somatic marker hypothesis posits a direct link between "emotional experiences" and behavior[11].) Until such models are adopted, commonplace, and understood, neuroscience tools cannot be as disruptive as they should be.

10. Richard P. Bagozzi, Mahesh Gopinath, and Prashanath U. Nyer, "The role of emotions in marketing." Academy of Marketing Science Journal, *Spring 1999, pp. 184–202. (Cited 1,791 times according to Google Scholar.)*

11. Antonio Damasio, Looking for Spinoza: Joy, sorrow and the feeling brain. *Harcourt, 2003.*

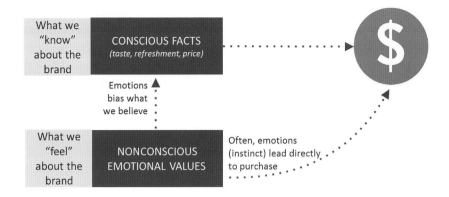

FIGURE 14.1
Nielsen's model of decision making is used to understand the role of emotion in advertising. This model is based on the work of several people, notably Antonio Damasio's somatic marker hypothesis.

Another example of a disconnect between the way research today is conducted and what we know from neuroscience and psychology is in the understanding of human memory. As discussed earlier, much of market research is based on the ability of a consumer to answer a question, and this includes questions on what consumers remember about advertising. Measures of recall, whether used in the pretest of an ad or in tracking the performance of the ad over time, rely on conscious memory (and often an accurate description of the ad) as evidence that the ad's impressions and memories have been retained by the consumer. Moreover, if the ad, or key elements of the ad, are not recalled, the assumption is that the ad, or those "forgotten" elements of the ad, could not have had an impact on the consumer. Underlying this entire approach is the assumption that human memory is like computer memory. The memory, once created, is retained in its original form and can be retrieved when needed, including at the point of purchase. Current learning on memory paints a quite different portrait including the fact that memories come in explicit (conscious and retrievable) and implicit (neither conscious nor retrievable by direct questioning) forms and that there are different types of explicit memory. So the assumption that the inability to remember an ad when questioned about it is an indication that the ad has failed to have an impact may in fact not be a true one.

14.2 EARLY IMPACT OF NEUROSCIENCE-BASED LEARNING

Disruptions do not always announce themselves loudly. The early signs for the research industry that the way they were practicing their art might not be wholly

The assumption that the inability to remember an ad when questioned about it is an indication that the ad has failed to have an impact may in fact not be a true one.

sound were quite subtle. In the late 1970s, VOPAN Market Research entered the market with the claim that they could use voice pitch analysis (which is where the acronym VOPAN came from) to get a more accurate read on whether consumers were really interested in a product. For example, two different concepts that had the same levels of stated purchase intent in a concept test could be found through voice pitch analysis to actually have very different levels of potential. The company is no longer in business (although voice pitch analysis itself is still in use) as client acceptance of the offer appears to have been weak. Similar attempts to introduce galvanic skin response (GSR) in the 1990s were met with limited acceptance. One reason for this is the difficulty, particularly at that time, in convincing marketers of the added value these approaches could bring. As noted earlier, without widespread knowledge and acceptance of a new model of consumer motivations, the need for these techniques is not obvious.

Possibly the first credible sign that consumers did not behave the way marketers always thought they did was the Advertising Research Foundation's 1990 study called the Copy Research Validity Project. This study examined the validity of multiple measures traditionally used in copy testing to see which were the most predictive of the results of split-cable advertising testing.[12] In a report on this study, Russell Haley stated that "Undoubtedly the most surprising finding of this study was the strong relationship found to exist between the likability of the copy and its effects on sales."[13] It had long been felt that such a soft measure of affect could not be a meaningful predictor. This set off a long and often controversial discussion in the ad testing industry, but in the end little was done with this finding other than incorporating this measure into standard copy tests. But it was most frequently used as diagnostic; that is, a measure used to explain other measures rather than directly predictive (as noted earlier, even today this is the role that neuroscience-based measures often play). Because the concept of likeability did not fit with the conventional theories on what made an ad effective, there was no way to incorporate it into the decision-making process except as a diagnostic. The lack of theory inhibited the understanding and application of this finding.

In 2001, Robert Heath published a monograph titled *The Hidden Power of Advertising*.[14] This was the first significant attempt to introduce a new model to the world of advertising and ad testing that was based around work from the academic and scientific community, drawing heavily on the work of several psychologists and neuroscientists with a particular focus on the work of Antonio Damasio.

When he authored this book, Heath was at the University of Bath but had spent many years as an ad agency planner. Over that time, he came to believe that the current measurement approaches were not effective at measuring certain types of ads. In particular, he stated that ads that were more "emotional" in nature could be processed by consumers with little to no attention actually paid to the ads. Thus, they would not be remembered using standard recall approaches but had an impact on the consumer nonetheless. He developed a model he called the "Low Attention

---

Because the concept of likeability did not fit with the conventional theories on what made an ad effective, there was no way to incorporate it into the decision-making process except as a diagnostic. The lack of theory inhibited the understanding and application of this.

12. *Split-cable testing uses an experimental design where two matched panels of consumers receive different ads. Purchases of these panel members is tracked to allow identification of which ad had the greatest impact on sales.*

13. *Russell I. Haley, "The ARF Copy Research Validity Project."* Journal of Advertising Research, *Vol. 40, No. 6, 2000, pp. 114–135.*

14. *Robert Heath,* The hidden power of advertising. *Admap Publications, 2001.*

Box 14.1
Robert Heath's Model on How Emotional Advertising Works to Build Brands

1. The more emotive an ad...

2. The more you like it...

3. The more you trust it...

4. The *less* attention you pay to it...

5. The more it affects you emotionally...

6. The more it builds brand values and relationships...

7. The less well it performs in recall and persuasion-based research.

Processing" model. He advocated using recognition measures to assess whether advertising was leaving an impression with the consumer. Because most ad research at the time used a form of recall measurement, his view was hotly debated. Over time this model became fairly well-accepted, and it may be the first true evidence of how neuroscience and psychology can disrupt marketing and market research, in this case by developing a new model of how advertising works. Heath has since gone on to write a more complete overview of his theories on how advertising works called *Seducing the Subconscious: The Psychology of Emotional Influence in Advertising*. His theory on how emotional advertising works to build brands, as outlined in this book, is described in box 14.1.

This model became fairly well-accepted, and it may be the first true evidence of how neuroscience and psychology can disrupt marketing and market research, in this case by developing a new model of how advertising works.

14.3   WHERE NEUROSCIENCE IS TODAY

By now it should be evident that for neuroscience to have a strong influence in how market research is done and used, two factors need to be addressed:
1. Adoption of new models of consumer behavior that are consistent with how neuroscientists and psychology now view it.

2. Adoption of tools from neuroscience that can address the parameters of these models.

There is some progress on the first front as leadership from associations such as ESOMAR, the Neuromarketing Science and Business Association (NMSBA), the World Advertising Research Center (WARC), and the Advertising Research Foundation (ARF) have focused on these learnings, as well as the tools themselves, in multiple conferences. Of great assistance has been the publication of books such as Daniel Kahneman' s seminal *Thinking, Fast and Slow*, which has instilled the concepts of System 1 and System 2 thinking broadly in the industry. At least one company—Brainjuicer—even refers to themselves as the System 1 company and names their products after this (System 1 Brand Tracking, System 1 Pack Test, etc.).

Also, books by industry practitioners such as Roger Dooley's *Brainfluence: 100 Ways to Persuade and Convince Consumers with Neuromarketing* and Steve Genco's *Neuromarketing for Dummies* have helped translate the concepts of neuroscience to practical marketing terms.

In 2012, Nielsen, the world's largest market research company, acquired the high-profile Neurofocus organization. Neurofocus was one of the pioneers in the neuromarketing industry, and the acquisition was seen as a sign that the industry was coming of age.[15] Nielsen upped the ante in 2015 with the acquisition of Innerscope Research, another of the industry pioneers. Meanwhile, both Ipsos and Millward Brown, two other large global research organizations, set up departments within their organization that focus on neuroscience.

However, as of this writing in 2015, it would be premature to say that neuroscience has disrupted the industry. The GreenBook organization's most recent survey of methods used shows that only 5% of organizations surveyed claimed to have used a neuromarketing or biometric technique in the past quarter.[16] While dollar figures are not available, this is likely a good estimate of the share of neuroscience techniques among all research dollars spent for quantitative research. Note also that there is little growth in the number over the previous two quarterly reports (figure 14.2). There is room for growth. This is also evidence that the two principles laid out to enhance adoption have not yet been fully realized.

The remainder of this chapter will focus on this expected growth and how that will in fact disrupt market research.

14.4 MARKET RESEARCH SURVEYS TODAY AND TOMORROW

Direct questioning is the most widely used approach in market research. It is used in all forms of qualitative research, concept testing, ad testing, segmentation, product testing, and equity research. The questions have been tested, scales devised, and validations performed so that today most researchers are very comfortable with the questions and what they can learn from them. Moreover, as data collection has moved online and data processing has become more automated, the cost to collect survey data has gone down. This familiarity and efficiency is another reason that market researchers have strong attachments to surveys. The following section will look at some common approaches for survey-based research. We will then look at how neuroscience approaches can disrupt these methods.

The GreenBook organization's most recent survey of methods used shows that only 5% of organizations surveyed claimed to have used a neuromarketing or biometric technique in the past quarter.

15. Source: http://www.nielsen.com/us/en/press-room/2011/nielsen-acquires-neurofocus.html. *Nielsen Press Release, May 26, 2011.*

16. Greenbook Research Industry Trends Report, Fall 2014 *New York AMA Communication Services, New York, NY, 2014.*

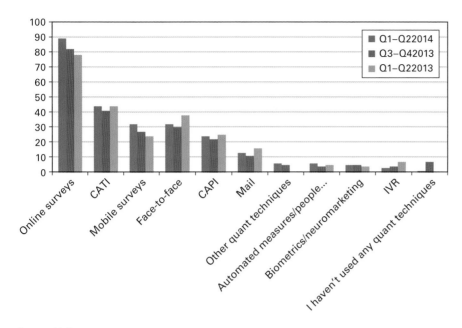

FIGURE 14.2
Quantitative methods used: Trend Q1 2013 to Q2 2014; base 817 Q1–Q2 2014; 2229 Q3–Q4 2013; 0 to 1372 Q1–Q2 2013. CATI, computer-assisted telephone interviewing; CAPI, computer-assisted personal interviewing; IVR, inbound voice recording.

14.4.1 CONCEPT TESTING

14.4.1.1 TODAY

When developing a new product for launch, one of the most important things manufacturers do is to have consumers assess a "concept." The concept is the basic premise behind the product and can take many forms:

- Concept statements are simple word statements (no images) that generally provide the consumer with a brief description of the product and its features and benefits. These statements are usually only one or two sentences long, and consumers can be asked to evaluate several of them at a time. Based on this, consumers are asked to indicate how likely they are to buy the product and why, how unique they feel the product is, and often to rate the brand on a limited number of different dimensions and compare it to competitive products. The manufacturer will compare these data to their historical results, particularly for those products with known success and databases to make the decision on whether to proceed with developing the product.

- Concept boards are a more advanced version of the concept statement and often include a picture of the product in use, package shots, a more complete benefit statement, mentions of any flavor/scent varieties, and pricing. As such, the concept board comes closer to an ad for a product than the concept statement, although usually the rules around concept development say that the concept should not be actively "selling" the product. The purpose here is to give the consumer more information and visual cues to gain more accurate information on how appealing this idea actually is. Consumers will be asked how likely they are to buy the product, uniqueness in the category, value for the money, as well as ratings and competitive comparisons. The latter two are often used to understand the *drivers* of purchase interest; that is, what specific features of the product are the most important in creating interest in the product. This information can be used to create future marketing materials.

Results from tests of concept boards can be compared to historical results or databases to understand the potential for the product. Many companies can also use this information in conjunction with their proprietary algorithms and a preliminary marketing plan (distribution, pricing, advertising spend, trade promotion, etc.) to actually make a volume forecast. As such, this stage is an important gate to the future of this particular product, and getting it right is crucial.

- Video concept boards go one step further by putting the concept into a video that can range in length anywhere from 30 seconds to several minutes. This is often used when the manufacturer feels that the idea cannot adequately be expressed in a static image. The consumer questioning and the use of the results is very similar to what is done with the concept boards.

14.4.1.2 TOMORROW

Concept testing has been criticized for using very rational measures of consumer interest, including purchase intent, on the basis that the question requires too much thought and thus is inconsistent with the automatic/habitual purchasing that are so frequently exhibited by consumers. Yet this criticism seems misguided as the whole purpose of new products and new ideas is to *disrupt* that very behavior. So asking a thoughtful question such as "how likely are you to buy this product" is not as inconsistent with behavioral science as it might be when dealing with a habitually purchased product. But neuroscience can still disrupt the concept testing in several ways, including:

Marketers will realize that how the product idea is presented is as important as the content of the idea.

1. Production of the concept board: Consumer decisions are driven by far more than the words used to describe the functional benefits that the product delivers. Understanding the role that emotion plays in the eventual decision, marketers will realize that how the product idea is presented is as important as the content of the idea. While the early screening is unlikely to show much change given the efficiency inherent in the screening process, changes will come in the production of

the more complete descriptions of the concept. These can include visual or aural cues designed to be indicative of the emotional benefits of the product. It is also likely that multiple concepts will be tested with the variance in the emotional cues. This would be in contrast to testing today where, if multiple boards are tested, it is to alter the description of the functional benefits to see which combination is most effective (although this likely will continue). One noticeable change will be more use of video to portray these cues, and they will end up looking more like ads (although likely longer the typical 30-second ad).

2. Measurement will go beyond the survey. Just as the VOPAN organization recognized in the 1970s that there is more than the spoken word to the consumer's answer, marketers will employ techniques to understand just how engaged the consumer truly is with the concept and elements of the concept. While we can speculate on which neuroscience techniques would be used for this type of work (electroencephalography, implicit association test, and biometrics), the world of neurotechnology is evolving quickly enough that this could become dated. Better to focus on what should be measured in this instance rather than how it would be measured. Combining the explicit interest with the implicit measures of engagement will provide better insights to the potential of the idea.

> Marketers will employ techniques to understand just how engaged the consumer truly is with the concept and elements of the concept.

3. Analytic techniques will evolve to include measurement from the neuroscience-based measures both in understanding the overall potential of the idea and in understanding what drives that potential. Implicit techniques (such as the implicit association test) could be particularly useful here in understanding exactly how the consumer reacted to the concept beyond what is already learned from explicit survey measures. One outcome of both the analytic techniques and the more complete presentation of the concept through the video boards is that marketers will have a better idea how to translate the concept into actual marketing communications.

14.4.2 ADVERTISING TESTING
14.4.2.1 TODAY

Advertising, particularly television advertising, is one of—if not the biggest—expenditure that a marketer makes. Ensuring the quality of the commercial is of vital importance as it can make the difference between a successful brand and one that does not survive. As noted earlier, advertising testing was first used when Procter & Gamble began using the DAR test to see if people could remember an ad, and its sponsor, the day after it aired. The more people who could remember the ad, the better it was felt to be. Since this practice started in the 1950s, advertising testing has changed a lot while at the same time changing very little.

Evaluation of ads is done throughout the development process. Early in the process, qualitative research (either in-depth interviews or focus groups) is used to fine-tune what the final ad will look like. As the ad nears final production, it will often go through quantitative testing for the purpose of qualification. That is, does the ad meet minimal quality standards? If not, it will either be killed or retooled so it can meet those standards. The goal is to ensure that weak ads are not put on-air.

Today, most of qualification testing (more commonly known as "copy testing" or "pretesting) is based around two key measures of success:

1. A measure of whether consumers can remember the ad. This has evolved over time from a pure recall question to more of a recognition-based metric. This is generally coupled with an unaided branding question ("Who was the ad for?").

2. A motivation measure, usually in the form of a preference or purchase intent measure. The results are measured against a control cell or a database to understand if the ad has moved interest in purchasing the product.

Most pretesting systems look at a combination of these two metrics as indicative of success. In addition to these measures, data will be collected on:

- Communication: What messages did consumers take away from the ad? This can be compared to the client's communication objectives to see if the ad is strategically on-target.

- Brand ratings: Consumers are asked to assess the brand on a number of different dimensions such as quality, taste, or other dimensions specific to the category or brand. Comparing these to other ads, a database, or to the results from a group not exposed to the ad helps the advertiser understand if the ad is having a positive impact on attitudes toward the brand.

- Likeability: Do consumers like the ad? This is often used to explain why persuasion, communication, or attitudinal data may be strong or weak. Likeability is most commonly assessed with a five-point scale with the endpoints of "like very much" and "dislike very much." This measure took on greater focus within the industry when ARF released the results of their Copy Research Validity Project, in which a "strong relationship [was] found to exist between the *likeability* of the copy and its effects on sales."[17] While there was advocacy from some quarters, particularly advertising agencies[18] at the time this report was released, to use likeability as a key performance metric, few used it in this way. Instead, it became a standard question and one often used heavily in diagnosing why the ad performed as it did.

- Ad profile questions: These are similar to the likeability question in that they ask the consumer to evaluate the ad on several dimensions, including affective ones. These typically include terms such as "confusing," "irritating," "like to see again," and so forth.

- The concept of emotion in advertising is often dealt with in several ways. The first is to rely on the likeability measure as an indication of response.

17. Haley, "The ARF Copy Research Validity Project."

18. For example, see A. Biel "Love the ad. Buy the product? Why liking the advertising and preferring the brand aren't such strange bedfellows after all." Admap, Vol. 26, 1990, pp. 21–25.

Box 14.2
Tracking Ad and Brand Awareness

Unaided: The consumer is given only the category name as a cue. Example: Have you seen any advertising recently for toothpaste?

Aided: The brand name is added as another cue. Example: Have you seen any advertising recently for Colgate toothpaste?

The second is to focus on specific feelings (e.g., happy, sad, irritated) in the survey and have consumers assess how strongly they agree (or disagree) that the descriptor describes their reaction to the ad. These data can be compared to other ads and/or to databases to profile the consumer response to the ad.

Once launched, the progress of the advertising is often monitored through a tracking study. Typically, data are collected on a daily basis and then reported on a rolling 4-week period. This is done to allow the analyst to align changes in the media plan or other environmental factors with changes in key brand metrics.

Data typically tracked include both brand and advertising data, including:

- Advertising: Unaided and aided recall of advertising, recognition of specific ads, and sources of awareness (television, online, print, outdoor, etc.).

- Brand: Unaided and aided brand awareness, recent use of brands in category, brand buy next, purchase interest for all brands in category, and ratings on multiple dimensions for each brand in the category. In addition, metrics designed to measure brand equity are often included so that these can be monitored (brand equity is explored in more depth later in this chapter).

Data from tracking studies are used to monitor whether the advertising is performing as expected, monitor competitive performance, and understand whether there are meaningful changes in the positioning and understanding of the brand (box 14.2).

14.4.2.2 TOMORROW

The industry has already recognized that ad testing, particularly at the pretesting phase, is the most likely to be disrupted. The traditional methods relied on highly rational and thoughtful measures with little insight into how the advertising engages with the consumer emotionally. Some work has already started in this area as many companies are incorporating various forms of neuroscience measurement with the most frequent being automated, online facial coding and forms of implicit measurement including implicit association testing and timed-response testing.

Other firms, including Nielsen, Neuro-Insight, and Innerscope,[19] use neuroscience measurements as their primary measures.

So the measurement aspect is well on its way to becoming real. But what is lacking is a model that helps incorporate what technology measures into a decision framework. The industry continues to rally around the idea that conscious memory and stated behavioral intentions (more commonly known as persuasion) are the lead indicators of a successful ad. There are numerous issues with this, including:

- The use of measures of conscious memory as an absolute indicator of whether an ad has left an impression with the viewer. Remembered means the ad was successful; not remembered means it was not. Yet memory research tells us that there are many facets of memory. The questions used are designed to tap into conscious and primarily episodic memory. Yet advertising can quite easily create implicit memories, and sometimes memories are not stored as an ad; they are stored as part of the brand memory. Robert Heath points out in his work that classic measures of recall are biased against certain styles of advertising, specifically those processed at low levels of attention[20] (which he says are likely those ads that rely on emotion). This is more evidence that the methods of determining whether an ad has left an impression are incomplete.

- There is no role, except a diagnostic one, in this model for emotion. If the persuasion measures are adequate, the ad is seen as successful even if the measures of emotion are weak. This implies that building an emotional connection with consumers is not a primary role of advertising. Neuroscience-based models of consumer behavior would suggest otherwise.

And this points to where pretesting may be the most disrupted by neuroscience in the future: the role and measurement of memory and the role of emotion.

Implicit memories cannot be measured by surveys, so neuroscience-based techniques are the only way to understand if the memory system is being activated by the ad in prelaunch testing. This measurement could take several forms, including functional magnetic resonance imaging (fMRI) or electroencephalography (EEG) to measure whether memory is activated and implicit techniques to gain a sense of what was encoded. Survey measures still serve a valuable role in understanding conscious memory, but the analyst needs to understand that this may not provide a complete picture of the impressions left by the ad.

Current models of how advertising works need to be completely retooled to reflect the fact that emotions can lead directly to behavior without conscious reflection on the decision. This means that building emotional values is a key goal of advertising, as is repeated reinforcement of those emotional values.

Survey measures still serve a valuable role in understanding conscious memory, but the analyst needs to understand that this may not provide a complete picture of the impressions left by the ad.

19. Innerscope Research was acquired by Nielsen in 2015 and is now part of the Nielsen Consumer Neuroscience division.

20. For more on low-attention processing, see Heath, The hidden power of advertising; and Robert Heath, Seducing the subconscious: The psychology of emotional influence in advertising. Wiley-Blackwell, 2012.

So the pretesting system of the future would have these features:

- Neuroscience measurement simultaneous with exposure to measure emotional engagement and memory activation.

- Survey-based measures of communication, behavioral intention, and key brand metrics (such as equity metrics), and implicit testing to understand the extent of memories that have been left.

This is a fairly heavy package of measurement being applied, suggesting that this future may not be realized until further cost efficiencies in technology and measurement come into play. Keep in mind that today, much of the prelaunch testing is done using online data collection because of its cost efficiency. But today there are only a limited number of techniques (e.g., automated facial coding) that can be used online. And these may not have the power to measure all that is required. So there is a distance between the ideal world outlined here and the practical and cost-conscious real world.

The above discussion focuses on how neuroscience can improve the selection and qualification of ads by providing a more complete picture of what the ad is accomplishing. But these same measures are useful in another important area—indicating how to improve and optimize the ad's performance before it goes on-air. Survey-based tools have attempted for many years to provide insights into exactly which areas of an ad are working and which need improving by using techniques such as "dials" to monitor moment-to-moment response, direct questioning on a segment-by-segment basis, or just open-end questions on what consumers like and dislike about the ad. The problem with all of these approaches is that consumers simply cannot accurately reconstruct their in-the-moment responses. First of all, they are not consciously aware of all of their responses (in particular, the key emotional responses), and they have a tendency to simplify and rationalize their responses. Those neuroscience techniques that have good temporal resolution (i.e., the response can be time locked to what the consumer was experiencing at the time of the response) can provide more complete insight on the consumer experience with the ad. EEG measures are particularly effective at this because of the frequency with which the brain waves are read (figure 14.3). Certain biometric responses and facial coding also have reasonable temporal resolution and can be used for this purpose.

The use of neuroscience techniques can finally help ad pretesting realize its long-promised purpose of both *qualifying* an ad as one that will perform well in-market and provide a strong return on investment (ROI) and *optimizing* the ad.

In-market monitoring (tracking) of advertising can also be disrupted by the same factors. This monitoring is essentially a memory test. What brands can you remember? What ones have you used? What ads have you seen recently? Where

> Consumers simply cannot accurately reconstruct their in-the-moment responses.

> The use of neuroscience techniques can finally help ad pretesting realize its long-promised purpose of both qualifying an ad as one that will perform well in market and provide a strong return on investment (ROI) and optimizing the ad.

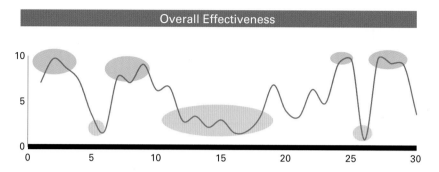

FIGURE 14.3
Second-by-second responses from EEG can help the ad agency optimize the ad performance (*x* axis, seconds; *y* axis, score).

have you seen them? All these questions assume the infallibility of memory. Remembering (either unaided or aided) is a sign of success; not remembering is a sign of failure. As an understanding of how memory works becomes more prominent in the tracking world, this paradigm will change. This will happen in two ways:

1. Improvements in how memories are cued to provide a more complete picture of what consumers have retained. Simple prompts and the focus on the importance of unaided recall will diminish to be replaced by a broader understanding that all memories are meaningful, regardless of how they are retrieved. The improvements in cueing will include things like the use of recognition-style cues (e.g., actual video from the ad) and contextual cues to help the consumer better place when and where he or she saw the ad.

2. An understanding that not all memories can be retrieved by direct questioning. To get at how ads have affected implicit and associative memories, implicit techniques such as implicit association testing will become a standard part of tracking surveys.

14.4.3 PACKAGE TESTING
14.4.3.1 TODAY
While the amount of money the marketer spends on packaging is less than that spent on advertising, many consumer goods marketers see packaging as one of the most important parts of their marketing programs because it is present at the "first moment of truth"; that is, at the shelf, the point where the consumer is deciding which product to actually buy. Consequently, many advertisers spend considerable amount of money on package testing. Generally, these tests revolve around two questions:

FIGURE 14.4
In an online find test, consumers are shown a virtual shelf and asked to find the product. In this case, they might be asked to find the Heinz Ketchup, and the time until they click on it will be recorded.

1. How visible is my package on the shelf? Will consumers see it as they scan the shelf to decide what to buy?

2. What does my pack design convey to consumers about my product? What messages do they take away? Is the branding clear?

Like ad testing, package testing approaches do not vary that much across companies. They tend to focus on the package in two ways. The first is an assessment of the visibility of the package in a competitive array (e.g., a shelf set). This is often referred to as a "find test." The second part, which can be done either as a separate study or after the find test, focuses on the consumer reaction to the pack itself.

- In the find test, consumers are shown a shot of the pack of interest and then shown a shelf array that includes the products they would typically see in a store including competitive products and those that are typically adjacent to this category (figure 14.4). They are asked to find the target package and pick it up (live testing) or click on it (online testing) to indicate they found it. The time until they find it is recorded with faster find times deemed as better. This task is often repeated with the package in different locations to get a more robust read on visibility.

- In the package evaluation, consumers are shown the package in isolation. This can be either a mock-up of a proposed package or the actual one. If the testing is done online, they are often shown a three-dimensional image that they can turn to examine. With in-person testing, they are given a physical product. After examining the package, they are asked a series of survey questions that typically include a purchase intent question, a question about what messages were communicated by the packaging likes and dislikes of the package, and brand and package descriptor ratings. Results are evaluated by comparison to the existing package, competitive packages, and/or databases.

14.4.3.2 TOMORROW

Traditional approaches to packaging treat the pack as another form of rational communication and stress the importance of how quickly the package can be found. While these functions are undoubtedly true—consumers can pick up the pack and scan for new information on things such as ingredients, nutrition, directions, and, most important, pricing—communication goes far beyond the rational messages on the package. The package can be thought of as another memory trigger. Effective packaging should trigger conscious memories of what the consumer already knows about the product from prior experiences (i.e., it should trigger the semantic memory system) but also elicit nonconscious, emotional experiences. Given earlier discussions on the importance of this latter system in influencing behavior, you can see the importance of the package at accomplishing this task. Neuroscience measures are an ideal way to understand *whether* a package elicits conscious memories and *which* elements of the package are the best at doing so. This information provides additional insight to the researcher in understanding which package might be the most effective but is also useful to the designer in understanding how to improve the packaging. Implicit testing to understand the associations that are triggered by the package will complement the response information.

Neuroscience measures are an ideal way to understand whether a package elicits conscious memories and which elements of the package are the best at doing so.

One of the great unanswered questions is just how important is it for consumers to quickly find the package? Conventional wisdom says that finding it faster means it is more likely that the consumer will actually buy the product in the store. But there is a difference between seeing something and responding to it. The consumer, in the find test task, may actually identify the product and click on it quickly. But what if there is no emotional response when the consumer notes the package? What if there is minimal memory activation when he or she sees it? Is this meaningful? You can understand why just finding the package quickly is not enough. But integrating a measure of response with the timed task provides that meaning.

14.4.4 BRAND EQUITY RESEARCH
14.4.4.1 TODAY

Equity research is designed to understand how consumers value a brand. While there are many definitions, it is often defined by the behavior that high equity elicits including greater brand loyalty, resistance to competitive marketing activity, or lower-price sensitivity. Regardless of which of these is the definition, the importance of strong brand equity to the marketer is obvious.

Unlike concept, ad, and package testing, there is considerable variance in how different research suppliers evaluate equity. One common form is known as the DREK model, which forms the basis for the Young & Rubicam Brand Asset Valuator (BAV) model. DREK stands for differentiation, relevance, esteem, and knowledge. These are defined as[21]:

Differentiation: BAV's Differentiation refers to how do the brand's offering differs from its rivals.Relevance: BAV's Relevance refers to how closely can the consumers relate to the brand's offering and is a significant driver for a brand's penetration.

Esteem: BAV's Esteem refers to the consumer perception about the brand. Whether a brand is popular or not, whether it delivers on its stated promises- all this contribute in building up the esteem of the brand.

Knowledge: BAV's Knowledge refers to the degree of awareness about a brand in the minds of its consumers. This is very important in building a brand and making the consumers understand of what the brand actually stands for and its implicit message to the consumers.

The BAV model postulates that brands grow in that order (difference to relevance to knowledge) and that the brands with the strongest consumer commitment have all of these. Brands also decline in that order with knowledge still strong for declining brands, with difference, relevance, and esteem in decline or low.

In addition to these high-level constructs, consumers are often asked to rate the brands in the category on a substantial number of dimensions (the BAV study includes 48 standard dimensions) including both functional and "higher order" emotional benefits. Analyzing these data allows the marketer to draw a picture of how consumers value the brand as well as which elements of the brand consumers view as unique and which are at parity or worse to competitors.

14.4.4.2 Tomorrow

The brand equity modules, while quite elegant and sophisticated, are completely devoid of any form of nonconscious measurement. They, like the other research tools of today discussed in this chapter, are built on the assumption that all elements that consumers associate with a brand are accessible by the conscious and thus can be measured through surveys. But brands, maybe more than any other element of the marketing mix discussed here, are incredibly complex. Brands are not bundles of functional benefits that the consumer can add up to determine the overall value of the brand to them. They are the composition of any and all experiences and exposures the consumer has ever had with the brand including actual use, advertising, pricing, packaging, word of mouth, and so on. And those experiences become associated in many ways with the elements that define the brand: the name, the logo, the packaging, and various icons that become symbols of the brand. For example, think of Nike and the Swoosh. That element by itself, devoid of any explicit branding, triggers not only the Nike name but all the rich associations that brand has accumulated over the years.

21. Source: MBASkool, Brand Asset Valuator (BAV) http://www.mbaskool.com/business-concepts/marketing-and-strategy-terms/1859-brand-asset-valuator-bav.html.

And not all of these associations are conscious. If we think about the concept of automatic or habitual purchasing, it is the brand and its symbols that trigger this behavior. The implicit values and associations are embedded in the consumer's mind, and it is these that trigger this behavior. Brand equity research of the future will provide the researcher and the marketer with insight to values and associations as discussed more fully in chapter 10. This can include any or all of the following:

- An understanding of the consumer's instinctive nonconscious response when he or she sees the brand, its logo, or other icons that trigger memories of the brand.

- An understanding of exactly which elements of the brand are uniquely and strongly associated with the brand and thus can also serve as these triggers. The marketing scientists at the Ehrenberg-Bass Institute in Australia refer to these as "Distinctive Brand Assets" and define them as follows:

  "An element is only an asset if it fulfills the following criteria:

  - Unique: The element evokes the brand, and not competitors.

  - Famous: Most, if not all consumers should know the element represents the brand name."[22]

> Brand equity research of the future will provide the researcher and the marketer with insight to values and associations.

Understanding which elements of your brand are both unique and distinctive and the nonconscious values that are triggered by the Distinctive Brand Assets will help the marketer better understand how to harness and improve the consumer's connection to the brand.

There are a number of approaches that can be used to understand the nonconscious reaction when exposed to the brand including fMRI and EEG. In addition, implicit testing such as implicit association testing can provide more detailed insight into exactly what is associated with the brand. These insights will be combined with survey data that will likely use many of the equity models that currently exist.

Learning from behavioral economics suggests that context is another factor that can influence consumer decisions. For example, Coca-Cola may have great value to you when eating at a fast-food restaurant but little value at a fine-dining restaurant. Any measure of brand equity that does not incorporate some form of context will not give a true reading of how consumers perceive and value the brand.

> Any measure of brand equity that does not incorporate some form of context will not give a true reading of how consumers perceive and value the brand.

22. Excerpted from Ehrenberg-Bass Institute, "Measure your distinctive assets." https://www.marketing science.info/wp -content/uploads/ 2015/08/Measure-Your -Distinctive-Assets.pdf, 2015.

14.5 THE RESEARCHER OF THE FUTURE

The discussion in the chapter so far has focused on how neuroscience will disrupt market research in terms of new measures and new models. But marketing and research are ultimately driven by humans, so it would be naïve to assume that anything will change if the people themselves do not change. To adapt and to lead the disruption, the researcher of the future will need a different skill set than what has historically been needed. And it is not just the role of neuroscience that drives this need. Two of the bigger trends in the research industry are the learnings from neuroscience and the increasing focus on "big data." The latter means a need for the researcher to understand increasingly complex statistical applications to derive learning from these massive data sets. Neuroscience requires an intimate under-standing of how the brain works and how that influences behavior. When you combine these skills with the other areas of knowledge that a researcher needs (including finance, management, economics, basic statistical analysis, psychology, sociology, oral and written communication skills, an understanding of experimen-tal design, and project management training), it becomes overwhelming for any one individual to be an expert in all. This suggests that the researcher of the future will be more specialized than currently. In fact, in organizations or groups that special-ize in areas where neuroscience will be the most disruptive (advertising testing, for example), it is reasonable to assume that trained neuroscientists will be part of the staff. But the researcher, the person whose responsibility is to turn the data from studies that may include surveys as well as one or more neuroscience tech-niques into meaningful insights, will need to understand the basic premises behind the workings of the brain. The need for this education will occur within the walls of the universities, where business school classes in neuroscience are already becoming common (e.g., the Fox School of Business at Temple University includes the Center for Neural Decision Making whose mission includes "investigat(ing) the neurobiological bases of human behavior, preference formation, and decision making"[23]), and in ongoing educational programs such as seminars by the Burke Institute.

In organizations or groups that special-ize in areas where neuroscience will be the most disruptive (advertising testing, for example), it is reasonable to assume that trained neuroscientists will be part of the staff.

23. Source: Temple University, Fox School of Business, www.fox .temple.edu/cms _research/institutes -and-centers/center -for-neural-decision -making/.

KEY TAKEAWAYS

- The idea that all factors that people use to make decisions are accessible by direct questioning has dominated market research practice for years.

- While the idea that the subconscious could influence behavior has been in popular science for years, marketers' first experiences with how this worked tended to be negative due to ethical concerns. These concerns had a negative influence on how marketers perceived the use of neuroscience for marketing and research purposes.

- But the biggest barrier, and one that still exists, is that our mental models of why people behave as they do have not been updated. They remain primarily focused on rational reasons. Even with a broader understanding of how the nonconscious can influence behavior (thanks to books such as Daniel Kahneman's *Thinking, Fast and Slow*), the lack of a model that shows how to integrate this learning into behavioral models has slowed the adoption of neuromarketing.

- Some estimates say that the share of research dollars that are invested in marketing research projects is as low as 5%.

- The areas of research most likely to be disrupted by neuroscience are concept testing, advertising testing, package testing, and evaluation of brand equity.

DISCUSSION QUESTION

APPLE "1984"

During the 1984 Super Bowl, Apple ran an ad titled "1984" (the ad can be found on YouTube),[24] now thought to be one of the greatest Super Bowl ads ever created (and possibly one of the best ads period). The ad was used to launch the first Macintosh computer and actually aired the only time nationally during the Super Bowl. Yet it is credited with the success of the Macintosh that continues even today.

Steve Jobs described the objective of the ad as follows:

> [...] It is now 1984. It appears IBM wants it all. Apple is perceived to be the only hope to offer IBM a run for its money. Dealers initially welcoming IBM with open arms now fear an IBM dominated and controlled future. They are increasingly turning back to Apple as the only force that can ensure their future freedom. IBM wants it all and is aiming its guns on its last obstacle to industry control: Apple. Will *Big Blue* dominate the entire computer industry? The entire information age? Was George Orwell right about 1984?[25]

Yet according to at least one source,[26] this ad almost did not air. The ad was tested by survey-based copy testing company ASI Market Research and reportedly received a score of 5 on their 43-point scale of how effective the ad would be at persuading people. The agency that commissioned the test elected not to take this information to Apple.

Question: Discuss how neuroscience might have been used to get a better read on why this ad was as successful as it is reported to have been? What did the survey-based copy test miss? What approaches would you recommend for testing an ad like this?

24. For more detail on this ad and the product launch, see Steve Jobs's introduction of the commercial at a sales meeting in 1983. Available at https://www.youtube.com/watch?v=lSiQA6KKyJo/.

25. From Steve Jobs's keynote address to employees in 1983. Available at https://www.youtube.com/watch?v=lSiQA6KKyJo/.

26. Aaron Taube, "How the greatest Super Bowl ad ever—Apple's '1984'—almost didn't make it that far." Business Insider, January 22, 2014. Available at www.businessinsider.com/apple-super-bowl-retrospective-2014-1/.

CHAPTER 15

ETHICS IN CONSUMER NEUROSCIENCE

JULIA F. TRABULSI, MARIA CORDERO-MERECUANA, DANIELA SOMARRIBA, AND MANUEL GARCIA-GARCIA

15.1 INTRODUCTION

As technologies continue to evolve and grow in capabilities, the ethics of research has become an important topic of discussion in academia and the media. Within several decades, neuroscience research has grown from a budding academic field to a widely used resource for both scientists and marketers alike. The ethical approach of neuroscience research—or *neuroethics*—is important to consider when designing a consumer neuroscience study.

15.2 THE HISTORY OF NEUROETHICS

The term *neuroethics* was coined in 2002 by William Safire, chairman of the Dana Foundation and writer for the *New York Times*, to describe a growing multidisciplinary field that stems from bioethics and links the fields of neuroscience, medical bioethics, philosophy, law, cognitive science, and public policy (Marcus 2002). Neuroethics is used to describe the ethics of neuroscience and examines the ethics surrounding the technology of neuroscience research and how its findings are used in society (figure 15.1).

Ethical considerations of consumer neuroscience vary little from those that exist for market research and biomedical human subject research. The ethics of biomedical research came under scrutiny in the mid-twentieth century after a lack of regulation resulted in numerous reports of human subject mistreatment. For example, throughout the Tuskegee syphilis study, syphilis diagnoses and treatment

Neuroethics is used to describe the ethics of neuroscience, or examining the ethics surrounding the technology of neuroscience research and how its findings are used in society.

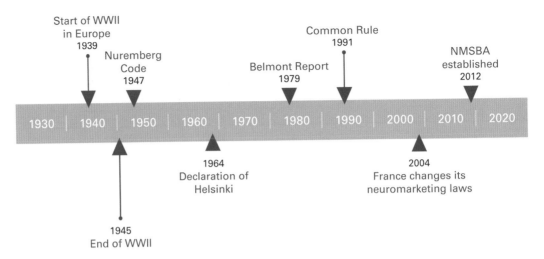

Figure 15.1
Historical events in neuroethics.

were withheld from disadvantaged, rural, black males for the sake of science (Brandt 1978). Biomedical research was conducted on prisoners during World War II, leading to the establishment of the Nuremberg Code in 1947, which placed an ethical framework around biomedical research conducted on human subjects (Nuremberg Code 1949).

Neuroethics: a growing multidisciplinary field that stems from bioethics, linking fields of neuroscience, medical bioethics, philosophy, law, cognitive science, and public policy.

The Nuremberg Code: the first widely recognized code to provide guidelines on ethical human subject research.

15.2.1 Regulatory Ethical Guidelines for Human Subject Research

The Nuremberg Code was the first widely recognized code to provide guidelines on ethical human subject research. Established after World War II, the code outlines 10 principles for human subject protection and places strong emphasis on informed consent (box 15.1).

The Declaration of Helsinki (1964) stemmed from the principles in the Nuremberg Code and inspired the creation of ethical review boards globally, including institutional review boards (IRBs) in the United States and the International Ethical Guidelines for Biomedical Research Involving Human Subjects (World

Box 15.1
The Nuremberg Code

1. The voluntary consent of the human subject is absolutely essential. This means that the person involved should have legal capacity to give consent; should be so situated as to be able to exercise free power of choice, without the intervention of any element of force, fraud, deceit, duress, over-reaching, or other ulterior form of constraint or coercion; and should have sufficient knowledge and comprehension of the elements of the subject matter involved, as to enable him to make an understanding and enlightened decision. This latter element requires that, before the acceptance of an affirmative decision by the experimental subject, there should be made known to him the nature, duration, and purpose of the experiment; the method and means by which it is to be conducted; all inconveniences and hazards reasonably to be expected; and the effects upon his health or person, which may possibly come from his participation in the experiment. The duty and responsibility for ascertaining the quality of the consent rests upon each individual who initiates, directs, or engages in the experiment. It is a personal duty and responsibility which may not be delegated to another with impunity.

2. The experiment should be such as to yield fruitful results for the good of society, unprocurable by other methods or means of study, and not random and unnecessary in nature.

3. The experiment should be so designed and based on the results of animal experimentation and a knowledge of the natural history of the disease or other problem under study, that the anticipated results will justify the performance of the experiment.

4. The experiment should be so conducted as to avoid all unnecessary physical and mental suffering and injury.

5. No experiment should be conducted, where there is an *a priori* reason to believe that death or disabling injury will occur; except, perhaps, in those experiments where the experimental physicians also serve as subjects.

6. The degree of risk to be taken should never exceed that determined by the humanitarian importance of the problem to be solved by the experiment.

7. Proper preparations should be made and adequate facilities provided to protect the experimental subject against even remote possibilities of injury, disability, or death.

8. The experiment should be conducted only by scientifically qualified persons. The highest degree of skill and care should be required through all stages of the experiment of those who conduct or engage in the experiment.

9. During the course of the experiment, the human subject should be at liberty to bring the experiment to an end, if he has reached the physical or mental state, where continuation of the experiment seemed to him to be impossible.

Box 15.1
(continued)

> 10.   During the course of the experiment, the scientist in charge must be prepared
>   to terminate the experiment at any stage, if he has probable cause to believe,
>   in the exercise of the good faith, superior skill, and careful judgment required
>   of him, that a continuation of the experiment is likely to result in injury, dis-
>   ability, or death to the experimental subject.

Source: Nuremberg Code (1949).

Medical Association 2001). These regulatory bodies ensure protection of human subject rights, including those regarding privacy, informed consent, coercion, withdrawal, and beneficence.

In 1979, the Belmont Report was authored to protect the rights of human subjects participating in research. The report addressed three major ethical concerns of human research and established regulatory guidelines to prevent human subject mistreatment. It outlined proper obtainment of informed consent, stated that research must maximize benefits while minimizing risks, and created guidelines for selection of subjects as a means to protect vulnerable populations from exploitation and harm (National Commission for the Protection of Human Subjects of Biomedical and Behavioral Research 1978). The Belmont Report heavily influenced federal regulations for biomedical and behavioral human subject research in the United States, affecting all government-funded human research under the Federal Policy for Protection of Human Subjects, also known as the "Common Rule" (HHS 1991).

15.3   CONSUMER NEUROSCIENCE IN PRACTICE: ETHICAL CONCERNS IN THE FIELD

When discussing the ethical concerns surrounding consumer neuroscience research, skeptics and critics of the field focus on two major issues: (1) how the data are being collected and (2) how the data are being used.

The two most widely discussed concerns surrounding the use of neuroimaging technology are those of privacy and informed consent.

The first issue includes the scientific process of data collection, study design, and execution. Concerns include informed consent, protection of vulnerable populations, privacy, ethical recruiting practices and compensation, training and certifications held by personnel exempt from academic research guidelines, and upholding scientific rigor within businesses not held to academic standards of scientific research.

The two most widely discussed concerns surrounding the use of neuroimaging technology are those of privacy and informed consent. According to McCabe (Olteanu 2014), *privacy* is defined as the ability of a person to control the extent, timing, and circumstances of sharing oneself—be it physically, behaviorally, or intellectually—with others. Given that the nature of neuroscience methods is to tap into the nonconscious, unmodulated response of the subject, it could be argued that the participant is unaware of the extent of the information he or she is providing and therefore unable to maintain privacy and comprehensive consent.

Privacy: the ability of a person to control the extent, timing, and circumstances of sharing oneself.

Informed consent: subjects are fully informed of the procedure, the risks, how their information will be used, and the outcome of the study.

15.3.1 INFORMED CONSENT

Informed consent is crucial to the ethical practice of human research, especially in the field of consumer neuroscience research. According to governing bodies regulating human subject research, participants must be fully informed of the procedure, the risks, how their information will be used, and the outcome of the study. There must also be open feedback with the participants about the scope of the research, how the information they relinquish will be used, and the possibility of accessing results. To this extent, the subject must be capable of providing signed consent and understanding the implications of the studies in which they participate.

It is vital to consider vulnerable populations who may be unable to truly provide consent, such as minors or populations with cognitive disabilities. Coercion should be avoided when recruiting and compensating human subjects for research participation, and it is important to avoid uneven distribution of population demographics.

It can be argued that the human subjects participating in consumer neuroscience studies are unaware of the information obtained using neuroscience methods, as responses are captured at a subconscious level. In this case, the subjects are not fully aware of the information they divulge. Is this unethical? Is this different from passively observing a subject's behavior or obtaining online behavioral data? An interesting comparison is the use of social media data to analyze human behavior. Both Facebook and OkCupid have received backlash upon publication of research using data mined from their sites (Albergotti and Dowskin 2014). In 2014, a study was published revealing that Facebook had manipulated the emotional content of text seen by nearly 700,000 users, without obtaining explicit consent or providing an opportunity to opt out (Kramer, Guillory, and Hancock 2014). Though critics

It can be argued that the human subjects participating in consumer neuroscience studies are unaware of the information obtained using neuroscience methods, as responses are captured at a subconscious level.

Box 15.2
Informed Consent Exercise

In 2012, social media giant Facebook conducted large-scale research on its users by manipulating emotional cues on its site. Users could not opt in or opt out of the study. Informed consent was obtained via the user agreement under a product testing clause.

1. In what ways is this different from the informed consent obtained for human subjects who participate in consumer neuroscience studies?

2. Subjects give consent to participate in a study and have their data analyzed. Does it still count as informed consent if they:
   a. Are fully aware of what information they divulged to researchers?
   b. Are aware that they are divulging behavioral information, but cannot be sure exactly what their behavior will reveal?
   c. Are aware that they are divulging information, but due to the complex nature of brain activity, cannot be sure exactly what their activity will show?

3. For the above, what protections would you put in place to ensure that the human subjects are as informed as possible and full consent is obtained?

(See Kramer, Guillory, and Hancock 2014.)

were quick to point out the potential ethical transgressions of the study, and the editors of the publishing journal expressed concerns regarding ethical best practices shortly after publication, the study was deemed to be within ethical guidelines for informed consent by both the IRB and the journal. It was stated that informed consent was obtained upon agreement of the user terms and conditions, and that as a private entity not receiving government funding for research, Facebook was under no obligation to conform to the Common Rule. Similarly, online behavioral data are analyzed regularly by websites such as OkCupid (Rudder 2014). As in consumer neuroscience research, the subjects know that their data are being analyzed, but they may not understand precisely what information they divulge. Because of this, it is important to design ethical protocols when obtaining consent and ensure that human subjects are informed to the greatest extent possible (box 15.2).

15.3.2 Privacy

Concerns exist regarding how individuals' privacy will be maintained, who ultimately owns brain scans, whether scans can be sold to other persons or institutions, and what happens to incidental findings revealed by the scans (Wolf et al. 2008). An *incidental finding* is a discovery concerning a research participant that has potential health importance that was revealed while conducting research for other purposes. Such issues are indicative of both possibilities and dilemmas that lie ahead at the intersection of marketing and neuroscience (Wilson, Gaines, and Hill

2008). Transgressions are particularly egregious when manipulation occurs without explicit awareness, consent, and understanding.

The use of information gathered through consumer neuroscience research poses its own set of ethical concerns in regard to protecting the rights of human subjects, collecting and promoting valid results, and using research findings for non-maleficence. McCabe defines *confidentiality* as the process of protecting an individual's privacy. This pertains to treatment of information that an individual has disclosed in a relationship of trust, with the expectation that the information will not be divulged to others without permission (Olteanu 2014.). With respect to consumer neuroscience, this means that human subject data can only be distributed to outside parties with express consent from the subject, and the subject must be informed of all the ways his or her information will be used. In order to protect subject data, many researchers avoid disclosing individual data and prevent personal identifiers from being linked to results.

Incidental finding: a discovery concerning a research participant that has potential health importance that was revealed while conducting research for other purposes.

Confidentiality: the process of protecting an individual's privacy; it pertains to treatment of information that an individual has disclosed in a relationship of trust, with the expectation that the information will not be divulged to others without permission.

The second main issue of neuroethics surrounds the use of data collection and the moral, social, and legal effects of neuroimaging studies on the future of society as a whole (Roskies 2002). Many of the concerns raised regarding the moral and societal implications of consumer neuroscience include confidentiality of thought, validity of research for describing consumer behavior, use of research findings for financial gains, or exploiting knowledge of human behavior for non-benevolent means. In a more futuristic sense, consumer neuroscience must ethically account for the protection of vulnerable populations from exploitation and protection of the consumer's right to make autonomous decisions, both of which have potential to be called into question if there is a lack of regulatory guidelines and adequate oversight. The validity of this research being extrapolated to a larger population and providing meaningful results to clients is another concern.

15.3.3 MANIPULATION

If the ethics of conducting consumer neuroscience is not addressed, there is concern that marketers could use results to design irresistible "super-ads" to drive consumer behavior, for good or evil. The worry is that super-ads will remove the consumer's autonomy and ability to choose the products he or she purchases. Additionally, critics want to ensure that consumers do not fall prey to marketers promoting products or lifestyles that could bring harm to a consumer, such as

Human subject data can only be distributed to outside parties with express consent from the subject, and the subject must be informed of all the ways his or her information will be used.

Consumer neuroscience must ethically account for the protection of vulnerable populations from exploitation and protection of the consumer's right to make autonomous decisions, both of which have potential to be called into question if there is a lack of regulatory guidelines and adequate oversight.

cigarette and alcohol campaigns. Largely, these concerns are rooted in a general misunderstanding of the field, yet they have been targeted and addressed by regulatory bodies.

Is it possible to create super-ads? Consumer neuroscience can be used to help marketers communicate their messages more effectively to the consumer at a basic level, and insights gleaned can help inform and shape best practices for future marketing campaigns. However, insights from an individual advertisement do not necessarily translate to another advertisement, and sweeping claims cannot be made across the board, as there are too many variables in stimuli. Additionally, it is unlikely that advertisements can manipulate users' behavior beyond their free will.

It is unlikely that advertisements can manipulate users' behavior beyond their free will.

15.4   Regulatory Guidelines for Ethical Research

Organizations and guidelines have been established to address the above concerns and uphold ethics in privacy and informed consent.

15.4.1   Health Insurance Portability and Accountability Act

The Office for Civil Rights enforces the Health Insurance Portability and Accountability Act (HIPAA) Privacy Rule, which protects the privacy of individually identifiable health information. Additionally, the HIPAA Security Rule sets national standards for the security of electronically protected health information. The HIPAA Breach Notification Rule requires covered entities and business associates to provide notification after a breach of unsecured, protected health information. The confidentiality provisions of the Patient Safety Rule protect identifiable information from being used to analyze patient safety events and improve patient safety.

15.4.2   Institutional Review Boards

Companies that perform any kind of behavioral research are required to register with an institutional review board subsequent to a 2009 change to the Belmont Report. The Office for Human Research Protections (OHRP) provides leadership in the protection of the rights, welfare, and well-being of subjects involved in research conducted or supported by the U.S. Department of Health and Human Services (HHS). The OHRP helps ensure this by providing clarification and guidance, developing educational programs and materials, maintaining regulatory oversight, and providing advice on ethical and regulatory issues in biomedical and social-behavioral research.

15.4.3   Belmont Report

As a result of several highly publicized abuses, the Department of Health and Human Services and the Department of Health, Education, and Welfare enacted the National Research Act in 1974. This resulted in the creation of the National Commission for the Protection of Human Subjects of Biomedical and Behavioral Research. Currently, the report is divided into five subparts:

Subpart A is the basic set of protections for all human subjects of research conducted or supported by HHS and was revised in 1981 and 1991, with technical amendments made in 2005.

Three of the other four subparts provide added protections for specific vulnerable groups of subjects.

Subpart B, issued in 1975, and most recently revised in 2001, provides additional protections for pregnant women, human fetuses, and neonates involved in research.
Subpart C, issued in 1978, provides additional protections pertaining to biomedical and behavioral research involving prisoners as subjects.
Subpart D, issued in 1983, provides additional protections for children involved as subjects in research.
Subpart E, issued in 2009, requires registration of institutional review boards (IRBs) which conduct review of human research studies conducted or supported by HHS.

In the Belmont Report, the following are considered and defined: (1) the boundaries between biomedical and behavioral research and the accepted and routine practice of medicine, (2) the role of assessment of risk-benefit criteria in the determination of the appropriateness of research involving human subjects, (3) appropriate guidelines for the selection of human subjects for participation in such research, and (4) the nature and definition of informed consent in various research settings.

15.4.4 NEUROMARKETING SCIENCE AND BUSINESS ASSOCIATION

Because many of the regulatory guidelines on ethical human subject research pertain largely to clinical and academic research rather than business or marketing, the Neuromarketing Science and Business Association (NMSBA) created a Code of Ethics for its members. According to the NMSBA Code of Ethics, participation in research should be entirely voluntary, participants should have the freedom to withdraw at any time, informed consent must be obtained, and procedures, risks, and use of information must be explained in clear terms that are easily understood by a participant. The International Chamber of Commerce and European Society for Opinion and Marketing Research (ICC/ESOMAR) International Code on Market and Social Research also suggests a framework of self-regulation in which companies that conduct consumer neuroscience research studies compromise to conduct all research in a way that guarantees both integrity on the part of the researchers and the protection of the research participants.

Participation in research should be entirely voluntary, participants should have the freedom to withdraw at any time, informed consent must be obtained, and procedures, risks, and use of information must be explained in clear terms that are easily understood by a participant.

15.5   Concerns about Scientific Validity

15.5.1   Predictive Validity and Limitations

Acknowledging limitations of neuroimaging technologies is important when making claims about consumer neuroscience. Most commonly, consumer neuroscience methodologies examine neurophysiologic markers for attention, affect, memory, and desirability, which are related to the effectiveness of messaging and communication, although these do not provide the ability to explicitly interpret consumer thoughts.

How strongly do these neurophysiological markers predict in-market behavior? In a collaboration between researchers at Temple University and the New York University Stern School of Business, a study was conducted to evaluate the link between various advertising research methodologies and in-market purchasing behavior. The study found neurophysiological measures to be predictive of a real-world, market-level response to advertising (Venkatraman 2015). Additionally, market researchers have linked consumer neuroscience measures to actual purchasing behavior and Twitter engagement (Smith and Brandt 2015).

Although these methods have been shown to reliably tap into attention, emotion, memory, and desirability, and these measures have been validated as predictors of in-market behavior, the scope of these technologies does not include the ability to read the minds of consumers, as some would believe. Misleading claims in the media must be avoided in order to prevent misinterpretation of these technological capabilities and understand the limitations of this type of research.

15.5.2   Scientific Rigor on a Global Scale

When conducting consumer neuroscience research across international waters and among varying cultures, how is scientific rigor ensured at a global scale? Reproducibility of research becomes a potential concern when conducting research at a large, multinational company. As businesses are in the interest of turning a profit, to what extent do business priorities such as cycle-time reduction and cost savings outweigh scientific interest in methodological rigor? At one consumer neuroscience firm, researchers have studied the reproducibility of results using their standard methodology, finding no significant difference across advertisements and across locations, indicating not only that neuroscience is a reliable measurement for advertising research, but also that methodologies are rigorous and standardized across labs (Gurumoorthy et al. 2017). Upholding rigorous standards in scientific methods is crucial when conducting and reproducing reliable research at a grand scale. Like in academia, consumer neuroscience researchers can apply strict methodology to all data collection and analysis through ongoing training and certification of technicians and applying the same processes to data analysis across

Although these methods have been shown to reliably tap into attention, emotion, memory, and desirability, and these have been validated as predictors of in-market behavior, the scope of these technologies does not include the ability to read the minds of consumers, as some would believe.

the board. Initiated in 2014, the Neurodata Without Borders (NWB) project brings together researchers across the world and establishes standards for neurophysiological data collection internationally (see https://crcns.org/NWB). Consumer neuroscience can utilize these standard protocols as well in order to address the risk of variability and reliability between global labs.

15.5.3   RISK OF REVERSE INFERENCE

With all neuroimaging research, researchers must avoid falling to the reverse inference fallacy. *Reverse inference* refers to the process of inducing reasoning from an observation to a particular process not directly tested but associated via other research. As noted by Murphy et al. (2008), interpreting study results accurately becomes a challenge due to the complexity of studying and explaining human behavior. When the results of a research study are not easily explained, there is a risk that the scientists and technicians interpreting the results may be tempted to associate results to metrics that cannot be proven to directly correlate to the material being tested.

A famous example of reverse inference is the case of neuroscientist James Fallon, who used an MRI scan of his brain to diagnose himself as a psychopath (Thorpe 2014). Fallon noticed that his brain scan showed abnormally low activity in some frontal lobe areas, which other research has suggested is typical in psychopathic individuals. These areas of the brain have been associated with empathy and moral reasoning. Fallon, then, concluded that because his own brain matched the functional profile of a psychopathic brain, then he also must be a psychopath, despite his lack of aggressive behavior and lack of direct evidence.

Reverse inference: the process of inducing reasoning backward from an observation to a particular process not directly tested but associated via other research.

Population exclusion: the exclusion of certain demographics because of the need to minimize variables in neuroscientific research, skewing results to a specific demographic rather than representing an entire population.

15.5.4   POPULATION EXCLUSION

It is worth noting the potential for validity to be skewed to certain demographics while excluding others because of the need to minimize variables in neuroscientific research. This limitation is referred to in this chapter as *population exclusion*. In many cases, neuroscientific studies use right-handed, healthy individuals, excluding subjects with physiological or psychological disorders and people who have suffered traumatic brain injuries. Because consistency is important in the analysis of neuroimaging data, researchers screen participants for factors such as medication use, physical brain trauma, neurological disorders, vision disorders, and age in

Neuroscience is not only a reliable measurement for advertising research, but also methodologies are rigorous and standardized across labs.

order to obtain a sample of similar brains. As an example, some left-handed individuals process language in the right hemisphere, and other left-handed individuals process language in the left hemisphere, while language processing is more reliably located in the left hemisphere for right-handed individuals (Day 1977). To ensure consistent localization of language processing for data analysis, researchers will screen participants for handedness, excluding left-handed individuals in many neuroimaging studies. These screening processes allow researchers to limit variables to dependent and independent variables so that they can ensure the findings are a direct result of the factor they intended to study. However, because certain populations are consistently filtered out from results, population exclusion does occur. This begs the question: Are the results from a specific population transferrable to the population as a whole? This pertains not only to consumer neuroscience but also to much of neuroimaging research overall. Concerns about population exclusion are inherent to this type of research and are no different than those that already exist within the scientific rigors of academia; however, these exclusions are not typically inherent to historical market research methodology and pose an interesting limitation for market researchers to consider when using consumer neuroscience tools.

> Exclusions are not typically inherent to historical market research methodology and pose an interesting limitation for market researchers to consider when using consumer neuroscience tools.

15.6   Critics of Consumer Neuroscience Research

Research findings have the power to inform marketing and messaging and should be presented with the intent of benefiting society rather than inciting harm. While critics of consumer neuroscience argue that misuse of data could have a negative impact on society by shifting the power from the consumer to the seller (Carr 2008), consumer neuroscience research can also be used to gain invaluable insight into decision making overall.

15.6.1   Commercial Alert

A number of entities have enforced regulations on consumer neuroscience or have expressed concerns, urging lawmakers to take action. Gary Ruskin of Commercial Alert, an organization aiming to protect populations from the negative effects of neuromarketing, expressed concerns that neuromarketing could potentially be used to promote harm. Ruskin cited three potential scenarios for misuse of consumer neuroscience: promotion of the sale or consumption of products harmful to the consumer, promotion of false political propaganda messages, and proliferation of degrading values. While it is acknowledged that consumer neuroscience could produce more effective messaging (whether benevolent or maleficent), this is an example of the false perception that neuromarketing is a brainwashing tool.

> Potential scenarios for misuse of consumer neuroscience: promotion of the sale or consumption of products harmful to the consumer, promotion of false political propaganda messages, and proliferation of degrading values.

In order to combat the perceived maleficence of consumer neuroscience as a whole, commercial researchers have committed to benefiting the community through pro bono work on public service announcements and nongovernmental organization (NGO) advertising campaigns. However, even companies that abide by the NMSBA Code of Ethics may still do research on products known to cause harm, such as tobacco or alcohol.

15.6.2 NEUROIMAGING LAWS IN FRANCE

In 2004, France took a stand against the misuse of neuroimaging for commercial use or financial gain by passing a law stating, "'Brain-imaging methods can be used only for medical or scientific research purposes or in the context of court expertise" (Oullier 2012). Because of the misguided, negative perception of consumer neuroscience in the public sphere, several companies using the technology for market research purposes choose to not disclose this fact in order to protect their image from criticism. However, several researchers have spoken out that there are no outstanding ethical concerns with regard to consumer neuroscience use.

15.7 ARGUMENTS IN SUPPORT OF NEUROSCIENCE FOR MARKET RESEARCH

Lee, Broderick, and Chamberlain (2007) argue that there are no ethical reasons why neuroscience should not be used in the marketing realm, but rather, the use of such technology benefits society with increased knowledge of how consumers respond to stimuli and make decisions. Many of the issues posed by the ethics of consumer neuroscience are often overinterpreted and exaggerated—scientists believe that there is no single source of decision making, or a "buy button" per se, leaving little ability for manipulation. Thus, neuroethics should be used to help inform and establish industry standards for practice in order to uphold privacy, confidentiality, and consumer rights. As new technology is continually developed and utilized in both marketing and academic research, ethical guidelines provide the framework to protect populations from exploitation and the negative impact of technological advances.

Fugate (2007) takes a "knowledge is power" approach to countering criticism of consumer neuroscience, arguing that it is compatible with consumer interest, as data can be used to learn about consumers' own harmful, covert behavioral patterns that they perform without awareness, such as impulsive buying or excessive consumption. Establishment of neuroethics guidelines simply creates a framework around research to protect and benefit society, rather than cause harm to any one person or to populations as a whole.

Neuroethics guidelines simply create a framework around research to protect and benefit society.

15.8   Looking at the Future of Consumer Neuroscience Research

Anticipating ethical challenges is crucial in designing effective research methods, with a focus on tackling ethical problems that infringe upon human subject rights to privacy and confidentiality or are a violation of consumer rights. Consumer neuroscience can arm society with knowledge about consumer behavior and purchase decision-making. While it may be argued that this knowledge could potentially be used to market products with ill effects or to exploit consumers' behavioral patterns for financial gains, it could also be used to identify and prevent negative behavioral patterns, such as overeating or excessive gambling. It is the ethical responsibility of marketers, advertisers, and researchers to use these technologies and research findings for the benefit of society.

At present, there are still misconceptions in the public domain about consumer neuroscience as a field, including its capabilities and its intended goals. As we look toward the future, it is important for consumer neuroscientists to continue academic research and publications in order to bring greater knowledge, transparency, and awareness. Equally important is to use this research to continue shaping and improving research protocols to ensure privacy, validity, scientific rigor, and respect for the rights of consumers and human subjects.

> It is important for consumer neuroscientists to continue academic research and publications in order to bring greater knowledge, transparency, and awareness.

Key Takeaways

- Ethical considerations of research became an important topic of conversation after multiple controversial research practices had come to light in the face of lax regulations, such as the Tuskegee syphilis study.

- The Nuremberg Code, the Declaration of Helsinki, the Belmont Report, HIPAA, and IRBs all were created in an effort to protect the rights of human subjects participating in research.

- Because many regulatory guidelines pertain largely to clinical and academic research, the Neuromarketing Science and Business Association Code of Ethics was drafted to ensure ethical consumer neuroscience research as it pertains to businesses and market research.

- Major ethical considerations within consumer neuroscience are (1) whether research participants fully understand and can consent to the information being used, even though they may be less aware of what information is gathered; and (2) whether populations who did not consent to or participate in research are losing their right to privacy and autonomous decision-making by extrapolation.

- While advertisements may be improved to better communicate desired messages to consumers, the reach of these improved advertisements does not push consumers beyond their free will, easing the concerns of many critics.

DISCUSSION QUESTIONS

1. What sets consumer neuroscience apart from clinical research in terms of ethical responsibility?

2. What are the major ethical concerns of consumer neuroscience research?

   a. How have these been addressed?

   b. What concerns are outstanding?

3. In what ways are human subject rights protected by regulatory guidelines?

EXERCISES

1. If you were designing a consumer neuroscience study, how would you keep ethics in mind for the following:

   a. Subject recruiting and incentives

   b. Subject age

   c. Subject demographic

   d. Interpretation of results

2. For the following case study, how would you interpret the results? Be careful to avoid reverse inference.

   A company uses EEG and eye tracking to collect data for a consumer neuroscience study. Fifty females, aged 21–55, are shown an advertisement for a new product and then compare it to a competitor brand. After the data are analyzed, the data show the competitor brand resonates more strongly with the population tested. In the commercial advertisement of the new product, the main character using the product never shows his/her face. The commercial advertisement of the competitor brand shows a family interacting with each other.

References

Albergotti, R., and E. Dowskin. 2014. Facebook study sparks soul-searching and ethical questions. *Wall Street Journal*. Available at www.wsj.com/articles/facebook-study-sparks-ethical-questions-1404172292.

Brandt, Allan M. 1978. Racism and research: The case of the Tuskegee syphilis study. *Hastings Center Report* 8 (6): 21–29.

Carr, Nick. 2008. Neuromarketing could make mind reading the ad-man's ultimate tool. Guardian, April 3, 2008. Available at www.theguardian.com/technology/2008/apr/03/news.advertising/.

Day, James. 1977. Right-hemisphere language processing in normal right-handers. *Journal of Experimental Psychology: Human Perception and Performance* 3 (3): 518.

Fugate, Douglas L. 2007. Neuromarketing: A layman's look at neuroscience and its potential application to marketing practice. *Journal of Consumer Marketing* 24 (7): 385–394.

Gurumoorthy, R., K. Kasinathan, V. Karapoondinott, and M. E. Smith. 2017. Reproducibility in consumer neuroscience: Focus on advertising research. [Under review.] *JMR, Journal of Marketing Research*.

HHS (Department of Health and Human Services). 1991. Common Rule. Available at www.hhs.gov/ohrp/regulations-and-policy/regulations/common-rule/index.html.

Kramer, Adam D. I., Jamie E. Guillory, and Jeffrey T. Hancock. 2014. Experimental evidence of massive-scale emotional contagion through social networks. *Proceedings of the National Academy of Sciences of the United States of America* 111 (24): 8788–8790.

Lee, Nick, Amanda J. Broderick, and Laura Chamberlain. 2007. What is "neuromarketing"? A discussion and agenda for future research. *International Journal of Psychophysiology* 63 (2): 199–204.

Marcus, Steven J. 2002. Neuroethics: Mapping the field. In Proceedings of the Dana Foundation Conference. Chicago: University of Chicago Press.

Murphy, Emily R., Judy Illes, and Peter B. Reiner. 2008. Neuroethics of neuromarketing. *Journal of Consumer Behaviour* 7 (4–5): 293–302.

National Commission for the Protection of Human Subjects of Biomedical and Behavioral Research. 1978. *The Belmont report: Ethical principles and guidelines for the protection of human subjects of research.* Bethesda, MD: ERIC Clearinghouse.

Code, Nuremberg. 1949. *Trials of war criminals before the Nuremberg military tribunals under Control Council Law no. 10.* vol. 2., 181–182. Washington, DC: U.S. Government Printing Office.

Olteanu, M. 2014. Neuroethics and responsibility in conducting neuromarketing research. *Neuroethics* 8:191–202.

Oullier, O. 2012. Clear up this fuzzy thinking on brain scans: France has banned commercial applications of brain imaging. *Nature. Worldview* 483 (7387): 7.

Roskies, Adina. 2002. Neuroethics for the new millennium. *Neuron* 35 (1): 21–23.

Rudder, Christian. 2014. We experiment on human beings! [blog] Available at https://blog.okcupid.com/index/php/we-experiment-on-human-beings/

Smith, Michael E., and David Brandt. 2015. Reliability and predictive validity in consumer neuroscience: Examples from advertising, packaging, and programming research. Paper presented at the 5th Interdisciplinary Symposium on Decision Neuroscience, May 16, 2015, Massachusetts Institute of Technology, Cambridge, MA.

Stromberg, Joseph. 2013. The neuroscientist who discovered he was a psychopath. *Smithsonian* 22 (November). Available at www.smithsonianmag.com/science-nature/the-neuroscientist-who-discovered-he-was-a-psychopath-180947814/.

Thorpe, Lexie. 2014. Reverse inference: Neuroscience's greatest fallacy? Knowing Neurons.com. Available at http://knowingneurons.com/2014/02/12/reverse-inference-neurosciences-greatest-fallacy/.

Venkatraman, Vinod, Angelika Dimoka, Paul A. Pavlou, Khoi Vo, William Hampton, Bryan K. Bollinger, et al. 2015. Predicting advertising success beyond traditional measures: New insights from neurophysiological methods and market response modeling. *JMR, Journal of Marketing Research* 52 (4): 436–452.

Wilson, R., J. Gaines, and R. P. Hill. 2008. Neuromarketing and consumer free will. *Journal of Consumer Affairs* 42 (3): 389–410.

Wolf, Susan M., Frances P. Lawrenz, Charles A. Nelson, Jeffrey P. Kahn, Mildred K. Cho, Ellen Wright Clayton, et al. 2008. Managing incidental findings in human subjects research: Analysis and recommendations. *Journal of Law, Medicine & Ethics* 36 (2): 219–248.

World Medical Association. 2001. World Medical Association Declaration of Helsinki. Ethical principles for medical research involving human subjects. *Bulletin of the World Health Organization* 79 (4): 373.

CHAPTER 16

FUTURE OF CONSUMER NEUROSCIENCE

KIMBERLY ROSE CLARK

16.1 INTRODUCTION

In 1990, Michael Gazzaniga, the "Father of Cognitive Neuroscience," declared the nineties to be the "Decade of the Brain." Indeed, this era gave rise to technologies and "neuro" insights more rapidly and comprehensively than the prior four decades combined. Since then, the turn of the millennium has proved a proliferation of that early foundational work and spawned advancements not only in research tools but also in the subfields and applications within neuroscience. Integrated learnings from cognitive, social, and affective neurosciences, along with psychonomics, have culminated in the field of consumer neuroscience and its applied sister, neuromarketing.

Many from both academia and the private sector anticipate a bright future in the utility of research findings garnered from brain and body measures. In a review of applied neuroscience methodology's integration with consumer psychology, Plassmann, Ramsøy, and Milosavljevic (2012) revealed that since the turn of the millennium, exponential growth has occurred in the amount of academic references focused on consumer neuroscience, the number of neuromarketing companies founded, and the frequency of Google hits for both terms (figure 16.1).

At the time of writing this chapter, a Google search for the term "Neuromarketing" yields 738,000 hits, while the term "consumer neuroscience" is rising steadily at 28,400 hits. On final revision nearly two years later, those numbers rose to 2,770,000 and 54,500 respectively.[1]

The groundswell of interest in neuromarketing stems from the proven utility of neuroscientific tools in the academic sector. Prior to positron emission

> The groundswell of interest in neuromarketing stems from the proven utility of neuroscientific tools in the academic sector.

[1]. Key word searches were conducted on June 30, 2015 and February 15, 2017.

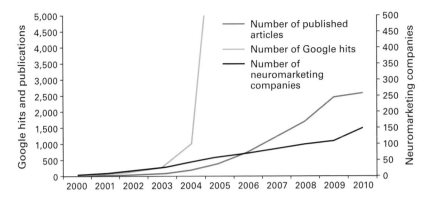

FIGURE 16.1
Growth of research applying neuroscience to marketing over time. Source: Adapted from Plassmann, Ramsøy, and Milosavljevic (2012).

tomography (PET) and functional magnetic resonance imaging (fMRI), it was not possible to observe metabolic changes linked to neural processes. Such activity has been associated with changes in the underlying processes that occur during certain types of decision making (Sanfey et al. 2003; Hsu et al. 2005; Fehr and Camerer 2007; Tom et al. 2007). Academic research aimed at understanding the dynamic nature of decision making at the neural level lends itself to application in the consumer world. The processing of changes resulting from a consumer's exposure to marketing stimuli, such as advertisements, brand and pricing information, emotional influencers, product availability, and spatial framing, has the power to better inform the marketing and advertising sectors (Kenning and Plassmann 2008; Karmarkar, Shiv, and Knutson 2015). In the early stages of the field, Ariely and Berns (2010) summed up the anticipated hope for neuromarketing's success in reporting that many academics and branders alike intuited that neuroimaging would provide marketers with information that is not obtainable through conventional marketing methods. In the short time since their prediction, the field of consumer neuroscience has become sophisticated in the ways in which researchers have applied findings from social, affective, cognitive, and decision neuroscience. For example, an understanding of social interactions related to fairness and reciprocity, metalizing, empathy, self-regulation, and emotion regulation can serve to better understand the predisposition of the consumer (Smidts et al. 2014).

During the same era, practitioners outside and intermixed with academia were born, conducting research within consumer contexts via tools measuring psychophysiologic information of the consumer with the initial purpose of informing information systems research (Dimoka et al. 2010) and organizational research (Lee and Chamberlain 2007). Such tools have also been shown to serve as proxies to neural processes, such as galvanic skin response (GSR) or electrodermal activity

(EDA), respiration changes, heart rate and heart rate variability, and changes in electrodermal activity of the scalp (via electroencephalography, or EEG) along with facial and microfacial expressions (Riedl et al. 2010). The advantage to such tools is their cost and ease of implementation within natural consumption contexts, which lends to a generalizability in the nature of the information garnered about the consumer that functional imaging does not. Through a two-pronged approach, academia's consumer neuroscience and practitioners' neuromarketing methodologies reached a critical mass in societal interest.

16.2   RESEARCH STANDARDS

Despite the many advances in methodological innovations and the integration of academic subdisciplines to advance neuromarketing, as well as an increased awareness of the field, neuromarketing has continued to oscillate in its acceptance in the market researcher's toolbox, exemplified by ebbs and flows in media coverage (Botswick 2010; William 2010). Its popularity follows a Gartner-like "hype cycle" (Linden and Fenn 2003) in the S-shaped rise and fall of its acceptance in market research because of a historical lack of replicability in research findings, past overclaims of the technology from early field practitioners, and a limitation in the standards of practice adopted by those who employ neuromarketing measures (figure 16.2).

> Through a two-pronged approach, academia's consumer neuroscience and practitioners' neuromarketing methodologies reached a critical mass in societal interest.

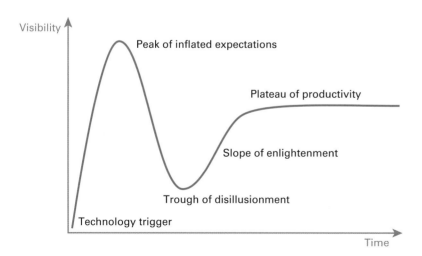

FIGURE 16.2
Gartner's hype cycles offer a summary of relative maturity of technologies in a specific industry or discipline. They provide both a scorecard to separate hype from reality and a model to assist enterprises in choosing when and what types of technologies to adopt.

It is more accurate to anticipate a future where industry decision-makers will embrace the added utility of measures based in neuroscience as tools that assist standard measures by increasing predictive models of the consumer choice.

Vendors in neuromarketing's future must be able to bridge the gap between understanding neural or biologically derived measures and associating those measures as the cause of a specific consumer outcome.

2. Neuromarketing Science and Business Association founder, Carla Nagel, identified this issue across neuromarketing vendors in her April 24, 2015, essay "Five Global Trends in Neuromarketing."

3. In neuroscience, an ROI is defined as a specific anatomic region of interest within the brain related to neural activity. In business, ROI is defined as the return on investment a business achieves as a result of an investment outlay.

Lynda Shaw, a cognitive neuroscientist who specializes in employing positive emotional cues in business, believes that "businesses are in reality in 2015 only still just applying a cursory nod to the impact of neuroscience on retaining and attracting new customers." Historically, market researchers have maintained a reticence in adopting novel neuroscientific measures (Shaw 2015).

Those coming from the market research industry focus on meaningful and reliable consumer insights that are born out of a number of measures rooted in psychology, behavioral economics, consumer psychology, and traditional, explicit measures of recalled experience and anticipated desires. It is unlikely that the future of the market research industry will trade out these familiar methods for full replacement by measures of the nonconscious. It is more accurate to anticipate a future where industry decision-makers will embrace the added utility of measures based in neuroscience as tools that assist standard measures by increasing predictive models of consumer choice.

Steve Genco coauthored the first book on the field of neuromarketing for lay audience consumption, entitled *Neuromarketing for Dummies* (Genco, Pohlmann, and Steidl 2013). In it, he discusses four requirements that practitioners of neuromarketing techniques had heretofore not been able to meet, which include establishing connections to behavior and business applications, scalability, trustworthiness, and an ability to meaningfully contribute to consumer insights. These issues will continue to be of critical importance to the acceptance of the application of neuroscience-based measures into real-world pursuits. Fortunately, advances are well under way to tackle these issues as academics and research vendors in the field continue meaningful dialogue on each of these key points.

16.2.1 CONNECTING BEHAVIOR AND BUSINESS OUTCOMES

One of the largest hurdles in establishing the field of applied consumer neuroscience has been the "explanation challenge"[2] of suppliers to provide concise and relevant definition to the market research industry. This challenge can be, in part, attributed to the present-day issues of reliability and validity in measures collected from nonconscious brain and body measures. In standard research methods courses, a common example is often shown to determine whether a methodology employed to address a research question is both a valid and reliable data source (figure 16.3).

Internal validity can be explained as the approximate truth about inferences regarding cause-effect or causal relationships. Vendors in neuromarketing's future must be able to bridge the gap between understanding neural or biologically derived measures and associating those measures as the cause of a specific consumer outcome. I have referred to this issue for some time now as how to resolve the "ROI to the ROI,"[3] and it is one that must be targeted by those in both consumer neuroscience and neuromarketing to achieve a robust understanding of the field's utility. In other words, neuromarketers must be able to create logical and sensible ties between regions of neural activity in the brain (regions of interest) and the

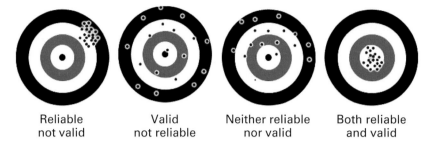

Reliable
not valid

Valid
not reliable

Neither reliable
nor valid

Both reliable
and valid

FIGURE 16.3
Although a commonly used illustration to depict issues of reliability and validity in experimental measures, these considerations are especially poignant in the application of neuroscientific tools onto commercial research questions.

return on investment marketers demand from their research initiatives. The temporal precedence, or cause and effect, relationship between brain and body measures and consumer decisions will continue to increase over time and with continued study.

External validity is determined by the extent to which the results of a particular study can be generalized to other situations and to other populations, which is highly relevant for market researchers who desire to understand the impact of a marketing campaign or a brand message on their target audience. Data collected in a laboratory setting, or "clean room," regarding a consumer's choice may not generalize to the same choice made in the "real world." An appraisal of empirical studies that link neural activity to behavior had suggested up to 70% relied on fMRI, which is limited in establishing external validity of the data obtained through this medium (Kable 2011). For example, consider a scenario where fMRI is used to identify neural activity related to product price evaluations when a subject's sole focus is only on the task at hand and on limiting his or her physical movements. These stringent instructional parameters are likely to manifest different neural processing and product valuations when the same individual is in the context of a grocery aisle considering similar evaluations of product price.

Construct validity is considered the degree to which a test measures what it claims, or purports, to be measuring. This issue is one that has been challenging for some vendors specializing in nonconscious measures but is especially acute for practitioners who collect data via ambulatory electroencephalography.

Electroencephalography is a measure of electrical activity in the brain using small, flat metal disks (electrodes) attached to the scalp. Its use as a tool in neuromarketing is primarily to ascertain emotional responses toward advertisements and for package testing. While there is an overwhelming amount of literature in affective neuroscience using EEG, some neuromarketing vendors have created ambulatory EEG devices that collect data from behaving consumers in natural

Data collected in a laboratory setting, or "clean room," regarding a consumer's choice may not generalize to the same choice made in the "real world."

selling environments. EEG data capture in laboratory settings requires participants to remain as motionless as possible in order to minimize artifacts in the data that result from movement. Vendors who utilize ambulatory EEG in consumer assessments face the issue of construct validity when interpreting their data as their data preprocessing (cleaning) often eliminates many of the frequencies produced. This preprocessing is done prior to data analysis in order to eliminate signal noise stemming from motion that naturally occurs in a freely moving consumer. The question then becomes: Are these vendors throwing out signal that also measures the consumer emotions they are trying to capture?

A second issue related to construct validity during data capture in this field occurs for pupillometric responses collected by eye-tracking devices. Much research has been done linking changes in pupil diameter to various levels of arousal (Garrett, Harrison, and Kelly 1989; Laeng, Sirois, and Gredebäck 2012). In various consumer contexts, lighting levels can often override pupil responses that might stem from emotional arousal. No matter the measure, practitioners must be able to provide meaningful linkage between the data captured and the measure they are trying to ascertain.

16.2.2 TRUSTWORTHINESS

Establishing trustworthiness in use of the methods based on measures from neuroscience will be enhanced when practitioners in the field agree upon definitive neurobiologies of such consumer neuroscience constructs. Once common definitions are put in place, a shared language will be possible. This will allow those on the market-research side the power to conduct longitudinal studies and meta-analyses through use of data collected across multiple measures from a variety of neuromarketing vendors.

The trust in metrics obtained from neuroscientific tools will continue to increase moving forward when vendors espouse a practice of transparency in their research designs and explanations of how data are collected, how artifacts are accounted for in the data,[4] the types of filtering processes chosen in data streams, and the levels of significance adopted in reporting findings. Given the proprietary nature of some neuromarketing firms who specialize on one or two measures, there are and will continue to be black boxes in data processing. With the surge in patents for tools based on neuroscientific measures, transparency will continue to increase because of their public nature which will allow for clearer conceptions regarding the data-capture techniques of neuromarketing.

At the present day, some firms can be considered the rising tide that will work to lift all ships with respect to trustworthiness in the transparent manner in which they choose to foster an environment of openness and shared communication. Applied Brain and Vision Sciences (ABVS) is ahead of the industry in its fostering of transparency.[5] ABVS provides their clients with all necessary preprocessing algorithms for assistance in understanding the analyses of data collected through their firm's hardware and software. Vendors that behave in this manner

A shared language will be possible to allow those on the market-research side the power to conduct longitudinal studies and meta-analyses through use of data collected across multiple measures from a variety of neuromarketing vendors.

4. Artifacts are considered those interference signals caused by irrelevant occurrences to the data, such as motion of eye blinks or gum chewing during an EEG session, which act to confound the data and impact the overall validity of findings.

5. See http://www.abvsciences.com.

will be at the forefront of replicability in findings, which clients of the future will demand. Such transparency will enable end-users easier ability to communicate and compare findings, which will in turn ease their comfort level in employing the tools of neuromarketing.

In addition, trust will be allayed when vendors come together in addressing how sample sizes are established. There is positive support from recent work by Dmochowski et al. (2014) in establishing a justification for using small sample sizes during brain-based measures in data collection. Dmochowski's lab used evoked encephalographic responses to record neural activity from a group of naïve individuals while viewing popular, previously broadcast television content. They then compared this small sample's response to the broad audience response derived from social media activity and audience ratings. His group determined that the level of intersubject correlation in the evoked encephalographic responses predicted the expressions of interest and preference among thousands. In other words, data collected from a small sample can be positively and significantly correlated with a larger population.[6]

While this is positive evidence in terms of cost containment on subject recruitment, successful vendors in the field of neuromarketing must consider a client's holistic agenda in their research program when determining the appropriate sample power. A neuromarketer's subject samples must align with the client's overall research agenda, giving the need to integrate and discuss data from multiple methodologies. As sensitivity in nonconscious measures continues to increase, demographics, personality traits, and affective states will be integrated along with traditional measures in order to understand and predict how various populations process specific brand information. This will in turn lead to an ability of branders to microsegment consumers with an extreme level of detail. Understanding the consumer at this level will allow branders to "narrowcast" highly specified content to consumers across target moments.

16.2.3 BENCHMARKING FOR THE FUTURE

All three components of validity have been hurdles to neuromarketing's future, but those in academia and the private sector are addressing such issues by establishing research benchmarks. For example, as mentioned in previous chapters, a recent study funded by the Advertising Research Foundation (ARF) and run in collaboration with Temple University's Fox School of Business and New York University (Venkatraman et al. 2014) was launched to evaluate the efficacy of various data types on subsequent performance of advertisements. In their paradigm, a number of implicit and explicit measures were collected during the viewing of multiple television ads. Their results hint at limitations in both internal and construct validity in some implicitly derived measures such as eye tracking, biometrics, and electroencephalography that are used as predictor variables in present-day neuromarketing initiatives. In fact, their results suggest that only fMRI-related activity significantly explained the fluctuation in ad performance.[7]

> Transparency will enable end-users easier ability to communicate and compare findings, which will in turn ease their comfort level in using the methodology of neuromarketing.

6. A term Dmochowski refers to as "neural consistency."

7. Activity in the ventral striatum is the strongest predictor of real-world, market-level response to advertising.

While the ARF studies are a disappointment to some vendors of neuromarketing, they have been essential to building a solid foundation for future research in the application of the field by establishing benchmarks to define success. Moving ahead, such issues of validity will resolve as academics and private vendors continue to collaborate to create a common set of definitions for common metrics and best practices.

16.3   The Future Tools of Consumer Neuroscience

In the futurescape of consumer neuroscience, the methodologies used to capture nonconscious brain and body measures will be less of a focus than utility of metrics produced. Those in the field and on the client side will need to maintain plasticity in the adaptation of novel technologies that will collect nonconscious data. With processing speeds becoming ever faster, hardware footprints becoming ever smaller, and data storage moving to centralized clouds, new technology and sensory-specific contexts will be constant catalysts for change in the field. New technologies available within the advertising industry will, along with novel tools of consumer measurement, give rise to the next iterations of the industry and the discipline. In tandem, they will provide critical correlates that will make bridging brain- and body-based measures with behavior more seamless.

16.3.1   Stand-Off Technologies

As with native advertisements in websites, the importance of measuring in-context marketing will be a critical step to move the field of neuromarketing forward. Just as video cameras are commonplace in consumer environments of today, the future will hold a continued increase in the use of crowd-sourced analytics derived from nonconscious behaviors of multiple consumers simultaneously through use of *stand-off* technology, or hardware and software that collects human subject data without physically touching a person. Thermal imaging was recently utilized by the Transportation Security Administration (TSA) in airports to collect nonconscious measures of international fliers due to concerns of international carriers of Ebola and more recently Middle East respiratory syndrome (MERS) (Sawitta Lefevre 2014). By removing the need to explicitly interview each passenger and by not having to rely on a passenger's self-reported body temperature allowed the TSA increased efficiency and accuracy by simply observing the body temperatures of deplaning passengers.

Video-based data capture will also be increasingly used as a stand-off measure to assess visual attention, arousal levels, and overall affect of consumers in real time, within consumer environments. Market researchers of today measure gross behaviors of consumers in contexts to ascertain the effectiveness of visual merchandising campaigns. Behavioral frequencies and durations are currently collected as

With processing speeds becoming ever faster, hardware footprints becoming ever smaller, and data storage moving to centralized clouds, new technology and sensory-specific contexts will be constant catalysts for change in the field.

(a) Input

(b) Magnified

FIGURE 16.4
Eulerian video magnification provides a means to capture biological information from the consumer in a "stand-off" fashion. Photo credit: Michael Rubinstein.

part of this type of video-based data mining. Forging ahead, video-based data will integrate data collected from other stand-off measures related to consumer affect, based on facial expression analysis,[8] and arousal, based on heart rate and heart rate variability (figure 16.4).[9]

16.3.2 WEARABLES

While stand-off measures will increase in use for crowd analytics within natural environments, wearables will have an equivalent value to the field of applied consumer neuroscience in the type of tethered specificity of consumer information they will afford. Currently, large providers such as Samsung, Apple, and Fitbit provide commercial-grade peripheral nervous system measures including heart rate, respiration rate, and blood glucose monitoring. Makers of these accessories were primarily interested in creating self-monitoring devices in order for consumers to have access to their physical statistics to achieve fitness goals. Wearable utility moving ahead will assist in continual data capture of individuals that will populate data sets to aid in *deep learning*, which is a kind of self-study mechanism utilized by machines. Rather than being programmed by a set of fixed rules, computer algorithms that harness deep learning actually learn how to achieve a task independently. Once provided with enough biological, neurologic, behavioral, and location data from inputs such as wearables, deep-learning predictions related to

8. Emotient, Noldus FaceReader, and Affectiva are three pioneering firms to first utilize stand-off methodology in facial expression analysis, using "action units" of muscle combinations known as FACET to classify emotion.

9. Eulerian video magnification allows magnification of video to visualize microscopic changes that are otherwise invisible to the naked eye, such as changes in blood flow beneath the skin's surface.

consumers within novel contexts will be possible. The application of deep learning onto consumer-based initiatives will allow the marketers of tomorrow to predict ad content that consumers will most likely desire. This will change the way marketers behave. Reactive campaigns based on consumer ratings will be replaced by proactive campaigns based on deep learning that will predict the most efficacious ads *a priori*.

As crowd-based and tethered technologies become part of the neuromarketer's toolbox, the commercial environments of tomorrow will work to embed sensors in environments that will enhance and broaden the utility of wearables. In the near future, wearables will be able to interact with the consumer on the basis of a rudimentary binary choice of whether or not he or she is physically present in a retail space or within a category of a space. For example, transmitters of location information may be read by apps on wearables in order to cue relevant ads for a shopper in that context, to link them to a particular website, or to remind them of an anticipated need, such as an item on a planned grocery list. When married to applications based on neuroscience, wearable tech will ultimately be charged with sensing particular psychophysiologic states, such as a dip in glucose. As an example based on academic literature, that ebb in glucose levels can be linked to evidence of a decrease in self-control or self-regulation (Baumeister and Vohs 2007). Connecting the dots to application, a targeted advertising message could then be cued specifically for a consumer in that state to suggest an impulse purchase he or she would otherwise not consider with in-tact self-regulatory stores in place.

16.3.3 VIRTUAL REALITIES

The Centennial Generation, also referred to as "Gen Z,"[10] is already fully immersed in online environments, and they will continue to come of age in a dualistic world where the line between digital and physical will have been erased by embedded technologies that take advantage of virtual reality.[11] The opportunities for consumer applications will continue to grow as virtual environments become more sophisticated. One means by which virtual realities will manifest application onto consumer marketing initiatives is in addressing storytelling techniques used by ad creatives. Present-day marketers capitalize on the value of storytelling to create persuasive narratives in their marketing communications. Moving into the future, virtual-reality environments will present virtual atmospheric information while simultaneously capturing and integrating brain and body responses from the experiencer related to the environment. This will allow creatives to present brand information that goes beyond storytelling in order to create a new type of interactive marketing communication based on *story making*. Story making will "gamify" advertisements by presenting dynamic experiences embedded within the promotional narrative on the basis of biological feedback of the experiencer. For example, consider a virtual world where you have the ability to browse a hotel or restaurant located on the other side of the world. If the virtual environment had "smart"

Wearable utility moving ahead will assist in continual data capture of individuals that will populate data sets to aid in deep learning, which is a kind of self-study mechanism utilized by machines.

10. Centennials are the generation after Millennials and were born starting in 1997.

11. Oculus Rift and Magic Leap are two major firms specializing in virtual reality.

capacity to incorporate neurologic and biological inputs, the consumer's experience could change dynamically on the basis of his or her real-time attentional, affective, or engagement levels related to the environment. Future advertisements will eventually marry virtual reality with the tools of neuroscience to detect a consumer's disinterest related to a product and either instantly swap one product out for another or replace its context to enhance a different product attribute.

The current movement of the advertising industry is to address the *so-lo-mo* trend in consumer demand[12] by generating more customized content for their target audiences. For example, retailers will adopt one-to-one e-commerce that will feature personalized home pages and purchase incentives based on individual consumer data. An integration of a consumer's nonconscious responses, discussed later in the chapter as neurographics, will become an essential component in the mix of consumer data to determine optimal personalization.

With the flood of new technology being especially poignant in this field, the questions that will continue to be most pressing in advancing market research will be:

- Are the tools employed to answer a research question sufficient to measure the efficacy of the initiative?

- What types of data streams will new tools produce?

- How will such novel data streams be integrated into a larger body of metrics to augment the utility of extant or "dark" data?

- Will new metrics and technology be required to measure new user interfaces?

16.4   MARKETING AND MEASURING TO ALL FIVE SENSES

The senses of sound, smell, taste, and touch have a greater influence on a consumer's perception than they are aware of (Morrison et al. 2011; Sugiyama et al. 2015), and by creating novel combinations of sensory prompts that typically connect with consumers at a subconscious level, such *polymodal* sensory marketing will garner attention through all senses, which has been shown to increase exploration and engagement in the context of consumer environments (Tullman and Clark 2004). Bricks-and-mortar retail environments will need to up the engagement and "retailtainment" they offer in order to compete with the ever-increasing online retail channels such as Amazon, Echo, and Dash. Addressing a holistic, polymodal sensory environment will work to achieve their continued place in future consumer considerations of retail channels, as stores of the future will focus less on purchase-oriented and more on experience-oriented avenues to resonate

Story making will "gamify" advertisements by presenting dynamic experiences embedded within the promotional narrative on the basis of biological feedback of the experiencer.

Retailers will adopt one-to-one e-commerce that will feature personalized home pages and purchase incentives based on individual consumer data.

The modes of sensory communication will necessarily diversify traditionally visual and auditory-only modes of marketing and promotional content toward a broader set of sensory outputs that include olfactory, somatosensory, and gustatory cues.

12. So-lo-mo *is a growing movement of consumers who wish to be impacted by social, local, and mobile marketing campaigns.*

The presence of specific olfactory cues effectively persuades consumers. Aromas that conjure the recall of childhood memories have been shown to facilitate the intention to adopt new or novel products.

13. *U.S. Patent No. 20130284821 A1. Electronic scents may be transmitted on a stand-alone basis, unaccompanied by other sensory stimulus, or as part of a multisensory experience. Examples of multisensory experiences include theatrical motion pictures, television programming, sound recordings, or e-books accompanied by one or more scents. These scents may be coordinated with content elements, such as the scent of horses accompanying the motion picture* High Noon, *the scents of beer and leather accompanying a sound recording of "When You're a Jet" from* West Side Story, *or the musty scent of a cellar in an e-book version of Poe's* The Cask of Amontillado.

14. *Scent-generator technology has the ability to sense, transmit, and receive scent-enabled digital media such as web pages, video games, movies, and music. The sensing part of this technology works by using olfactometers and electronic noses.*

with consumers. Visionary selling environments are already beginning to crop up in the form of "destination malls" to adapt to market demands by providing innovative experiential environments (Dobrian 2015). Such spaces will present multisensory cues to shoppers at an ever-increasing pace.

Future advances in multisensory marketing communications both in physical commercial environments and online will require research to address the impact of polymodal sensory inputs in consumer choice. The modes of sensory communication will necessarily diversify traditionally visual and auditory-only modes of marketing and promotional content toward a broader set of sensory outputs that include olfactory, somatosensory, and gustatory cues. In our future where the Internet is embedded in elements at the point of purchase, clicking the "buy button" in a physical space will be facilitated by multiple routes of sensory persuasion.

16.4.1 SMELL

Olfaction, or smell, is the only sense with a direct connection to the brain's limbic system and hippocampus—areas of the brain that have long been known to be involved in emotion and memory (Damasio 1998; Eichenbaum et al. 1999) and have been linked to brand preference and recall in extant consumer neuroscience research (McClure et al. 2004). A wealth of academic research has shown that the presence of specific olfactory cues effectively persuades consumers. Aromas that conjure the recall of childhood memories have been shown to facilitate the intention to adopt new or novel products (Ibrahim 2015). Olfactory cues have also been shown to serve as a proxy for product quality (Rimkute, Moraes, and Ferreira 2015). Ambient scents have been shown to effectively affect consumers' spatial perceptions in retail environments, which in turn influence customers' feelings of power and, thus, product preference and purchasing behavior (Madzharov, Block, and Morrin 2015).

As in-store and in-home scent-generating technologies[13] merge into mainstream marketing communications,[14] their ability to persuade consumer attention, emotion, and memories will be key considerations in developing future metrics in consumer neuroscience.

16.4.2 TASTE

In the same polymodal vein, marketing influencers on gustatory perception will increasingly be considered important cues to incorporate into the success metrics of consumer neuroscience. A seminal study in the nascent field of consumer neuroscience, mentioned in previous chapters, highlights the impact of marketing actions, such as manipulation of pricing information, on changes in the neural representations of experienced pleasantness (Plassmann et al. 2008). Using fMRI, the researchers collected brain signals based on blood oxygen level–dependent activity while subjects tasted wines that, contrary to reality, they believed to be different and sold at different prices. The findings of the researchers show that by increasing the price of a wine, both subjective reports of "flavor pleasantness" as well as blood oxygen level–dependent activity in the medial orbitofrontal cortex increased. The medial orbitofrontal cortex is an area that has been widely shown to encode experienced pleasantness during experiential tasks (O'Doherty et al. 2003; Kringelbach 2005). Moving ahead, increases in advertising and promotional content that either covertly or overtly primes gustatory cues will be at the forefront of testable content using neuroscientific measures. Linking bio measures to neural activity that evokes positive flavor pleasantness will allow experimental testing in native contexts, such as within a grocery store, to efficiently measure a campaign's success.

16.4.3   TOUCH

The increase of haptic and somatosensory information will become available through novel input/output (I/O) devices via home computers to effectively change our online purchase decisions. For example, inFORM technology[15] (Follmer et al. 2013) will shrink in size over time and become commercialized for consumer use to allow users the ability to interact with digital information in a physical manner.

This will enable consumers to have the capacity to include a product's touch and feel into their consideration sets when deciding among online products or in determining their willingness-to-pay for items dependent on their perceived weight. The importance of haptic cues on product perception has been known for some time. For example, the weight of a product has been shown to serve as a proxy for quality (Piqueras-Fiszman and Spence 2012).

Consider for a moment how your purchase decisions might change if you were allowed to compare the weight of two different shoes you might plan to purchase online. As marketers increase use of the sense of touch in their initiatives, neuromarketers will adopt measurement parameters to measure nonconscious cues derived from haptic and somatosensory information.

16.5   KNOWLEDGE

The increased utility of research based in nonconscious brain and body measures will undoubtedly be realized as knowledge from previously disparate fields of study is formally synthesized under the umbrella of consumer neuroscience. Offerings of formal training in the field will explode in both the academic and private sectors through courses taught online,[16] in collegiate classrooms, and across the private sector as business-to-business (B2B) educational workshops. At present, a handful of business schools, such as Stern, Fox, Harvard, and University of Michigan, teach courses in consumer neuroscience. Recently, Ivy League schools, such as Dartmouth College, have launched courses in consumer neuroscience for

---

Advertising and promotional content that either covertly or overtly primes gustatory cues will be at the forefront of testable content using neuroscientific measures.

Neuromarketers will adopt measurement parameters to measure nonconscious cues derived from haptic and somatosensory information.

15. inFORM is a dynamic shape display that can render three-dimensional content physically, so users can interact with digital information in a tangible way. inFORM can also interact with the physical world around it; for example, moving objects on the table's surface. Remote participants in a video conference can be displayed physically, allowing for a strong sense of presence and the ability to interact physically at a distance.

16. The first online course in consumer neuroscience and neuromarketing was offered in fall 2014 by the Copenhagen School of Business.

undergraduate majors in neuroscience, psychology, and economics. It is clear such courses serve as bellwethers for other institutions to follow suit.

16.5.1 ACADEMIA

In support of shared knowledge and communication regarding the field's definitions, standards, and ethics, there will continue to be a burgeoning growth of specialized organizations to foster the fields of consumer neuroscience and neuromarketing. In the academic arena, satellite symposia on consumer neuroscience have cropped up. In the past few years, the large and long-standing Society for Neuroeconomics has had the insight to offer a satellite symposium on consumer neuroscience (the Consumer Neuroscience Satellite Symposium) during its main convention. In addition, a powerful cross-institutional collaboration among academics from the business schools of MIT, Harvard, Stanford, and the University of Michigan has culminated in an annual Interdisciplinary Symposium for Decision Neuroscience known as the "Truth Serum Conference,"[17] which has grown year after year in the number of attendants and contributors. These events are conduits between the academy and business, and their primary purpose is to highlight academically derived original research related to affected consumer attention, engagement, memory, and purchase decision information, such as price valuations and willingness-to-pay scenarios. Events such as these will continue to grow within the field of neuroscience. In 20 years' time, the Consumer Neuroscience Satellite Symposia and Truth Serum Conferences may well find their attendance numbers on par with the present-day Society for Neuroscience and American Psychological Association (APA) events, which currently number in the thousands.

16.5.2 COMMERCIAL SECTOR

As the academic front has begun to build the bridge to the private sector, organizations such as the Neuromarketing Science and Business Association (NMSBA) have sprung up with business-oriented perspective, working to achieve academic-like standards in practice within the community of neuromarketing vendors. While still in its infancy, the NMSBA has a global reach, representing 91 countries at the time of writing of this chapter.[18] The collaborative environment of this organization's annual Neuromarketing World Forum has launched work to make significant societal contributions by industry members, including a recent multi-lab initiative deemed "Neuro Against Smoking." As the industry advances, this organization will continue to define the rubric of the measures and will serve as a quality service mark in which to vet vendors.

16.5.3 MARRYING THE OLD WITH THE NEW

There is currently developing an unprecedented need to understand and integrate measures derived from neuroscience into the larger body of traditional market research. As a result, intermediary firms are beginning to spring up in this white

Firms will be charged with designing and integrating nonconscious measures garnered from the brain and body with traditional explicit self-report measures collected from surveys and focus groups.

17. See http://truthserum.mit.edu/ISDN2015/?page_id=36/.

18. Source: NMSBA (www.nmsba.com/countries).

space between science-oriented methodological specialists and advertising marketers and creatives. Such firms will be charged with designing and integrating nonconscious measures garnered from the brain and body with traditional explicit self-report measures collected from surveys and focus groups. Consultancies of this nature will be methodologically agnostic and serve as a stop-gap for quality control to effectively separate the wheat from the chaff with respect to vendor credibility. The future will hold no room for the "snake oil" salesmen present in the first iteration of neuromarketing's evolution (U.K. Essays 2013).

Like a puzzle coming together whose sum is greater than any one part, a cross-pollination of expertise will explode between academic and private-sector parties. Along with such third-party "interpreter" firms that bridge the gap between academia and business, a spreading activation of interdisciplinary personnel will become the norm for successful businesses. There will be a back- and-forth movement of professionals who bring expertise in neuroscience onto the client side and client-based expertise into neuromarketing firms. Large firms such as Coca-Cola, Walmart, and Maritz Holdings[19] are already breaking ground in adopting a diverse workforce that includes expertise in consumer neuroscience. Firms such as these will increase their rate of adoption and use of the practices of employing and measuring heuristic-driven, academically derived hypotheses in training their sales forces and justifying the rationale of predicted return on investment.

The inevitable mainstream synthesis of neuroscience and business in market research initiatives will yield a diverse, yet integrated, methodological suite of analytics. As a result of this adoption and integration, new standards in success metrics will exist. Consumers in traditional market research initiatives are segmented with respect to demographics, psychographics, and need states (Schaninger and Sciglimpaglia 1981; Carpenter and Moore 2006). Each of these segmentation mechanisms brings a level of insight that is meaningful, yet is unidimensional in terms of uncovering the holistic picture in decoding the consumer decision-making process.

16.6   DATA

Consumers in the present day are categorized and segmented by market researchers on the basis of information such as psychographics, demographics, income and education levels, number in household, and type of need state. As the field of consumer neuroscience advances in integrative measures, a new type of consumer breakout will be possible: one derived from *neurographics* and *neurosegmentation*. These will provide a critical piece to the puzzle of the consumer's narrative, and that is the process of *how* decisions are made. With the inclusion of nonconscious measures in the mix with traditional market research tools, a parsing of how consumers access, process, and activate against products and services will become

There will be a back-and-forth movement of professionals who bring expertise in neuroscience onto the client side and client-based expertise into neuromarketing firms. Large firms such as Coca-Cola, Walmart, and Maritz Holdings are already breaking ground in adopting a diverse workforce that includes expertise in consumer neuroscience.

19. Maritz's mission is to understand, enable, and motivate people to unleash their hidden potential, enabling people to do things differently by developing their strengths, knowledge, and confidence. The company designs employee incentive and reward programs and customer loyalty programs. It also plans corporate trade shows and events and offers traditional market research services such as the creation of product-launch campaigns. Its programs are designed to help its clients improve workforce quality and customer satisfaction.

possible. Evidence of the increased efficacy of nonconscious information has already been evidenced in academic findings in predictive consumer choices (Tusche, Bode and Haynes 2010). The "real world" will hold a multitude of context and cultural variations of test conditions where neuroscientific tools will be harnessed for optimal prediction of future consumption choices.

Neurosegmentation of the consumer will become a reality through a kind of sabermetric[20] approach to data analytics. In order to achieve such "uber metrics," a determination of which methods yield the most efficacious measures will first need to be accomplished. The output from those measures will then be weighted appropriately depending on the relative utility to the research question at hand in order to create powerful derivatives of the primary metrics.

A historic issue in the field of neuromarketing is that of limited scalability in terms of generalizing results from measures of the brain and body to larger populations. Branders often demand that research results must maintain an ability to predict outcome behaviors of mass consumer segments, such as social shares or purchases. Given the small sample sizes typically tested using brain and body measures, scalability of neuromarketing measures can often be at odds with brander's research objectives. In an attempt to remedy this disconnect, some early vendors of brain and bio-based measures from the first iteration of neuromarketing had adopted a stance that all brains behave in a similar fashion in response to like stimuli. While it is enticing to embrace the notion that we share consistent and similar representations of neural processing of stimuli, "one of the major frontiers of or neuromarketing lies in building an understanding of the ways in which different societies relate to companies, advertisements and brands (Karmarkar 2011). In other words, practitioners of applied consumer neuroscience will adopt the philosophy that individuals are dynamic and each of us maintains psychological and cultural differences and can very well be differentially affected by our experience of an environment. Moreover, prior goals and learned biases add a level of complexity to individual behavioral outcomes. Such individuality based on traits and states will allow for unprecedented precision in the neurosegmentation of consumer processes previously discussed and ensure a continued reliance on the integration of nonconscious and consciously derived measures in research contexts. As a result, "neocontextual" applications will be possible that will maintain the ability to match emotional resonance of branded content with congruent neurosegmentations of interest from the consumer population. In fact, branders of the future may embrace more targeted messaging to specific consumer segments of interest rather than defining mass messaging solutions that may miss the mark on creating meaningful emotional connections with an intended audience.

Consumer neuroscience is rapidly moving toward the adoption of efficient translation and interpretation environments that will be able to address the glut of eventual data that the neurosegmentation of consumers will afford. Such

A new type of consumer breakout will be possible, derived from neurographics and neurosegmentation. These will provide a critical piece to the puzzle of the consumer's narrative, and that is the process of how decisions are made.

20. In the United States, baseball is an extraordinarily researched game. In the book Money Ball by Michael Lewis (2003), sabermetrics is used to effectively assemble competitive teams on the basis of assessments of derivative measures of relevant player statistics.

environments will incorporate powerful analytics that bridge the gap that exists among disparate types of data sets culled from multiple sources. Text analytics, neural measures, implicit association measures of emotion such as FAC, IATs, and ZMET,[21] and traditional measures of self-report and demographic information will no longer be considered in piecemeal by market researchers, but instead will be integrated through machine learning and the use of neural networks for unprecedented predictive power from multimodal data streams. Data processing and storage advances have dovetailed with recent research incentives, such as The BRAIN Initiative and The Human Brain Project, to suggest that we are now just beginning to catch a glimpse of the predictive power of "Big Neuroscience."

Individuality based on traits and states will allow for unprecedented precision in the neurosegmentation of consumer processes.

16.7 CONCLUSION

In 1980, MIT Media Lab founder Nicholas Negroponte was famously quoted as saying, "Computing isn't about [the form factor or interface] computing anymore. It's about living." In the same vein, the futurescape for the field of consumer neuroscience will not be centered on the technology of measurement devices du jour. Instead, it will be about the most accurate and efficient predictors of human behavior at the earliest point in time along the consumer's decision-making journey.

Negroponte's prediction of where neuroscience will be in 30 years paints a world in which neuroscientists will eventually tackle the limitations of our visual system's attentional bottleneck by creating ingestible information in the form of neural prosthetics (Negroponte 2014). He predicts we will literally be able to eat Shakespeare. Until that time, the field of consumer neuroscience will continue to evolve in its definitions, standards, and measures to gain unprecedented insights to the consumer.

21. FAC refers to Paul Eckman's seminal facial action coding system in facial expression analysis. IATs refers to a variety of implicit association tasks, which rely on analyses of reaction-time analysis in binary choice tasks. ZMET refers to the Zaltman Metaphor Elicitation Technique (ZMET), a patented market research tool that elicits both conscious and especially unconscious thoughts by exploring people's nonliteral or metaphoric expressions.

KEY TAKEAWAYS

- The four requirements that neuromarketing techniques must meet in order to become standard methodological tools in marketing and advertising research of the future are:

  o The establishment of connections between behavior and business applications

  o Scalability

  o Trustworthiness

  o Creation of meaningful contributions to consumer insights

- In the future, vendors of applied consumer neuroscience techniques will be able to overcome current hurdles in the reliability and validity of their metrics.

- Common definitions of neuromarketing metrics will create a shared language that will allow market researchers an ability to perform longitudinal studies and meta-analyses across data sets from multiple measures across vendors.

- Academic and business-oriented organizations that foster consumer neuroscience and neuromarketing will continue to grow and tackle issues of standards and ethics in practice.

- Intermediary firms will populate the current white space between science-oriented methodological specialists and advertising marketers and creatives to assist in the interpretation and application of neuromarketing data.

- A cross-pollination of expertise will occur in advertising and neuromarketing firms to facilitate the future understanding and utility of neuromarketing measures.

- Future advances in multisensory marketing communications both in physical commercial environments and online will require neuromarketing research to address the impact of polymodal sensory inputs in research paradigms.

- Neuromarketers of the future will be less reliant on hardware tethered to participants and instead harness the untapped power of wearables and stand-off measures of data capture.

- A new type of consumer breakout will be possible, derived from neurographics and neurosegmentation. These will provide a critical piece to the puzzle of the consumer's narrative, and that is the process of how decisions are made, illustrated by specific temporal activation of neural systems.

- Metrics collected from brain and body measures will assist the deep learning of computers and improve predictive models of future consumer behaviors.

- While humans share common neural processes to respond to the physical world, the future of applied consumer neuroscience will capitalize on the individual processing differences among our species. Individual brains are unique, maintaining psychological and cultural differences and can vary in neural processes as a result of genetics, culture, and experience. Prior goals and learned biases add a level of complexity to individual behavioral outcomes. Such individuality based on traits and states will allow for unprecedented precision in the neurosegmentation of consumer processes.

DISCUSSION QUESTIONS

1. As the application of consumer neuroscience becomes mainstream, discuss two potential consumer-centric research applications that measures of the brain and/or body might address more accurately than traditional measures of self-report.

2. With the increase in the "Internet of Things" (meaning the Internet will be available in everyday objects beyond desktop computers and mobile devices), what things might someday collect brain or physiologic measures for commercial purposes?

3. What issues might neuromarketers face utilizing crowdsource data collection? How might they mitigate those issues before they arise?

4. Conduct an Internet search for academic research related to polymodal persuasion. Briefly discuss the findings of this research and its potential commercial application.

5. Give two examples of how individual brains or neural processes have been shown to differ.

REFERENCES

Ariely, D., & Berns, G. S. (2010). Neuromarketing: The hope and hype of neuroimaging in business. *Nature Reviews. Neuroscience*, 11(4), 284–292.

Baumeister, R. F., & Vohs, K. D. (2007). Self-regulation, ego depletion, and motivation. *Social and Personality Psychology Compass*, 1(1), 115–128.

Botswick, W. 2010. Waiter, there's pseudoscience in my soup: Campbell's chooses "neuromarketing" over consumer feedback in rebranding it's iconic soup cans. Fast Company. Available at https://www.fastcompany.com/1554158/waiter-theres-pseudo-science-my-soup.

Carpenter, J. M., & Moore, M. (2006). Consumer demographics, store attributes, and retail format choice in the US grocery market. *International Journal of Retail & Distribution Management*, 34(6), 434–452.

Damasio, A. R. (1998). Emotion in the perspective of an integrated nervous system. *Brain Research. Brain Research Reviews*, 26(2), 83–86.

Dimoka, A., Banker, R. D., Benbasat, I., Davis, F. D., Dennis, A. R., Gefen, D., et al. (2010). On the use of neurophysiological tools in IS research: Developing a research agenda for NeuroIS. *Management Information Systems Quarterly*, 36(3), 679–702.

Dmochowski, J. P., Bezdek, M. A., Abelson, B. P., Johnson, J. S., Schumacher, E. H., & Parra, L. C. (2014). Audience preferences are predicted by temporal reliability of neural processing. *Nature Communications*, 5, 4567.

Dobrian, J. 2015. Destination malls create a sense of place. [special advertising section] *Wall Street Journal*, May 13, C9.

Eichenbaum, H., Dudchenko, P., Wood, E., Shapiro, M., & Tanila, H. (1999). The hippocampus, memory, and place cells: Is it spatial memory or a memory space? *Neuron*, 23(2), 209–226.

Fehr, E., & Camerer, C. F. (2007). Social neuroeconomics: The neural circuitry of social preferences. *Trends in Cognitive Sciences*, 11(10), 419–427.

Follmer, S., Leithinger, D., Olwal, A., Hogge, A., & Ishii, H. (2013). inFORM: Dynamic physical affordances and constraints through shape and object actuation. *UIST*, 13, 417–426.

Garrett, J. C., Harrison, D. W., & Kelly, P. L. (1989). Pupillometric assessment of arousal to sexual stimuli: Novelty effects or preference? *Archives of Sexual Behavior*, 18(3), 191–201.

Genco, S. J., Pohlmann, A. P., & Steidl, P. (2013). *Neuromarketing for dummies*. Hoboken, NJ: John Wiley & Sons.

Hsu, M., Bhatt, M., Adolphs, R., Tranel, D., & Camerer, C. F. (2005). Neural systems responding to degrees of uncertainty in human decision-making. *Science*, 310(5754), 1680–1683.

Ibrahim, N. 2015. *Back to the future: Effects of olfaction induced episodic memories on consumer creativity and innovation adoption*. Doctoral dissertation. Department of Marketing and Consumer Studies, University of Guelph, Ontario.

Kable, J. W. (2011). The cognitive neuroscience toolkit for the neuroeconomist: A functional overview. *Journal of Neuroscience, Psychology, and Economics*, 4(2), 63.

Karmarkar, U. R 2011. Note on neuromarketing. Harvard Business School Background Note 512-031.

Karmarkar, U. R., Shiv, B., & Knutson, B. (2015). Cost conscious? The neural and behavioral impact of price primacy on decision making. *JMR, Journal of Marketing Research*, 52(4), 467–481.

Kenning, P. H., & Plassmann, H. (2008). How neuroscience can inform consumer research. *IEEE Transactions on Neural Systems and Rehabilitation Engineering*, 16(6), 532–538.

Kringelbach, M. L. (2005). The human orbitofrontal cortex: Linking reward to hedonic experience. *Nature Reviews. Neuroscience*, 6(9), 691–702.

Laeng, B., Sirois, S., & Gredebäck, G. (2012). Pupillometry a window to the preconscious? *Perspectives on Psychological Science*, 7(1), 18–27.

Lee, N., & Chamberlain, L. (2007). Neuroimaging and psychophysiological measurement in organizational research. *Annals of the New York Academy of Sciences*, 1118(1), 18–42.

Lewis, M. (2003). *Moneyball: The art of winning an unfair game*. New York: Norton.

Linden, A., & Fenn, J. 2003. *Understanding Gartner's hype cycles*. Strategic Analysis Report No. R-20–1971. Stamford, CT: Gartner, Inc.

Madzharov, A. V., Block, L. G., & Morrin, M. (2015). The cool scent of power: Effects of ambient scent on consumer preferences and choice behavior. [oil]. *Journal of Marketing*, 79(1), 83–96.

McClure, S. M., Li, J., Tomlin, D., Cypert, K. S., Montague, L. M., & Montague, P. R. (2004). Neural correlates of behavioral preference for culturally familiar drinks. *Neuron*, 44(2), 379–387.

Morrison, M., Gan, S., Dubelaar, C., & Oppewal, H. (2011). In-store music and aroma influences on shopper behavior and satisfaction. *Journal of Business Research*, 64(6), 558–564.

Negroponte, N. 2014. Nicholas Negroponte: A 30 year history of the future. TED Talk. [video] Available at www.ted.com/talks/nicholas_negroponte_a_30_year_history_of_the_future?language=en.

O'Doherty, J., Winston, J., Critchley, H., Perrett, D., Burt, D. M., & Dolan, R. J. (2003). Beauty in a smile: The role of medial orbitofrontal cortex in facial attractiveness. *Neuropsychologia*, 41(2), 147–155.

Piqueras-Fiszman, B., & Spence, C. (2012). The weight of the bottle as a possible extrinsic cue with which to estimate the price (and quality) of the wine? Observed correlations. *Food Quality and Preference*, 25(1), 41–45.

Plassmann, H., O'Doherty, J., Shiv, B., & Rangel, A. (2008). Marketing actions can modulate neural representations of experienced pleasantness. *Proceedings of the National Academy of Sciences of the United States of America*, 105(3), 1050–1054.

Plassmann, H., Ramsøy, T. Z., & Milosavljevic, M. (2012). Branding the brain: A critical review and outlook. *Journal of Consumer Psychology*, 22(1), 18–36.

Riedl, R., Banker, R. D., Benbasat, I., Davis, F. D., Dennis, A. R., Dimoka, A., et al. (2010). On the foundations of NeuroIS: Reflections on the Gmunden Retreat 2009. *Communications of the Association for Information Systems*, 27(1), 15.

Rimkute, J., Moraes, C., & Ferreira, C. (2015). The effect of scent on consumer behaviour. *International Journal of Consumer Studies*, 40(1), 24–34.

Sanfey, A. G., Rilling, J. K., Aronson, J. A., Nystrom, L. E., & Cohen, J. D. (2003). The neural basis of economic decision-making in the ultimatum game. *Science*, 300(5626), 1755–1758.

Sawitta Lefevre, A. 2014. Asia on alert with thermal cameras, doctors as Ebola declared global risk. *Reuters*. Available at www.reuters.com/article/2014/08/08/us-health-ebola-asia-idUSKBN0G80TZ 20140808.

Schaninger, C. M., & Sciglimpaglia, D. (1981). The influence of cognitive personality traits and demographics on consumer information acquisition. *Journal of Consumer Research*, 8, 208–216.

Shaw, L. 2015. *The importance of neuroscience in business. Press release available at* http://www.personneltoday.com/pr/2015/05/the-importance-of-neuroscience-in-business/.

Smidts, A., Hsu, M., Sanfey, A. G., Boksem, M. A. S., Ebstein, R. B., Huettel, S. A., et al. (2014). Advancing consumer neuroscience. *Marketing Letters*, 25, 257–267.

Sugiyama, H., Oshida, A., Thueneman, P., Littell, S., Katayama, A., Kashiwagi, M., et al. (2015). Proustian products are preferred: The relationship between odor-evoked memory and product evaluation. *Chemosensory Perception*, 8, 1–10.

Tom, S. M., Fox, C. R., Trepel, C., & Poldrack, R. A. (2007). The neural basis of loss aversion in decision-making under risk. *Science*, 315(5811), 515–518.

Tullman, M. L., & Clark, K. R. (2004). Revitalizing visual merchandising—Restoring balance to retail environment entails engaging all five senses. *Chain Store Age*, 63–68.

Tusche, A., Bode, S., & Haynes, J. D. (2010). Neural responses to unattended products predict later consumer choices. *Journal of Neuroscience*, 30(23), 8024–8031.

Essays, U. K. 2013. Neuromarketing holy grail or snake oil psychology essay. Available at https://www.ukessays.com/essays/psychology/neuromarketing-holy-grail-or-snake-oil-psychology-essay.php?cref=1.

Venkatraman, V., Dimoka, A., Pavlou, P. A., Vo, K., Hampton, W., Bollinger, B., et al. (2014). Predicting advertising success beyond traditional measures: New insights from neurophysiological methods and market response modeling. *JMR, Journal of Marketing Research*, 52(4), 436–452.

William, J. 2010. Campbell's Soup neuromarketing redux: There's chunks of real science in that recipe. Fast Company. Available at https://www.fastcompany.com/1558477/campbells-soup-neuromarketing-redux-theres-chunks-real-science-recipe.

CONTRIBUTORS

Fabio Babiloni, Sapienza University of Rome

Davide Baldo, Ipsos Neuroscience and Behavioral Sciences

David Brandt, Nielsen Consumer Neuroscience

Moran Cerf, Kellogg School of Management, Northwestern University

Yuping Chen, National Taiwan University

Patrizia Cherubino, Sapienza University of Rome

Kimberly Rose Clark, Department of Psychological and Brain Sciences, Dartmouth College; Merchant Mechanics

Maria Cordero-Merecuana, Emory University School of Medicine

William A. Cunningham, Rotman School of Management, University of Toronto

Manuel Garcia-Garcia, Advertising Research Foundation

Ming Hsu, Haas School of Business, University of California, Berkeley

Ana Iorga, Buyer Brain

Philip Kotler, Kellogg School of Management, Northwestern University

Carl Marci, Harvard Medical School; Nielsen Consumer Neuroscience

Hans Melo, University of Toronto

Kai-Markus Müller, The Neuromarketing Labs

Brendan Murray, Nielsen Consumer Neuroscience

Ingrid L. C. Nieuwenhuis, Nielsen Consumer Neuroscience

Graham Page, Millward Brown

Hirak Parikh, The Neuromarketing Labs

Dante M. Pirouz, Ivey Business School, University of Western Ontario

Martin Reimann, Eller College of Management, University of Arizona

Neal J. Roese, Kellogg School of Management, Northwestern University

Irit Shapira-Lichter, The fMRI Center, Cognitive Neurology Clinic and Neurology Department, Beilinson Hospital, Rabin Medical Center, Israel

Daniela Somarriba, Nielsen Consumer Neuroscience

Julia F. Trabulsi, Nielsen Consumer Neuroscience

Arianna Trettel, BrainSigns

Giovanni Vecchiato, Sapienza University of Rome

Thalia Vrantsidis, University of Toronto

Sarah Walker, Millward Brown

INDEX

Ad Council, 161, 162, 261
Addictive behavior, 258
Advertising, 10, 37, 80–82, 107, 121, 169, 172, 175, 176, 200–202, 237, 238, 265, 282, 283, 286, 287, 291, 293, 327, 333, 343
Advertising Research Foundation (ARF), 169, 286, 287, 327, 343
Advertising testing, 284, 286, 291, 301, 302
 persuasion measures, 294
 pretesting, 147, 292–295
 recall measurement, 287
Affect, 1, 32, 43, 58, 96, 100–102, 106, 113, 149, 157, 158, 160, 174, 175, 185, 187, 190, 192, 193, 197, 199, 200, 201, 203–206, 225, 237, 243, 250, 259, 260, 261, 286, 312, 328, 329, 332
Affective circumplex, 155
Affective neuroscience, 238
Affective states, 175, 327
Algorithms, 9, 160, 189, 249, 252, 253, 271, 272, 277, 290, 326, 329
Amygdala, 3, 10, 27, 28, 31, 32, 51, 55, 71, 89, 148, 155, 156, 161, 170, 172, 173, 175, 199, 205, 228, 261
Analytics, 17, 86, 89, 269, 270, 274, 277, 328, 329, 335–337. See also Big data
Anchoring, 250, 252, 253
Approach/withdrawal, 95
Arousal, 5, 43, 82–84, 92, 96, 101, 115, 148, 153, 155, 156, 159–161, 166, 167, 172–174, 274, 326, 328, 329, 340
ASI Market Research, 302
Attention
 associative, 5, 6, 7, 11, 13, 17, 26, 28, 30, 32–34, 36, 41, 43, 46, 60, 61, 74, 76, 77, 80, 82–84, 88, 90, 94, 95, 102–116, 120, 121, 140, 148, 149, 157, 162, 165, 166, 168, 169, 175, 176, 186, 189, 200, 219, 245, 254, 257, 258, 260, 262, 268, 276, 286, 294, 312, 328, 331–334
 bottom-up, 28, 33, 34, 36, 103, 105, 107, 109, 110, 112, 116, 120, 121
 goal-oriented, 106
 top-down, 28, 34, 36, 57, 103, 105, 106, 112, 120, 121
Attentional resources, 109, 157

Basic emotion theory, 152–154, 157
Behavioral economics, 177, 300, 324
Belmont Report, 304, 306, 310, 311, 316
Beta-adrenergic antagonists, 166
Big data, 67, 86, 216, 243, 269, 270, 272, 277, 301

Binet, 151, 165, 172
Biology, 61, 153, 158, 173, 237, 238
Biometrics, 85, 114, 115, 120, 121, 160, 167, 168, 170, 211, 291, 327
Blood glucose monitoring, 329
Blood oxygen–level dependent (BOLD), 69, 332, 333
Box office sales, 169
Brainjuicer, 288
Brain Vision (SBVS), 94
Brand, 65, 80, 82, 101, 121, 127–129, 201, 205, 224–230, 235–239, 288, 292, 293, 298–300, 341
 asset valuator, 299
 awareness, 178, 226, 293
 DREK model, 299
 equity, 121, 225, 298
 image, 226
 knowledge, 199, 225, 227, 229–231, 235, 236
Burke Institute, 301

Camerer, Colin, 14, 19, 156, 172, 205, 233, 234, 238, 322, 340
Cerf, Moran, 93, 97, 98, 188, 343
Cognitive neuroscience, 34, 174, 238
Cognitive processing, 236, 260, 261
Commercial, 16, 37, 41, 67, 72, 77, 80, 81, 84, 89, 100, 122–126, 129–132, 138, 139, 142, 144, 146, 148, 159, 160, 172, 252, 272, 291, 302, 315, 317, 318, 325, 329, 330, 332, 338, 339
Compulsive shopping, 258
Concept testing, 288, 302
Conceptualization, 157, 209
Construct-based model, 156
Consumer behavior, 11, 13, 16, 32, 33, 58, 170, 177, 237, 259–261, 263, 274, 275, 287, 294, 309, 316
Consumer insights, 107, 324
Consumer response
 habitual, 34, 236, 290, 300
Copy Research Validity Project, 286
Crowdsourcing, 328
Customer lifetime valuation (CLV), 224, 225

Damasio, Antonio, 9, 158, 284–286
Decision making, 3, 5–10, 12, 13, 30, 32, 33, 36, 80, 88, 91, 116, 121, 141, 158, 179, 180, 182, 187, 193, 197, 200, 201, 204–206, 223, 233, 237–239, 242, 247, 256, 263, 268, 285, 314, 315, 322, 340

Decision making (cont.)
  process, 10, 14, 18, 32, 77, 91, 112, 113, 158,
    177, 178, 183, 189, 192, 194, 196, 197, 199,
    200, 204, 224, 229, 233, 235, 237, 259, 270,
    273, 275, 278, 286, 316, 317, 335, 337, 340,
    341
Declaration of Helsinki, 304, 316, 319
Deep learning, 329
Diagnostic, 8, 163, 170, 284, 286, 294
Distraction, 6, 103, 105, 109, 121, 227
Dooley, Roger, 288
Dopamine, 26, 27, 34, 212–214, 217–221,
    237
Drinking, 144, 199, 257
Drucker, Peter, 281

Ehrenberg-Bass Institute, 300
Ekman, Paul, 78, 79, 152, 153, 163, 173
Electrocorticography (ECG)
  heart rate, 5, 30, 86, 89, 92–94, 99, 115, 122,
    160, 161, 166–168, 170, 174, 180, 211, 323,
    329
Electrodermal activity (EDA), 65, 95, 99, 115,
    174, 322, 323. See also Galvanic skin
    response
Electroencephalography (EEG), 8, 9, 15, 16,
    65, 67, 69, 70, 72–78, 80, 81, 84, 85,
    88–102, 109, 114, 120, 122, 130–132, 145,
    146, 160–164, 167, 169, 170, 172, 211, 215,
    216, 235, 247, 249, 250, 261, 273–275,
    278, 279, 291, 294–296, 300, 317, 323,
    325–327
Electrophysiology, 5
Embodiment, 166
Emotions, 9, 10, 14, 17, 21, 27, 30–33, 36, 51,
    55, 60, 69, 79, 82, 90, 96, 131, 141, 142,
    152, 153, 155–158, 165, 172–176, 182, 187,
    189, 197, 199, 237, 247, 252, 283, 284, 294,
    326
Empathy, 313, 322
Engagement, 29, 90, 206
ESOMAR, 282, 287, 311
Executive Function, 30
External validity. See Generalizability
Eye-tracking, 79, 83, 84, 93, 113, 114, 146,
    162, 168, 326

Facial action coding (FACS), 16, 78, 79, 82,
    83, 90, 92, 121, 160, 284, 293, 295
  micro facial expressions, 78, 79, 163, 164,
    173
Fear, 6, 11, 27, 79, 89, 90, 92, 152, 153,
    155–157, 173–175, 180–182, 189, 228, 230,
    239, 302
Federal Communications Commission (FCC),
    283
Feelings, 3, 21, 27, 57, 69, 170, 187, 192, 196,
    202, 208, 213, 225, 227, 293, 332
Fixations, 41, 82, 85, 113, 196
  count, 168

Forgetting curve, 138
Frontal asymmetry, 95, 163
Functional magnetic resonance imaging
    (fMRI), 9, 15, 16, 19, 65, 67, 69–74, 76–78,
    80, 84, 85, 88, 90–93, 100, 101, 115, 144,
    145, 148, 160, 164, 165, 167, 170, 172, 174,
    176, 195–199, 210–213, 215, 216, 219, 220,
    235, 245, 246, 259–261, 265, 273, 274, 278,
    294, 300, 322, 325, 327, 332, 343

Gallup, George, 281
Galvanic skin response (GSR), 16, 65, 94, 115,
    122, 160, 211, 286, 322
Gamification, 330, 331
Generalizability, 323

Habits, 5, 28, 189, 225, 229, 234, 235, 238,
    239, 257, 259, 263
Haley, Russell, 286
Haptics, 333
Heath, Robert, 1, 10, 286, 287, 294
Hippocampus, 27, 29, 31–33, 51, 55, 89,
    134–136, 140, 142–145, 149, 170, 172,
    230–232, 332, 340

Iconic brand assets, 141, 143, 148
Implicit association task (IAT), 16, 65, 77, 86,
    88, 163, 173, 181, 235, 291
Implicit techniques, 291
Implicit testing, 163, 298
Impulsive purchase, 210
Informed consent, 306–308, 310, 311
Innerscope, 166–170, 288, 294
Institute of Practitioners in Advertising (IPA),
    165
Internal validity, 324
Ipsos, 288, 343

James, William, 5, 9, 103, 104

Kahneman, Daniel, 10, 287, 302
Keller, Kevin, 223–227, 230, 231, 238
Kotler, Phillip, 233, 238, 256, 264, 281, 343

Laddering, 283
Lexical decision task, 145
Liking, 139, 140, 167, 208, 210, 212, 215, 217,
    218, 292
Low-involvement theory, 111
Loyalty, 55, 119, 196, 206, 212–214, 223, 226,
    234, 235, 237, 238, 298, 335

Machine learning, 231, 270–272, 277, 278,
    337
Marketing mix models, 197
Market research, 1, 13, 14, 17, 107, 131, 153,
    159, 160, 165, 170, 281, 282, 284, 285, 287,
    288, 300, 301, 303, 314, 316, 324, 331, 335,
    337
Medial temporal lobe (MTL), 134

MediaPost, 166, 174
Memory, 2, 17, 25, 26, 28–34, 51, 55, 57, 71,
    74–77, 80, 85, 89, 94, 101, 102, 105, 109,
    110, 113, 121, 134–149, 162, 166, 170, 172,
    174–176, 179, 189, 195, 201, 225, 227–235,
    237–239, 265, 275, 285, 294–296, 298, 312,
    332, 334, 340, 341
  episodic, 229, 239
  explicit, 285
  implicit, 139
  recognition measures, 287
  semantic, 111, 229, 230, 235
Mere exposure effect, 139
Microsegment, 327
Millward Brown, 181, 288, 343
Mimoco, 168, 169
Mismatch negativity, 107, 121, 253
Mood, 6, 43, 60, 82, 108, 152, 181, 213,
    219
Movies, 112, 172, 208, 332
  trailers, 169, 172

National Association of Broadcasters (NAB),
    283
Neocontextual, 336
Neocortex, 32, 55, 134–136, 140, 142, 145,
    149
Neuhaus, Carolyn, 219
Neuroethics, 259, 303, 304, 309, 315
Neurofocus, 288
Neurographics, 331, 336, 338
Neuron, 34, 93, 101, 172, 173, 205, 206, 217,
    218, 238, 239, 279, 340
Nielsen, 161, 162, 166, 167, 175, 211, 261,
    265, 285, 288, 294, 343
NMSBA, 17, 287, 304, 311, 315, 334
Nonconscious, 10, 14, 15, 68, 91, 113, 117,
    118, 158–160, 163, 166, 168–170, 189, 195,
    298–300, 302, 307, 324, 325, 327, 328, 331,
    333–336. See also Unconscious
Nucleus accumbens, 27, 31, 70, 210–213, 215,
    217–220, 246, 252, 274
Nudges, 256, 263, 270
Nuremberg Code, 304–306, 316

Old-new effect, 144, 145
Olfaction, 35, 340
Opioids, 213, 217
Optimizing, 59, 265
Orbitofrontal cortex (OFC), 8, 32, 89, 198, 215,
    333, 340

Package testing, 113, 296–298, 302, 325
Packard, Vance, 282
Personality traits, 86, 232, 327, 341
Persuasion, 261
Physiology, 61, 173
Pleasure center, 207, 215
Positron emission tomography (PET), 67, 93,
    215

Prediction, 34, 86, 141, 206, 209, 211, 214,
    217, 218, 239, 249, 267–270, 272–277, 279,
    322, 336, 337
Price-to-product fit, 247
Pricing, 14–16, 44, 63, 67, 71, 74, 90, 92, 100,
    116, 117, 119, 143, 160, 165, 183, 191,
    196–198, 203, 210, 225, 241–247, 249–253,
    282, 298, 325, 333, 334, 340
Priming, 60, 145, 149, 164, 181, 254
Privacy, 17, 306–310, 315–317
Propranol, 166
Psychological construction, 152–158, 160,
    175
Public service announcement (PSA), 162
Pupillometry, 326, 340
Purchases, neural predictors of, 19, 101, 254

Rangel, Antonio, 113, 121, 198, 205, 206, 233,
    234, 238, 341
Respiration, 5, 85, 92, 93, 99, 115, 160, 323,
    329
Retailtainment, 331
Retrieval cue, 138, 141, 142

Sales, 10, 34, 101, 131, 165, 167–169, 171,
    192, 204, 211, 213, 231, 243, 256, 282, 286,
    292, 302, 335
Saliency, 31, 33, 34, 60, 105, 106, 112, 113,
    121
Sample sizes, 164, 327, 336
Scalability, 324, 336
Schema, 43, 130
Self-regulation, 311, 322, 330
Self-report, 159, 160, 167, 235, 259, 334, 335,
    337, 339
Snake oil, 335, 341
Social marketing, 255–257, 259, 261–263,
    265
Social neuroeconomics, 340
So-lo-mo, 331
Somatic marker, 158, 159, 173, 182, 284, 285
Somatosensorial experience, 30, 35, 38, 157,
    331–333
Starch, Daniel, 281
Subliminal
  advertising, 37, 282, 283
  messages, 283
Super Bowl, 100, 167, 170, 174, 175, 195,
    302
Surveys, 12, 60, 100, 144, 146, 192, 242, 243,
    249, 252, 288, 291, 293, 297, 300, 302
  direct questioning, 285, 295, 296, 301
System 1, 180–186, 190, 209–211, 215, 216,
    244, 287, 288
System 2, 180, 182–184, 186, 209, 210, 244,
    287

Television advertising, 109, 161, 166, 167,
    282, 291
Tethered technologies, 330

Theory of cue reactivity, 259
Transcranial magnetic stimulation (TMS), 77
Twitter, 167, 312

Valence, 2, 96, 100, 146, 153, 155, 159, 174, 225
Vicary, James, 60, 282, 283
Virtual reality, 269, 330, 331

Wanting, 169, 208, 212, 215, 217, 219, 220
Wearable devices, 86, 216, 320
Willingness-to-pay (WTP), 76, 205, 241–244, 247, 249, 250, 252, 253, 333, 334
Willpower, 189, 190, 193
World Advertising Research Center (WARC), 287

Yoon, Carolyn, 198, 206, 224, 239